TECHNOLOGY, GROWTH AND COMPETITIVENESS

Technology, Growth and Competitiveness

Selected Essays

Jan Fagerberg

Professor of Economics, University of Oslo, Norway

Edward Elgar

Cheltenham, UK • Northampton, MA, USA

F.W. Olin College Library

Published by
Edward Elgar Publishing Limited
Glensanda House
Montpellier Parade
Cheltenham
Glos GL50 1UA
UK

Edward Elgar Publishing, Inc.
136 West Street
Suite 202
Northampton
Massachusetts 01060
USA

A catalogue record for this book
is available from the British Library

Library of Congress Cataloguing in Publication Data
Fagerberg, Jan.
    Technology, growth and competitiveness : selected essays / Jan Fagerberg.
        p. cm.
    Includes index.
    1.Technological innovations–Economic aspects.2.Economic development.3.
    Competition, International.4.Labor economics.5.Economics.6.Schumpeter, Joesph
    Alois, 1883-1950. I.Title.

    HC79.T4 F33 2002
    338'.064–dc21

                                                                2002024471

ISBN 1 84064 859 7

Printed and bound in Great Britain by Bookcraft Ltd

Contents

PART III   TECHNOLOGY AND COMPETITIVENESS

Acknowledgements

The author and publishers wish to thank the following who have kindly given permission for the use of copyright material.

Blackwell Publishers Ltd for articles: 'Heading for Divergence? Regional Growth in Europe Reconsidered' with B. Verspagen, *Journal of Common Market Studies*, **34** (3), September 1996, 431–48; 'International Competitiveness', *The Economic Journal*, **98**, June 1988, 355–74.

The Century Foundation for article: 'Vision and Fact: A Critical Essay on the Growth Literature', in *Unconventional Wisdom: Alternative Perspectives on the New Economy*, J. Madrick (ed.), The Century Foundation Press, 2000, 299–320.

CERUM for article: 'Diffusion, Structural Change and Intra-Regional Trade: The Case of Nordic Countries 1961–1983', in *Innovation, Industrial Knowledge and Trade*, B. Johansson and C. Karlsson (eds), CERUM, Umeå, 1990, 19–35.

Continuum International Publishing Group for article: 'Small Open Economies in the World Market for Electronics: The Case of the Nordic Countries' with B. Dalum and U. Jørgensen, in *Small Countries Facing the Technological Revolution*, C. Freeman and B.-Å. Lundvall (eds), Pinter Publishers, 1988, 113–38.

Elsevier Science for article: 'A Technology Gap Approach to Why Growth Rates Differ', *Research Policy*, **16** (2–4), August 1987, 87–99.

Forum for Development Studies for article: 'East Asian Growth: A Critical Assessment' with A. Cappelen, *Forum for Development Studies*, **2**, 1995, 175–95.

Macmillan Press for article: '"Modern Capitalism" in the 1970s and 1980s' with Bart Verspagen, in *Growth, Employment and Inflation*, M. Setterfield (ed.), 1999, 113–26.

Oxford University Press for articles: 'Europe at the Crossroads: The Challenge from Innovation-Based Growth', in *The Globalizing Learning Economy*, D. Archibugi and B.-Å. Lundvall (eds), 2001, 45–60; 'User–Producer Interaction, Learning and Comparative Advantage', *Cambridge Journal of Economics*, **19**, 1995, 243–56; 'Technology and Competitiveness', *Oxford Review of Economic Policy*, **12** (3), 1996, 39–51.

Taylor and Francis for articles: 'Technology, Growth and Unemployment across European Regions' with B. Verspagen and M. Caniëls, *Regional Studies*, **31** (5), 1997, 457–66; 'The Method of Constant Market Shares Analysis Reconsidered' with G. Sollie, *Applied Economics*, **19**, 1987, 1571–83.

Chapter 7 was first circulated as NUPI Report No. 107, May 1987, Norwegian Institute of International Affairs, Olso.

Chapter 14 was first circulated as NUPI Working Paper No. 526, January 1995, Norwegian Institute of International Affairs, Oslo.

Introduction

This book has it origins in a research project that I undertook in the mid 1980s. The project, the main aim of which was to explain why some countries succeed much better than others in generating growth and competitiveness, was supposed to run from 1983 to 1986. Yet somehow it became a never-ending story. The reason for this, I think, had to do with the scope of the project which I now (with hindsight) can see was too large and ambitious, and the fact that I became severely hooked on this type of research and never really wanted to stop. One important output from this research was my Ph.D. thesis, 'Technology, Growth and Trade – Schumpeterian Perspectives', submitted to the University of Sussex in 1988. Three of the chapters in this book were also included in my thesis (Chapters 7, 9 and 12). In addition I have included 12 other articles that, in various ways, supplement and extend the analysis that was presented in the thesis. Hence, what is presented here is a far more complete analysis of the relationship between technology, growth and competitiveness than anything I have published to date. Each chapter is self-contained and may be read independently of the other chapters.[1] In this introduction I try to outline the story of how I came to view global dynamics in the way I do and to summarize the main arguments of the subsequent chapters.

How I got started
The idea of undertaking research in this area came to me in the early 1980s when I was working as a civil servant in the Planning Department of the Norwegian Ministry of Finance. Within the department I became responsible for the analysis of international economic trends and Norwegian trade performance. When I started to work on this I was quickly confronted with the view, widely accepted at the time, that the competitiveness of a country (see Chapter 12) could be measured by the unit labour cost of its manufacturing industry relative to that of its trading partners (in a common currency). The argument behind this view seemed to be that, if unit costs go up relative to that of trading partners, this would harm exports and favour imports, with foreseeable negative consequences for growth, employment and welfare. The policy implication of this was of course wage restraint. Heard the story before?

Although the logic of the argument may seem convincing at first glance, it appeared to me that there was a logical flaw in it: it did not take into account quality differences. Higher prices could equally well reflect higher quality, which, in turn, might justify higher wages. From this perspective higher growth in relative unit labour cost (RULC) could just as well be seen as an indicator of growing quality relative to other countries or increasing – rather than deteriorating – competitiveness. In developing this view I was strongly influenced by two people who had thought much more about this issue than myself, namely François Chesnais of the Department for Science, Technology and Industry at the Organization for Economic Cooperation and Development (OECD) (whom I had come to know during a visit to the OECD the year before) and Bengt-Åke Lundvall at the IKE-group of the University of Aalborg.[2] Both of them argued that competitiveness should be analysed as a dynamic phenomenon, that is, in a growth perspective, and that so-called 'non-price factors' (and, hence, 'technology') were equally if not more important than variations in wage costs and prices. This I found very attractive.

I do not think I convinced anyone in the ministry when I started to question the then common wisdom, but I convinced myself sufficiently to ask the Director of the Department, Per Schreiner, for permission to do a small project on this during the first months of 1982. Little did I know when I started that the report (based mostly on secondary sources) I submitted a few months later would come to have a lasting influence on my professional life. This had to do with a request from a former colleague, Terje Røed Larsen, who at the time was setting up a 'think-tank' for the Federation of the Norwegian Trade Unions, to publish the report as a working paper. I asked Schreiner if he accepted this, which he did. However, he did certainly not foresee (nor did I) that Larsen would use his great entrepreneurial talent (which later brought him fame as a mediator in the Middle East conflict) to persuade a newspaper in Oslo to use most of its front page on my report under the heading 'Research shows that wage costs do not matter for competitiveness'. The fact that wage negotiations between employers and trade unions were under way at the same time (which was hardly a coincidence) increased the public interest enormously, and the alleged findings of my research became one of the main themes in the media for some time. This made my position in the Ministry quite uncomfortable. I was happy, therefore, when, later the same year, I was awarded a three year fellowship from the Norwegian Research Council for the Humanities and Social Sciences (NAVF) to do research on competitiveness.[3]

In mid 1983 I left the Ministry to start my new career as a researcher. The Research Council did not provide an office, so my first task was to find one. Initially, I got one at the Research Department of the Central Bureau of Statistics in Oslo, a large research organization with a highly experienced staff and an excellent library (from which I received first class service). While there I entered into a very rewarding collaboration with Gunnar Sollie who – like me – was interested in the relationship between structural changes in international trade and trade performance.[4] In 1985 I moved to a tenured position at the (much smaller) Department for International Economics and Development Economics at the Norwegian Institute for International Affairs (NUPI), also in Oslo. There I was equipped with my own computer, excellent library support and was free to pursue my own research interests.[5] I stayed at NUPI on a full time basis until 1996 (interrupted, though, by several periods abroad) when I moved to my present position at the University of Oslo.

How I came to think differently
Why did I come to view things so differently from my colleagues in the Ministry and most other Norwegian economists? Actually, when I entered university I had no intention of becoming an economist. My wish was to become a journalist. I had already worked on a newspaper for short periods. When I asked the senior editor what he considered to be the best educational background for a journalist, he said that the most efficient education was learning on the job, but that a few years' exposure to the university might be helpful as well. Following this advice I enrolled as a student at the University of Oslo (my home town) with the ambition of taking an undergraduate

course in political science. On the completion of this course in 1973 I moved on to history and to the (recently founded) Regional College in Telemark and one year later to economics and to the University of Bergen.[6]

Compared to studying history, a multi-faceted subject full of life, studying economics was like a cold shower. The approach I was presented with appeared overly static in focus and based on a simplistic view of human behaviour. I still remember the first lecture. The lecturer started by making a number of assumptions about human behaviour and similarly for firms from which he no doubt was going to make a number of deductions for the working of markets and the economy in general. However, he never got that far, because he was repeatedly interrupted by students asking him how these assumptions could be justified. Unfortunately, he was never able to answer these questions. As the weeks passed by we learnt that this practice – making far-reaching deductions from ad hoc assumptions with little if any empirical backing – was common in the discipline. Although this did not make anyone any happier, it calmed down the situation. Teaching continued in the usual way, and we[7] on our side concluded that if we were going to learn something about the working of the real economy (in contrast to its textbook version), it would probably have to be outside the classroom.

My 'out of classroom' activities included, among other things, studying classic texts – and interpretations – on political economy and long-run economic and social change. I read widely on the subject, including classics such as Adam Smith, David Ricardo and Karl Marx, and interpretations such as those by Mark Blaug, Maurice Dobb, Luigi Pasinetti and Joseph Schumpeter.[8] Through Rune Skarstein, who at that time worked as a researcher at The Christian Michelsen Institute in Bergen, I became familiar with Sraffa's work and the controversy between the neoclassicals and the neo-Ricardians. However, the most central authority in these days was of course Marx and I joined a cross-disciplinary seminar on Marx's '*Capital*', led by a philosopher, Hans Ebbing, that lasted three full terms. Like many others in those days I started to ask myself to what extent this theory could be of relevance for understanding contemporary economic developments. What I particularly had in mind was the strong economic downturn that the capitalist world was experiencing at the time. Here, Marx had an interesting theory to offer: (technological) competition, he argued, forced capitalists to invest in new machinery. This would in the short run improve the competitiveness of the individual capitalist but have negative repercussions on long-run profitability (the rate of profit) in the economy as a whole. Eventually this would cause investment to shrink and a crisis to appear. Could the depression of the mid 1970s be understood in this light? I wrote a term paper on the issue and became very excited about it.

I left Bergen for Oslo in the summer of 1976 having completed my undergraduate degree. However, the idea of doing more research on the interaction between growth and crisis became more and more irresistible, so I decided to write a master's thesis on the subject. Initially, my idea was to combine a theoretical and historical approach to the subject and major within (economic) history, but the academic in charge of economic history at the History Department of the University of Oslo at the time was not at all enthusiastic about the idea. So I ended up enrolling as a graduate student in economics at my old department in Bergen but, except for the academic year 1979–80, I continued to live and work in Oslo (where I had a part time job in the

Information Department of the Ministry of Environment). However, working part time on a thesis with little, if any, contact with teachers and students was a lonely process, and it would surely have ended in failure had I not come into contact with the Nordic Summer University (NSU), which hosted study groups in a variety of disciplines and themes (with a common Nordic session every summer). Through my participation in the group on political economy I had the opportunity to discuss my research with others and was introduced to many (for me) new topics and approaches. I also got to know many people with whom I have been in close contact to this very day.[9]

I graduated from the University of Bergen in 1980 with a thesis on 'Theories of Growth and Crises within Classical Political Economy'. The thesis consisted of a series of chapters comparing and discussing the contributions from writers such as Smith, Ricardo, Malthus, various underconsumptionists, Marx (in particular), Keynes and post-Keynesian growth theorists (particularly Domar). In my view the possibility for a 'market glut' caused by a mismatch between production and demand was inherent in capitalism and could be provoked for a number of reasons. It was argued that such incidents ought to be distinguished from long periods characterized by slow growth, increasing unemployment and so on, which were more likely to be caused by fundamental imbalances in the economy of the type discussed by Ricardo, Marx and some of the post-Keynesians. To me it seemed as if there was a common ground among these writers in how they looked at long-run economic growth. On the one hand they emphasized the immense potential of the capitalist machine (as an engine of economic progress), on the other that this potential could only be realized if matched by appropriate institutions (such as, for instance, property rights, workers' rights, income distribution rules, patterns/routines/rules of competition etc.).[10] Hence, following this view prolonged periods of economic depression might be seen as a structural imbalance between the conditions for economic progress on the one hand and the prevailing institutional system on the other. I found this way of looking at things very attractive.

Searching for a theory of growth and trade
This is the title of an article I wrote during my first year of research (Fagerberg 1984). The reason I decided to undertake such a search was that I realized that the kind of 'political economy of growth' framework within which I had worked did not provide sufficient guidance for the type of research I wished to undertake. It provided a focus, that growth and competitiveness problems needed to be analysed in a long-run, dynamic perspective, but not much more. Hence, I started to search for theoretical and empirical contributions that shared this focus but went beyond the general analyses I had encountered hitherto. I decided to cast the net rather widely and identified at least four different strands that potentially might be of some relevance for the research I wished to undertake, namely:

- neo-Ricardian theory,
- the regulation school,
- post-Keynesian theory,
- neo-Schumpeterian theory.

The search process consisted of a combination of travelling and reading. In the summer of 1983 I went to a summer school in Trieste in Italy. It was a combined neo-Ricardian/post-Keynesian venture with many of the leading figures within these strands lecturing. My inclination was that there was more promise in the post-Keynesian than in the neo-Ricardian strand. This impression was much strengthened during the summer course. However effective Sraffa (1960) may have been as a critic of neoclassical formalism, it occurred to me the attempts to build a positive theory on the basis of his critique were misguided. To me it seemed to be an abstract scheme totally void of any real understanding of human behaviour/interaction and, as such, not at all superior to the neoclassical theorizing that it wished to replace.

The post-Keynesian strand was more promising in these respects since it placed human behaviour (satisficing rather than maximizing) and institutions at the core. However, many of the post-Keynesians whom I met in Trieste seemed to focus on a rather limited set of issues, often related to money/monetary policy in one way or another. Important as this may be in itself I found it to be of little help in my research endeavour. However, this does not extend, it should be said, to all researchers carrying this label, at least not if you include writers such as Nicholas Kaldor, John Cornwall and Anthony Thirlwall. Kaldor (1978, 1981) and Thirlwall (1979) were at the time clearly the most well-known critics of the established wisdom of competitiveness, and my work on this topic took their arguments as a point of departure (see Chapters 12 and 16). Cornwall's treatise on 'Modern Capitalism' from 1977 is one of the best books on economics I have ever read and it has influenced me a lot. What I found especially attractive was his strong emphasis on growth as transformation, that is, as a process of qualitative (and structural) change, in which the success (or lack of such) of individual countries to a large extent depends on their ability to transform economic, social and institutional structures.

In the spring of 1984 I went to Paris as a visiting fellow at CEPREMAP for some months to study the regulation approach.[11] I was very well received by both Robert Boyer and Pascal Petit and I benefited greatly from interacting with them.[12] The regulation approach had a lot in common with the kind of approach I had developed in my master's thesis, for example, it combined Marx's dynamic theory of capitalist development with Keynesian and post-Keynesian features. Compared to Marx the regulationists were more specific when describing the productive forces and the corresponding institutional requirements. Furthermore, while Marx wrote about the type of mechanization that characterized the period following the so-called 'industrial revolution', the regulationists focused on the scale-intensive, mass-consumption production system that developed in the United States about a century ago (and which later diffused to Europe) and its assumed institutional counterparts (such as, for instance, collective bargaining). While I found much of this quite sensible, I could not help recognizing that the regulationists essentially took the scale-based production system for given, and that there was no explanation of how such systems emerge, change through time, grow (or decline) and so on.

From reading John Cornwall's work I recognized that Schumpeter heavily influenced his theory of growth as transformation, and I therefore decided to read more of Schumpeter's work in the original.[13] Schumpeter, it occurred to me, was writing in the classical tradition from Smith, Ricardo and Marx, but enriched it by adding a much more refined analysis of the role of technology and innovation for long-run economic growth. The core of his argument, that growth is driven by technological competition, was taken from Marx, as Schumpeter himself readily admitted.[14] However, while Marx exclusively focused on investments in new generations of machinery (and hence on process innovation), Schumpeter combined the idea of technological competition with a broader understanding of innovation as a social and cumulative process. Innovation to Schumpeter was a new combination – developed for a commercial purpose – of existing knowledge and resources. Thus, following this view innovation is by its very nature a systemic phenomenon.[15] In addition to process innovation Schumpeter also included other types such as the development of new products, the use of new raw materials or intermediary products, the exploitation of new markets and the introduction of new ways to organize business (Schumpeter 1934, 1943).

It struck me that the Marx–Schumpeter model of technological competition was potentially a very fruitful framework for analysing not only competition among firms but also relationships among nations. Just as some firms were innovators while others were imitators, some countries stayed at the technological frontier while others lagged behind. It might be objected, though, that to apply an approach developed for firms to countries may be methodologically suspect (although very common in economics). My argument for doing it, in this particular case, is that countries, regions and firms can all be viewed as innovation systems with sufficient internal coherence (structure) to qualify as analytical units in the model/approach. In fact, economic historians had played with similar ideas for quite some time (see, in particular, Gerschenkron 1962; Abramovitz 1979) and there had also been some attempts by trade economists to analyse the interaction between growth and trade from this perspective (Posner 1961; Vernon 1966). However, much of this work was based on a pure leader–follower dichotomy, and had difficulties in dealing with dynamic aspects such as, for instance, innovation among followers or 'change of technological leadership'. It occurred to me that by taking advantage of the deeper understanding on innovation diffusion offered by Schumpeter this type of work could be substantially sharpened and refined.

One (systemic) aspect on which Schumpeter put a good deal of emphasis is the tendency towards 'clustering' of innovations in time and space. He saw this as related to phenomena such as business cycles and 'long waves'. While studying Schumpeter's account of this I also consulted some of the other contributions on long waves that were published at that time such as Mensch (1979), Maddison (1982), Clark *et al.* (1982) and van Duijn (1983). However, what I considered to be of importance for my research was, not so much the exact regularity or causal structure of such 'waves', as the fact that it was possible to distinguish between different 'technological systems' that were dominant at different times and which differed in terms of internal dynamics, conditions of diffusion and institutional requirements. My hunch was that by taking such differences into account it would perhaps be possible to explore better why some countries were more successful than others in certain types of activities and why some countries succeeded much more than others in exploiting the international process of innovation and diffusion to their benefit.

Putting ideas to work

These were some of the ideas I set out to explore.[16] However, although my ideas were to a large extent inspired by the revival of Schumpeterian thinking, I had been in little direct contact with the advocates of the so-called neo-Schumpeterian theory.[17] In October 1985, I joined a group of economic historians from the Norwegian 'technology history project' (with which I had become partly associated) who were going to visit the Science Policy Research Unit (SPRU) in Sussex, UK. During this visit I was lucky enough to get the opportunity to give a staff seminar there. I remember that Christopher (Chris) Freeman, Keith Pavitt and Luc Soete were all present, and that they were very positive both to the main thrust of my arguments and to the empirical techniques I had used to support them. I realized that SPRU was probably the best academic environment around at the time for this type of research, and I began to play with the idea of turning the research I had started into a thesis there. I applied to and was (after some negotiation) accepted as a part time Ph.D. student at SPRU/University of Sussex.

During the following years I had several shorter stays at SPRU, the longest being in the autumn of 1986 when I stayed one full term. During these years I had a lot of fruitful interaction with several members of the staff, particularly Chris Freeman, Keith Pavitt and Nick von Tunzelmann (who became my supervisor). Chris Freeman also invited me to take part in the big IFIAS project, which was then already well under way, and which in 1988 resulted in the volume *Technical Change and Economic Theory*, edited by Giovanni Dosi, Christopher Freeman, Richard Nelson, Gerald Silverberg and Luc Soete. This gave me a chance to write about growth theory and its applications (Fagerberg 1988b) and combine it with my own stuff, and in connection with this I received a lot of stimulating feedback from the other participants, particularly Richard Nelson, who (I now realize) obviously knew most of the growth literature much better than I did.

In the same year the IFIAS book (at the time called 'the bible' by younger scholars) was published, my SPRU days came to an end with the defence of my thesis in the autumn. The thesis, entitled 'Technology, Growth and Trade: Schumpeterian Perspectives', combined a more macro-oriented approach, based on the application of the Marx–Schumpeter model of technological competition to the study of growth and competitiveness, with a more sectoral focus exploring the changing competition of international trade, its causes and the ability of individual countries to face the challenge. Hence, in contrast to my master's thesis, which ended up being purely theoretical, the doctoral thesis had a clear empirical basis, drawing on a variety of data sources (including, for instance, national accounts, trade data,[18] R&D data and patent statistics). Many of those data were not easily available and a great deal of time had been spent on searching for relevant data and transforming them to a format suitable for my purpose.

Perhaps the most important achievement was the formulation of a Schumpeterian growth model ('technology gap model') that could be extended to take into account trade and competitiveness as well and its subsequent application to post-war data for a sample of countries on different levels of development (see, in particular, Chapters 1 and 12, and the Appendix on p. 287). Following Schumpeter, the model assumes that both innovation and diffusion of technology fuel economic growth. However, in contrast to much previous work in this area, it was emphasized that innovation is not something that occurs only in the technologically leading country, from which it diffuses to other countries at different speeds. Innovation, it was argued, is a pervasive phenomenon in contemporary capitalism, and may be an important source of growth in poorer countries as well (though not necessarily in the same proportion as in a frontier nation).[19] Moreover, it was emphasized that successful imitation (or diffusion) often involves innovation as well, and that innovation and imitation generally draw on many of the same capabilities or resources. R&D capabilities, for instance, were shown to be crucial for both innovation and imitation.

Thus, 'catch-up' is not something that comes easy (as traditional neoclassical theory used to suggest, see Chapter 6). Successful catch-up, it was shown, normally involves both an extensive upgrading of the technological infrastructure and a rapid transformation of the composition of output and international trade (see Chapters 7–9 and 11). Arguably, the historical evidence tells us that policy has had an important role to play in such processes. The most clear-cut examples of this were of course Japan and the Asian NICs (Korea and Taiwan in particular). This evidence remains a matter of considerable controversy, however. For instance, the role of policy in the catch-up of Japan and the Asian NICs has been disputed by the World Bank in its study of the 'The East-Asian Miracle' (World Bank 1993). Aadne Cappelen and I discuss these issues in some detail in Chapter 3 of this book.

As argued above the 'technology gap model of economic growth' is not only applicable to the question of 'why growth rates differ' across countries, but can be used to analyse differences in performance among other entities as well. What matters is that it is possible to identify a 'system of innovation' with sufficient internal structure and coherence to qualify as a unit in the analysis. It has been suggested that such systems are more likely to be found at the regional than the national level, particularly in the case of the larger economies (Braczyk *et al.*, 1998). Chapters 4–5, which result from my close collaboration during the 1990s with Bart Verspagen,[20] put this idea into practice by applying the technology gap model to the growth performance of European regions. As suggested by the theory, the potential for diffusion and R&D capabilities were found to be important factors behind the observed growth differences across European regions. However, the outcome was strongly affected by structural and social factors, such as a large agricultural sector and high long-term unemployment, which were shown to contribute to the failure of many poorer regions fully to exploit the potential for diffusion.

Refining the analysis

After the defence of my doctoral thesis, I thought a lot about publishing it as a book but I never came that far. There were two reasons for this. First, I felt that more research was needed in order to arrive at a really comprehensive understanding of the relationship between technology, growth and competitiveness. In particular, I felt that although the thesis to some extent dealt with the consequences of the changing structure of international trade for countries with different patterns of specialization, and the role of trade (and specialization) as a medium for 'catching up', it did too little in terms of explaining how specialization was generated, sustained (or altered) and what the long-run consequences might be. Second, at that time there was a lot happening in this area on the theoretical front, such as the advent of the 'new growth theory', and I wanted some time to consider the possible consequences of this for my work.

The first opportunity to do more research on specialization came while I was working (lecturing) in Aalborg during the academic year 1987–88. The IKE-group was at the time under some pressure from fellow economists in Denmark with less heterodox inclinations. One of the suggestions that came up in the internal discussions within IKE, and which I strongly supported, was to write a book in English that presented their research for an international audience. In the end what came out of this was the highly influential volume on *National Systems of Innovation* edited by Bengt-Åke Lundvall (Lundvall *et al.* 1992). Building on earlier work by Lundvall (1985, 1988) and Andersen *et al.* (1981), I contributed to a study on the relationship between learning-based advantages, acquired through domestic user–producer interaction, and the international competitiveness of countries. In fact, I found the impact of such learning on competitiveness to be quite substantial. A revised and extended version of that study is included here as Chapter 13.

However, specialization is not only affected by local learning, important as it may be. It also has to do with differences in competitive conditions across sectors and industries, cross-country differences in capabilities, resources, market size and so on, and the willingness of firms and governments to devote resources to R&D. I include two articles written during the first half of the 1990s which explore these issues in some detail (Chapters 14 and 15). The results presented in these two articles emphasize the central role played by technological capability and R&D for international competitiveness in a whole range of industries. This clearly illustrates the crucial fact that innovation is a pervasive phenomenon that matters in most industries/sectors, although the forms it takes and the sources it depends on may, as pointed out by Pavitt (1984, 1988), differ considerably. A particular issue that is explored in these two chapters, and in a different manner in Chapters 9–10 as well, is to what extent small countries are at disadvantage in so-called 'high-tech' (R&D intensive) industries, as some neoclassical theorizing in this area indeed suggests.[21] This is, of course, an important question for policy makers, particularly in small countries. The research reported here indicates that there are some industries for which large domestic markets appear to be an important competitive factor and where firms from small countries consequently may face some additional constraints. However, these constraints often tend to be of a rather 'soft' character and may in many cases be overcome through appropriate strategies and/or policies. Arguably, this is an area where policy really matters.[22]

That innovation is a pervasive phenomenon in modern capitalism does of course not imply that all innovations are of equal importance. On the contrary, as pointed out already by Schumpeter, some clusters of innovations (or technological systems) may have a very large impact, what Chris Freeman calls 'technological revolutions' (Freeman and Perez 1984), while others are fairly marginal. The pay-offs to growth are clearly larger in the former case than in the latter. However, the nature of such pay-offs change through time as new technologies develop and expand, while older technologies become progressively less important. It follows that a pattern of specialization that has been very favourable for growth in the past may under changed circumstances have lost much its dynamism. Illustrations of such changes can be found in Chapters 7–9, which analyse the structural changes in OECD trade and its impact on specific countries, and in Chapter 11 for the European Union as a whole.

In the mid 1990s the European Union launched its Targeted Socio-Economic Research Program (TSER), the first large-scale European research program in this area. Like many others, Bart Verspagen and I thought that it might be fun to take part in this new activity. One of the topics that we singled out for research was the relationship between technology, specialization and growth in Europe over the long term. We started to contact others and soon found ourselves at the centre of a large network of enthusiastic people. Some of the participants were also part of other networks that considered applying to the TSER programme. So why not join forces? In that way the project grew very large with more than 50 researchers involved, and Bart – who became the coordinator of the project (labelled 'Technology, Economic Integration and Social Cohesion', TEIS) – had a hard time trying to keep everything on track. The project soon divided into three working groups, one of these coordinated by me. One of the main outputs of that work was the book *The Economic Challenge for Europe: Adapting to Innovation Based Growth*, edited by Paolo Guerrieri, Bart Verspagen and myself (Fagerberg *et al.* 1999), a summary of which is included here as Chapter 11.

It is argued in Chapter 11 that the technological dynamics in the capitalist world has changed considerably in recent decades. In most of the post-war period growth in Europe has been based on the scale-based technological system that originated in the USA around a century ago (and later diffused to Europe). European policies (including integration efforts) have to a large extent been geared to getting the maximum out of this potential. However, more recently the scale-based technological system has been replaced by a science-based one with ICT [23] as the most important part of the main engine of growth in the capitalist world. These changes, it is suggested, call for a reassessment of many established practices, institutions and policies. The chapter discusses how policy may be adjusted in order to get the most out of the current technological dynamics. [24]

A broader view?

The opportunity to place my own research in a broader setting came in 1991 with a request from Keith Smith of the STEP group in Oslo to write an overview paper on technology and growth for Norwegian policy makers. [25] When I sent a draft of the paper to Moses (Moe) Abramovitz, with whom I had been in contact for some time, [26] he reacted by inviting me to submit a substantially revised and expanded version to *The Journal of Economic Literature* (of which he was one of the editors). I was of course very pleased with this suggestion, not the least because it gave me an opportunity to work with Moe, whose work on 'catching up' had been an important source of inspiration for me in my own research. The paper, which was finalized during my stay at the IRPS (Graduate School for International Relations and Pacific Studies), [27] University of California San Diego during the academic year 1993–94, went through several rounds of revisions and was finally published in September 1994 (Fagerberg 1994). Moe's many insightful comments and suggestions substantially improved the content and exposition and contributed to a broadening of my understanding of processes of economic growth and 'catching up' processes. My understanding of the latter was also improved by my stay at the IRPS, which allowed me to follow lectures on Asian catch-up by area specialists such as Chalmers Johnson, Stephan Haggard and others (and to read their accounts of these processes).[28]

When I started to do research in the mid 1980s, mainstream growth theory had been a stagnant field for decades and was no longer able – if it ever had been – to generate a meaningful agenda for applied research. What happened during the 1970s and 1980s was that this agenda was taken over by more heterodox writers, many of whom were inspired by Schumpeterian ideas, my own work being no exception. However, I recognized from the reading I then undertook that there were important changes underway in the way mainstream looked at growth. Some of it, it should be said, was not so novel, as it based itself entirely on the idea of 'learning by doing' as a source of growth, an idea that had been widespread among growth theorists at least since the early 1960s. Yet it seemed to me that the approach suggested by Paul Romer in his seminal paper from 1990 (Romer 1990) made a real difference in this regard, since in that paper he incorporated the Schumpeterian idea of R&D-based innovation as the prime source of growth.[29] Hence, what in my view had happened was that at least some mainstream economists adopted parts of the Schumpeterian research agenda. This seemed to me to be a very positive development, as it might open up, I hoped, more promising discussions between economists with different theoretical inclinations and give new and more meaningful directions for empirical research in this area.

With hindsight, I may have been slightly over-optimistic. Rather than a more open-minded scholarly discourse, what we primarily have obtained is a swarm of imitators (to use a Schumpeterian term) trying to achieve academic credit by making relatively marginal changes and refinements in the formal models suggested by Romer and others, often without much concern for the validity of the assumptions they have to make in order to arrive at the desired results. In that respect, much of the recent revival of formal growth theorizing is no better than the kind of economics I encountered when I first enrolled as a student in the 1970s. There may be more gains in the applied area but these have taken long to materialize and are (as shown in Chapter 6) still relatively modest. In fact, the overwhelming majority of applied research that followed in the wake of the first 'new growth' models consisted of testing so-called conditional convergence models (also called 'Barro-equations'). This represents nothing new since similar exercises have been frequent in the applied literature on growth and development since the early 1970s. The reason for this is of course that such empirical tests can be made consistent with different theoretical perspectives. Hence, without further qualifications, such tests are not well suited for discriminating between different theories or increasing our understanding of the growth-inducing mechanisms pointed to by the new growth theories. This is not to say there is no empirical work available that can be used to shed light on the relationship between innovation and growth. In fact, there is by now a lot of work on issues such as science policy, research policy, innovation activities, diffusion of innovations and so on published in books and specialized journals such as *Research Policy*. However, most of this has been going on for a long time and is not specifically related to the new growth theories.

Maybe I expected too much. Perhaps I was so enchanted by the fact that someone in the neoclassical camp finally took innovation and diffusion of technology seriously, that I forgot to ask the crucial question of to what extent the way they modelled it was really adequate. In part, this was only natural since the new growth theory of Paul Romer and others and the 'technology gap theory' that I had used as a framework for my own research had a lot in common. Both constructs focused on the interaction between innovation and diffusion of technology as the prime source of growth, and in both cases diffusion – or 'spillovers' in the new growth framework – played a major role. There were, however, also some important differences. While the new growth theory is a typical formal theory, that is, 'an abstract structure set up to enable one to explore, find and check logical connections' (Nelson 1994, p. 292–3), the technology gap theory is much closer to what Nelson has called 'appreciative theorising', that is, theorizing close to the empirical substance which attempts to identify, interpret and understand important empirical relationships without necessarily putting the insights thus obtained into a formal (mathematical) model. Hence, the new growth theory is in a (formal) theoretical sense much more ambitious than the technology gap theory since the former insists on explaining both innovation and diffusion of technology – as well as their mutual interactions – within a unified, mathematical framework.

So, how is innovation explained within the type of new growth theories discussed here? The answer is simple: innovation is just like any other activity. In principle there is no difference between innovation and, say, shoe repair. Both activities are assumed to be carried out by profit-seeking entrepreneurs endowed with perfect knowledge and foresight about all factors relevant for their activities. The reason why the former activity is more conducive to growth than the latter has nothing to do with the activity in itself but with so-called externalities (or 'spillovers') that are assumed to be more frequent in the former case. Is this a valid understanding of how innovation occurs? It was certainly not Schumpeter's view as he described it in his *Theory of Economic Development* (1934). For Schumpeter, innovation was something special, and it required much more than ordinary economic activities. He was careful to distinguish between innovators, which he saw as driven essentially by the joy of creating, a competitive spirit (as in sports) and the pleasure of having success, and the surrounding managerial and financial infrastructure for which standard profit-oriented behaviour could perhaps be assumed. Since the motives of innovators are complex, and only partially related to economic gains, he held it as likely that innovation, in principle, could thrive under quite different institutional 'arrangements'. The answer to the question of what such arrangements might look like could only be found, he argued, 'by detailed observation of the psychology of entrepreneurial activity ... for given times and places' (Schumpeter 1934, p. 94). Later in life Schumpeter acknowledged that organized R&D within large firms was one such arrangement (Schumpeter 1943), although he did not go very far in analysing the nature of innovation within this (for him) new setting.[30] However, introducing the organizational aspect arguably adds to (rather than reduces) the complexity of the phenomenon under study, as testified by the rapidly increasing literature on how the organization of innovation activities differs across nations, sectors, industries and firms.[31]

Does this difference in views really matter? Yes it does. Take for instance the design of policies in this area. If you believe in the neoclassical story, this is only a question of providing the right economic incentives to profit-seeking entrepreneurs. If for some reason the government wants to increase innovative activity, what it has to do is to raise the rewards to it by, say, improving intellectual property rights, providing subsidies and so forth. However, if the motivations of innovators are more complex and dependent on, say, organizational, institutional or cultural contexts or factors, such an 'economistic' approach to policy may totally fail to generate the warranted results.

This is where I would like to end this exposition. To explore what shapes innovation in firms, organizations and society at large requires both empirical investigations and theoretical guidance and interpretation. It should come as no surprise that new growth theorizing, based as it is on a simplistic and one-sided view of how innovation occurs, has failed to provide a guide to the development of a really new agenda for applied research in this area. To do that, I will argue, one needs a broader view that draws on insights from not only economics but other disciplines as well, such as – for instance – history, business studies, sociology and cognitive science. Arguably, the extreme division and specialization of the social sciences that we have seen developing in the post-war period may have diverted attention from important factors behind long-run economic development that, like innovation, cannot be properly understood from a narrow disciplinary perspective.

Acknowledgements

I wish to thank my co-authors, Marjolin Caniëls, Ådne Cappelen, Bent Dalum, Ulrik Jørgensen and Bart Verspagen for their permission to include joint work in this book and Dymphna Evans for her patience and support during the time it took to finalize it. Furthermore, I am indebted to Ådne Cappelen, Nanna Frogg, Einar Lie, Keith Pavitt, Luc Soete and Bart Verspagen for comments on various drafts of the introduction. A special thanks to Kristine Bruland who read all the drafts and came up with a large number of detailed suggestions for improvements. The responsibility for any remaining error is mine, however.

Notes

1. The price to be paid for this is that there is some overlapping, especially in cases where articles use the same data source. This applies for instance to Chapters 7–10 in Part II and Chapters 13–14 in Part III which all use the same data base on international trade.
2. I had met Bengt-Åke Lundvall a few years earlier through the Nordic Summer University and had in this way became acquainted with the work he and other members of the IKE-group were doing on competitiveness. Chenais' work I became aware of through internal OECD documents that I gained access to through my job in the ministry (Chesnais 1981).
3. I am indebted to Professor Tor Rødseth, my former supervisor in Bergen, and Professor Gudmund Hernes who backed the application. I knew Hernes, who had previously been Professor of Sociology in Bergen and one of the lead researchers in 'Maktutredningen' (a research programme on the power structure in Norway), from his time as junior minister ('statssekretær') in the Planning Department. His intellectual and moral support was very important to me, especially in the in the early phase when my ideas were regularly attacked in the media and I, as a public servant, was prevented from defending them publicly.
4. Gunnar Sollie and I knew each other from Bergen where we both were graduate students in economics. At the Bureau he was working on a project on intra-Nordic trade with which I became partly associated. Together we developed a new method for assessing the effects of structural changes in international trade on trade performance that put more emphasis on the ability of each country to adapt to changing patterns of demand. Our ideas were set out in a paper which was later published in *Applied Economics* (included here as Chapter 8). The method was subsequently used by, among others, the OECD.

Sadly, Gunnar did not live long enough to experience the appreciation of our joint work as he died prematurely (of cancer) shortly before the article was published.

5.   I am grateful to the people at NUPI who made this possible. This includes Jens Andvig, Valter Angell, Daniel Heradstveit and the Director at the time, the late Johan Jørgen Holst. At NUPI I also received first-class assistance from the administrative staff, particularly Eilert Struksnes and Liv Høivik, and the two librarians, Dagfrid Hermansen and Tore Gustavsson.

6.   The Regional College in Telemark was one of several universities/colleges in Norway offering undergraduate history, and I chose it because I had heard that the course was really excellent. I was not disappointed. As for economics I was left with little choice since at the time the University of Bergen was the only Norwegian University offering standard undergraduate courses in economics.

7.   With 'we', I am referring to a group of students who shared these views. Central in this group were my two friends from Oslo, Trond Erik Seem and Erik Horn, who also enrolled as economics students, and with whom I shared an apartment close to the university. This apartment soon became a veritable 'hot-house' for critical thinking about economic, social and political issues with study groups, meetings and informal discussions in the late evenings. It is a sad fact that both Erik and Trond died prematurely, both in their forties. How I miss their company!

8.   Blaug (1958), Dobb (1973), Pasinetti (1974) and Schumpeter (1954). Other interpretations that influenced me a lot at the time include Bleaney (1976) and Shaikh (1978).

9.   This includes, for instance, Ådne Cappelen and Lars Mjøset from the local study group in Oslo with whom I have over the years written several papers on Norwegian economic policy. Our first analysis was published (in Norwegian) as Cappelen *et al.* (1984) as part of an NSU-initiated project on economic policy formation in the Nordic area. For more recent analyses in English see Fagerberg *et al.* (1990, 1992). Mjøset (1987) puts the Norwegian experience in a comparative perspective. On the Nordic level I met, among others, Bengt-Åke Lundvall, Esben Sloth Andersen and Bent Dalum from the newly founded Aalborg University Centre in Denmark.

10.   To support this interpretation I will briefly mention three examples of this way of looking at things. The first is Ricardo's discussion of the Corn Laws, in which the prevailing institutional set up (including the rules for allocating income across social classes) was seen as incompatible with the productive potential of the capitalist machine. Hence, if institutional change was not allowed, this would – according to Ricardo – lead to stagnation. A second and more far-reaching example of this way of thinking is Marx's distinction between the productive potential of the capitalist machine, which he called 'forces of production', and the surrounding institutional system, which he called 'relations of production'. He argued that in the long run the latter would constrain the former and hence had to be changed. Third and last, I will point to an example form post-Keynesian growth theory, in which it is argued that an institutional system that divides income between workers and capitalists according to certain rules is a prerequisite for long-run growth in capitalist economies (see Pasinetti 1974, pp. 86–102).

11.   See, in particular, Aglietta (1979) and Boyer (1988a).

12.   At the time Robert Boyer was doing a lot of work on formalizing this dynamic based to a large extent on Kaldorian ideas (Boyer and Petit 1981, Boyer 1988b). With my background in growth theories of the 'political economy' type I thought it would be fun to try to do the same within such a framework, so I devoted a lot of time on it while there. It proved to be quite complicated but with some good advice I finally succeeded. The paper, which initially circulated as a working paper from CEPREMAP, was finally published as Fagerberg (1991).

13.   This I have never regretted, and I think that there would be much less confusion about Schumpeter (and other classics as well) if people took the time to read the classic texts in the original rather than relying on the secondary literature that in many cases, it has to be said, does more harm than good. The three texts I read at the time, all in English, were *Theory of Economic Development* (1934), *Business Cycles I–II* (1939) and *Capitalism, Socialism and Democracy* (1943). The *Theory of Economic Development* is generally regarded as the basic introduction to Schumpeter's thinking, and deservedly so. *Capitalism, Socialism and Democracy*, by contrast, was clearly the most amusing read. However, although difficult to comprehend at times, I found *Business Cycles* to be very informative, since in that work Schumpeter offered a good deal of analysis and commentary on actual economic developments.

14.   See, for example, Schumpeter (1943), pp. 31–2 and pp. 82–3 (cited after the fourth edition, 1954).

15.   In my view this both explains and justifies the many recent attempts to introduce system concepts to the analysis of innovation and diffusion such as 'national systems of innovation', 'regional systems of innovation', 'sectoral systems of innovation', 'technological systems' and the like (for overviews and further references see Freeman 1995 and Edquist 1997).

16.   I develop these ideas in more detail in Fagerberg (1984) and in the introductory chapter of my thesis (Fagerberg 1988a).

17. My first direct encounter with the proponents of this approach was, I believe, at a Nordic Summer University workshop in Copenhagen in March 1983 in which Chris Freeman and Carlota Perez gave a joint presentation (published as Freeman and Perez 1984). I was struck by the vigour and fruitfulness of their approach.

18. The trade data used in this book are mostly drawn from a database constructed by Bent Dalum, Aalborg University Centre and myself on the basis of trade data supplied by the OECD (on tape). I am indebted to Bent for his help and encouragement in using trade data in analyses of structural change and competitiveness. Without his assistance the analysis presented here would certainly have been less rich.

19. This implies, of course, that knowledge is conceived quite differently from the traditional public good approach of neoclassical economics. For an extended discussion see Chapter 6 and Fagerberg (1994).

20. I got to know Bart Verspagen when he was a Ph.D. student in Maastricht towards the end of the 1980s and was struck by the similarity of our approaches. At the time I was acting as Head of the Department of International Economics and Development Economics at NUPI and I invited Bart to come to NUPI as a guest researcher and stay with us for a few weeks. Bart had, as part of his Ph.D. thesis, developed a non-linear version of the technology gap model that allowed for both 'catching up' and 'falling behind' and which greatly impressed me (Verspagen 1991). This was the start of a very rewarding relationship. In the early/mid 1990s we started on Bart's suggestion to do joint work on European regions. Our common interest in the relationship between technology and growth has also resulted several other papers (see, Fagerberg and Verspagen 2000 and Chapter 2 in this volume). We have also edited two books (Fagerberg *et al.* 1994, 1999) and have organized several workshops and conferences together.

21. The logic behind this assertion is the simple one that when there are increasing returns to scale, as is commonly assumed to be the case in these industries, unit costs are a decreasing function of the volume of production. Under such circumstances one might expect that firms with access to large markets would outperform those who operate in smaller markets. The argument is a tricky one, however, because the outcome depends on 'market access' which is notoriously difficult to define and measure in open economies.

22. See, in particular, the case study on electronics presented in Chapter 10.

23. There is a strong and very robust correlation between high growth in manufacturing productivity growth and an increasing presence in electronics broadly defined. See Fagerberg (2000 and Chapter 2 in this volume).

24. For an analysis of how the increasing importance of ICT technologies affects global competition and the competitiveness of countries see Meliciani (2001).

25. This paper was published as a STEP working paper (8/92). An English version was presented to the International Joseph A. Schumpeter Society in Kyoto in August 1992 and published in *Evolutionary Economics* a few years later (Fagerberg 1995).

26. I received a letter from Moe, whom I did not know at the time, in 1988, expressing strong interest for my research. He rightly saw it as a continuation and extension of his own work on catching up. Thereafter, I continued to send him papers, and on several occasions he replied with comments and encouragements. In 1993 I had the pleasure to receive him in Norway at a conference in part organized by me. The proceedings, including a paper by Moe, were published as Fagerberg *et al.* 1994.

27. I am grateful to IRPS and to the Dean at that time, Peter Gourevitch, for inviting me and providing me with such excellent working facilities.

28. See, in particular, Johnson (1982), which I really enjoyed reading. I also learnt much from the accounts by Amsden (1989), Haggard (1990) and Wade (1990).

29. Since the publication of Romer (1990) there have been many new theoretical contributions in this area; see Aghion and Howitt (1998) for an extended account. I will not discuss these further here since I intend to focus on arguments that appear to be common to all R&D-based new growth models.

30. See, in particular, Schumpeter (1943), ch. XII, pp. 131–4. He thought that this might ease innovation and, hence, increase its speed considerably, but did not analyse the issue in depth.

31. See, for instance, Malerba and Orsenigi (1997) and Lam (2000).

References

Abramovitz, M. (1979). 'Rapid growth potential and its realisation: the experience of capitalist economics in the post-war period', in Malinvaud, E. (ed.), *Economic Growth and Resources: Vol. 1. The Major Issues*, London: Macmillan, pp. 1–30.

Aghion, Philippe and Howitt, P. (1998). *Endogenous Growth Theory*, Cambridge, MA: MIT Press.

Aglietta, M. (1979). *A Theory of Capitalist Regulation. The U.S. Experience,* London: NLB.

Amsden, A.H. (1989). *Asia's Next Giant: South Korea and Late Industrialization*, New York: Oxford University Press.

Andersen, E.S., Dalum, B. and Villumsen, G. (1981). *International Specialisation and the Home Market*, Aalborg: Aalborg University Press.

Blaug, M. (1958). *Ricardian Economics: A Historical Study*, New Haven: Yale University Press.

Bleaney, M. (1976). *Underconsumption Theories: A History and Critical Analysis*, London: Lawrence and Wishart.

Boyer, R. (1988a). 'Technical change and the theory of regulation', in Dosi, G. et al. (eds.), *Technical change and economic theory*, Pinter, London, pp. 67–94.

Boyer, R. (1988b). 'Formalizing growth regimes within a regulation approach', in Dosi, G. *et al.* (eds), *Technical Change and Economic Theory*, London: Pinter, pp. 608–30.

Boyer, R. and Petit, P. (1981). 'Progrès technique, croissance et emploi: un modèle d'inspiration Kaldorienne pour six industries européenes', *Revue Economique*, **32**: 1113–53.

Braczyk, H.J. *et al.* (1998). *Regional Innovation Systems*, London: UCL Press.

Cappelen, Å., Fagerberg, J. and Mjøset, L. (1984). 'Den norske modellen', *Nordisk tidskrift för politisk ekonomi*, No. 15/16: 75–108.

Chesnais, F. (1981). 'The Notion of International Competitiveness', Discussion Paper DSTI/SPR/81.32, OECD, Paris.

Clark, J., Freeman, C. and Soete, L. (1982). *Unemployment and Technical Innovation: A Study of Long Waves and Economic Development*, London: Pinter.

Cornwall, J. (1977). *Modern Capitalism: Its Growth and Transformation*, London: St. Martin's Press.

Dobb, M. (1973). *Theories of Value and Distribution since Adam Smith: Ideology and Economic Theory*, Cambridge: Cambridge University Press.

Dosi, G., Freeman, C., Nelson, R., Silverberg, G. and Soete, L. (eds) (1988). *Technical Change and Economic Theory*, London: Pinter.

Edquist. C. (1997). *Systems of Innovation. Technologies, Institutions and Organisations*, London: Pinter.

Fagerberg, J. (1984). 'På søking etter en teori om utenrikshandel og vekst', *Nordisk tidskrift för politisk ekonomi*, No. 17: 40–62.

Fagerberg, J. (1988a). 'Technology Growth and Trade. Schumpeterian Perspectives', Ph.D. thesis, University of Sussex, Brighton.

Fagerberg, J. (1988b). 'Why growth rates differ', in Dosi, G. et al. (eds), *Technical Change and Economic Theory*, London: Pinter, pp. 432–57.

Fagerberg, J. (1991). 'Technology and regulation in a classical model of economic growth', *European Journal of Political Economy*, **7**: 299–312.

Fagerberg, J. (1994). 'Technology and international differences in growth rates', *Journal of Economic Literature*, **32**: 1147–75.

Fagerberg, J. (1995). 'Convergence or divergence? The impact of technology on "why growth rates differ"', *Journal of Evolutionary Economics*, **5**: 269–84.

Fagerberg, J. (2000). 'Technological progress, structural change and productivity growth', *Structural Change and Economic Dynamics*, **11**: 393–411.

Fagerberg, J. and Verspagen, B. (2000). 'Productivity, R&D Spillovers and Trade', in van Ark, B., Kuipers, S.K. and Kuper, G.H. (eds), *Productivity, Technology and Economic Growth*, Dordrecht: Kluwer Academic Publishers, pp. 345–60

Fagerberg, J., Cappelen, Å., Mjøset, L. and Skarstein, R. (1990). 'The decline of social-democratic state capitalism in Norway', *New Left Review*, No. 181: 60–94.

Fagerberg, J., Cappelen, Å and Mjøset, L. (1992). 'Structural change and economic policy: the Norwegian model under pressure', *Norwegian Journal of Geography*, **46**(2): 95–107.

Fagerberg, J., Verspagen, B. and von Tunzelman, N. (eds) (1994). *The Dynamics of Technology, Trade and Growth*, Aldershot: Edward Elgar.

Fagerberg, J., Guerrieri, P. and Verspagen, B (eds) (1999). *The Economic Challenge for Europe: Adapting to Innovation Based Growth*, Cheltenham: Edward Elgar.

Freeman, C. (1995). 'The "National System of Innovation" in historical perspective', *Cambridge Journal of Economics*, **19**: 5–24.

Freeman, C. and Perez, C. (1984). 'Long waves and new technology', *Nordisk tidskrift för politisk ekonomi*, No. 17: 5–14.

Gerschenkron, A. (1962). *Economic Backwardness in Historical Perspective*, Cambridge, MA: Belknap Press.

Haggard, S. (1990). *Pathways from the Periphery: The Politics of Growth in the Newly Industrializing Countries*, New York: Cornell University Press.

Johnson, C.A. (1982). *MITI and the Japanese Miracle: The Growth of Industrial Policy, 1925–1975*, Stanford: Stanford University Press.

Kaldor, N. (1978). 'The effect of devaluations on trade in manufactures', in Kaldor, N. (ed.), *Further Essays on Applied Economics*, New York: Holmes & Meyer, pp. 99–116.

Kaldor, N. (1981). 'The role of increasing returns, technical progress and cumulative causation in the theory of international trade and economic growth', *Economic Applique* (ISMEA), **34**: 593–617.

Lam, A. (2000). 'Tacit knowledge, organisational learning and societal institutions: an integrated framework.', *Organization Studies*, **21**: 487–513.

Lundvall, B.-Å. (1985). *Product Innovation and User–Producer Interaction,* Aalborg: Aalborg University Press.

Lundvall, B.-Å. (1988). 'Innovation as an interactive process – from user–producer interaction to the National System of Innovation', in Dosi, G. *et al.* (eds), *Technical Change and Economic Theory,* London: Pinter, pp. 349–69.

Lundvall, B.-Å. (1992). *National Systems of Innovation: Towards a Theory of Innovation and Interactive Learning,* Pinter: London.

Maddison, A. (1982). *Phases of Capitalist Development,* Oxford: Oxford University Press.

Malerba, F. and Orsenigo, L. (1997). 'Technological regimes and sectoral patterns of innovative activities', *Industrial and Corporate Change,* **6**: 83–117.

Meliciani, V. (2001). *Technology, Trade and Growth in OECD Countries. Does Specialisation Matter,* London: Routledge.

Mensch, G. (1979). *Stalemate in Technology,* Cambridge, MA: Ballinger Publishing Company.

Mjøset, L. (1987). 'Nordic economic policies in the 1970s and 1980s', *International Organization,* **41**(3): 403–56.

Nelson, R.R. (1994). 'What has been the matter with neoclassical growth theory?', in Silverberg, G. and Soete, L. (eds), *The Economics of Growth and Technical Change,* Aldershot: Edward Elgar, pp. 290–324

Pasinetti, L.L. (1974). *Growth and Income Distribution: Essays in Economic Theory,* Cambridge: Cambridge University Press.

Pavitt, K. (1984). 'Patterns of technical change: towards a taxonomy and a theory', *Research Policy,* **13**: 343–74.

Pavitt, K. (1988). 'International patterns of technological accumulation', in Hood, N. and Vahlne, J.E. (eds), *Strategies in Global Competition,* London: Croom Helm.

Posner, M.V. (1961). 'International trade and technical change', *Oxford Economic Papers,* **13**: 323–41.

Romer, P.M. (1990). 'Endogenous technological change', *Journal of Political Economy,* **98**: S71–S102.

Schumpeter, J. (1934). *The Theory of Economic Development,* Cambridge, MA: Harvard University Press.

Schumpeter, J. (1939). *Business Cycles: A Theoretical, Historical, and Statistical Analysis of the Capitalist Process I–II,* New York: McGraw-Hill.

Schumpeter, J. (1943). *Capitalism, Socialism and Democracy,* New York: Harper.

Schumpeter, J.A. (1954). *History of Economic Analysis,* New York: Allen & Unwin.

Shaikh, A. (1978). 'An introduction to the history of crises theories', in *US Capitalism in Crises,* URPE, USA, pp. 219–41.

Sraffa, P. (1960). *Production of Commodities by Means of Commodities: Prelude to a Critique of Economic Theory,* Cambridge: Cambridge University Press.

Thirlwall, A.P. (1979). 'The balance of payments constraints as an explanation of international growth rate differences', *Banca Nazionale del Lavoro Quarterly Review,* **32**: 45–53.

Van Dujin, J.J. (1983). *The Long Wave in Economic Life,* London: Allen & Unwin.

Vernon, R. (1966). 'International investment and international trade in the product cycle', *Quarterly Journal of Economics,* **80**: 190–207.

Verspagen, B. (1991). 'A new empirical approach to catching up or falling behind', *Structural Change and Economic Dynamics,* **2**: 359–80.

Wade, R. (1990). *Governing the Market. Economic Theory and the Role of Government in East Asian Industrialization,* Princeton: Princeton University Press.

World Bank (1993). *The East Asian Miracle. Economic Growth and Public Policy,* New York: Oxford University Press.

PART I

TECHNOLOGY AND GROWTH

A technology gap approach to why growth rates differ *

Jan FAGERBERG

Economics Department, Norwegian Institute of International Affairs, P.O. Box 8159, 0033 Oslo 1, Norway

This paper contains a discussion and test of the technology gap approach to development and growth. The basic hypotheses of the theory are tested on pooled cross-sectional and time-series data for 25 industrial countries for the period 1960–1983. The sample includes, in addition to 19 OECD countries, 6 of the most important industrial economies from the non-OECD area. The findings of the paper confirm that there exists a close correlation between the level of economic development, measured as GDP per capita, and the level of technological development, measured through R&D or patent statistics. Furthermore, for the group of 25 countries as a whole, technology gap models of economic growth are found to explain a large part of the actual differences in growth rates, both between countries and periods. As expected, both the scope for imitation, growth in innovative activity and "efforts" to narrow the gap (investment) appear as powerful explanatory factors of economic growth. However, when the non-OECD countries, and later USA and Japan, are removed from the sample, the explanatory power of the technology variables, especially growth in innovative activity, diminishes.

1. Introduction

Why do growth rates differ? When students of economic growth nearly thirty years ago started to study this question, they expected differences in the supply of capital and labour to be of utmost importance. Much to their surprise, differences in the growth of capital and labour explained [1] only a small part of the actual differences in growth between nations (Abramowitz [1], Solow [32], Denison [9]). One of the consequences of these paradoxical findings was to put technology in the forefront of theoretical and empirical studies of growth. Solow [32] and others extended the neoclassical theory of growth by including technology as a third factor of production in addition to capital and labour. According to this approach, technology should be regarded as a free good, growing at a constant, exponential rate.

The technology gap approach, developed by Posner [24], Gomulka [11], Cornwall [7,8] and others, also emphasizes the crucial role of technology in the process of economic growth, but from a radically different perspective. According to this approach, the international economic system is characterized by marked differences in technological levels and trends, differences which can only

* This is a revised version of a paper presented at a Seminar at Science Policy Research Unit, University of Sussex, on 17 October 1985. The research presented in the paper has been supported financially by the Norwegian Institute of International Affairs (NUPI) and the Norwegian Research Council for Social Sciences and the Humanities. Andreas Lindner at the Science, Technology and Industry Indicators Unit, OECD, and Paul Claus at World Intellectual Property Organisation have both been very helpful in furnishing me with unpublished data on patent activities. Furthermore, I want to thank the participants at the seminar and colleagues at NUPI for comments and proposals for improvements, retaining, of course, sole responsibility for the final version.

[1] The term "explain" in the present context refers primarily to the fit of a regression. Obviously, neither the models in "the growth accounting" literature, nor "the technology gap" models to be developed later, can claim to be "explanations" in the sense that all relevant functional relationships and variables are included. While economic development is shaped by a large number of interrelated factors, of which many cannot be easily quantified, the models discussed and developed in this paper include only a few variables, all on a very high level of aggregation. Therefore, the tests presented in this paper cannot be expected to explain all the observed differences in growth between countries. What they can do is to test the explanatory power of a few vital variables and in this way increase our understanding of economic processes and give directions for future research. The "growth accounting" debate is in my view an excellent example of this.

Research Policy 16 (1987) 87–99
North-Holland

be overcome through radical changes in technological, economic and social structures. The main hypotheses of the technology gap approach to economic growth may be summarized as follows:

(1) There is a close relation between a country's economic and technological level of development.
(2) The rate of economic growth of a country is positively influenced by the rate of growth in the technological level of the country.
(3) It is possible for a country facing a technological gap, i.e. a country on a lower technological level than the countries on "the world innovation frontier", to increase its rate of economic growth through imitation ("catching up").
(4) The rate at which a country exploits the possibilities offered by the technological gap depends on its ability to mobilize resources for transforming social, institutional and economic structures.

Hypotheses 1 and 2, laid down in the seminal contributions by Posner [24] and Gomulka [11], may be regarded as the basic hypotheses of the technology gap theory. Curiously enough, with one notable exception (Pavitt and Soete [23]), very little empirical research has been done in order to test these hypotheses. In contrast to this, the "catching up" hypothesis (3) has been tested extensively, using the level of economic development as a proxy for technological development (Gomulka [11], Singer and Reynolds [30], Cornwall [7,8] and others). [2] The results seem generally to support this hypothesis. Regarding the last hypothesis, the research process is still in an early phase, but the results so far seem to support this hypothesis also (Parvin [21], Cornwall [7,8], Abramowitz [2]).

The purpose of this paper is to test the basic hypotheses of the technology gap theory and analyse the differing growth performance of the industrial countries during the last twenty years. For this purpose it was found necessary to include in the sample, in addition to 19 OECD countries, 6 of the most important industrial economies from the non-OECD area: Brazil, Argentina, Mexico, Korea (South), Hong Kong and Taiwan. In the next section the relation between levels of eco-

nomic and technological development is discussed and tested. With the results in mind, the third section presents a test of a technology gap approach to "why growth rates differ".

2. Economic and technological levels of development

Most people, economists or not, would probably agree with the proposition that economic and technological levels of development are closely related. But they would probably disagree on how levels of technological development should be defined and measured. Following traditional neo-classical theory, the level of technological development of a country depends primarily on the relation between capital and labour. The technology gap theorists on the other hand relate the technological level of a country to its *level of innovative activity*. A high level of innovative activity means a high share of "new" goods in output and an extensive use of "new" techniques in production. Since "new" goods command high prices and "new" techniques imply high productivity, it follows that countries with a comparatively higher level of innovative activities also tend to have a higher level of value-added per worker, or GDP per capita, than other countries. [3] Of course, a country may increase its level of economic development by mainly imitating activities, but it cannot, according to the way of reasoning sketched above, surpass the most advanced countries economically without passing them in innovative activities as well.

Measures of technological level and/or innovative activity may be divided into "technology input" measures and "technology output" measures (Soete [31]). Of the former type, expenditures on education, research and development and employment of scientists and engineers may be mentioned, of the latter, patenting activity. Regarding the former type, these measures may be said to be related to the innovative capacity of a country as well as its capacity for imitation, since a certain scientific base is a precondition for successful

---

[2] For an overview, see Choi [6].

[3] This is the argument with runs through the whole "neotechnological" tradition, from Kravis [14] to Posner [24], Vernon [33] and Hirsch [13]. For a more recent formulation, see Krugman [15].

imitation in most areas. [4] This study confines itself to one "technology input" measure, R&D. Patenting activity, on the other hand, is more directly related to inventive activity and process and product innovation than to imitation.

The main problem concerning R&D as an indicator of technological level is that the data generally are of poor quality, especially for years earlier than 1970, and for non-OECD countries. Yearly time-series dating back to the early 1960s exist for a few countries only. Another problem is whether or not military R&D should be included. [5] Patent statistics, on the other hand, are available for a lot of countries and for long time-spans. Furthermore, studies on the relation between patenting activity and R&D on the firm or industry level seem to indicate a close relation between patenting activity and R&D. [6] Differences in national patenting regulations have made it more difficult to compare patenting activities across countries. [7] But, as pointed out by Soete [31], this problem may be significantly reduced by limiting the analysis to patenting activities of different countries in one common (foreign) market. Contrary to Soete who used foreign patenting in USA as indicator, this paper uses foreign patenting on the world market. [8] This has several ad-

vantages. [9] First, it gives data for USA, which is of great importance in an analysis of technological gaps and trends. Second, the propensity to patent in the US market probably varies more than the propensity to patent in foreign markets in general.

Figure 1 compares the development of average civil R&D as percentage of GDP, patenting activity (less domestic patents) and average GDP per capita in constant 1980 prices for the OECD countries between 1963 and 1982. [10] All variables are expressed relative to average 1963–82 to facilitate comparison. Before 1973, the R&D and patent indicators show a relatively similar pattern. During the 1960s both show a strong upward trend, strongest for patents, with peaks in 1968/69, followed by a slowdown in the early/mid 1970s. It is an interesting fact that both indicators peak several years before GDP per capita, indicating that innovative activity cannot be seen as a mere reflection of economic activity. After 1973, however, patenting activity continues to decline, while the growth in R&D picks up again from 1979 onwards. This general slowdown in patenting activity affects most countries except Japan, Finland and the Asian NICs. However, in general the diverging trends in the two technology indicators in the last years (after 1978) should be interpreted with great care because new international patenting channels may have influenced the general pro-

---

[4] The role of R&D as a necessary precondition for imitation is emphasized by, among others, Freeman ([10], p. 185) and Mansfield et al. ([18], p. 209).

[5] I have chosen to exclude military R&D. The main reason for this is that if included, the size of the military sector of a country, relative to the military sectors of other countries, would have influenced the rank of the country relative to other countries in terms of technological level. For instance, a country like Japan, which for political reasons does not have a military sector, would have obtained a lower rank in terms of technological level if military R&D had been included.

[6] This was pointed out already by Schmookler ([26], pp. 44–55) in a case study of USA for the year 1953. More recent evidence pointing in the same direction may be found in Griliches ([12], especially ch. 1 and 3).

[7] Nevertheless Soete [31] found a quite close correlation between levels of domestic patenting and R&D expenses in a cross-country study covering the business enterprise sector in 19 OECD countries.

[8] That is: Total patent applications of residents in country x in all countries which report patent applications to WIPO (World Intellectual Property Organisation) less patent applications by residents of x in country x.

[9] A possible disadvantage is that since patent regulations differ between countries, and several studies show that the level of external patent applications of a country is correlated with the level of its exports, external patent applications of a country may be influenced by the geographical breakdown of its export. However, case studies show that external patenting is not significantly affected by differences in patent regulations between countries. Thus, this problem is probably not of major importance. Differences in "attractiveness" between countries in relation to patenting from abroad seem mainly to depend on the size and level of economic development in the recipient country. Also the level of exports and subsidiaries of MNEs of the patenting country in the recipient country seem to be of importance, but here the direction of causation is not at all clear. For discussion and tests of the relation between external patenting and characteristics of the patenting and the recipient country the reader is referred to Schiffel and Kitti [25], Bosworth [4,5] and Basberg [3].

[10] The reader is referred to the appendix for further information regarding sources and methods.

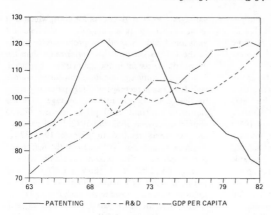

PATENTING   ---- R&D   —·—GDP PER CAPITA

Fig. 1. Technology indicators 1963–82 (OECD).

pensity to patent through the established national channels. [11]

Tables 1 and 2 present indexes of technological level for 25 countries in the periods 1960/63–68, 1969–73, 1974–79 and 1980–82/83. The first index is based on patent statistics, while the second is based on R&D data. In both cases the sources and methods are the same as in fig. 1 above. Both indexes are expressed relative to average in the period (average level = 1). To construct an index of technological development based on patent statistics, it was necessary to normalize the levels of patenting activity according to the size of the country and the propensity to patent in foreign markets. This was done by dividing the number of patent applications filed by residents of a country in foreign markets by the number of inhabitants and the share of exports in GDP in the country. The reason for including the degree of openness of the economy in the index is that the propensity to patent in foreign markets is assumed to be dependent on the importance of the

[11] Since 1 June 1978 national channels for filing applications for patents have been supplemented by a European channel (EPC) and an international channel (PCT). If the applications filed through these channels are added to the data supplied through the WIPO member countries, the measure of patenting activity would show an upward trend (OECD [20]).

Table 1
Index of technological level (patent data) [a]

	1960–68	1969–73	1974–79	1980–83
USA	5.091	4.701	3.342	3.391
Japan	0.509	1.113	1.430	2.053
FRG	2.561	2.502	2.542	2.228
France	1.527	1.459	1.347	1.276
UK	1.460	1.218	0.987	1.081
Italy	0.534	0.502	0.486	0.593
Canada	0.536	0.486	0.545	0.561
Austria	0.765	0.769	0.844	0.802
Belgium	0.477	0.379	0.351	0.285
Denmark	0.734	0.853	1.037	0.837
Netherlands	1.045	0.952	0.956	0.850
Norway	0.305	0.326	0.463	0.396
Sweden	2.517	2.216	2.457	2.222
Switzerland	5.601	5.820	5.796	5.152
Finland	0.313	0.500	0.786	1.178
Ireland	0.090	0.110	0.118	0.143
Australia	0.403	0.516	0.691	0.925
New Zealand	0.251	0.284	0.440	0.563
Spain	0.172	0.158	0.200	0.184
Brazil	0.011	0.013	0.022	0.026
Argentina	0.045	0.070	0.068	0.068
Hong Kong	0.015	0.015	0.036	0.067
Taiwan	0.011	0.010	0.028	0.075
Korea	0.001	0.003	0.007	0.016
Mexico	0.025	0.027	0.031	0.027
Standard dev.	1.461	1.423	1.296	1.193

[a] The index is defined as follows: Index = [PAT/ (POP•X/GDP)], relative to average of the sample, where PAT = Patent applications filed in other countries; POP = Population; X = Exports in constant prices; GDP = Gross national product in constant prices.

Table 2
Index of technological level (R&D data) [a]

	1963–68	1969–73	1974–79	1980–82
USA	1.821	1.558	1.413	1.407
Japan	1.636	1.576	1.584	1.711
FRG	1.581	1.681	1.689	1.740
France	1.690	1.338	1.218	1.211
UK	1.745	1.505	1.340	1.400
Italy	0.774	0.775	0.707	0.703
Canada	1.254	1.004	0.869	0.914
Austria	0.436	0.537	0.747	0.841
Belgium	1.200	1.206	1.113	
Denmark	0.654	0.836	0.788	0.776
Netherlands	1.963	1.840	1.624	1.363
Norway	0.818	1.030	1.096	0.928
Sweden	0.971	1.100	1.316	1.472
Switzerland	2.595	2.025	1.933	1.661
Finland	0.414	0.740	0.820	0.885
Ireland	0.589	0.651	0.658	0.573
Australia	1.091	1.056	0.812	0.725
New Zealand	0.523	0.669	0.682	
Spain	0.174	0.229	0.284	0.290
Brazil			0.528	0.435
Argentina	0.218	0.176	0.284	0.363
Hong Kong				
Taiwan	0.425			
Korea	0.305	0.291	0.495	0.602
Mexico	0.120	0.176		
Standard dev.	0.665	0.537	0.454	0.450

[a] Civil R&D in percentage of GDP relative to average in the sample.

home market relative to export markets.

The indexes of technological level reveal several interesting facts. Firstly, as can be seen from the standard deviations, the absolute differences in technological levels between countries are greater on the patent-based index than on the index based on R&D data. This is consistent with the assumption that patent statistics measure innovative activities, while R&D data measure both innovative

and imitating activities. Secondly, the ranking of the countries is very similar on the two indexes. For instance, the seven technologically most advanced countries in the early 1960s, according to patent statistics, were Switzerland, USA, FRG, Sweden, France, UK and the Netherlands. With one exception these countries also were the technologically most advanced according to R&D statistics. A similar relation holds for later periods. Thirdly, the two indexes give broadly the same picture of the changes in relative technological position through time. Both indexes show an increase in the technological levels relative to other countries for countries like Japan, Finland, and Korea, and a similar decrease for "old superpowers" like US, UK and the Netherlands. Furthermore, it may be noted that both indexes show a decreasing technological gap (measured in terms of standard deviation) from the early 1960s to the early 1980s. But this process seems to have slowed down in the late 1970s.

Table 3 presents a formal test of the relation between the two measures of technological level. Since the relation between them is non-linear, and the ranking is what interests most, the test is performed by calculating the Spearman rank correlation separately for each period. The test shows a strong positive correlation between the two rankings, significant at a 1 percent level at a one-tailed test. Table 3 also presents similar tests of the relation between the technological level on the one hand, and the level of economic development measured as GDP per capita in fixed prices on the other hand. In both cases a positive correlation existed between the two rankings, significant at a 1 percent level at a one-tailed test.

In summary, the results of this section support the general hypothesis of the technology gap theory of a strong positive relation between the level

Table 3
Rank correlations – economic and technological level

	1960/63–68	1969–73	1974–79	1980–82/83
R&D index/ Patent index [a]	0.784	0.829	0.839	0.827
R&D index/ GDP per capita [a,b]	0.642	0.677	0.709	0.701
Patent index/ GDP per capita [b,c]	0.837	0.826	0.838	0.795

[a] Sample = 20.
[b] Fixed prices, at the price levels and exchange rates of 1980.
[c] Sample = 25.

of technological and economic development. [12] However, this is only a first step in testing the theory. Of particular interest is whether or not the technology gap theory may explain the differing growth performance of industrial countries in the post-war period. This will be discussed in the next section.

3. Technology gaps, innovation and economic growth

The technology gap approach, following Schumpeter [27–29], analyses economic growth as the combined result of two conflicting forces; innovation which tends to increase technological gaps, and imitation or diffusion which tends to reduce them. Countries on a comparatively low economic and technological level may realize higher growth rates than other countries by exploiting the potential for imitation. But this is certainly no "law". It depends both on their own efforts and the innovative efforts of the more advanced countries in increasing the "gap".

Attempts to test models which explain economic growth (or productivity growth) as a function of both technology gaps and efforts or "capacity" for exploiting the gap, have been made by Parvin [21], Cornwall [7,8], Marris [19] and Lindbeck [16]. In general, these studies show that both technology gaps, measured (in different ways) by GDP per capita, and efforts in exploiting it, measured by investment ratios, have significant influences on growth. However, a common omission in all these models and tests is that they do not include any variable measuring differing trends in innovativeness between countries, as pointed out by Pavitt [22]. According to Pavitt, this is a major weakness, because innovation plays an increasingly important role in the process of growth.

Pavitt and Soete [23] have tried to extend the models developed by Cornwall [7,8] and others by including US patents per capita and growth in US patents. The model was tested for seven different

time periods using cross-sectional data for the period 1890–77 covering 14 OECD countries. The results do not seem to indicate any stable relations between the variables involved for the period as a whole. Surprisingly, the "gap" variable (relative GDP per capita) does not seem to influence economic growth, except for the period 1970–77, and then with an opposite sign of what could be expected. A significant positive effect of patent growth on economic growth between 1950 and 1970 turns to a significant negative effect in the period 1970–77. The level of patents does not seem to matter much, except for the last period and then with a negative sign. Pavitt and Soete also tested alternative models, replacing either economic growth with productivity growth as the dependent variable, or patent statistics with R&D statistics as independent variables. The results were not qualitatively different, with the exception that the "gap" variable performed better when productivity growth was taken as the dependent variable.

Generally, the results obtained by Pavitt and Soete cannot be interpreted as fully supporting the technology gap approach. Pavitt's assumption of the increasing importance of innovativeness for growth does not seem to get any support at all. One possible reason for this somewhat disappointing result may be the inclusion of both a technological level variable and an economic level variable in the same model. These variables reflect to a high degree the same basic relationship, and are – as shown by Pavitt and Soete themselves – closely correlated. By including both types of variables in the same model, and by estimating on cross-sectional data only, a problem of multicollinearity appears.

Although the general approach of this paper is quite close to that of Pavitt and Soete, the test presented in the following differs from their test in several respects. Firstly, in terms of model specification, the model does not include more than one "gap" variable; GDP per capita. This variable was preferred for two reasons: (1) As shown in the previous section, the ranking according to GDP per capita and patent- or R&D-based indexes of technological development was quite close. (2) The other two indexes have some disadvantages compared with the GDP index. The patent index clearly overestimates the absolute differences in technological level between countries, and R&D data do not exist for several countries and periods.

---

[12] This confirms the results obtained earlier by Pavitt and Soete [23]. They tested the correlation between GDP per capita, US patents per capita and R&D expenditure per capita in selected years up to 1977 for a sample of 14–15 OECD countries. The results indicated a positive and significant correlation between economic and technological level, especially after 1963.

A second difference between this test and that of Pavitt and Soete is that the sample in this test is not limited to OECD countries, but includes some of the more important industrial countries of the non-OECD area as well. The importance of including these countries in testing a technology gap theory can hardly be questioned. Thirdly, the present test differs from that of Pavitt and Soete in the method of estimation. While Pavitt and Soete estimated on cross-country data from different periods, this test uses a pooled time-series cross-country data set. Both methods, of course, have their advantages and problems, but in the present context the latter method should be more efficient because it uses more information. [13]

In general, the model tested contains three variables; the potential for imitation, the efforts mobilized in exploiting this potential and the growth of innovating activity. For reasons mentioned above, GDP per capita (TG) was chosen as a measure of the potential for imitation. As in most other studies the investment share (INV) was chosen as an indicator of the efforts in exploiting the potential for imitation. This is, of course, a simplification since institutional factors obviously are very important for imitation and the associated structural changes to take place. But the share of investment may also be seen as the outcome of a process in which institutional factors take part; i.e. differences in the size of the investment share reflect differences in institutional systems as well. To measure growth in innovative activity, growth in patent applications abroad (PAT) was chosen. In theory, growth in R&D could have been used instead, but since R&D data are lacking for several countries and periods, this was not possible.

The following variables were used:

GDP_i = growth of gross domestic product in country i in constant prices

TG_i = gross domestic product per capita in country i in constant 1980 market prices (1000 US $)

PAT_i = growth of patent applications from residents of country i in other countries

INV_i = gross fixed investment in country i as percentage of GDP in constant prices

W = growth of world trade in constant prices

Since annual observations are heavily affected by short-run fluctuations, average values of the variables covering whole business cycles were calculated, using the "peak" years 1968, 1973, 1979 and 1983 (final year) to separate one cycle from the next. As mentioned above, this gives a pooled cross-country time-series data set with a maximum of 100 observations for each variable. Further information regarding the data is given in a separate appendix to this paper.

Two different versions of the model were tested:

(1) $GDP = f(TG, PAT, INV)$,
(2) $GDP = f(TGa, PATa, INVa, W)$.

The first model may be regarded as a pure "supply-side" model where economic growth is supposed to be a function of the level of economic development TG (negative), the growth of patenting activity PAT (positive) and the investment share INV (positive). However, it can be argued that this model overlooks that differences in the overall growth rate between periods also are heavily affected by other factors, especially differences in economic policies. According to Maddison [17], who generally favours a technology gap approach to economic growth, the economic slowdown in the 1970s could partly be explained by too "cautious" economic policies. The second model takes this into account by assuming that the average growth rate of all countries is determined by the growth of world demand, but that the deviations from this average growth rate are determined by the three technology gap variables mentioned above. It may be regarded, then, as an extreme "Keynesian" version of the general technology gap model. In this version, all variables (except the growth rates of GDP and world demand) are expressed as the difference between the value of the variable for country i and the average value of the variable for all countries in the sample. [14]

---

[13] Cross-country estimates are confined to the relation between variables at a specific point of time. Pooled data sets combine this information with information on the overall changes in, for instance, growth, technology gaps and growth of innovative activity through time.

[14] This implies that the average value of each of the variables TGa, PATa, INVa in each period in this transformed data set is defined as zero. Thus, the growth rate (GDP) of an "average" country, defined as having average values of these three variables, would be determined exclusively by the growth in world demand (W) (and the constant term).

To test the sensitivity of the results for changes in sample and periods, each model was tested for three different samples: (1) all countries, (2) OECD countries and (3) small and medium-sized OECD countries (SMD = OECD countries less USA and Japan), and three periods: (a) 1960–83, (b) 1960–73 and (c) 1974–83. To test for serial correlation in the residuals of the cross-sectional units, we used the Durbin–Watson statistics adjusted for gaps (DW(g)). [15] The results are given in table 4.

For the period as a whole, the technology gap models explain a large part of the actual differences in growth rates, both between countries and between periods. As expected, both GDP per capita, patent growth and the investment ratio appear as powerful explanatory factors of economic growth, even if the effect of GDP per capita decreases somewhat when the non-OECD countries are removed from the sample. Both models give essentially the same picture, but the effect of growth in patenting activity is somewhat smaller in the "Keynesian" model than in the "supply-side" model. This is not surprising since in the "Keynesian" model the general slowdown in economic growth in the 1970s is explained by the slowdown in world demand, while in the "supply-side" model this is taken care of mainly (but not exclusively) by the slowdown in patenting activity. Both models go a long way in explaining the differences in economic growth, both between countries and periods, but in terms of fit the "Keynesian" is in general the most successful one. [16]

When the models are estimated on data before and after 1973, some interesting results emerge. Notably, for all three groups of countries, the effect of GDP per capita decreases from 1960–73 to 1974–83, while the effect of the investment

ratio increases. Keeping in mind that the technology gaps were significantly reduced from the 1960s to the 1970s, one possible explanation is that the cost of imitation has increased as the distance to the world innovation frontier has decreased. Another interesting result is that when the non-OECD countries, and later USA and Japan, are removed from the sample, the "technology variables" become gradually less important, even if the signs of the coefficients do not change. For the group of OECD countries, patent growth ceases to influence growth after 1973, and for the group of small and medium-sized developed countries this variable does not seem to have significant effects on economic growth, neither before, nor after 1973. In general, for this group of countries, the patent growth variable may explain some of the slowdown in the 1970s, but it does not explain "why growth rates *differ*" between countries.

The last result calls for some reflection. Obviously, it is not very surprising that technology gap models are better suited for a sample of industrial countries on different levels of development than for a sample of countries on approximately the same level of development. But it is surprising to find that differences in the growth of innovative activities seem to have strong effects on the differing growth performance of industrial countries in general, but much less so for the developed countries, especially the small and medium-sized ones. In terms of data, it is not difficult to see why. For the period as a whole, only a few countries have trends in innovative activities that differ much from other countries; Japan, Finland, Korea, Taiwan, Hong Kong and to some extent Brazil. When the majority of these countries is excluded from the sample, it is not surprising that the importance of the variable is reduced.

To test the sensitivity of this result for the way data were handled, two additional tests were carried out. First, for the OECD countries as well as the SMD countries, a three-year lag was introduced for the patent growth variable. This did not alter the result significantly. Second, a cross-country regression was carried out for the period 1979–83, replacing the patent growth variable based on WIPO statistics with the growth of total external patent applications *including patent applications through international channels (EPC / PCT)*. Because of data limitations, only 11 countries were included in the regression. The result was

---

[15] This test was suggested to me by Professor Ron Smith of Birkbeck College, London. What it implies is that we leave out the differences between the residuals of different cross-sectional units, and the corresponding residuals, from both the numerator and the denominator, thereby reducing the number of observations by one per cross-sectional unit. Given the short time series, this test was applicable to the 1960–83 period only.

[16] This may be interpreted in support of Maddison's view, i.e. that differences in demand policies between periods have significant effects for economic growth, and that a large part of the economic slowdown in the 1970s may be explained in this way.

Table 4
The technology gap approach tested

All countries, 1960–83 (N = 99)
GDP = 2.04 − 0.19TG + 0.18PAT + 0.13INV, R^2 = 0.67
    (1.99) (−3.90) (7.79)   (3.21)   SER = 1.56,   DW(g) = 1.56
    **   *   *   *

GDP = 0.29 − 0.19TGa + 0.13PATa + 0.14INVa + 0.55W, R^2 = 0.75
    (0.97) (−4.64)   (5.47)   (3.70)   (12.62)   SER = 1.35,   DW(g) = 1.56
           *   *   *

OECD countries, 1960–83 (N = 76)
GDP = 1.02 − 0.14TG + 0.18PAT + 0.16INV, R^2 = 0.68
    (1.03) (−2.46) (6.62)   (4.07)   SER = 1.21,   DW(g) = 1.81
         *   *   *

GDP = 0.51 − 0.13TGa + 0.09PATa + 0.16INVa + 0.51W, R^2 = 0.79
    (2.20) (−2.72)   (2.86)   (4.87)   (14.35)   SER = 0.98,   DW(g) = 2.36
    **   *   *   *   *

SMD countries, 1960–83 (N = 68)
GDP = 0.44 − 0.17TG + 0.16PAT + 0.19INV, R^2 = 0.60
    (0.38) (−2.74) (5.26)   (3.82)   SER = 1.22,   DW(g) = 1.81
         *   *   *

GDP = 0.46 − 0.14TGa + 0.03PATa + 0.15INVa + 0.50W, R^2 = 0.78
    (2.04) (−3.04)   (1.02)   (3.76)   (14.55)   SER = 0.90,   DW(g) = 2.26
    **   *   *   *

All countries, 1960–73 (N = 49)
GDP = 3.02 − 0.32TG + 0.10PAT + 0.17INV, R^2 = 0.54
    (2.26) (−4.00) (2.41)   (2.80)   SER = 1.47
     **   *   *   *

GDP = 5.78 − 0.31TGa + 0.13PATa + 0.14INVa − 0.09W R^2 = 0.60
    (2.10) (−4.11)   (3.09)   (2.43)   (−0.30)   SER = 1.39
    **   *   *   *

OECD countries, 1960–1973 (N = 38)
GDP = 1.91 − 0.18TG + 0.09PAT + 0.17INV, R^2 = 0.50
    (1.54) (−2.17) (2.06)   (3.16)   SER = 1.10
    ***   **   **   *

GDP = 5.10 − 0.21TGa + 0.12PATa + 0.15INVa − 0.02W, R^2 = 0.59
    (2.20) (−2.62)+ (2.95)   (2.91)   (−0.07)   SER = 1.02

SMD countries, 1960–73 (N = 34)
GDP = 4.01 − 0.14TG + 0.02PAT + 0.08INV, R^2 = 0.12
    (2.72) (−1.61)   (0.46)   (1.07)   SER = 1.00
    *   ***   ****

GDP = 3.01 − 0.18TGa + 0.05PATa + 0.08INVa + 0.21W, R^2 = 0.26
    (1.33) (−2.13)   (1.16)   (1.25)   (0.80)   SER = 0.94
    ***   **   ****   ****

All countries, 1974–83 (N = 50)
GDP = −1.82 − 0.10TG + 0.12PAT + 0.24INV, R^2 = 0.70
    (−1.27) (−2.01) (4.13)   (4.48)   SER = 1.29
      ****   **   *   *

GDP = 0.32 − 0.11TGa + 0.11PATa + 0.22INVa + 0.59W, R^2 = 0.75
    (0.81) (−2.22)   (4.26)   (4.43)   (4.63)   SER = 1.19
      **   *   *   *

OECD countries, 1974–83 (N = 38)
GDP = −1.74 − 0.08TG + 0.03PAT + 0.21INV, R^2 = 0.51
    (−1.51) (−1.43) (0.65)   (5.01)   SER = 0.91
    ***   ***   *

Table 4 (continued)

GDP = $0.72 - 0.07\text{TGa} + 0.03\text{PATa} + 0.19\text{INVa} + 0.43\text{W}$, (2.35) (−1.29) (0.62) (4.76) (4.18) ** **** * *	$R^2 = 0.59$ SER = 0.84
SMD countries, 1974–83 ($N = 34$) GDP = $-2.34 - 0.10\text{TG} + 0.03\text{PAT} + 0.24\text{INV}$, (−1.90) (−1.72) (0.71) (4.93) ** ** *	$R^2 = 0.51$ SER = 0.89
GDP = $0.64 - 0.09\text{TGa} + 0.02\text{PATa} + 0.21\text{INVa} + 0.44\text{W}$, (1.94) (−1.60) (0.55) (4.44) (4.07) ** *** * *	$R^2 = 0.58$ SER = 0.84

Method of estimation: Ordinary least squares
* = significant at a 1% level (one-tailed test); ** = significant at a 5% level (one tailed test); *** = significant at a 10% level (one-tailed test); **** = significant at a 15% level (one-tailed test).
SER = Standard error of regression; DW(g) = Durbin–Watson statistics adjusted for gaps.

that when USA and Japan were included, the patent growth variable was significant, otherwise not.

Many of the countries included in the test, among them the non-OECD countries, had a very low level of patenting activity in the early 1960s (and still have) compared to other countries. It may be dangerous to draw conclusions from high growth rates when the initial levels were very low. However, in terms of R&D, where the initial levels were higher, the tendencies seem to be the same for countries where data exist. Japan had a very high share of civil R&D in GDP in the early 1960s compared to other countries. Nevertheless, its share has grown very rapidly and currently enjoys the highest level in the world. Finland and Korea both had rather low shares compared to other countries in the 1960s, but they grew very rapidly throughout the 1970s, and both countries have now (1982/83) shares close to the average of the sample. Thus, the available evidence seems to support that these countries have followed a separate way of development characterized by rapid imitation, high growth in innovative activities and rapid economic growth.

4. Conclusions

The main findings of this paper are the following:

(1) There exists a close correlation between the level of economic development, measured as GDP per capita, and the level of technological development, measured through R&D or patent statistics.

(2) Technology gap models of economic growth explain rather well the differences in growth between the industrialized countries as a whole in the post-war period. Both the scope for imitation, growth in innovative activity and "efforts" to narrow the "gap" (investment) seem to be powerful explanatory factors of economic growth. This has not changed qualitatively after 1973, but the scope for imitation seems to have decreased and the costs of imitation increased, compared with the 1960s.

(3) The models are less well suited in explaining the (much smaller) differences in growth between developed countries, especially the small and medium-sized ones, most of which are on approximately the same level of development.

The findings of this paper confirm that many of the small and medium-sized European countries have attained very high levels of GDP per capita with moderate levels of innovative activity. Thus, to explain the differences in growth between these countries in the post-war period, a much more detailed analysis of economic, social and institutional structures should be carried out. The prospects for this group of countries will partly depend on whether or not competition through innovation will be the dominant form of competition in international markets in the future. The decreased scope for imitation which is revealed in this study and the general upturn in R&D efforts during the last years may be taken as an indication of a growing importance of technological competition on the international level. If correct, this implies that the future growth of the small and medium-sized European countries in part depends on their ability to change the trend towards a stagnating innovative level compared to other countries.

Appendix

Methods

Growth rates are calculated as geometric averages for the periods 1960–68, 1968–73, 1973–79 and 1979–83, or the nearest period for which data exist. Levels and shares are calculated as arithmetic averages for the periods 1960–67, 1968–73, 1974–79 and 1980–83, or the nearest period for which data exist.

Sources

Real GDP per capita, 1980 market prices in US $:
Taiwan: *Statistical Yearbook of the Republic of China 1984*
Other countries: *IMF Supplement on Output Statistics*

Growth of gross domestic product in constant prices:
OECD countries: *OECD Historical Statistics 1960–1983*
Hong Kong, Taiwan and Korea 1960–73: E.K. Chen, *Hyper-growth in Asian Economies* (MacMillan, London, 1979)
Taiwan 1973–83: *Statistical Yearbook of the Republic of China 1984*
Hong Kong and Korea 1973–83 and Mexico, Argentina and Brazil: *IMF Supplement on Output Statistics*

Gross fixed capital formation as percentage of GDP:
OECD countries: *OECD Historical Statistics 1960–1983*
Taiwan: *Statistical Yearbook of the Republic of China 1984*
Other countries: *IMF Supplement on Output Statistics*

External patent applications:
OECD countries: *OECD/STIIU DATA BANK*
Other countries: World International Property Organisation (WIPO): *Industrial Property Statistics*, various editions and unpublished data.

Table A1
Growth of real GDP

	1960–68	1968–73	1973–79	1979–83
USA	4.5	3.3	2.6	0.7
Japan	10.5	8.8	3.6	3.9
FRG	4.2	4.9	2.4	0.5
France	5.4	5.9	3.1	1.1
UK	3.1	3.2	1.4	0.4
Italy	5.7	4.6	2.6	0.6
Canada	5.6	5.6	3.4	0.8
Austria	4.2	5.9	2.9	1.5
Belgium	4.5	5.6	2.2	0.9
Denmark	4.6	4.0	1.9	0.9
Netherlands	4.8	5.3	2.6	−0.3
Norway	4.4	4.1	4.9	2.3
Sweden	4.4	3.7	1.8	1.2
Switzerland	4.4	4.5	−0.4	1.4
Finland	3.9	6.7	2.4	3.3
Ireland	4.2	4.8	4.6	2.2
Australia	5.0	5.5	2.6	1.7
New Zealand	3.1	5.1	0.6	2.1
Spain	7.5	6.8	2.5	1.2
Brazil	8.5 [a]	9.3	6.8	0.8
Argentina	2.8	3.2	2.3	−1.9
Hong Kong	8.5	8.4	8.3	6.7
Taiwan	9.0	10.6	8.0	5.6
Korea	7.6	10.7	9.0	4.5
Mexico	6.7	6.6	5.9	2.6

[a] 1962–82.

Table A2
Real GDP per capita, 1980 market prices in US $

	1962–67	1968–73	1974–79	1980–82
USA	9,419	10,746	11,905	12,706
Japan	4,018	6,365	7,827	9,063
FRG	7,374	9,132	10,618	11,806
France	6,530	8,311	10,004	11,000
UK	6,836	7,788	8,726	9,054
Italy	3,972	5,075	5,864	6,486
Canada	7,310	8,961	10,624	11,157
Austria	5,139	6,624	8,180	9,198
Belgium	6,133	7,823	9,516	10,186
Denmark	8,264	9,889	10,975	11,571
Netherlands	7,070	8,857	10,214	10,586
Norway	7,993	9,550	11,668	13,385
Sweden	9,638	11,399	12,797	13,368
Switzerland	12,177	14,317	15,010	15,855
Finland	5,848	7,485	8,891	10,004
Ireland	3,285	4,059	4,718	5,024
Australia	7,796	9,429	10,262	10,775
New Zealand	6,135	6,890	7,495	7,249
Spain	3,056	4,047	4,935	5,054
Brazil	1,024	1,366	1,954	2,217
Argentina	2,166	2,583	2,786	2,652
Hong Kong	1,676	2,389	3,436	4,710
Taiwan	490	780	1,448	2,037
Korea	592	871	1,337	1,613
Mexico	1,227	1,546	1,844	2,133

The OECD data are adjusted WIPO data. Data for the non-OECD countries are compiled from published WIPO statistics except for Hong Kong, Korea and Taiwan 1975–83 where data are compiled by WIPO from unpublished sources. Unfortunately, the quality of the data for some of the non-OECD countries prior to 1975 is far from perfect. To avoid year-to-year fluctuations, caused mainly by bad statistics, from influencing the calculated growth rates, some efforts were made to adjust the growth rates accordingly (see table A3 for details).

R&D as percentage of GDP:
The R&D data are estimates based on the following sources:
OECD countries: *OECD Science and Technology Indicators, Basic Statistical Series (vol B (1982) and Recent Results (1984))*
Other countries: *UNESCO Statistical Yearbook* (various editions) and various *UNESCO surveys on resources devoted to R&D*

Military R&D expenditures were, following OECD, assumed to be negligible in all countries except US, France, FRG, Sweden and UK. The R&D data for these countries were adjusted downward according to OECD estimates. The estimates were taken from OECD, Directorate for Science, Technology and Industry: *The problems of estimating defence and civil GERD in selected OECD member countries* (unpublished). For other countries, civil and total R&D as percentage of GDP were assumed to be identical.

Population and export shares in GDP:
Data on population and export shares in GDP were taken from: *OECD Historical Statistics 1960–83, OECD National Accounts* (various editions), *IMF Supplement on Output Statistics, UN Monthly Bulletin of Statistics* (various editions) and *Statistical Yearbook of the Republic of China 1984*

Growth of world trade at constant prices:
The growth of total OECD imports was used as

Table A3
Growth in external patent applications

	1960–68	1968–73	1973–79	1979–83
USA	6.7	−1.7	−6.1	−4.3
Japan	22.8	10.9	0.9	1.0
FRG	5.2	0.7	−6.7	−8.7
France	6.3	0.5	−6.1	−4.8
UK	3.1	−2.4	−9.5	−2.2
Italy	5.9	0.6	−0.3	−8.7
Canada	5.7	2.9	−5.7	−3.2
Austria	4.5	3.0	−5.0	−6.5
Belgium	5.9	−5.8	−8.7	−4.4
Denmark	8.6	−3.0	−5.8	−2.9
Netherlands	2.2	−1.4	−4.6	−9.2
Norway	1.2	5.9	−6.2	−7.3
Sweden	5.3	0	−4.5	−4.9
Switzerland	5.2	0.6	−7.3	−9.1
Finland	10.0	8.1	4.0	4.2
Ireland	10.4 [a]	7.9	−2.7	−6.6
Australia	5.1	9.4	−1.7	−2.7
New Zealand	−0.7	10.3	1.7	−2.4
Spain	8.8 [a]	2.0	−2.7	−9.0
Brazil	7.5 [a]	16.0	3.4	−19.2
Argentina	16.3 [a]	1.4	−3.8	−15.9
Hong Kong	8.8 [a]	4.2	14.8	0
Taiwan	22.2 [a]	17.9 [b]	21.0 [d]	12.7
Korea	n.a.	13.5 [c]	16.3 [d]	18.9
Mexico	−0.6 [a]	4.8	−9.5	1.1

[a] 1969/70–1964/65.
[b] 1968–75.
[c] 1969–75.
[d] 1975–79.

Table A4
Gross fixed capital formation as percentage of GDP

	1960–67	1968–73	1974–79	1980–83
USA	18.0	18.3	18.3	17.4
Japan	31.3	34.7	32.0	30.4
FRG	25.2	24.4	20.9	21.5
France	22.3	23.3	22.7	20.9
UK	17.8	19.2	19.4	16.9
Italy	21.7	20.6	20.0	19.2
Canada	22.1	21.6	22.9	21.8
Austria	26.4	27.2	26.4	24.0
Belgium	21.6	21.7	21.9	18.3
Denmark	23.4	24.4	22.1	16.7
Netherlands	25.0	25.0	20.9	19.2
Norway	29.0	27.4	32.9	25.8
Sweden	23.9	22.6	20.6	19.2
Switzerland	28.0	27.9	22.7	23.6
Finland	26.6	26.2	27.2	24.9
Ireland	18.7	23.3	26.1	26.7
Australia	25.8	25.3	22.7	23.1
New Zealand	21.1	20.8	23.2	21.4
Spain	20.2	22.7	21.6	19.5
Brazil	18.6 [a]	25.3	27.2	21.7 [b]
Argentina	18.6 [a]	24.6	25.1	19.5 [b]
Hong Kong	26.7 [a]	21.7	28.1	32.8
Taiwan	15.4	23.1	27.8	28.3
Korea	17.4 [a]	25.6	30.3	28.2
Mexico	18.5 [a]	21.1	23.6	26.1 [b]

[a] 1962–67.
[b] 1980–82.

proxy (8.1, 9.4, 4.0, 1.3). The data were taken from: *OECD Historical Statistics 1960–1983*.

References

[1] M. Abramowitz, Resources and Output Trends in the United States since 1870, *Am. Econ. Rev.* 46 (1956) 5–23.

[2] M. Abramowitz, Rapid Growth Potential and its Realisation: The Experience of Capitalist Economies in the Post-war Period, in: E. Malinvaud (ed.), *Economic Growth and Resources* (London, 1979).

[3] L. Basberg, Foreign Patenting in the U.S. as a Technology Indicator, *Research Policy* 12 (1983) 227–237.

[4] D. Bosworth, The Transfer of U.S. Technology Abroad, *Research Policy* 9 (1980) 378–388.

[5] D. Bosworth, Foreign Patent Flows to and from the United Kingdom, *Research Policy* 13 (1984) 115–124.

[6] K. Choi, *Theories of Comparative Economic Growth* (Iowa State University Press, Ames, 1983).

[7] J. Cornwall, Diffusion, Convergence and Kaldor's Law, *Econ. J.* 85 (1976) 307–314.

[8] J. Cornwall, *Modern Capitalism. Its Growth and Transformation* (Martin Robertson, London, 1977).

[9] E.F. Denison, *Why Growth Rates Differ: Post-War Experience in Nine Western Countries* (Brookings Institute, Washington D.C., 1967).

[10] C. Freeman, *The Economics of Industrial Innovation*, 2nd edn (Frances Pinter, London, 1982).

[11] S. Gomulka, *Inventive Activity, Diffusion and Stages of Economic Growth*, Skrifter fra Aarhus universitets økonomiske institut nr. 24, Aarhus (1971).

[12] Z. Griliches (ed.), *R&D, Patents and Productivity* (Chicago University Press, Chicago, 1984).

[13] S. Hirsch, *Location of Industry and International Competitiveness* (Clarendon Press, Oxford, 1967).

[14] I. Kravis, "Availability" and Other Influences on the Commodity Composition of Trade, *Journal of Political Economy* LXIV (1956) 143–155.

[15] P. Krugman, A Model of Innovation, Technology Transfer and the World Distribution of Income, *Journal of Political Economy* 87 (1979) 253–266.

[16] A. Lindbeck, The Recent Slowdown of Productivity Growth, *Econ. J.* 93 (1983) 13–34.

[17] A. Maddison, *Phases of Capitalist Development* (Oxford University Press, New York, 1982).

[18] E. Mansfield, A. Romeo, M. Schwartz, D. Teece, S. Wagner and P. Brach, *Technology Transfer, Productivity and Economic Policy* (Norton, New York, 1982).

[19] R. Marris, How Much of the Slow-down was Catch-up?, in: R.C.O. Matthews, *Slower Growth in the Western World* (London, 1982).

[20] OECD, *Indicators of the Technological Position and Performance in OECD Member Countries during the Seventies*. Directorate for Science, Technology and Industry, Science and Technology Indicators, Working Paper No. 2 (1984).

[21] M. Parvin, Technological Adaptation, Optimum Level of Backwardness and the Rate of per Capita Income Growth: An Econometric Approach, *American Economist* 19 (1975) 23–31.

[22] K. Pavitt, Technical Innovation and Industrial Development, *Futures* (Dec. 1979) 458–470, (Febr. 1980) 35–44.

[23] K. Pavitt and L.G. Soete, International Differences in Economic Growth and the International Location of Innovation, in: H. Giersch (ed.), *Emerging Technologies: Consequences for Economic Growth, Structural Change, and Employment* (J.C.B. Mohr (Paul Siebeck), Tübingen, 1982).

[24] M.V. Posner, International Trade and Technical Change. *Oxf. Econ. Pap.* 13 (1961) 323–341.

[25] D. Schiffel and C. Kitti, Rates of Invention: International Patent Comparisons, *Research Policy* 7 (1978) 324–340.

[26] J. Schmookler, *Invention and Economic Growth* (Harvard University Press, Cambridge, MA, 1966).

[27] J. Schumpeter, *The Theory of Economic Development* (Oxford, 1934).

[28] J. Schumpeter, *Business Cycles I–II* (Mc Graw-Hill, New York, 1939).

[29] J. Schumpeter, *Capitalism, Socialism and Democracy* (London, 1947).

[30] H. Singer and L. Reynolds, Technological Backwardness and Productivity Growth, *Econ. J.* 85 (1975) 873–876.

[31] L. Soete, A General Test of Technological Gap Trade Theory, *Weltwirtschaftliches Archiv* 117 (1981) 639–659.

[32] R. Solow, Technical Change and the Aggregate Production Function, *Rev. Econ. Stat.* 39 (1957) 312–320.

[33] R. Vernon, International Investment and International Trade in the Product Cycle, *Quarterly Journal of Economics* (1966) 191–207.

[2]

'Modern Capitalism' in the 1970s and 1980s

Jan Fagerberg and Bart Verspagen

INTRODUCTION

The past decade has witnessed important changes in how economic growth is conceived by the economic profession. The traditional neoclassical model (Solow, 1956), based on the ideas of perfect competition, decreasing returns and exogenous technology (a global public good), has had to give way to more realistic approaches emphasizing among other things innovation (through R&D investments or learning in private firms), scale economics and market power.[1] This change of perspective was clearly anticipated by John Cornwall in his path-breaking study, *Modern Capitalism* (1977). Here he suggests a model of economic growth in which technological progress is endogenized, that is, an 'endogenous growth model' to use a more recent term. Manufacturing, Cornwall argues, plays an important role in this context, because it is the locus of technological progress, whether in the form of learning by doing (scale economics) or as the result of search activities by entrepreneurs. Hence his main focus is on what shapes growth in manufacturing (since this is considered to be the main source of overall growth).

A central issue in the recent discussions on economic growth is the so-called 'convergence controversy'. Do poor countries catch up with the rich ones and if so, why? Under the standard assumptions,[2] the traditional neoclassical model predicts that due to decreasing returns to capital accumulation, convergence in GDP per capita will more or less automatically occur.[3] This – as might be expected – was not Cornwall's position. He argued that although the existence of technology gaps between rich and poor countries does imply a potential for technological catch-up through imitation, the realization of this potential requires a lot of extra effort (and, in particular, investment). Hence, according to Cornwall's view, convergence is conditional on investment and other necessary supporting factors. He was probably the first to present empirical tests for what since has been dubbed 'conditional convergence', and to discuss the implications of this notion for long-run differences in growth between countries.

As Cornwall himself was the first to recognize, his theoretical perspective was richer than his modelling efforts or subsequent empirical work. For

113

instance, he pointed out that the prospects for growth were not the same across all manufacturing industries and that, indeed, some of them might be more important than others in fostering technological progress and hence growth. However, in his model and empirical tests he focused on manufacturing as a whole. His empirical work, mainly based on data for the 1950s and 1960s, gave some support to the idea of manufacturing as an 'engine of growth', as well as to his emphasis on investment-embodied catch-up as an important source of growth in manufacturing. In this chapter we return to these and related questions for a larger group of countries and a more recent time period. We ask: is there any evidence that manufacturing is an 'engine of growth' in this later period, and are all manufacturing industries equally conducive to growth? What does this more recent evidence have to say about the impact on growth of investment in physical capital compared to the impact of other supporting factors such as, for instance, education and R&D? Finally we raise the issue of what all this tells us about the working of contemporary 'modern capitalism' as compared to that of the 1950s and 1960s.

MANUFACTURING – AN 'ENGINE OF GROWTH'?

One of the most crucial hypotheses in *Modern Capitalism* is that of the manufacturing sector as the engine of economy-wide growth. Cornwall points to two main arguments for this.

First, the manufacturing sector displays dynamic economies of scale through so-called 'learning by doing' (Young, 1928; Kaldor, 1966, 1967). When production expands, the scope for learning and productivity increases becomes larger. Hence, the rate of growth of productivity in manufacturing will depend positively on the rate of growth of output in manufacturing (the Kaldor–Verdoorn Law).[4]

The second line of argument concerns the special role of the manufacturing sector in enhancing productivity growth through its linkages with the non-manufacturing sectors. Cornwall argues that the manufacturing sector is characterized by strong backward linkages, that is, increased final demand for manufacturing output will induce increased demand in many sectors 'further down the line'.[5] In other words, increased output in manufacturing, due to increased final demand, does not only lead to increased productivity in the manufacturing sector (the Kaldor–Verdoorn Law), but also to increased output and, perhaps, productivity in the sectors further down the line. In addition to these backward linkages, Cornwall emphasizes that the manufacturing sector also has many forward linkages, through its role as a supplier of capital goods (and the new technologies that these goods embody). In fact, he considers capital goods from the manufacturing sector to be the main carriers of new technology (Cornwall, 1977, p. 135). Moreover, although 'learning by doing' may be an important source of productivity growth in non-manufacturing industries as well, it is argued that the realization of this 'learning potential' will in many cases require capital goods supplied by the manufacturing sector.

Cornwall's model of economic growth can be summarized in two equations as follows (1977, p. 139):

$$\hat{Q} = c_1 + a_1 \hat{Q}_m \tag{9.1}$$

$$\hat{Q}_m = c_2 + a_2 \hat{Q} + dq_r + e(I/Q)_m \tag{9.2}$$

In these equations, Q is output, q_r is GDP per capita relative to the technology leader (the USA), I/Q is investment as a fraction of output, c, a, b, d and e are parameters and the subscript m indicates the manufacturing sector. Equation (9.1) states that manufacturing is the engine of growth, hence the parameter a_1 is expected to be positive, and larger than the share of manufacturing in GDP. Equation (9.2) introduces a feedback from overall demand growth on manufacturing production, hence a_2 is expected to be positive. In addition it allows for catching up by industrial latecomers (hence d is expected to be negative). The inclusion of the investment share (e positive) reflects Cornwall's emphasis on investment as a necessary supporting factor for successful catch-up.

Cornwall does not estimate equation (9.1), but refers to OLS estimates by Kaldor (1966), Cripps and Tarling (1973) and the UN (1970). Based on data for developed market economies in the 1950s and 1960s, these studies estimate a_1 to be about 0.6, more than twice the share of manufacturing in GDP. Hence, the evidence from these studies seems to support the hypothesis of manufacturing as an engine of growth. However, in Cornwall's model, both GDP growth and growth of manufacturing output are endogenous variables, and in that case equation (9.1) should have been estimated by a method other than OLS. Indeed, the OLS estimate of 0.6 may be seriously biased.

Looking at the model in equations (9.1) and (9.2) from a simultaneous equation perspective, one must conclude that the second equation is not identified. It does not satisfy the order condition, which says that the equation must exclude at least N-1 exogenous variables, where N is the number of equations in the model (in this case 2). Hence, it cannot be estimated by any estimation technique.[6] The first equation, however, is over-identified, and may be estimated by a single equation technique that takes the simultaneous equation bias into account, such as, for instance, the instrumental variables/two-stage least squares method (2SLS).

The analysis here will proceed by using such a procedure to estimate equation (9.1) for a large sample of countries. The sample includes 67 countries: 19 developed countries (including Japan), 6 countries from East Asia and the Pacific (excluding Japan), 18 countries in Latin America and the

Caribbean, 17 sub-Saharan African countries, and seven other countries (among which two oil exporters). We thus have a rather heterogeneous set of countries. The dependent variable is the growth rate of GDP in real terms over 1973–89 (taken from the Penn World Tables,[7] version 5.5). The independent variable is the growth rate of manufacturing value added (in fixed prices) for the same period, taken from World Development Indicators (World Bank).[8] However, for some of the developed countries, no data on manufacturing growth were available in World Development Indicators. For these countries data were taken from the STAN database (OECD). Both growth rates are average annual compound growth rates over the period specified.

To estimate the equation with the chosen (instrumental variable) technique, we need a number of exogenous variables (or instruments). The chosen variables are in most cases well-known from previous econometric work in this area: *initial GDP per capita* (in log form, taken from the Penn World Tables), *investments in physical capital* as a share of GDP (mean value over 1973–89, also from the Penn World Tables),[9] *education* (enrolment of the relevant age group in secondary education, from the World Development Indicators) and *inflation* (yearly average increase in the CPI 1973–89, taken from the World Development Indicators). Finally, and less conventionally, we include a variable for *technology investment*[10] as proxied by patents (taken out in the USA over the 1975–85 period per head of the population of the country in question, as recorded by the US Patent and Trademark Office).[11]

A well-known problem in estimations using cross-country data sets is the possible bias from inclusion of outliers, that is, countries with patterns that deviate from the other countries in the sample. If such countries are included, we may be lead to conclusions that in fact are not valid for the majority of the countries in our sample. We therefore adopt a procedure which identifies and excludes such outliers.[12]

The results of the instrumental variable/2SLS estimations are given in Table 9.1. The results for OLS are also provided for reference.[13] Estimates are reported for the three country groupings and for the sample as a whole. The three country groupings are the developed *market economies*, comparable to Cornwall's sample (though larger), the industrializing countries of *East Asia and Latin America* and a group of *other countries* (low-income), most of which are from sub-Saharan Africa.

In general, the results obtained by the instrumental variable/2SLS method are not very different from those obtained by OLS.[14] Hence, simultaneity bias does not seem to be an important problem here. This might indicate that the feedback from overall growth on manufacturing output is not so important after all, that is, that manufacturing growth is important for overall growth, but not the other way around.

For the sample as a whole there appears to be a significant positive relationship between manufacturing growth and GDP growth, with coefficient

Table 9.1   Estimation results for Cornwall's 'manufacturing as an engine of growth' equation, OLS and 2SLS, various countries, 1973–90

Eq. num	Est. method	Sample (n)	Manufacturing growth	Constant	Adj. R^2
1	OLS	Market economies (17)	0.104 (0.70)	0.024 (11.55***)	0.00
2	2SLS	Market economies (14)	0.083 (0.21)	0.024 (6.01***)	0.00
3	OLS	East Asia, Latin America (22)	0.721 (12.36***)	0.008 (3.20***)	0.88
4	2SLS	East Asia, Latin America (17)	0.829 (8.45***)	0.006 (1.82*)	0.83
5	OLS	Other countries (22)	0.371 (4.47***)	0.014 (3.00***)	0.47
6	2SLS	Other countries (15)	0.827 (2.86***)	–0.005 (0.35)	0.40
7	OLS	All countries, no dummies (61)	0.514 (10.54***)	0.014 (7.49***)	0.65
8	2SLS	All countries, no dummies (49)	0.488 (5.98***)	0.016 (5.62***)	0.49
9	OLS	All countries, dummies (61)	0.473 (8.45***)	Continent dummies	0.69
10	2SLS	All countries, dummies (45)	0.719 (4.54***)	Continent dummies	0.57

Note:
Values between brackets are absolute *t*-statistics. One, two and three asterisks denote significance at the 10%, 5% and 1% level, respectively, in a 2-tailed *t*-test.

estimates close to the 0.6 estimate cited by Cornwall, and significantly larger than the share of manufacturing in GDP at the 5 per cent level. This might be interpreted as supporting the idea of manufacturing as an engine of growth. But from inspecting the estimates for the three sub-samples it becomes clear that this result is very much dependent on the inclusion of countries other than the developed market economies. For the East Asia–Latin America group as well as the 'other countries', we find a highly significant and positive relationship between the two variables. However, for the developed countries the evidence is less clear. Initially, a significant and positive relationship was found for the developed market economies, but this result turned out to depend heavily on the inclusion of three outliers (Italy, Japan and Finland). When these countries were excluded, we found no evidence of a relationship between the growth of GDP and manufacturing growth.[15] Thus, although manufacturing may explain some of the difference in growth between the three outlier countries and the remaining developed countries in the sample, it clearly does not explain the differences in growth performance among the latter.

In summary, the results in this section indicate that for most developed market economies, manufacturing no longer plays the important role it was found to play in the 1950s and 1960s. This is in sharp contradiction to Cornwall's theory in *Modern Capitalism*, which posits that such a relationship should exist, particularly for developed countries.[16] However, Cornwall's argument on the relevance of manufacturing seems to hold good for a number of fast-growing 'newly industrializing countries' (NICs) as well as for some developing countries.

GROWTH AND TRANSFORMATION

In *Modern Capitalism*, Cornwall depicts growth as a process of qualitative change (transformation), with large and persistent differences in factor returns between dynamic and less dynamic activities. Hence, he points out, the economic success – or lack of such – of a country will to a large extent depend on its 'flexibility', that is, its ability to devote (transfer) resources to new and promising activities. As discussed in the previous section he attaches a lot of importance to the performance in manufacturing which he saw as the centre of technological progress in the economy. Within manufacturing, he especially emphasizes the importance of the chemical, electronic and machine tools industries, both as conduits of technological progress and suppliers of new and improved products and processes to the entire economy (1977, p. 135). These three industries, he notes, totally dominate 'the technology sector' of the economy. This raises the question of the relationship between the industries that make up what he terms 'the technology sector' and other manufacturing activities. To put it bluntly: are all parts of manufacturing equally conducive to growth?

As mentioned in the introduction, Cornwall also emphasizes the potential for catch-up in productivity through imitation for countries behind the world technology frontier. However, he is at pain to stress that this catch-up is far from a free ride. Among the supporting factors, he especially emphasizes the supply of skills (workers and entrepreneurs), materials and capital equipment (1977, p. 111). In his modelling efforts and subsequent empirical work, however, he confines attention to investment as a share of value added which, together with the potential for imitation (proxied by GDP per capita), is assumed to determine the growth of manufacturing output. Note that this relationship can be seen as a reduced form of the model discussed in the previous section (1977, p. 139).

In this section we will return to the relationship between growth, catch-up and structural change discussed by Cornwall, taking into account the possible impact on growth of structural changes within manufacturing, as well as that of other 'conditioning' factors, to use a more recent term. To do so, we need data that are less aggregated than those used earlier. UNIDO publishes data on manufacturing value added and employment for a large number of countries at different levels of development, and it seems natural to try to use these data here. The data cover both three- and four-digit ISIC, but the coverage of the latter is too restricted in terms of countries and time-span for our purposes. Since the relationship between productivity growth and structural change is of a long-term nature, a sufficiently long time-span is necessary. After examining the data, the years 1973 and 1990 were chosen, since this allows more countries to be included than any other combination of years spanning roughly two decades. The desire to include other conditioning factors, such as investments in education, physical capital and R&D, also limits the number of countries that can be included in the analysis. Furthermore, the analysis is confined to market economies (broadly defined). The final data set consists of forty countries from all parts of the world: Africa, America, Asia, Europe and Oceania. With the exception of the first, the data set appears quite representative (due to data problems only three African countries could be included).

The dependent variable in our analysis is the growth rate of labour productivity (not production). Labour productivity is defined as value added divided by employment measured at current prices and converted to US dollars by the exchange rate (as supplied by UNIDO). The entries for 1990 are deflated to constant 1973 dollars by dividing by an index reflecting the growth in US producer prices over the period. Hence, productivity growth as defined here reflects changes in the quantities of the products that a country produces, changes in the relative prices of these products and changes in the exchange rate. The use of current exchange rates introduces a possible bias, to the extent that the exchange rates of any country in 1973 and/or 1990 were seriously over- or undervalued. However, one should expect any such effect, although important from a short-run perspective, to be small over the longer run.

The hypothesis that we wish to test is that it matters for a country whether it puts its resources into expanding areas or chooses to concentrate its efforts on activities where prospects for growth are bleak. This hypothesis – obvious as it may seem – is not trivial since, as noted by Cornwall, it is often disputed by neoclassical economists. We define growth industries as the upper third of the distribution of the industries in our sample, ranked in terms of their productivity growth rates. The top-ranking growth industry during this period was electrical machinery (including electronics, arguably the technologically most progressive industry in recent decades). We therefore divide the growth industries into two groups, electrical machinery (ISIC 383) and high-growth (ISIC 351, 352, 341, 385, 382, 342, 313) and, for each country, calculate the change in the share of the manufacturing labour force that goes to these two groups. The assumption, then, is that if structural change does not matter for growth, then the changes in these shares should not be correlated with growth, at least not significantly so.

However, we have to take into account that structural change within the manufacturing sector is not the only factor that affects the growth of manufacturing productivity. If there are other omitted variables, and these tend to be correlated with our measures of structural change, we may get a biased estimate. To control for this, we include a number of variables that relate to the country as a whole and which may be thought of as characteristics of 'the national system of innovation', or the pool of factors available at the national level for manufacturing (and other sectors of the economy). Among the variables included are those emphasized by Cornwall: initial productivity (in manufacturing) and the ratio of investment to GDP. In addition, we include some of the variables fashioned in recent econometric work on growth such as primary and secondary education (share of age group enrolled) and export orientation/openness (exports as a share of GDP). In contrast to most analyses in this area, we also control for the effort devoted to innovation (R&D as a share of GDP), since this may be a source of growth in its own right. All of these variables are measured mid-period (1980 or closest available year).[17]

Table 9.2 contains estimation results for the growth of manufacturing productivity as a function of the increase in the employment shares of *high-growth* and *electrical machinery* industries and the other variables mentioned above. As in the previous section, we adopt a procedure that identifies and excludes outliers. This reduces the number of countries by between two and five depending on the specification.

Equations (1) and (4) report the results with only the two structural variables and a constant term (not reported) included, with and without continent dummies, respectively.[18] The latter may be thought of as a rough test of the impact of other non-identified factors that happen to be correlated geographically. Equations (2) and (5) repeat these regressions with education, investment and initial productivity, all in log form, included as conditioning factors, that is, we test to what extent structural change matters when the effects of other growth-inducing factors have been accounted for. The results are very clear. High productivity growth and increases in the share of resources devoted to the electrical machinery industry go hand in hand. A 1 per cent increase in the employment share of the electrical machinery industry implies about 0.5 per cent higher overall growth of manufacturing productivity. Increasing the share of employment going to other high-growth industries matters much less, though. The inclusion of other conditioning factors does not change these results to a significant extent, but the explanatory power of the model increases. Among the additional factors, education (especially secondary) is the most important.[19] Neither the share of investments in GDP nor the initial level of productivity seems to matter much for growth. The

Table 9.2   Structural change and productivity growth

	1	2	3	4	5	6	7	8
High growth	0.29	0.11	0.15	0.20	0.08	0.17	0.07	0.19
	(1.73) *	(0.62)	(0.79)	(1.17)	(0.59)	(1.07)	(0.34)	(1.59)
Electrical machinery	0.47	0.57	0.52	0.46	0.41	0.49	0.57	0.48
	(1.94) *	(2.98) ***	(2.91) ***	(2.26) **	(2.38) **	(2.79) ***	(3.01) ***	(2.69) ***
Primary education		3.51	3.11		2.85	4.21	5.67	6.79
		(0.96)	(0.79)		(0.82)	(1.34)	(1.31)	(1.34)
Secondary education		2.36	2.10		1.07	2.42		
		(1.99) *	(1.50)		(0.87)	(1.91) *		
Investment		−1.33						
		(0.69)						
Initial productivity		−0.58	−0.52		−0.42	−0.54	−0.60	−0.76
		(0.86)	(0.73)		(0.58)	(0.69)	(0.67)	(0.98)
Export share						−0.46		
						(0.62)		
R&D							1.03	0.74
							(1.49)	(1.20)
Interaction R&D – electrical machinery							0.01	0.23
							(0.04)	(1.22)
Continent dummies	No	No	No	Yes	Yes	Yes	No	Yes
R^2 $(\bar{R}^2)$	0.16	0.48	0.42	0.50	0.61	0.52	0.48	0.64
	(0.11)	(0.37)	(0.32)	(0.41)	(0.48)	(0.42)	(0.34)	(0.49)
N	35	35	34	34	34	35	29	32

Note:
Estimated with OLS. Absolute *t*-statistics in brackets under coefficients. One, two and three asterisks denote significance at the 10%, 5% and 1% level, respectively, in a two-tailed test. R^2 in brackets is adjusted for degrees of freedom.

same holds – surprisingly perhaps – for 'openness' as reflected in exports as a share of GDP (equation (6)).[20]

The two last equations in the table ((7) and (8)) take into account investments in R&D (measured as a share of GDP), which recent theorizing in this area would suggest as being important (see, for example, Romer, 1990). This leads to a reduction in the number of countries included. Doubts may also be raised about the quality and comparability of the R&D data. Anyway, for this sample of countries, secondary education and R&D are so closely correlated that only one of them can be retained. When R&D is chosen, the coefficient is positive as expected, but not significantly different from zero at the 10 per cent level.[21] We also include an interaction variable, reflecting the hypothesis that the effects of R&D investment on growth are larger if undertaken in conjunction with an expansion of the electrical machinery industry. This hypothesis, however, receives only very moderate support.

The results from this section give ample support to Cornwall's argument regarding the importance of flexibility, or the ability to transfer resources to technologically progressive areas, for productivity growth. Hence, transformation clearly matters for growth. However, Cornwall's emphasis on investment in physical capital in this context is not justified for the period under study here. Rather, the recipe for high growth of manufacturing productivity seems to be a combination of flexibility (targeting the right industries) and investments in skills.

QUO VADIS MODERN CAPITALISM?

Cornwall built his analysis of modern capitalism on a combination of two strands of thought: the Schumpeter–Svennilson view of capitalist development as a process of qualitative change driven by innovation and diffusion of technology, and the Kaldorian idea of static and dynamic economies of scale in manufacturing as the driving force behind economic progress in the industrialized world. Combining these (and other) insights into a coherent perspective on modern economic growth was an important achievement in itself. He also provided convincing evidence from a group of industrialized countries in the 1950s and 1960s that supported his interpretation of the events.

What we have done in this chapter is to update and extend his empirical analysis using a larger sample of countries and more recent data. We have found that the Schumpeter–Svennilson perspective of growth as a process of qualitative (and structural) change, and the emphasis on the importance of skills and flexibility, has a lot to commend it. On the second set of ideas the evidence is more ambiguous. At least for many of the technologically and economically most advanced countries, manufacturing does not seem to be the 'engine of growth' assumed by Kaldor and Cornwall. Rather, it is for countries in the process of industrialization (NICs) that manufacturing seems to matter most. This may have to do with the role of the manufacturing sector in acquiring foreign technology and generating learning and skills, in combination with forward and backward linkages, as argued by Cornwall in the case of the developed countries. However, it may also have to do with another issue discussed extensively by Cornwall (1977, ch. IV): the existence of persistent differences in productivity levels (and growth) between sectors ('the dual economy'), and the role of the manufacturing growth in speeding up the transfer of labour from low- to high-productivity activities (from agriculture to manufacturing, for instance).

The differences in findings between the studies cited by Cornwall and the present study may also reflect a change in the way 'modern capitalism' works. Arguably, the first decades after the Second World War constituted a period during which the diffusion of scale-intensive technology, from the USA to Europe and Japan, and learning from the use of these technologies, played a large role (Abramovitz, 1994). However, the role as 'engine of growth' has relocated to electronics and other industries characterized by a strong science base and heavy investments in R&D. Our results indicate that there is a strong, positive and very robust correlation between a country's performance in these new growth industries and the rate of growth of manufacturing productivity. This may indicate that there are strong positive spillovers from these kinds of activities, and that these spillovers, to some extent at least, are nationally embedded. However, there are reasons to believe that the technologies that emerge from the new growth industries (especially electronics), and the learning that follows, are equally (or even more) relevant in many service industries. This is, of course, consistent with the finding of this chapter that in most advanced countries, the distinction between manufacturing and services has lost much of its economic significance.

Notes

1. For overviews see Verspagen (1992) and Fagerberg (1994).
2. These include among other things a common technology, equally available to all countries (a global public good), identical saving rates (or more generally that the incentives to save are the same) and identical rates of labour force growth. See Fagerberg (1994) for an extended discussion.
3. If saving behaviour and labour force growth differ across countries, countries will still converge towards the same *rate of growth* of GDP per capita (given by exogenous technological progress), but the *levels* of GDP per capita in long-run equilibrium will differ. Hence, only countries that share the same characteristics (in terms of saving behaviour and labour force growth) will converge towards the

same level of GDP per capita. This is often called 'conditional convergence' (Barro and Sala-i-Martin, 1995).

4. There is an extensive literature on this topic, both theoretical and empirical, which it is beyond the scope of this chapter to summarize (see, for example, McCombie and Thirlwall, 1994).

5. An empirical approach to the study of such linkages is the so-called triangulation of input–output matrices (Cornwall, 1977, pp. 130–5). This procedure takes an input–output table and rearranges the order of the sectors (rows and columns) of the table such that (in the 'ideal' case) a sector only supplies to sectors listed above it, and only purchases from sectors listed below it. Hence, sectors ranked at the top tend to purchase large quantities from other sectors (further below) and supply mostly to final demand, while sectors ranked at the bottom tend to supply mostly to other sectors (instead of final demand), only being dependent on a limited number of other sectors for their inputs. Cornwall argues that work based on this methodology shows that manufacturing is a sector with strong backward linkages: it supplies a relatively large part of its output to final demand, and purchases large quantities of inputs from other sectors.

6. Cornwall solved the identification problem by estimating only the reduced form of the model, which is adequate for testing the overall explanatory power of the model. However, when one wants to test the role of manufacturing as an engine of growth separately from the other elements of the theory, this approach is not sufficient, because in general one can not calculate a parameter estimate for a_1 from the reduced form.

7. We use the RGDP variable, that is, real GDP in international prices using a Laspayeres price index.

8. Version on CD-ROM, 1997.

9. Due to data availability we use economy-wide investment as a share of GDP instead of investment in manufacturing as a share of manufacturing output.

10. See Fagerberg (1987, 1988) for discussion of different indicators of technology gaps and technology investment, and an analysis of the impact of technology gaps and technology investment on growth.

11. As with most of the literature in this area we use patents taken out in the USA, because this provides us with more consistent and economically relevant data than data drawn from a variety of different national sources.

12. This method identifies outliers by calculating the so-called hat-matrix, $X(X^T X)^{-1} X^T$, where X is the matrix of independent variables. Observations with entries larger than $2k/n$, where k is the number of independent variables, and n the number of observations in the regression, were excluded. See Belsley *et al.* (1980).

13. Note that the 2SLS estimates generally have fewer observations, due to missing values for some of the instrumental variables.

14. The 2SLS estimates are higher than the ones obtained by OLS in three cases, and in two cases it is the other way around. However, in no case are the 2SLS estimates significantly different from those obtained by OLS at a 5 per cent level of significance.

15. It is possible that the engine of growth equations as estimated here suffer from a bias due to omitted variables. Manufacturing may indeed be an important factor

explaining growth in other sectors, but there may be other factors explaining economy-wide growth, or growth in non-manufacturing sectors, which should have been taken into account when estimating the relationship. For instance, one might argue (see, for example, Cornwall, 1977, p. 133) that some of the factors explaining growth in manufacturing also explain economy-wide growth, that is, one may include some of the instrumental variables in our 2SLS procedure as exogenous variables in equation (1). We tested various equations from this perspective, but always found that the results reported above are robust to the inclusion of other possible explanatory factors. These results are available from the authors on request.

16.   More recently, Cornwall has argued that above a certain threshold level of development, the importance of manufacturing for growth should be expected to decrease, since the rise in income per capita encourages a shift in demand from manufacturing products towards services (see Cornwall and Cornwall, 1994a, 1994b). While this may be true, it does not explain the finding of no correlation at all between growth of GDP and growth of manufacturing for a cross-section of developed countries.

17.   The industry data (productivity and employment shares) are from UNIDO, investment and exports as shares of GDP and education from the World Development Report (World Bank, various editions), and R&D data are from OECD and UNESCO. In a few cases these data were supplemented with data from national sources.

18.   Oceania (Australia and New Zealand) is included in Asia in this study.

19.   In most cases, the countries that were identified as outliers (and hence excluded) were poor countries with low educational standards. In the initial estimations (with these countries included) education (especially primary education) had somewhat more impact.

20.   We also estimated a version more akin to Cornwall's reduced form, that is, with only initial productivity (Y_{73}) and investment (INV) as exogenous variables, and growth of labour productivity (G) as the endogenous variable. This model turned out to have very little explanatory power. The result was (absolute *t*-values in brackets):

$$G = 0.75Y_{73} + 3.19INV$$
$$\quad (1.32) \qquad (1.77)$$

$$R^2(\overline{R}^2) = 0.11(0.06)$$

21.   In the initial estimation (before exclusion of outliers) the impact of R&D was found to be both larger and significant (at the 1 per cent level).

References

Abramovitz, M.A. (1994) 'The origins of the postwar catch-up and convergence boom', in J. Fagerberg *et al.* (eds) *The Dynamics of Technology, Trade and Growth*, Aldershot, Edward Elgar

Barro, R. and X. Sala-i-Martin (1995) *The Theory of Economic Growth*, Cambridge, MA, MIT Press

Belsley, D.A., E. Kuh and R.E. Welsch (1980) *Regression Diagnostics: Identifying Influential Data and Sources of Collinearity*, New York, John Wiley & Sons

Cornwall, J. (1977) *Modern Capitalism: Its Growth and Transformation*, London, Martin Robertson

Cornwall, J. and W. Cornwall (1994a) 'Structural change and productivity in the OECD', in P. Davidson and J.A. Kregel (eds) *Employment, Growth and Finance: Economic Reality and Economic Growth*, Aldershot, Edward Elgar

Cornwall, J. and W. Cornwall (1994b) 'Growth theory and economic structure', *Economica*, 61, 237–51

Cripps, F. and R. Tarling (1973) *Growth in Advanced Capitalist Economics 1950–1970*, Cambridge, Cambridge University Press

Fagerberg, J. (1987) 'A technology gap approach to why growth rates differ', *Research Policy*, 16, 87–99

Fagerberg, J. (1988) 'Why growth rates differ', in G. Dosi *et al.* (eds) *Technical Change and Economic Theory*, London, Pinter

Fagerberg, J. (1994) 'Technology and international differences in growth rates', *Journal of Economic Literature*, 32, 1147–75

Kaldor, N. (1966) *Causes of the Slow Rate of Economic Growth of the United Kingdom*, Cambridge, Cambridge University Press

Kaldor, N. (1967) *Strategic Factors in Economic Development*, Ithaca, NY, Cornell University Press

McCombie, J.S.L. and A.P. Thirlwall (1994) *Economic Growth and the Balance-of-Payments Constraint*, London, Macmillan

Romer, P.M. (1990) 'Endogenous technological change', *Journal of Political Economy*, 98, 1002–37

Solow, R.M. (1956) 'A contribution to the theory of economic growth', *Quarterly Journal of Economics*, 70, 65–94

United Nations (1970) *Economic Survey of Europe 1969, Part 1*, New York, United Nations

Verspagen, B. (1992) 'Endogenous innovation in neo-classical models: a survey', *Journal of Macroeconomics*, 14, 631–62

Young, A. (1928) 'Increasing returns and economic progress', *Economic Journal*, 38, 527–42

3

FORUM FOR DEVELOPMENT STUDIES
NO. 2 – 1995

East Asian Growth: A Critical Assessment

Aadne Cappelen and Jan Fagerberg

The Agenda

It is a well established fact that a number of East Asian countries have had much faster economic growth than most other countries for several decades. From 1960 to 1990 the average GDP per capita increased by more than 5 per cent annually in countries like Hong Kong, Indonesia, Japan, Malaysia, Singapore, South Korea, Taiwan and Thailand. Their output in manufacturing increased even more rapidly and their share of world trade in manufactures was more than doubled. For a country like South Korea, whose level of GDP per capita equalled that of say Bangladesh and many African countries in 1960, the level is today more in line with that of low-income countries in Europe. This progress is not the result of favourable new terms of trade or caused by discoveries of valuable natural resources. Furthermore, this growth miracle has taken place in countries with relatively small income inequalities that have even been reduced during these decades of high growth. For students of economic growth and economic development in particular, the experience of these countries represents important material for 'testing' competing hypotheses. And of course the lessons for economic policy will very much depend on how one explains this growth miracle.

Among those studying catching-up processes, there is a long tradition – starting with Gerschenkron (1962) – for supporting an interventionist policy stance. Countries far behind the technology frontier, it is argued, usually lack many of the resources necessary for success in advanced industry. In addition, there may be important parts of society that resist change. To overcome these handicaps, such countries have to develop 'institutional instruments for which there was little or no counterpart in an established industrial country' (Gerschenkron, 1962:7). While Gerschenkron based his views on a study of European industrialisation, several students of the more recent

175

Aadne Cappelen and Jan Fagerberg

industrialisation efforts in East Asia, most notably Japan (Johnson, 1982; Freeman, 1987), South-Korea (Amsden, 1989) and Taiwan (Wade, 1990), have come to share his basic approach. The role of government, these authors argue, is to boost the growth of the technological capabilities of firms through providing finance and other supporting factors, cooperation and guidance, and (performance-related) economic incentives, *inter alia.*

Traditionally, neoclassical economists, for instance as represented by the World Bank (1991), have been rather critical towards the interventionist strand, emphasising instead the various problems attached to interventionism such as misallocation of resources, efficiency losses, rent-seeking behaviour and the like. The most important task for the government of a developing country, according to this view, is to 'get the prices right' so that economic agents face the right incentives. This clearly reflects the traditional neoclassical belief in the efficiency of markets. However, the advent of the new growth theory, with its emphasis on endogenous technological progress and externalities, has somewhat challenged the theoretical basis for this position (Romer, 1986, 1990; Grossman and Helpman, 1991). For instance, if there are positive externalities from accumulation of physical or human capital, or R&D investments, market solutions will normally lead to under-investment because private investors normally do not take these externalities into account when making decisions. Then, according to the new theory, governmental intervention that affects such investments positively, through the demand for – or supply of – funds, may raise growth. This holds even in the long run, provided that change in investment behaviour is there to stay, in contrast to what the traditional theory would predict. Similarly, if there are differences across sectors in the prospects for technological progress, it may pay off for a government to intervene in order to change the economic structure of the country towards technologically more progressive sectors, for instance by protecting the most promising activities from international competition (for a while).

The advent of the new growth theories has clearly broken the stalemate and opened for a more meaningful debate on policy issues related to catching-up processes. Even the World Bank now acknowledges, at least at a theoretical level, that Japanese-type interventionism may have positive growth-inducing effects. However, the World Bank study on the 'East Asian Miracle' (World Bank, 1993) downplays the positive impact that such policies have had in East Asia and may have elsewhere. It is argued that industrial policy (targeting certain industries) did not work in East Asia, and thus is of little rele-

East Asian Growth: A Critical Assessment

vance for other countries. Furthermore, the study points out, some of the attempts to increase investments, although successful in the East Asian case, rested on national control of the markets for capital and foreign exchange. These markets have since been deregulated almost everywhere. Thus the conclusion is that the East Asian experience in this field is probably not replicable. In other cases, the World Bank study argues, the policies may be too challenging institutionally. For instance, a highly competent and independent bureaucracy seems to be a must for successful interventionism, and most developing countries are, according to the report, far from meeting this requirement. The only aspect of the East Asian policy package that receives really wholehearted support is the emphasis on exports, which – incidentally – may also be consistent with the policy recipe of the traditional theory.[1]

It is impossible within the context of this article to discuss all aspects of this controversy,[2] and we will confine ourselves to the more narrow question of what the empirical evidence on growth presented in the report actually shows. This evidence consists mainly of a set of regressions between productivity growth, defined in different ways, and variables that are assumed to impact on this. There is also an attempt to take changes in the structure of production into account. The following sections contain a detailed presentation and assessment of the empirical work on growth, its methodological and theoretical underpinnings, and the derived policy conclusions. Then we discuss the impact of industrial policy, openness and income distribution (equality) on growth. We also briefly examine some other applied studies on East Asian growth that have been published in the wake of the World Bank report. Finally some tentative conclusions on the state of the art and the future research agenda in this area are offered.

What can Cross-country Regressions tell Us about the Causes of Economic Growth?

Comparative analyses are important in most social sciences and not least in development economics. To analyse East Asian growth from a comparative perspective, we need something to compare with, i.e., a control group. The importance of this choice should be stressed. To arrive at meaningful results, we have to assume that the growth of the countries in the control group is affected by the same variables, and roughly in the same way, as the East Asian countries. What is allowed to differ is the magnitude and, hence, impact of each explanatory variable in each case. For example, a variable that is commonly used to

Aadne Cappelen and Jan Fagerberg

explain economic growth is investment (usually measured as the ratio of investment to GDP). For a cross-country regression of the investment ratio on the growth rate of GDP, using one data point for each country, to be meaningful, changes in the investment ratio must affect the growth rate in the same way in all countries. This is a strong assumption that may be contested. For instance, it cannot be ruled out by definition that the impact of investment on growth differs across countries due to differences in, say, the working of capital markets or the returns on investments in new industrial projects. Similar considerations may apply for other variables such as, for instance, investments in education or R&D. Ideally, this possibility should be tested for, although this is not always possible with the available data sets (at least not to the extent one would wish).[3] However, it is important to keep this possibility in mind when choosing samples and assessing results.

Even when countries are relatively similar in most respects, there may be so-called country-specific factors at work, due to differences in culture, etc. To ignore such factors when they exist may seriously distort the results. For instance, if a country is an 'outlier' with regard to growth, but not necessarily with regard to the (independent) variables taken into account in the regression, the results may depend very much on whether you include that country or not. One method that is often recommended to deal with this problem is to test for country-specific effects. The simplest form of this is to let the constant term of the regression be country specific. However, this method is more data demanding. Instead of only using averages for a long time period, one needs several observations for each country. Again, data limitations often preclude this option. Apart from that, one also runs the risk of referring a large share of the observed differences in growth to unknown country-specific factors, when these may equally well be the outcome of some combination of other left-out variables.

Since there are many possible variables that could be brought into the analysis, one needs to be sure that the variables that are singled out for analysis really are the most important ones. However, the models applied to cross-country data sets are often rather tentative. This, combined with the fact that a large part of actual growth normally continues to be unaccounted for (i.e., a poor fit), imply that the results from such studies must treated with caution. There is always a risk of leaving out an important variable, the effect of which may then be picked up by one of the other variables in the regression. Besides careful consideration of specification, this points to the need for sensitivity testing, i.e., including other, possible explanatory variables. In

East Asian Growth: A Critical Assessment

practice a substantial amount of cross-country regression results are not robust, i.e., sensitive to changes in the number of variables (or countries) included, cf. Levine and Renelt (1992). Note that a failure to pass such sensitivity testing does not necessarily imply that the variable in question is unimportant for growth, just that the degree to which this is the case (or not) cannot be assessed with sufficient precision with the available data.

Indeed, the question of causality is a difficult one in regression analyses. In time-series analysis some methods have been suggested, based on the ideas that there generally is a time lag between cause and effect and that a casual factor, when taken into account, should increase the explanatory power of the regression. However, in cross-sectional analysis there is no way to test for the direction of causality.

The importance of these considerations will become clearer as we discuss some of the studies of the 'East Asian Miracle'. It all boils down to the point that it is not enough to present a cross-country regression for a selected group of variables and countries and claim that it tells us something important. One needs to consider the deeper issues, such as how 'equal' the countries are (and possible changes in this aspect during the period of investigation), the possibility of alternative explanations and variables, the direction of causality, etc. The fact that in some of these cases no clear-cut 'tests' are available is not an argument for ignoring these problems.

Does Accumulation explain It all?

The first shot at this issue in the recent World Bank report is a cross-country regression of the type that has become standard in the empirical literature for a sample of both industrialised and developing countries in the last decades. This regression, which includes explanatory variables reflecting the scope for catch-up and accumulation of physical and human capital, fits poorly and produces large, unexplained residuals for the East Asian countries. On this basis a decomposition of the growth performance of the East Asian countries is made. It is claimed that the results support the conclusion that 'between 60 and 90 percent of their output growth derives from accumulation of physical and human capital' (World Bank, 1993:58) and that other factors therefore are of lesser importance.

But this conclusion does not seem to be warranted. To see this, consider panel A in Table 1, which presents an overview of predicted growth and its sources for four country groupings: the so-called HPAEs (high-performing Asian economies),[4] Latin-America, sub-

Aadne Cappelen and Jan Fagerberg

Saharan Africa and the OECD. The presentation is based on a cross-country regression from the World Bank study, covering 113 countries and the period 1960-85.[5] What is most noteworthy is that the predicted impact of accumulation (education and investment) far exceeds predicted growth for all four country groupings (for three of them it also exceeds actual growth). The reason for this is very simple. The contribution from the scope for catch-up (GDP relative to USA), which normally is assumed to be a positive factor for countries behind the frontier, does in this decomposition take on a negative sign for all countries' groupings, i.e., it acts as a growth retardant (and more so the more developed the country is). This inflates the contribution from the remaining (positive) factors, since the sum of all contributions necessarily has to add up (to predicted growth). A consequence of this is that it is not meaningful to calculate the ratio between the contribution to growth from one or more positive factors (say, accumulation) and predicted (or actual) growth and interpret this as a measure of the explanatory power of the factors in question. Unfortunately, this is precisely what the World Bank study does. For all the HPAEs taken together, accumulation in per cent of actual growth amounts to 87 per cent (the last line in panel A), seemingly a reasonable figure, and consistent with the conclusion in the World Bank study. But for the three other country groupings included in the table, this ratio is around 200 per cent or more![6] The only reason why this ratio is not above 100 per cent for the HPAEs as well is that predicted growth is so much lower than actual growth.

Panel B presents an attempt to correct for the failure to take catch-up properly into account by assuming (as commonly done in many empirical studies of this type) that diffusion of technology follows a logistic curve. This means that the contribution to growth from diffusion of technology is an increasing function of the productivity gap (for the frontier country the contribution is zero).[7] When calculated in this way, accumulation explains slightly above, and catch-up slightly below, one-half of the predicted growth in the HPAEs. Note that since predicted growth falls short of actual growth, the shares of accumulation and catch-up in actual growth are lower.

There are, however, many methodological problems associated with growth decompositions of this type. For instance, many of the variables included in the analysis are proxies that may differ from the 'true' (unobservable) variables in several respects. Arguably, some of these problems may be less damaging for the analysis of growth differences across country groupings, since all countries may be affected more or less in the same way. Such an analysis is presented in panel

East Asian Growth: A Critical Assessment

C.[8] It turns out that only between one-fourth (HPEA – OECD) and one-half (HPAE – sub-Saharan Africa) of the actual differences in growth between the East Asian countries and other country groups may be 'explained' by this approach. Only in relation to the African countries does the decomposition attribute a large share of the actual difference in growth to differences in factor accumulation. *Vis-à-vis* the Latin American countries differences in factor accumulation 'explain' relatively little (around one-fifth of the actual difference). In relation to the OECD it is even worse – the unexplained part of the actual difference in growth increases markedly when differences in factor accumulation are drawn into the picture! In fact, the only factor that contributes to the superior growth performance of East Asia *vis-à-vis* the OECD countries is the scope for catch-up.

Table 1.
Contribution of Accumulation to Growth (per cent)

(A)   Calculated as in World Bank (1983)

	HPAE	Latin America	Sub-Saharan Africa	OECD
Constant	-0.7	-0.7	-0.7	-0.7
GDP per cap. rel. to USA	-0.7	-0.9	-0.4	-2.3
Primary education	2.4	2.3	1.2	2.9
Secondary education	0.7	0.5	0.1	1.3
Population growth	0.2	0.2	0.3	0.1
Investment (share in GDP)	1.4	1.0	0.8	1.5
Predicted growth	3.4	2.3	1.2	2.7
Of which accumulation	4.5	3.7	2.0	5.7
Accumulation in per cent of predicted growth	135.1	160.4	168.3	208.6
Actual growth	5.2	1.6	1.0	2.9
Accumulation in per cent of actual growth	87.2	236.9	199.4	197.0
Predicted growth in per cent of actual growth	64.5	147.7	118.4	94.4

Aadne Cappelen and Jan Fagerberg

(B) Catch-up taken more properly into account

	HPAE	Latin America	Sub-Saharan Africa	OECD
Constant	-5.0	-5.0	-5.0	-5.0
GDP per cap. rel. to USA	3.6	3.4	3.9	2.0
Primary education	2.4	2.3	1.2	2.9
Secondary education	0.7	0.5	0.1	1.3
Population growth	0.2	0.2	0.3	0.1
Investment (share in GDP)	1.4	1.0	0.8	1.5
Predicted growth	3.4	2.3	1.2	2.7
Catch-up in per cent of predicted growth + 5 %	43.2	45.8	63.1	25.4
Accumulation in per cent of predicted growth + 5%	54.3	51.1	32.6	73.5

(C) Accounting for differences in growth

	HPAE - Latin America	HPAE - Sub-Saharan Africa	HPAE - OECD
Source of difference in growth:			
GDP per cap. rel. to USA	0.2	-0.3	1.6
Primary education	0.2	1.3	-0.5
Secondary education	0.2	0.6	-0.6
Population growth	-0.0	-0.1	0.1
Investment (share in GDP)	0.4	0.6	-0.1
Total predicted difference	1.0	2.2	0.6
Actual difference	3.6	4.2	2.3
Predicted difference in per cent of actual difference	28.2	51.5	27.4

Notes
1. Sources and definitions as in World Bank (1993).
2. Accumulation is the sum of primary education, secondary education and investment.

East Asian Growth: A Critical Assessment

Squeezing down the Residual

While regression models of the type discussed above generally can be made consistent with different theories (and therefore often fail to distinguish between them), the second shot at this issue in the report explicitly takes the traditional neoclassical growth model, extended to take into account human capital, as its point of departure. Constant returns to scale, e.g. that a one per cent growth in all factors yields one per cent growth, are imposed, seemingly without testing. However, for the East Asian countries the residuals continue to be large (Table 2, first column). In an attempt to squeeze down the residuals, the model is re-estimated on a sample of industrial countries only, and the estimates thus obtained are imposed on the HPAEs on the grounds that these countries are so 'allocatively efficient'. This reduces the East Asian residuals somewhat, since it gives higher weights to physical and human capital (Table 2, second column). Finally, the estimated technological progress (residual) from the industrialised country sample is deducted, using the familiar neoclassical argument that technological progress is the same everywhere. What is left is then interpreted as increases in technological efficiency (i.e., catch-up). But there is not much left: only a few countries catch up following this definition, and the contribution to growth thus obtained is rather small.

The purpose of all this appears to be to support the view that the lion's share of East Asian growth can be explained by conventional sources, i.e., that there is no miracle to explain. But the analysis is unconvincing. First, what should be shown – that the world conforms to the traditional neoclassical assumptions – is simply taken for granted. Thus, interaction between technological progress and factor accumulation (i.e., externalities) is ruled out by assumption. It is possible that a model based on a competing perspective would have performed better or equally well on the same data. For instance, using a more flexible model (weaker assumptions), Kwon (1994) arrives at radically different results from those published by the World Bank.[9] Second, the handling of technology lacks internal consistency.[10] On the one hand it is assumed that all countries benefit to the same extent from technological progress, i.e., the traditional public good assumptions, on the other that large differences in technological levels of development continue to exist across countries (due to differences in 'technological efficiency'). However, if technology is a global public good, and technological progress is independent of factor accumulation, technological catch-up should be fast and easy! It is also disappointing to note that the results from decades of research on inno-

Aadne Cappelen and Jan Fagerberg

vation and diffusion of technology, indicating that technology is not at all a global public good, are completely ignored. Indeed, much of the literature in this area now depicts technological knowledge as a rather local affair, organisationally and culturally embedded, and inter-twined with other factors of production. Third, as shown in Table 2 (third column), the results end with a big paradox. For most countries 'technological efficiency', as calculated in this study, is continually decreasing, i.e., they become gradually less and less apt![11] How is this finding to be explained within this perspective?

Table 2. Squeezing down the "residual" (TFP)

	Mark 1	Mark 2	Mark 3
Hong Kong	3.6	2.4	2.0
Indonesia	1.3	-0.8	-1.2
Japan	3.5	1.4	1.0
Korea	3.1	0.2	-0.2
Malaysia	1.1	-1.3	-1.8
Singapore	1.2	-3.0	-3.5
Taiwan	3.8	1.3	0.8
Thailand	2.5	0.5	0.1
Latin America	0.1	-1.0	-1.4
Sub-Saharan Africa	-1.0	-3.0	-3.5

Notes:
Mark 1 is estimated as a country-specific fixed effect in a pooled cross-country time series regression covering 87 countries and 30 years and including variables for physical and human capital and labour. Constant returns to scale are assumed (Cobb-Douglas).
Mark 2 is calculated using weights obtained from a much smaller sample containg only developed countries.
Mark 3 is Mark 2 less the estimated TFP-growth for the developed countries.

Source: World Bank (1993) Tables A1.2-3

East Asian Growth: A Critical Assessment

The above criticism notwithstanding, the World Bank interpretation of events is not without some scholarly support. In two recent papers, Young (1993, 1995) has presented evidence suggesting that there is nothing miraculous to East Asian growth as long as factors such as labour participation, structural changes in the composition of GDP, education and investment are properly accounted for. The first of these studies is rather similar to the one just discussed (and subject to many of the same weaknesses), the second is a conventional growth account of the type well known from the older empirical literature in this area.[12] Young's interpretation of events has been embraced by Krugman (1994) in a paper entitled 'The Myth of Asia's Miracle': ' ... East Asian growth has been matched by input growth so rapid that Asian economic growth (...) ceases to be a mystery.' (ibid.:76). However, as Lucas (1993) points out,[13] that rapid growth of input and output tend to go hand in hand should come as no surprise. Indeed, this is something that would be consistent with most theoretical perspectives in this area! Rather the question is what causes what. The traditional neoclassical growth theory, which seems to underlie the Young-Krugman interpretation of events, has something to say about this but so have other perspectives. For the Young-Krugman interpretation to be credible, it is not enough to argue that the predictions of the theory seem to fit the evidence, when this evidence may equally well be consistent with other theoretical perspectives. Rather, what should be done is to show that the assumptions of the theory (on which the interpretation is based) suit the East Asian experience. Thus, one has to ask questions of the following type: Did perfect competition prevail (i.e., no large firms with market power, no economies of scale and so on) ? Was new technology equally available to all firms, domestically as well as abroad, independently of factor accumulation (and other efforts)? As long as these (deeper) questions are ignored, studies of the type presented by Young should be regarded as descriptions, reflecting among other things the underlying assumptions, rather than tests. It follows that exercises of this type are not well suited for making judgements on causality.

Industrial Policy – of no Value?

The third attempt by the study to throw some light on the lessons from East Asian growth is carried out at the industry or sector level. The general idea is that if interventionist politics had any impact it should be reflected in a superior performance in the promoted sectors. To asses this impact, the study points out, it is necessary to find out what

Aadne Cappelen and Jan Fagerberg

would have happened in the absence of interventionist politics. This is a valid point. But unfortunately the analysis of specific policies and their impact is totally neglected in favour of more indirect (and approximate) methods.

Three different approaches to the comparison of actual versus expected developments are pursued. The first is based on the assumption that the structure of GDP changes as the country climbs up the development ladder. Differences in country-size are also taken into account. While this approach may yield some general insights, it neglects the point that countries have different comparative advantages and follow different strategies (Rodrik, 1994). Thus, as the study points out, this approach is too rough to allow for a test of the impact of interventionism and other factors.

The second approach, based on neoclassical trade theory, seeks to establish a correlation between the changing composition of output during recent decades and wage and productivity levels for five East Asian countries. Neoclassical theory, it is argued, would suggest that growth would be fastest in sectors with low initial wage or productivity levels, while successful interventionism is assumed to lead to an association between high growth and high wage or productivity levels at the end of the period. This way of putting things is by no means obvious. For instance, one of the most influential arguments in favour of interventionism rests on the idea of 'coordination failure', i.e., the failure by the market to generate a set of actions that – if coordinated – would lead to highly profitable outcome. In this case there is no reason why the firms or industries concerned should not be characterised by low relative wages at the outset (prior to intervention or coordination). However, the data do not seem to provide much support for the hypotheses outlined in the World Bank study. For Hong Kong, Japan and Taiwan there is no correlation at all. Only for Korea and Singapore are there some significant results, but these generally go in opposite directions. Thus the results are at best inconclusive. However, the authors of the World Bank study do their best to explain away this rather obvious result. In the case of Singapore, for which the results support the 'interventionist' hypothesis, it is suggested that this result is also consistent with the neoclassical view, because of the changing factor endowments of that country during the period of investigation. Similarly, the disappointing result for Japan is explained away by alluding to the advanced state of its economy (which the theory apparently is not suited for). However, this means, as pointed out by Rodrik, that 'the empirical analysis was inappropriate to begin with!

East Asian Growth: A Critical Assessment

One wonders what the point of running regressions is if any result will be taken to confirm the authors' priors' (Rodrik, 1994:31).

A third approach calculates so-called 'total factor productivity growth rates' (what remains when the contribution from factor growth is deducted) at the industry level, and compares the performance of promoted and non-promoted industries. Again the result is mixed, with some evidence in favour of the interventionist stance in the case of Japan, less so for others, although this conclusion may be disputed. For instance, Wade (1994) argues that some of the sectors that the study regards as non-promoted, such as textiles, in fact were heavily promoted in some periods and countries. Another problem is – as before – that the calculations are based on very restrictive assumptions, such as those of perfect competition and constant returns to scale, which are not tested. Kwon (1994:636) argues that these assumptions 'are typically unsuitable for the estimation of rapidly growing economies'. Based on less restrictive assumptions, allowing *inter alia* for economies of scale, he arrives at results (for Korea) that essentially contradict those presented by the World Bank: 'Contrary to the World Bank's findings, ... productivity change has been higher in promoted sectors' (ibid.: 638).

Openness

The World Bank study makes a big point about the importance of exports/openness. Three main arguments are presented in support for this view. The first is that openness enhances productivity growth by promoting competition. That there is an effect on the level of productivity seems reasonable, but an effect on the growth of productivity is not obvious. Second, it is argued that export orientation increases foreign direct investments which again increase growth. It is, however, a well established fact that neither in Japan, South Korea nor in Taiwan did such investments play any significant role. The third argument is that export orientation leads to more contacts with foreign customers and that this contact enhances improvements in products. This argument is in line with the studies that emphasise the relations between producers and customers (Lundvall, 1988). But, following this literature, one should not necessarily expect a difference in the impact of domestic and foreign customers in this regard.

The World Bank uses different measures of openness in its study. One set of variables are export shares (exports as a share of GDP or manufacturing exports as a share of total exports). The other is an openness indicator due to Dollar (1992). Essentially this indicator is a

Aadne Cappelen and Jan Fagerberg

measure of exchange-rate distortions. The argument behind it is that a large gap between the official exchange rate and the black market rate may hamper exports and growth.[14] This is not necessarily an argument supporting openness as such. What it implies, perhaps, is that there may exist some policies that reduce both openness and growth. However, the empirical evidence presented in the World Bank study (tables 6.17-18) and elsewhere (Levine and Renelt, 1992) shows that the relationship between growth and openness, however defined, is rather fragile, i.e., sensitive to differences in specification and choice of sample, and may be subject to different interpretations.[15]

More generally, the problem is not so much to establish a correlation between, say, high growth of GDP and high export growth, but to determine what the direction of causation is. For instance, a recent study of the time pattern of exports and investment in Korea and Taiwan concludes that the most likely direction of causation is from investment to exports, i.e., from accumulation to openness, not the other way around (Rodrik, 1995). A similar conclusion is reached for Singapore in a recent study by Ahmad and Harnhirun (1995) using cointegration methodology. The authors state that 'One can infer from this that internally generated mechanisms and exports have a mutually reinforcing relationship with one another', and further that 'The policy implications of our investigation, though limited, are not sanguine for the hypothesis of export-led growth in the ASEAN region' (Ahmad and Harnhirun, 1995:331-2).

Following Rodrik (1994), one should look for special features in the East Asian economies before or around 1960 in order to 'explain' why economic growth 'took off' at around that time. The point is to try to provide a better set of conditioning variables than those emphasised by the World Bank (i.e. the investment or export ratio) which tend to be so closely correlated with economic growth that any causal inference is difficult to make. Rodrik suggests these countries stand out with a well educated labour force and a relatively even distribution of income and land compared to other developing countries at that time.

Is Equality Conducive to Economic Growth?

That there is a trade off between economic growth and equality is the received wisdom from neoclassical theory. However, the results from cross-country regression studies seem to suggest that this trade-off is not an empirical regularity. Indeed, the results in Rodrik (1994, 1995) support the opposite conclusion, i.e., that equality may increase eco-

East Asian Growth: A Critical Assessment

nomic growth. It is shown that a model incorporating variables reflecting the scope for catch-up, educational efforts and the distribution of property and land 'explains' the growth performance of the East Asian countries better than the models suggested by the World Bank. It so happens that these variables also 'explain' the investment ratio quite well. Hence, a well educated labour force and an equal distribution of income appear to foster both a good investment climate and fast economic growth.

An attractive feature of Rodrik's regressions is, as mentioned, that the independent variables are all dated around 1960 (and then used to explain developments during the following decades). This gives some credibility to the assumption of a causal relationship. On the other hand it might be argued that Rodrik's work is subject to some of the same caveats as most cross-country regression studies. For instance, due to the lack of data on income distribution in most countries, the sample is relatively small and country-specific factors are generally ignored.

Still, the results presented by Rodrik raises some intriguing questions on the relationship between income distribution and long-run economic growth. Can these results be supported by economic theory? Two lines of argument are usually pursued; perhaps most common is of a political nature, while the second focuses more on economic mechanisms.

According to traditional neoclassical theory, redistribution policies should be expected to distort market outcomes, making the economy less efficient and slowing down growth. It has been argued (Persson and Tabellini, 1994) that an economy characterised by an unequal distribution of income will be more prone to political pressures for redistribution, by, for instance, taxing investment and other growth-promoting activities, than an economy with a more egalitarian distribution of income. Thus, following this line of reasoning, a positive relationship between growth performance and equality might be expected. The essence of the argument, then, is that equality reduces the electoral demands for redistribution (by government). Note that it is an unequal distribution of pre-tax income that is the 'cause' of growth-reducing policies in this case.

Another argument linking growth and income distribution is provided by Alesina and Perotti (1993). They argue that an equal distribution of income reduces political tensions and supports political stability, thereby creating a stable environment for business, which promotes investment and economic growth. This argument is more related to post- than pre-tax distribution, and may be quoted in sup-

Aadne Cappelen and Jan Fagerberg

port of redistribution policies (as growth promoting). They also provide some empirical support for this view for a sample including, among else, some of the so-called HPAEs.[16]

However, there are also some arguments in favour of a positive relationship between equality and growth that focus less on policy. Again it is the post-tax distribution of income that matters. Two such arguments will be presented below. Murphy *et al.* (1989) argue that equality is one of the conditions for industrialisation because the middle class is the natural source for domestically produced manufactures (in their model, farmers are included in the concept of the middle class). They point to the well documented fact that in Japan and Taiwan the demand for manufactures by farmers (both consumer and investment goods) was important in the early phase of industrialisation. Arguments of a similar nature have been put forward in theories of industrialisation based on 'linkages' and 'clusters' where the development of new goods and industries is stimulated by the contact between the industry and its customers.

A second line of reasoning links income distribution to investment, cf. Bernanke and Gertler (1990), and is based on the assumption of capital market imperfections. Traditional neoclassical theorising tells us that equality leads to low savings, low investments and low growth. However, in the case of the East Asian countries it is well known that an egalitarian distribution of income has coexisted with, by international standards, very high household savings and investment ratios. How can this be explained? If capital markets are imperfect, in the sense that the rate of interest fails to clear the market, credit will to some extent be distributed through rationing (Stiglitz and Weiss, 1983). It is commonly assumed that this holds for the developing world, but it may apply to developed countries as well. If the extent of credit rationing is increasing with inequality, because it widens the gap between potential savers and lenders, this may, according to this way of reasoning, hamper investment. Hence, on these assumptions it might be argued that a redistribution of income may reduce the extent of credit rationing and increase investment (Bernanke and Gertler, 1990).

This short overview of possible approaches to the relation between income distribution to growth does not do full justice to the literature in this area. However, it should be sufficient to show that the positive correlation between economic growth and equality that characterises the countries of East Asia may be something more than just an artifact of the data. Good data are hard to come by, and there is a real need for more empirical work in this area. However, in the East Asian context,

East Asian Growth: A Critical Assessment

it appears well worth emphasising the role played by distributional policies.[17] In many of these countries land reforms after World War II resulted in a more equal distribution of land. The relatively egalitarian distribution of income that this resulted in has to a large extent prevailed (anf even increased) during the growth boom that followed.

Concluding Remarks

The World Bank study on East Asia was conceived as a response to the challenge to orthodoxy caused by the success of the Japanese model of economic development. The project was launched with the active backing of the Japanese government. It led to an impressive amount of high quality research as well as an increased attention to the factors behind the economic success stories in East Asia.

Besides all that, what are the lessons from the study and the ensuing debate? As pointed out previously, the study presents its conclusions in an admirably clear way. It so happens that these in most respects are in accordance with the traditional policy stance of the World Bank. Unfortunately, detailed scrutiny – here and elsewhere – has shown that many of these conclusions are open to objections. Indeed, the presentation of research results in the report has in some cases been shown to be biased. Further research is also necessary.

The main merit of the World Bank study on East Asia is that it has focused the attention of many clever people on the East Asian growth process. This has raised many interesting issues. For instance, does it matter what you do or (only) how you do it? The idea that some activities are more promising than others is as old as economics itself. The World Bank study approached the issue, but did not resolve it. The possible role of a relatively egalitarian distribution of income is another topic that the report and the debate that followed have helped to highlight. Furthermore, to what extent can the high growth in these countries be shown to be related to successful dealing with coordination failures? Are such failures important for the low growth (if any) in many poor countries today? Related to this, how can we explain that policies 'similar' to some of those at work in East Asia do not seem to have worked elsewhere? Indeed, a sharper focus on actual policies, their implementation (including the institutional setting) and results seems to be very relevant. Another important issue with far-reaching implications is what role the high degree of regulation and control of financial markets (and the markets for foreign exchange) played in the East Asian growth process. Is it really true, as argued by the World Bank, that these policies are not at all replicable due to

191

Aadne Cappelen and Jan Fagerberg

international system changes and that they, because of problems of 'rent-seeking', should be avoided anyway?

There are other policy questions as well that deserve more attention. As is well documented (and also discussed by the World Bank) many of the East Asian countries started their industrialisation with import substitution policies. The turn to a more outward oriented policy came in the 1960s. What has been the role of these different phases of policies and their timing for the development? Many of these countries received substantial support from the US in the 1950s and 1960s. Did this support increase the savings ratio and thereby prepare for the 'take-off'? Finally, what has been the role of agricultural reforms? After World War II several countries undertook land reforms. In South Korea the number of farmers owning their land increased from 50 per cent to 94 per cent due to the reform. This increased labour intensity and output per hectare as well as agricultural output. Their success in terms of output is thus not confined to manufacturing alone. Are there lessons to learn from these policies for other developing countries?

Thus, in our view, we are still closer to the beginning than to the end in our search for an understanding of how countries like Japan, Korea and Taiwan have managed to get where they are today. We may not have so many good answers yet. But at least we have some good questions.

Notes

1. In the traditional theory 'openness' to trade is regarded as important for 'getting the prices right'. In addition to this the recent World Bank study also emphasises the beneficial effects that trade may have for the acquisition of foreign technology.
2. Readers who want a broader overview of the debate may benefit from the papers in Fishlow *et al.* (1994) and the special issue of *World Development* (Vol. 22, No. 4, 1994). See also Amsden and Singh (1994) and Singh (1994, 1995).
3. Ideally one would wish many observations for each country. For a pure cross section one may experiment with identifying outliers or splitting samples. A method for endogenous split of samples within a cross-country framework has been suggested by Durlauf and Johnson (1992).
4. Hong Kong, Indonesia, Japan, Korea (South), Malaysia, Taiwan, Thailand and Singapore.
5. Coefficients and data are taken from tables 1.8-9 in World Bank (1993). The prediction/decomposition presented here is based on the first of the three regressions presented in Table 1.8 (i.e., without group dummies).
6. These numbers, it may be noted, cannot be directly read out of the tables in World Bank (1993), but they follow (indirectly) from the estimates and numbers presented there. It just requires a little bit of extra effort.
7. To see how this is done, consider the following simple model, adapted from Fagerberg (1988). Assume that GDP (Y) is a function of technology (T) and other factors (O):

East Asian Growth: A Critical Assessment

$$Y = f(T,O)$$

Let small letters denote growth rates, and e_T and e_O be the elasticity of GDP with respect to technology and other factors, respectively. Then the GDP growth may be expressed as:

$$y = e_T t + e_O o$$

Now, assume that t follows a logistic curve, so that t for any particular country may be written:

$$t = h - h \, (T/T_f),$$

where T_f is the level of technological development in the frontier country. Then by substitution we have:

$$y = e_T h - e_T h \, (T/T_f) + e_O o$$

The first two terms, then, are the contribution to growth from international diffusion of technology (catch-up). Since we know the estimates of $(e_T h)$ and (T/T_f) from tables 1.8-9 in World Bank (1993), we may use this formula to calculate the contribution from catch-up.

8. A similar analysis is presented in Table 1.9 in World Bank (1993), but in that case group-dummies (one constant term for each country group) were included. The theoretical basis for including such dummies is weak and we do not employ them. However, the qualitative results are the same as those presented here. If anything factor growth explains less of the actual differences when group-dummies are included.

9. The study by Kwon (1994) is limited to Korea.

10. For an overview of the theoretical and empirical work on the relation between technology and growth, see Fagerberg (1994).

11. This result, it may be noted, is the price to be paid for using other weights than those that were suggested by the regression containing developed as well as developing countries. The estimated ones are by definition those that explain the growth of the countries included in the best possible way, given the structure of the model. When other weights are imposed the quality of the predictions generally deteriorates.

12. Growth accounting became a popular empirical methodology around 1960 (following contemporary advances in formal modelling). What it does is to calculate the contribution to output growth from growth of inputs, using factor shares as weights. For instance, the contribution of labour is calculated as the growth of the labour force multiplied by the share of wages in value added. This procedure is based on the traditional neoclassical theory of growth (and its underlying assumptions). Central themes in this literature have been to what extent growth of inputs should be adjusted to take into account changes in quality and composition and whether explanatory factors other than input growth should be included or not. A useful survey is Maddison (1987). See also the discussion in Fagerberg (1994).

13. In a comment on Young's findings Lucas (1993: 257) points out that 'Correlations between investment ratios and growth rates, which tend to be positive, are frequently cited but do not settle anything. If growth is driven by rapid accumulation of human capital, one needs rapid growth in physical capital just to keep up (...)'. Similar arguments can be made from other perspectives.

14. See Rodrik (1994) for a detailed discussion of the Dollar index.

Aadne Cappelen and Jan Fagerberg

15. See, for instance, the following remark: 'One possible interpretation of these results is that a high concentration of manufactures exports relative to total exports, rather than openness, contributes relatively more to productivity change ...' (World Bank, 1993:321).
16. This view on the relationship between income distribution and stability has also been put forward as an explanation of why so many Latin American countries have been slow growers.
17. A special case is Malaysia, where the economic and political interests of ethnic Malays have been promoted by extensive regulations at the expense of the Chinese minority, probably leading to more equality than otherwise would have been the case.

References

Ahmad, J. and S. Harnhirum, 1995, 'Unit roots and cointegration in estimating causality between exports and economic growth: Empirical evidence from the ASEAN countries', *Economic Letters* 49.

Alesina, A. and R. Perotti, 1993, *Income Distribution, Political Instability and Investment*, NBER Working Paper No. 4486.

Amsden, A. H., 1989, *Asia's Next Giant: South Korea and Late Industralization*, New York: Oxford University Press.

Amsden, A. and A. Singh, 1994, 'The Optimal Degree of Competition and Dynamic Efficiency in Japan and Korea', *European Economic Review* 38.

Bernanke, B. and M. Gertler, 1990, 'Financial Fragility and Economic Performance', *Quarterly Journal of Economics*, 105.

Durlauf, S. N. and P. A. Johnson, 1992, 'Local versus Global Convergence: Across National Economies', *NBER Working Paper* No. 3996, Cambridge, MA: National Bureau of Economic Research.

Fagerberg, J., 1988, 'Why Growth Rates Differ', in G. Dosi *et al.* (eds.), *Technical Change and Economic Theory*, Pinter: London.

Fagerberg, J., 1994, 'Technology and International Differences in Growth Rates', *Journal of Economic Literature*, 32.

Fishlow, A. *et al.*, 1994, 'Miracle or Design? Lessons from the East Asian Experience', *Policy Essay*, No. 11, Washington, DC.: Overseas Development Council.

Freeman, C., 1987, *Technology policy and economic performance: Lessons from Japan*, London: Pinter Publishers.

Gerschenkron, A., 1962, *Economic Backwardness in Historical Perspective*, Cambridge (USA): The Belknap Press.

Grossman, G.M. and E. Helpman, 1991, *Innovation and Growth in the Global Economy*, Cambridge (USA): The MIT Press.

Johnson, C., 1982, *MITI and the Japanese Miracle: The Growth of Industrial Policy, 1925-1975*, Stanford: Stanford University Press.

Krugman, P., 1994, 'The Myth of Asia's Miracle', *Foreign Affairs*, 73.

Kwon, J., 1994, 'The East Asia Challenge to Neoclassical Orthodoxy', *World Development*, 22.

Levine, R. and D. Renelt, 1992, 'A Sensitivity Analysis of Cross-Country Growth Regressions', *American Economic Review*, 82.

Lundvall, B. Å., 1988, 'Innovation as an Interactive Process – from User-Producer Interaction to the National System of Innovation', in G. Dosi *et al.* (eds.), *Technical Change and Economic Theory*, London: Pinter.

Lucas, R. E., Jr., 1993, 'Making a Miracle', *Econometrica*, 61.

Maddison, A., 1987, 'Growth and Slowdown in Advanced Capitalist Economies: Techniques of Quantitative Asessment', *Journal of Economic Literature*, 25.

East Asian Growth: A Critical Assessment

Murphy, R. A. Shleifer and R. Vishny, 1989, 'Income Distribution, Market Size and Industrialisation', *Quarterly Journal of Economics*, 54.

Persson, T. and G. Tabellini, 1994, 'Is inequality harmful for growth?', *American Economic Review*, 84.

Rodrik, D., 1994, 'King Kong Meets Godzilla: The World Bank and The East Asian Miracle', in Fishlow *et al.*

Rodrik, D., 1995, 'Getting Interventions Right: How South Korea and Taiwan Grew Rich', *Economic Policy*, April.

Romer, P.M., 1986, 'Increasing Returns and Long-Run Growth', *Journal of Political Economy*, 94.

Romer, P.M., 1990, 'Endogenous Technological Change', *Journal of Political Economy*, 98.

Singh, A., 1994, 'Openness and the Market Friendly Approach to Development: Learning the Right Lessons from Development Experience', *World Development*, 22.

Singh, A., 1995, 'How Did East Asia Grow so Fast? Slow Progress Towards an Analytical Consensus', *UNCTAD Discussion Paper* No. 97, Geneva: UNCTAD.

Stiglitz, J.E. and A. Weiss, 1983, 'Credit Rationing in Markets with Imperfect Information', *American Economic Review*, 71.

Wade, R., 1990, *Governing the Market. Economic Theory and the Role of Government in East Asian Industrialisation*, Princeton: Princeton University Press.

Wade, R., 1994, 'Selective Industrial Policies in East Asia: Is The East Asian Miracle Right?', in Fishlow *et al.*

World Bank, 1991, *World Development Report: The Challenge of Development*, New York: Oxford University Press.

World Bank, 1993, *The East Asian Miracle. Economic Growth and Public Policy*, New York: Oxford University Press.

Young, A., 1994, 'Lessons from the East Asian NICs: A Contrarian View', *European Economic Review*, 38.

Young, A., 1995, 'The Tyranny of Numbers: Confronting the Statistical Realities of the East Asian Growth Experience', *Quarterly Journal of Economics*, 110.

Summary

Aadne Cappelen and Jan Fagerberg, 'East Asian Growth: A Critical Assessment', *Forum for Development Studies*, 1995:2, pp. 175-195.

It is a well-established fact that a number of East Asian countries have had much faster economic growth than most other countries for several decades. Many observers have held that this growth success is related to the interventionist policy stance that has characterised many of these countries. However, a recent World Bank study - *The East Asian Miracle* (1993) - downplays the positive role that such policies might have had (and may have elsewhere). This article contains a detailed presentation and assessment of the World bank's analysis of East Asian growth, including the derived policy conclusions. Among the topics discussed are the roles of industrial policy, openness and income distribution (equality) in East Asian growth.

4

Journal of Common Market Studies

Vol. 34, No. 3
September 1996

Heading for Divergence?
Regional Growth in Europe Reconsidered*

JAN FAGERBERG

NUPI, PO Box 8159,
Dep. N-0033, Oslo, Norway

BART VERSPAGEN

MERIT, University of Limburg,
PO Box 616, NL-6200 MD, Maastricht, the Netherlands

Abstract

This article analyses regional growth in the European Union (EU) in the post-war period. We examine the levels and growth of per capita GDP for a sample of 70 regions, covering six of the EU Member States. We find that after a slow, but steady reduction of differences in GDP per capita across European regions during most of the post-war period, there are now some signs of a reversal in this trend. This does not imply that differences in levels of productivity and income across European regions are now reduced to a negligible level. Rather, the explanation is that other variables, notably R&D effort, investment support from the EU, the structure of GDP and differences in unemployment have had a diverging impact. We also find some support for the idea of a 'Europe at

* An earlier version of this paper was presented at the CRENoS Conference on 'Economic Integration and Regional Gaps', 26–7 May 1995, Cagliari, Italy. Bart Verspagen's research has been made possible by a fellowship of the Royal Netherlands Academy of Arts and Sciences.

different speeds', with at least three different 'growth clubs' characterized by different dynamics, productivity and unemployment levels.

I. Introduction: What Drives Regional Growth-rate Differences?

In recent years there has been a surge in empirical work on growth. This work has, with few exceptions, focused on cross-country differences. Although convenient in terms of data availability, this tends to 'aggregate away' important differences between smaller geographic entities within countries. For example, in the dataset that we analyse below, the ratio of GDP per capita between the richest (Hamburg, Germany) and poorest region (Calabria, Italy) was about 3:1, while for the two countries as a whole the difference in GDP per capita was almost negligible (all comparisons for 1990). This implies that the difference in GDP per capita between the richest and poorest region in our sample is roughly the same order as the difference between Germany and a developing country such as Costa Rica or, alternatively, South Africa.[1] We can only guess what the differences would have been, had we been able to include countries like Ireland, Portugal, Spain or Greece.

Within the EU, such big differences in per capita GDP across regions have always been regarded as undesirable. Therefore, various policy measures to reduce these differences have been invented, such as the so-called structural funds, investment loans, etc. A vital question for the EU is, to what extent these policy instruments really help the relatively poor regions of Europe to catch up. The answer to this question, however, requires knowledge about what drives regional growth differences. What determines whether or not a region converges towards the average, falls behind or, alternatively, forges ahead of the others? This article attempts to throw some light on the issue, drawing on recent developments in economic theory and new and better data on regional developments across Europe.

Much of the contemporary policy discussion in Europe is based on the idea that convergence in income (and productivity) depends on convergence in certain macroeconomic characteristics (inflation, public sector deficit, external account, etc.). Hence, the focus has largely been on the question of, to what extent convergence in these factors can be achieved. The empirical basis of this way of looking at things seems to be at best weak. There is not much evidence supporting the assumption that macroeconomic characteristics have an impact on differences in growth rates, given that the influence of other factors is properly taken into account. The available evidence from cross-country samples clearly shows that the correlations – if any – between macroeconomic characteristics and growth are not robust (Levine and Renelt, 1992).

[1] According to the Penn World Tables, version 5.5.

The scholarly work on European convergence seems either to be based on the traditional neoclassical theory of economic growth (Barro and Sala-i-Martin, 1992), or to consist of measurement exercises without any specific theoretical base.[2] A central assumption in neoclassical growth theory is that technology is a public good, e.g. that all regions and countries benefit from technological progress, which is assumed to be exogenous, to the same extent. Another is that there are decreasing marginal returns to the accumulation of capital per worker. Hence, profit opportunities are better in poor regions or countries (where there is relatively little capital available for each worker) than in the rich ones. Thus, if markets are allowed to work, and everything else is assumed identical, poor regions (or countries) should be expected to outgrow the rich ones. In the end, they will share the same level of income and grow at the same rate. The role of government, then, is essentially that of letting markets work. Hence the emphasis in policy analyses on avoiding too much interference in the economy, but instead fostering a stable macroeconomic climate and a roughly similar set of incentives (over time and across regions and countries).

The neoclassical assumption of technology as a (global) public good does not carry much empirical support. On the contrary, decades of research on the creation and diffusion of technology within and across country borders has shown that technology is often a very local affair, embedded in firms, clusters of firms, regions and countries (Dosi, 1988). Although diffusion may – and does – take place, successful cases normally involve a host of other supporting factors (Fagerberg, 1988). These are facts that any theory that wants to throw light on the convergence–divergence phenomenon has to account for. Another problematic aspect is the assumption of constant returns to scale, effectively ignoring the substantial positive spillovers that investments in, say, education or R&D may have. This deficiency in the 'old' growth models has recently led to the so-called 'new growth theories' (Verspagen, 1992). It is our view that these problems support a call for more theoretical and empirical work on regional growth in Europe, as suggested by Neven and Gouyette (1995, p. 64).

As an alternative to the traditional neoclassical perspective in this area, we have in previous work analysed international growth rate differences from a 'technology-gap' perspective. Basically this is an application of Schumpeterian thinking to the international economy.[3] The main factors taken into account in this approach are the impact of differences in innovative efforts across countries,

---

[2] For instance, Neven and Gouyette (1995, p. 64) conclude that their work 'describes a pattern of regional evolution ... and ... offers little to explain it'.

[3] Although Schumpeter did not extend his analysis of innovation-diffusion to the international economy, this seems to be a quite natural way to proceed from his work. Indeed, the so called "neotechnological" trade theories of the 1960s were heavily inspired by Schumpeter (Posner 1961, Vernon 1966). More recent analyses of international economic developments drawing on Schumpeterian insights can be found in Dosi *et al.* (1990).

the potential for imitation and the capacity to exploit advances in technology, whether developed indigenously or elsewhere in the world (Fagerberg, 1987, 1988; Verspagen, 1991). This perspective, although less formal than many other approaches in this area, has the great advantage that it is consistent with the existing knowledge on innovation and diffusion processes. Many of the assumptions and derived predictions can also be made consistent with 'new growth theories' that focus on innovation as the driving force of capitalist development (Romer, 1990; Grossman and Helpman, 1991). Our earlier empirical work on cross-country samples confirms the importance of national technological capabilities (and other supporting factors) for successful catch-up. Real world catch-up is far from the easy, mechanical process envisaged by the traditional neoclassical approach in this area (see, e.g., Abramovitz, 1994).

What we will do in this article is to apply this framework to regional growth rate differences within Europe. Although 'national systems of innovation' (Lundvall, 1992; Nelson, 1993) may differ, such differences may be even more pronounced on a regional level. Indeed, much of the theoretical and empirical literature on technological systems focuses on regional differences. However, some of the other supporting variables commonly taken into account in cross-country studies may be less relevant at the regional level. For instance, many cross-country studies include the savings rate (or investment share) as an exogenous variable, although much theoretical work in this area points to saving and investment as endogenous. The inclusion of these variables may be defended on the ground that national capital markets differ and – in spite of recent developments – are poorly integrated, at least with respect to long-term investments in industrial projects. This argument does not apply to the regions within a country, and it may (arguably) also be of little relevance within the EU.

The rest of this article is organized as follows. Section II looks at the facts on convergence in levels of per capita GDP in the EU over the post-war period. Based on the finding that intra-European catch-up appears to have come to an end, Section III introduces some variables that may help to explain this pattern. It is shown that the potential for catch-up is not exhausted. What seems to have happened is that other factors, among them some related to EU policies, have pushed towards divergence. Section IV looks in more detail at the hypothesis of a 'Europe at different speeds'. The analysis seems to suggest that there exist at least three different 'growth clubs' characterized by differences in unemployment levels, as well as the impact of the variables taken into account in the analysis. Section V summarizes the arguments and considers the lessons for policy-making.

II. Convergence or Divergence in Productivity Levels across European Regions?

To what extent do the regions of Europe converge towards a growth path characterized by roughly similar levels of income (GDP per capita)? Previous work in this area (Barro and Sala-i-Martin, 1991; Sala-i-Martin, 1994; Neven and Gouyette, 1995) indicates that convergence takes place, but at a rate too slow to be consistent with the traditional neoclassical growth model (Solow, 1956).[4]

To answer this question, we present in Table 1 (A) estimates for different periods between 1950 and 1990.[5] The data comprise 70 regions from six EU member countries.[6] For the period up to 1970, the results indicate that substantial catch-up took place. The estimate suggests that the poorest region of Europe grew 4.3 per cent faster than the richest one. However, the impact of catch-up on growth became gradually weaker through time. For the period 1970–90, the results suggest that the poorest region would grow 2.4 per cent faster than the richest one. For the most recent subperiod, the 1980s, there is not much evidence at all for catch-up.

One way to compare these results with previous work is to calculate how long it would take for the poorest region to catch up with the richest one. For the 1950s and 1960s the results suggest that, starting in 1950, it would take roughly 50 years to eliminate the difference between the poor and the rich. This is consistent with previous work by Barro and others. The results for the 1970s and 1980s, when taken together, are broadly consistent with this pattern: starting in 1970 it would take around 30 years to close the remaining gap. Thus, in both cases the results suggest that the gap would be closed around the year 2000. However, the results for the 1980s do not confirm this pattern.[7] This raises the question of whether the

---

[4] The Solow model predicts that the growth path of any country or region converges to a steady state, which, on the assumptions of labour mobility (or equal growth rates of the population) and public technological knowledge, is the same for every country. Barro and Sala-i-Martin (1992) show that such a convergence process can be represented by the following equation:

$$\hat{y} = a - \frac{1 - e^{\beta T}}{T} \log(y_0)$$

where y is per capita GDP, or productivity, T is the period over which convergence takes place, and a hat (^) represents a proportionate growth rate. This process has been termed 'ß-convergence' (Barro and Sala-i-Martin 1991). Other measures of convergence include σ-convergence (the coefficient of variation), or ergodic distributions deriving from a Markov-chain process. Neven and Gouyette (1995) show that these different measures provide consistent results.

[5] We subsitute the exponent term on the r.h.s. of the equation in note 3 by a single coefficient, enabling the interested reader to calculate the value of ß.

[6] The countries were Belgium, France, Germany, Italy, Netherlands and the United Kingdom. The appendices to this paper list sources, precise definitions and the regional breakdown of the countries.

[7] This finding is consistent with a slowdown in convergence since the mid-1970s observed in country-data (see, e.g., Verspagen, 1995).

Table 1: Europe – Convergence or Divergence in Income Levels

	Constant	$LG_{\text{start year}}$	$R^2 (R^2$–adj.)	n
A. Testing the convergence hypothesis				
1950–70				
(1.1)	0.066 (18.2)	–0.029 (5.84)	0.39 (0.38)	68
1970–90				
(1.2)	0.060 (13.3)	–0.018 (5.94)	0.31 (0.30)	68
1980–90				
(1.3)	0.028 (4.12)	–0.006 (1.51)	0.02 (0.01)	67
B. Including country dummies				
1950–70				
(1.4)	*DUMMIES*	–0.019 (9.64)	0.89 (0.89)	68
1970–90				
(1.5)	*DUMMIES*	–0.006 (1.82)	0.54 (0.51)	68
1980–90				
(1.6)	*DUMMIES*	0.0005 (0.12)	0.37 (0.32)	67

Notes: The dependent variable is the average annual compound growth rate of GDP per capita over the period; LG = log of GDP per capita; *DUMMIES* = France, Germany Italy, Belgium/Netherlands and UK; absolute value of t-statistics (corrected for heteroscedasticity) in brackets behind parameter estimates; n = number of regions included in the test.

post-war trend towards convergence in productivity and income across Europe has now come to an end.[8]

The slow, but steady convergence prior to the 1980s that this and other studies have documented cannot automatically be quoted in support of a Solow-type growth model. Actually, based on reasonable parameters, Solow-type models predict much faster convergence. Similar results have been shown to hold for cross-country samples. To explain this discrepancy, it has been argued (e.g. Sala-i-Martin, 1994) that either the concept of capital has to be substantially broadened (for instance by including educational efforts) or one has to revert to a framework that focuses on technology diffusion. Opting for the first alternative, Barro and Sala-i-Martin (1991, 1992) have chosen to augment the production function with human capital and other factors (so-called 'conditional ß-convergence'). Following the second option, we have in previous work included

[8] Neven and Gouyette (1995) conclude that there are different trends for convergence in the 1980s for north and south Europe. Given that we extend our data backwards to 1950, and will collect additional data for the 1980s used below, we cannot include as many regions as they have in their sample. This implies we have only a few southern regions in our sample, and cannot test for different trends over the 1980s between the North and the south.

variables reflecting efforts to develop and implement technology. However, for the present sample of European regions, data for conditioning variables are generally not available before 1980 (see the next section).

As a rough test of the impact of other, unidentified conditioning variables, we have in Table 1 (B) repeated the same regressions including country-specific constants (so-called fixed effects). In general, when country dummies are included, the estimated contribution from catch-up to faster growth for the poor regions is lower than in the case without country dummies. For instance, for the period 1950–70, our model (without dummies) predicts that the poorest region would grow 4.3 per cent faster than the richest one. With dummies, the contribution from the catch-up factor is estimated to be only 2.8 per cent (still a substantial number). For the period 1970–90 the introduction of dummies reduces the estimated contribution of catch-up from 2.4 to 0.8 per cent. For the most recent subperiod there is no contribution whatsoever from the catch-up factor when dummies are included. These results must be interpreted with care since the country-specific variables taken into account here reflect a number of factors about which we know very little. What is important is that these results confirm (and strengthen) our earlier results on the weakening of the catch-up process through time.

Thus, for what they are worth, the results indicate that the post-war trend towards convergence in levels of productivity and income levels across Europe may have come to an end. This is not a result of a process in which the differences in income and productivity across Europe have been reduced to a negligible level, as one might expect. On the contrary, these differences remain quite substantial: in 1990 the ratio of GDP per capita between the richest and poorest region was approximately 3:1 (compared to approximately 4:1 40 years earlier). This is not a result which is easily explained by Solow-type models.

III. Accounting for the Diverging Trends of the 1980s

How to account for this apparent shift in trend? This is what we try to explore in the following. It is our contention that the potential for catch-up through imitation might still be present in the 1980s, but that the realization of this potential depends on other factors which have to be taken into account to reveal the true impact of diffusion on growth. Furthermore, there might also be diverging factors at work, perhaps most notably differences in innovative activity, which also have to be taken into account.

The basic model that we wish to apply is one in which productivity growth depends on the scope for catch-up, efforts devoted to innovation, the capability to exploit advances in technology commercially (independent of origin) and other, relevant factors. In doing so, we encounter the problem that data are not easily forthcoming, particularly not for technological activities. Soete (1981) distinguishes between 'technology output measures' (e.g. patents) and 'technology input measures' (e.g. R&D). The former are often regarded as better measures of innovative efforts than the latter, which often reflect efforts related to both innovation and diffusion. R&D, for instance, clearly matters for both (Cohen and Levinthal, 1989). In this case we have two available data sources, R&D employees in the business sector (RDE) and the number of EU-sponsored R&D projects (RDP). Both are in a sense 'technology input' indicators, reflecting the supply of skilled labour and financial support to R&D, respectively. Thus, these variables do, to some extent, reflect both innovative efforts and the capability to exploit technological advances commercially.

To these variables we add others that may contribute to the explanation of differing regional performance. Following the theoretical literature in this area, we adopt the assumption that investment is endogenous. But we allow for an exogenous component, the support to investment projects from EU sources (EUI). We also test for the sensitivity of including investment as an exogenous variable. Furthermore, we investigate the possibility that differences in economic structure may have an impact on productivity growth. This hypothesis, well known from the development literature, rests on the assumption that the prospects for productivity growth are much better in 'modern' sectors than in 'traditional' sectors, such as agriculture. In order to examine this issue, we include the share of agriculture in employment (AGR), which is expected to act as a growth retardant, as one of the independent variables. Another set of factors that are commonly assumed to impact on growth are those related to the labour market, such as wage-setting, skill-mismatches, migration, etc. Unfortunately, we do not have data on such variables. What we do know something about is the outcome of these process, i.e. the rate of unemployment (UE), which we shall use here as a rough proxy.

Five different sets of regressions are presented (Table 2). The first includes the scope for catch-up, R&D efforts and directed credit (investment loans), the second uses European transfers instead of investment loans, the third adds differences in economic structure and unemployment. The fourth and fifth test for the sensitivity of including investments and country dummies, respectively. Each set contains two regressions, one using R&D employment, the other using R&D projects, as measure of innovative efforts or the capability to exploit technology. The former is based on fewer observations than the latter, since we lack data on R&D employment for the UK and the Netherlands.[9]

Generally, the inclusion of R&D efforts (RDE or RDP) and directed credit (EUI) leads to a significant increase in the explanatory power of the model (2.1

---

[9] The correlation between our two R&D variables is nearly perfect, thus indicating that the RDP variable measures R&D input in general, rather than the EU-support aspect.

Table 2: Accounting for the Lack of Convergence in the 1980s (1980–90)

	Constant	Independent Variables		R^2 (R^2-adj.)	n
(A) The impact of R&D and directed credit					
(2.1)	0.018 (1.90)	0.009 RDE (3.45)	1.349 EUI (4.38)		
		−0.004 LG_{80} (0.90)		0.21 (0.16)	49
(2.2)	0.037 (3.45)	0.131 RDP (2.84)	0.692 EUI (2.17)		
		−0.011 LG_{80} (2.19)		0.16 (0.12)	64
(B) The impact of R&D and EU Structural Funds					
(2.3)	0.035 (3.34)	0.0005 RDE (2.05)	−0.225 RDF (2.17)		
		−0.009 LG_{80} (1.82)		0.07 (0.01)	49
(2.4)	0.055 (4.63)	0.107 RDP (2.13)	−0.417 RDF (3.70)		
		−0.017 LG_{80} (3.12)		0.16 (0.12)	64
(C) Allowing for differences in economic structure and unemployment					
(2.5)	0.057 (2.70)	0.008 RDE (3.03)	1.396 EUI (4.04)		
		−0.037 AGR (1.72)	−0.061 UE (1.71)		
		−0.017 LG_{80} (2.24)		0.27 (0.19)	49
(2.6)	0.131 (9.54)	0.092 RDP (2.57)	0.795 EUI (3.92)		
		−0.072 AGR (5.47)	−0.194 UE (7.45)		
		−0.041 LG_{80} (8.19)		0.47 (0.42)	63
(D) Adding investment in physical capital					
(2.7)	0.092 (3.19)	0.008 RDE (2.83)	1.797 EUI (3.46)		
		−0.041 INV (1.48)	−0.037 AGR (1.57)		
		−0.129 UE (2.45)	−0.026 LG_{80} (2.67)	0.33 (0.22)	46
(2.8)	0.136 (9.12)	0.107 RDP (3.20)	0.942 EUI (3.51)		
		−0.021 INV (0.89)	−0.067 AGR (4.69)		
		−0.197 UE (6.80)	−0.041 LG_{80} (8.64)	0.49 (0.43)	61
(E) Testing for the impact of country dummies					
(2.9)	DUMMIES	0.001 RDE (3.59)	0.523 EUI (0.80)		
		−0.005 INV (0.16)	−0.038 AGR (1.85)		
		−0.108 UE (2.05)	−0.023 LG_{80} (2.60)	0.42 (0.25)	46
(2.10)	DUMMIES	0.100 RDP (3.08)	0.108 EUI (0.23)		
		0.008 INV (0.27)	−0.041 AGR (1.94)		
		−0.155 UE (3.25)	−0.027 LG_{80} (3.56)	0.56 (0.47)	61

Notes: The dependent variable is the average annual compound growth rate of GDP per capita over the period; RDE = R&D personnel in business enterprise per 1000 labour force; RDP = number of R&D projects undertaken with support from the EU divided by population; EUI = investment loans from the European Investment Bank and the New Community Investment scheme divided by GDP, 1985-87; RDF = transfers under the European Regional Development Funds scheme, divided by GDP, 1985-87; INV = gross fixed capital formation as a share of GDP; UE = unemployment rate; AGR = share of agriculture in GDP; LG = log of GDP per capita; DUMMIES = France, Germany, Italy, Belgium/Netherlands and UK; absolute value of t-statistics (corrected for heteroscedasticity) in brackets behind parameter estimates; n = number of regions included in the test.

and 2.2). Both variables enter the equations with the expected sign, which is also (highly) significant. The same holds when economic structure (AGR) and unemployment (UE) are added (2.5 and 2.6). Using transfers under the so-called European Regional Development Funds scheme instead of the EU investment loans, leads to a quite different result. In this case, EU support turns up with a significantly negative coefficient, indicating that this type of support goes to the slow-growing regions. While it is beyond the scope of this article to analyse the differences in impact between these different forms of EU support in more detail, the explicit investment character of the EUI variable, as well as its form of a loan instead of a transfer, seem to be a plausible explanation for the result reported here.

Adding the share of investment in GDP (INV) leads to a much smaller increase in the fit, and the variable itself enters with a negative sign, not significantly different from zero at the per cent level (2.7 and 2.8). This is not what would be expected had it been exogenous. Thus, there is not much support in the data for including investment as an explanatory variable in addition to the others. The introduction of country dummies (2.9 and 2.10) also leads to a rather modest increase in the explanatory power, when account is taken of the reduction in the degrees of freedom. The most notable impact of the inclusion of country dummies is that it renders the investment loans variable with a less significant and lower impact on growth. This suggests that EU credits are not randomly distributed across countries, e.g. that these policies systematically favour some member countries.

With respect to the impact of R&D, the results are as expected, and the estimated impact is remarkably robust across different specifications.[10] Thus, the results lend clear support to a perspective that emphasizes the importance of R&D efforts for growth. A high share of agriculture in GDP and high unemployment act as growth retardants, as predicted, but the estimates are not always significantly different from zero. However, the relatively large increase in explanatory power associated with the introduction of these variables suggests that these factors do play an important role and should be taken into account.

Finally, given the additional explanatory factors taken into account here, the scope for catch-up regains its role as an important explanatory factor behind regional growth rate differences. This holds also when country dummies are included. Indeed, the impact turns out to be quite substantial.[11]

[10] There is only one exception, when R&D employment (RDE) is used and country dummies are included (2.7). The estimated impact of R&D efforts is still positive and significantly different from zero at the 1 per cent level, but the coefficient is markedly smaller than in the other regressions.
[11] Other factors left apart, the results suggest convergence to a common income level within a few decades. This holds when both R&D efforts and structural factors are taken into account (regressions 2.3–2.8). When structural factors are not taken into account (regressions 2.1–2.2), the estimated contribution from the catch-up factor is much smaller, and the time period necessary for closing the gap much longer.

IV. Europe at Different Speeds?

The results in the previous section are by no means a full account of what drives differences in economic growth in Europe. An obvious shortcoming of the regressions so far is the implicit assumption that all regions obey the same simple linear relation between growth and a number of independent variables. The idea of 'convergence clubs' (Baumol, 1986) or, alternatively, 'Europe at different speeds' contests this simple mechanic notion of growth. Rather than opting for a geographical split of our sample (as in Neven and Gouyette, 1995), we ask whether we can find a set of regional groupings characterized by differences in how the variables taken into account work. Thus we adopt, with some small modifications, the methodology suggested by Durlauf and Johnson (1992). Basically, this consists of ordering the observations in increasing order of a control variable and then find the sample split that minimizes the residual variance. Durlauf and Johnson suggest two methods. In the first, the number of splits is arbitrarily given, and is based solely upon one variable.[12] The second method is based on a branching approach. This starts by splitting the complete sample into two on the basis of the variable that gives the best fit (this is done by applying the first method with only one split for each of a number of control variables, and picking the one which yields the best fit). This procedure is then repeated for each of the resulting subsamples, until the degrees of freedom become too small, or the split into subsamples becomes insignificant.[13]

We limited the analysis to the largest of our two samples (the one with R&D projects, RDP, instead of R&D employment, RDE). Moreover, variables in Table 2 which were generally not significant at a level higher than 5 per cent (AGR, INV) were also left out of the regressions. The variables that were retained were initial GDP per capita, R&D efforts and European investment support. Although the correlation between unemployment and growth was quite high, the direction of causality is not clear; indeed it might be argued that unemployment is an endogenous variable. Rather than opting for a simultaneous model, for which we do not have all the necessary variables, we decided to include unemployment as a control variable for splitting up the sample. In principle, we applied the second Durlauf and Johnson method, but it turns out that for the three samples that we present here, the two methods lead to the same splits.[14]

---

[12] One would for example order the sample in increasing order of initial per capita GDP, assume a split into three subsamples, and then, by minimizing the residual variance, find the two optimal points at which to split the sample.

[13] Durlauf and Johnson apply a rather complicated, but, as they themselves admit, still ad hoc, method of deciding where to stop sub-branching the sample. We have used less formal judgement to decide when to stop sub-branching.

[14] We also experimented with LG_{80} and RDP as control variables, but neither of those variables could produce a split with a lower residual sum of squares, relative to the split based upon unemployment levels.

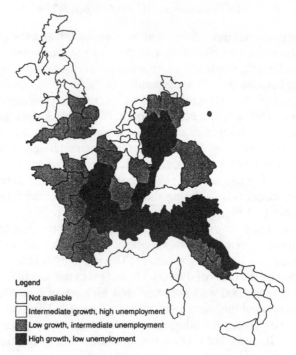

Figure 1: Growth Clubs in Europe

Table 3: Europe at Different Speeds – Searching for a Pattern

	Constant	RDP	EUI	LG_{80}	R^2 (R^2–adj.)
High unemployment ($n = 23$)					
(3.1)	0.059 (2.94)	0.065 (0.81)	0.211 (0.52)	–0.020 (2.06)	0.33 (0.22)
Intermediate unemployment ($n = 19$)					
(3.2)	0.013 (2.66)	0.355 (4.27)	–2.771 (2.18)	–0.050 (2.42)	0.62 (0.54)
Low unemployment ($n = 21$)					
(3.3)	0.009 (0.39)	0.053 (1.75)	0.740 (2.66)	0.003 (0.29)	0.16 (0.10)

Notes: The dependent variable is the average annual compound growth rate of GDP per capita over the period; *RDP* = number of R&D projects undertaken with support from the EU divided by population; *EUI* = investment loans from the European Investment Bank and the New Community Investment scheme divided by GDP, 1985–87; *LG* = log of GDP per capita; absolute value of *t*-statistics (corrected for heteroscedasticity) in brackets behind parameter estimates; *n* = number of regions included in the test.

Table 4: Means of the Three 'Growth Clubs' for the Variables in the Equations

Variable	High UE	Intermediate UE	Low UE
RDP	0.020	0.024	0.022
EUI	0.0031	0.0015	0.0025
LG_{80}	2.12	2.32	2.42
g	0.017	0.015	0.019

Notes: g = average annual compound growth rate of GDP per capita over the period; *RDP* = number of R&D projects undertaken with support from the EU divided by population; *EUI* = investment loans from the European Investment Bank and the New Community Investment scheme divided by GDP, 1985-87; *LG* = log of GDP per capita.

The results suggest three different 'growth clubs' in Europe (Table 3). Table 4 summarizes the means of the variables included in the model for these three regional groupings, and Figure 1 gives an idea of the geographical spread of the groups. First, there is a high unemployment group, which is characterized by low initial productivity, average growth of productivity, little R&D (RDP) but quite substantial EU investment loans. In this group, we find most of the northern regions in the UK, many of the southern regions in Italy, all of the BENELUX regions in our sample, as well as individual regions in other countries.[15] On the whole, this seems to be the group where many 'peripheral' regions are found. For this group, neither R&D efforts nor investment support from the EU seem to matter much. Indeed, the only factor which appears to have some impact on the differences in productivity within this group is the scope for catch-up.

The second group is one of average unemployment. This group is characterized by average initial productivity, low productivity growth, little investment support (EUI), but a high level of R&D (RDP). Many of the large urban regions of the EU (such as west Berlin, Bayern, London, Rome, but not Paris) belong to this group. There is also quite a substantial number of French regions here, of an industrial or rural character (such as Picardie or Bretagne). For these regions, the scope for imitation and R&D efforts explain a lot. Surprisingly, investment support from the EU enters with a negative sign. Thus, in this group, the investment support from the EU seems to go to the slow growers. The catch-up term is also significant, and the estimated value (impact) is much higher than in the other two groups.

For the third group (low unemployment) this pattern is reversed. Here, the scope for imitation does not matter (in fact, it has a non-significant positive coefficient), but investment support from the EU appears very important and, to some extent, also R&D efforts. The regions in this group are the real 'winners' in our sample. Not only do they have lower unemployment, they also have higher

[15] For the exact listing of regions according to group, see appendix.

GDP per capita and faster growth than the others. Here we find 'well-known growth poles', such as the North of Italy and Paris, as well as other French regions.

Thus, if these results are to be believed, EU support to R&D and investment only impacts positively on growth in regions for which the rate of unemployment is below a certain threshold level. In regions with high unemployment, i.e. where the problems are most manifest, these policies seem largely ineffective.

V. Concluding Remarks

For most of the post-war period, income and productivity levels across the regions of the European Union have been converging. The evidence considered in this article suggests that this slow, but steady convergence in productivity levels may gradually have come to an end during the 1980s. It was argued that a perspective that takes innovation diffusion and other, diverging factors into account, may explain this shift of trend. The results suggest that the potential for catch-up by poorer regions through diffusion is still there, but that its impact is masked by diverging factors, most notably differences in R&D efforts, EU investment support (but not the so-called European Regional Development Funds), industrial structure and unemployment.

It is perhaps a troubling fact that some of these 'diverging' variables are policy instruments at the Community level. However, the finding that these policies have little impact on the poorest regions in Europe is also confirmed by our analysis of different 'growth clubs' in Europe. The results indicate that there exist at least three different of such 'growth clubs', each with its own dynamics. For the group of regions where the problems are most manifest (high unemployment, low GDP per capita), both R&D support and direct credit seem rather inefficient. This clearly points to the need for a better understanding of how these policies work in different environments. Another area in need of more research is the relation between growth and unemployment across European regions. The finding that growth and unemployment are strongly inversely related certainly begs new questions about the nature and cause of this relationship.

Taken as a whole, we think that these results are important for the ongoing European policy debate about cohesion. In case our results can withstand further scrutiny (e.g. when including data for other countries, which may become available in the future), there are certainly important policy lessons to be learned about the working of investment support, knowledge generation and diffusion, and the economic role of unemployment.

Appendix A: Regions Used in the Regression, and the Composition of the 'Growth Clubs'

NUTS Code	Country	'Growth Club'*	Name
R11	Germany	na	Schleswig-Holstein
R12	Germany	na	Hamburg
R13	Germany	2	Niedersachsen
R14	Germany	2	Bremen
R15	Germany	3	Nordrhein-Westfalen
R16	Germany	3	Hessen
R17	Germany	3	Rheinland-Pfalz
R1A	Germany	1	Saarland
R18	Germany	1	Baden-Württemberg
R19	Germany	2	Bayern
R1B	Germany	2	Berlin (West)
R71	UK	1	North
R72	UK	1	Yorkshire-Humberside
R73	UK	2	East Midlands
R74	UK	2	East Anglia
R75	UK	2	South East
R76	UK	2	South West
R77	UK	1	West Midlands
R78	UK	1	North West
R79	UK	1	Wales
R7A	UK	1	Scotland
R7B	UK	1	Northern Ireland
R311	Italy	3	Piemonte
R312	Italy	3	Valle d'Aosta
R313	Italy	3	Liguria
R32	Italy	3	Lombardia
R331	Italy	3	Trentino-Alto Adige
R332	Italy	3	Veneto
R333	Italy	3	Friuli-Venez. Giulia
R34	Italy	3	Emilia-Romagna
R353	Italy	3	Marche
R351	Italy	2	Toscana
R352	Italy	2	Umbria
R36	Italy	2	Lazio
R37	Italy	1	Campania
R381	Italy	3	Abruzzi
R382	Italy	1	Molise
R391	Italy	1	Puglia
R392	Italy	1	Basilicata
R393	Italy	1	Calabria
R3A	Italy	1	Sicilia
R3B	Italy	1	Sardegna

R21	France	3	Région Parisienne
R221	France	1	Champagne
R222	France	2	Picardie
R223	France	1	Haute Normandie
R224	France	3	Centre
R225	France	2	Basse Normandie
R226	France	2	Bourgogne
R23	France	2	Nord
R241	France	2	Lorraine
R242	France	3	Alsace
R243	France	3	Franche-Comte
R251	France	2	Pays de la Loire
R252	France	2	Bretagne
R253	France	2	Poitou-Charentes
R261	France	2	Aquitaine
R262	France	2	Midi-Pyrenees
R263	France	3	Limousin
R271	France	3	Rhône-Alpes
R272	France	3	Auvergne
R281	France	1	Langedoc-Roussillon
R282	France	na	Provence-Côte d'Azur
R283	France	na	Corse
R41	Netherlands	1	Noord
R42	Netherlands	1	Oost
R47	Netherlands	1	West
R45	Netherlands	1	Zuid
R51	Belgium	1	Vlaanderen
R52	Belgium	1	Wallonie
R53	Belgium	na	Brussel

* Growth clubs: (1) high unemployment, (2) intermediate unemployment, (3) low unemployment.

Appendix B: Definitions and Sources of the Variables Used

LG: GDP per capita in 1985 PPP to the ECU. Constructed using nationwide GDP deflator. Source for underlying data: Molle (before 1980), EUROSTAT (1980 and beyond), OECD (GDP deflators before 1980).

g: Average annual compound growth rate of *LG*, over the period specified in the text or tables.

EUI: Investment loans over the period 1985–87 (under the European Investment Bank and the New Community Instrument scheme) divided by GDP for the same period. Source for the underlying data: EUROSTAT.

RDF: Transfers under the European Regional Development Funds scheme, divided by GDP, 1985-87. Source for the underlying data: EUROSTAT.

RDP: Number of R&D projects undertaken with support by one of the programmes of the European Commission (mainly so-called Framework Programmes) over the period 1980–90, divided through by population in 1990. Projects are assigned to regions by means of their primary contractor. Source: CORDIS Database, European Commission.

UE: Unemployment rate (1983), defined as 1 − persons employed/labour force. Source for underlying data: EUROSTAT. (These data differ from the official EUROSTAT regional unemployment data, based upon survey data, which contain less valid observations.)

RDE: R&D personnel in business enterprise per 1000 labour force. Source for underlying data: EUROSTAT.

INV: Gross fixed capital formation as a fraction of GDP. Source for underlying data: EUROSTAT. Note: values for United Kingdom scaled down by using OECD data on nationwide investment/GDP ratio (scale factor: 0.31), values for Italy scaled up by factor 1000 to correct for apparent mistake in EUROSTAT units.

AGR: Share of agriculture in employment. Source for underlying data: Molle (before 1980), EUROSTAT (from 1980 onwards).

References

Abramovitz, M.A. (1994) 'The Origins of the Postwar Catch Up and Convergence Boom'. In Fagerberg, J., Verspagen, B. and Von Tunzelmann, N. (eds), *The Dynamics of Technology, Trade and Growth* (Aldershot: Edward Elgar).

Barro, R. J. and Sala-i-Martin, X. (1991) 'Convergence across States and Regions'. *Brookings Papers on Economic Activity*, No. 1, pp. 107–82.

Barro, R. J. and Sala-i-Martin, X. (1992) 'Convergence'. *Journal of Political Economy*, Vol. 100, pp. 223–51.

Baumol, W. J. (1986) 'Productivity Growth, Convergence, and Welfare: What the Long-run Data Show'. *American Economic Review*, Vol. 76, No. 5, December, pp. 1072–85.

Cohen, W. M. and Levinthal, D. A. (1989) 'Innovation and Learning: The Two Faces of R&D'. *Economic Journal*, Vol. 99, September, pp. 569–96.

Dosi, G. (1988) 'Sources, Procedures and Microeconomic Effects of Innovation'. *Journal of Economic Literature*, Vol. 26, pp. 1120–71.

Dosi, G., Pavitt, K. and Soete, L. G. (1990) *The Economics of Technical Change and International Trade* (London: Harvester Wheatsheaf).

Durlauf, S. N. and Johnson, P. A. (1992) 'Local versus Global Convergence: Across National Economies'. *NBER Working Paper* No. 3996 (Cambridge, Ma: National Bureau of Economic Research).

Fagerberg, J. (1987) 'A Technology Gap Approach to Why Growth Rates Differ'. *Research Policy,* Vol. 16, No. 2–4, August, pp. 87–99.

Fagerberg, J. (1988) 'Why Growth Rates Differ'. In Dosi, G. *et al.* (eds), *Technical Change and Economic Theory* (London: Pinter), pp. 432–57.

Fagerberg, J. (1991) 'International Competitiveness'. *Economic Journal,* Vol. 98, pp. 355–74.

Fagerberg, J. (1994) 'Technology and International Differences in Growth Rates'. *Journal of Economic Literature,* September, Vol. 32, pp. 1147–75.

Grossman, G. M. and Helpman, E. (1991) *Innovation and Growth in the Global Economy* (Cambridge, Ma: MIT Press).

Levine, R. and Renelt, D. (1992) 'A Sensitivity Analysis of Cross-Country Growth Regressions'. *American Economic Review,* Vol. 82, No. 4, September, pp. 942–63.

Lundvall, B. Å. (ed.) (1992) *National Systems of Innovation – Towards a Theory of Innovation and Interactive Learning* (London: Pinter).

Molle, W. (1980) *Regional Disparity and Economic Development in the European Community* (Westmead: Saxon House).

Nelson, R. R. (ed.) (1993) *National Systems of Innovation: A Comparative Study* (Oxford: Oxford University Press).

Neven, D. and Gouyette, C. (1995) 'Regional Convergence in the European Community'. *Journal of Common Market Studies,* Vol. 33, pp. 47–65.

Posner, M. V. (1961) 'International Trade and Technical Change'. *Oxford Economic Papers.*

Romer, P. M. (1990) 'Endogenous Technological Change'. *Journal of Political Economy,* Vol. 98, No. 5, October, pp. S71–S102.

Sala-i-Martin, X. (1994) 'Regional Cohesion: Evidence and Theories of Regional Growth and Convergence'. *CEPR Discussion Paper* No. 1075 (London: Centre for Economic Policy Research).

Soete, L. (1981) 'A General Test of Technological Gap Trade Theory'. *Weltwirtschaftliches Archiv,* Vol. 117, pp. 638–60.

Solow, R. M. (1956) 'A Contribution to the Theory of Economic Growth'. *Quarterly Journal of Economics,* February, Vol. 70, No. 1, pp. 65–94.

Vernon, R. (1966) 'International Investment and International Trade in the Product Cycle'. *Quarterly Journal of Economics,* Vol. 80, pp. 190–207.

Verspagen, B. (1991) 'A New Empirical Approach to Catching Up or Falling Behind'. *Structural Change and Economic Dynamics,* Vol. 2, No. 2, December, pp. 359–80.

Verspagen, B. (1992) 'Endogenous Innovation in Neo-Classical Growth Models: A Survey'. *Journal of Macroeconomics,* Vol. 14, No. 4, Fall, pp. 631–62.

Verspagen, B. (1995) 'Convergence in the Global Economy. A Broad Historical Viewpoint'. *Structural Change and Economic Dynamics,* March.

5

Regional Studies, Vol. 31.5, pp. 457–466

Technology, Growth and Unemployment across European Regions

JAN FAGERBERG*, BART VERSPAGEN† and MARJOLEIN CANIËLS†

**Education in Society, Science and Technology, Faculty of Social Sciences, University of Oslo, Sognsveien 70, Postbox 1108 Blindern, N-0317 Oslo, Norway*

†*Maastricht Economic Research Institute on Innovation and Technology (MERIT), University of Maastricht, PO Box 616, 6200 MD Maastricht, The Netherlands*

(Received September 1996; in revised form November 1996)

FAGERBERG J., VERSPAGEN B. and CANIËLS M. (1997) Technology, growth and unemployment across European regions, *Reg. Studies* **31**, 457–466. The process of convergence in GDP per capita levels across European regions came to a halt in the 1980s, although the differences in GDP per capita remain substantial. Moreover, these differences are related to similarly persistent differences in unemployment rates. This paper argues that a perspective which, in addition to other factors, takes into account differences across regions in innovation and diffusion of technology may explain these findings. A simultaneous equation model with GDP per capita growth, employment growth and migration as endogenous variables is proposed and estimated using data for 64 European regions in the 1980s. The results show that innovation and the diffusion of technology are indeed important factors behind European growth in the 1980s. However, due to a lack of own R&D capabilities, most poor regions fail to take advantage of the more advanced technologies available elsewhere. The growth of the poor regions is also hampered by an unfavourable industrial structure (the predominance of agriculture). As a consequence, growth of GDP per capita in the poorer regions is not substantially faster than in the richer ones (where growth is fuelled by much larger R&D efforts and a more advanced industrial structure). Although employment in poor regions actually grows somewhat faster than in the rich ones, so does labour supply, preventing a (relative) reduction in their rates of unemployment.

Convergence   Unemployment   R&D   Innovation   Economic growth   European regions

FAGERBERG J., VERSPAGEN B. et CANIËLS M. (1997) La technologie, la croissance et le chômage à travers les régions européennes, *Reg. Studies* **31**, 457–466. La convergence du PIB par tête à travers les régions européennes fut interrompue aux années 1980, bien que les écarts du PIB par tête restent non-négligeables. Qui plus est, ces écarts se rapportent aux écarts des taux de chômage qui persistent également. Cet article laissent supposer que ces résultats pourraient s'expliquer à partir d'une approche qui met en considération à travers les régions les écarts d'innovation et de diffusion de la technologie, parmi d'autres facteurs. Un modèle d'équations simultanées comportant des variables endogènes, à savoir l'augmentation du PIB par tête, la montée de l'emploi et la migration, se voit proposer et estimer à partir des données sur soixante-quatre régions européennes aux années 1980. Les résultats laissent voir que l'innovation et la diffusion de la technologie sont d'importants facteurs à l'origine de la croissance européenne aux années 1980. Toujours est-il qu'à défaut de la R et D, la plupart des régions défavorisées ne profitent pas des technologies plus avancées qui sont disponibles ailleurs. Une structure industrielle défavorable empêche aussi les régions défavorisées (vu l'importance du secteur agricole). Par conséquent, le PIB par tête dans les régions défavorisées n'augmente pas sensiblement plus rapidement par rapport à celui des régions plus riches (où la croissance est alimentée par des efforts de R et D beaucoup plus importants et par une structure industrielle plus avancée). Non seulement

FAGERBERG J., VERSPAGEN B. und CANIËLS M. (1997) Technologie, Wachstum und Erwerbslosigkeit in europäischen Regionen, *Reg. Studies* **31**, 457–466. Der Vorgang einer Konvergenz der im eigenen Land pro-Kopf erzielten Bruttosozialprodukthöhen in europäischen Regionen kam in den achtziger Jahren zum Erliegen, obschon weiterhin beträchtliche Unterschiede in den im eigenen Land pro-Kopf erzielten Bruttosoziaprodukten bestehen. Diese Unterschiede stehen außerdem in Bezug zu ebenso beharrlichen Unterschieden in der Erwerbslosenrate. Der vorliegende Aufsatz vertritt die Auffassung, daß diese Befunde sich durch eine Perspekive erklären ließen, die außer anderen Faktoren auch Unterschiede in Innovation und Verbreitung von Technologie in den Regionen in Betracht zieht. Es wird ein Gleichungssystem des Zuwachses des im eigenen Lande erzielten Bruttosozialprodukts, der Zunahme der Erwerbstätigkeit und der Wanderung als endogene Veränderliche vorgeschlagen und berechnet, dem Daten der achtziger Jahre für 64 europäische Regionen zugrunde gelegt wurden. Die Ergebnisse zeigen, daß Innovation und die Verbreitung von Technologie tatsächlich wichtige Faktoren sind, die hinter dem Wachstum der achtziger Jahre standen. Mangels eigener Fähigkeiten in Forschung und Entwicklung gelingt es jedoch den meisten armen Regionen nicht, Vorteile aus höher entwickelten, an anderen Orten zur Verfügung stehenden Technologien zu ziehen. Das Wachstum der armen Regionen wird zudem durch eine ungünstige Industriestruktur (Überwiegen der Landwirtschaft) gehemmt.

0034-3404/97/050457-10 ©1997 Regional Studies Association

l'emploi augmente quelque peu plus rapidement dans les régions défavorisées que dans les régions riches, mais l'offre d'emploi aussi, ce qui empêche une baisse (relative) de leurs taux de chômage.

Convergence   Chômage   R et D   Innovation
Croissance économique   Régions européennes

Folglich nimmt das im eigenen Lande per Kopf erzielte Bruttosozialprodukt in den ärmeren Regionen nicht wesentlich schneller zu als in den wohlhabenderen (wo das Wachstum von weitaus größeren Anstrengungen in Forschung und Entwicklung, sowie einer höher entwickelten Industriestruktur angeheizt wird). Obwohl Erwerbstätigkeit in armem Gebieten tatsächlich etwas schneller als in reichen zunimmt, trifft das Gleiche auf das Angebot an Arbeitskräften zu, was eine (obschon relative) Senkung der Erwerbslosenrate verhindert.

Konvergenz   Erwerbslosigkeit
Forschung und Entwicklung   Wirtschaftswachstum
Europäische Regionen

INTRODUCTION

During most of the post-war period, differences in GDP per capita between European regions have been on the decrease. Seemingly, the regions of Europe were on a steady, albeit slow, path towards convergence in GDP per capita. Not any more. Research shows that for the most recent decade (the 1980s) differences in GDP per capita levels were essentially unchanged (NEVEN and GOUYETTE, 1995; FAGERBERG and VERSPAGEN, 1996).[1] This change in trend is not the result of a process through which the differences in GDP per capita across European regions have been reduced to a negligible level. On the contrary, these differences remain rather substantial. In the data set we analyse below, GDP per capita in the poorest region in 1990 was only about one-quarter of that in the richest region. Moreover, as we show in the next section, these differences seem to be related to equally persistent differences in levels of unemployment: regions with a low level of GDP per capita tend to have much higher unemployment and vice-versa.[2] How are these findings to be explained? This is the question we address in the third section of this paper. There are, of course, many possible approaches that could be applied to increase our understanding of this issue. As far as the issue of growth is concerned, the neoclassical model of economic growth (SOLOW, 1956) has been the standard frame of analysis. However, it has been shown that predictions derived from this framework are not consistent with the observed growth pattern of European regions in the post-war period (SALA-I-MARTIN, 1996). Moreover, as argued in more depth elsewhere (FAGERBERG, 1994), the Solow model is based on assumptions that cannot be easily defended. An example is the assumption that technology is a public good. In contrast, we have in previous work (FAGERBERG, 1987; 1988; VERSPAGEN, 1991; CANIËLS, 1996) analysed growth differences from a perspective that acknowledges the joint private–public character of technology. Following this perspective, innovations diffuse through time and space, but diffusion depends on capabilities, efforts and structural factors. In other

words diffusion is not an instantaneous and costless process (as suggested by Solow-type models).

In an earlier paper (FAGERBERG and VERSPAGEN, 1996) it was shown that a perspective that takes differences across European regions in innovation and diffusion of technology (and supporting factors) into account has a good deal to offer when analysing growth. What we try to do in this paper is to broaden this perspective by also taking into account differences in employment growth and migration flows. This can only be done in a coherent way if it is acknowledged that variables such as GDP per capita growth, employment growth and migration flows are in fact interdependent. We therefore adopt a framework of analysis that takes this into account. The results confirm that these interdependencies are indeed strong, i.e. that the factors that impact on GDP per capita growth also are important for employment growth, and the other way around.

EUROPEAN REGIONS IN THE 1980s

The sample consists of 64 European regions from four different countries: (West) Germany, France, Italy and Spain. The source is the Eurostat REGIO database.[3] For some variables we have data for other countries as well (Belgium, the Netherlands, Portugal and the UK), but because these countries have missing values for some of the key variables considered here, such as R&D, employment or migration, we exclude them from the analysis. Thus, compared to our previous work (FAGERBERG and VERSPAGEN, 1996), this sample has a more 'southern twist'. The variables employed in this study may be divided into two groups. First, the variables that we wish explain, i.e. those we have chosen to regard as endogenous. There are three of them, and they are all expressed as growth rates or flows: growth of GDP per capita; employment growth; and migration flows. These variables are clearly interdependent: higher growth is likely to lead to more jobs, and job availability is generally recognized as an important impetus to migration. The latter, in turn, should be expected to feed back on GDP per capita.

If inward migrants are relatively productive people, a positive effect may be envisaged. But if they tend to be rather unproductive, their addition to the population may actually lead to a fall in GDP per capita.

The second group consists of variables characterizing the environment in which change is taking place. These variables, normally expressed as levels or shares, are assumed to have an impact on the changes that take place, but not the other way around (i.e. they are exogenous).[4] Typically, these variables change very slowly, so for a period of a decade or so, they can be taken as given. Examples include the industrial breakdown of GDP, the composition of the labour force, population density. In the longer term, of course, many such variables undergo important changes, which would then have to be taken into account. Ideally, one would have wished to test for the assumed stability of such structural factors. But due to lack of annual data this was not possible. However, in the case of the rate of unemployment, which might be considered as one of the more problematic cases, we have at least two observations – one towards the beginning and one towards the end of our period. In Fig. 1 these observations are plotted against each other. The figure confirms that the distribution is essentially stable.

The definitions of the variables are as follows: GQ stands for the average annual compound growth rate of GDP per capita (in 1990 PPPs – Purchasing Power Parities – to the Ecu) over the period 1980–1990; Q is the level of GDP per capita in 1980;[5] GE is the average annual compound growth rate of employment (in persons) over 1983-89, and GN the average annual compound growth rate of the labour force (in persons);

Wage is the sum of wages divided by employment, 1989 (in 1990 PPPs to the Ecu); RDE is R&D employment in business enterprises in 1985 as a percentage of the labour force; PA is population density in 1985 (in thousands of persons per km^2); UE is the unemployment rate in 1983;[6] MIR is the mean net inward migration per thousand persons in the labour force over 1983–89; and AGR, IND and SER are the shares of agriculture, industry and services in total 1983 employment, respectively.

One of the novelties of this data set compared to the one we used in previous work is the inclusion of data for employment and net migration. Note, however, that the migration data used in this paper only counts migration within countries, not across. This implies an underestimation of total migration, but perhaps not a very serious one, since cross-border migration flows in Europe are known to be small. However, the data also include persons that are not in the labour force. Hence, the data may in fact overestimate the actual flows of economically active migrants. Still, migration flows appear small (see Table 1). In fact, in most regions, migration adds/subtracts far less than 0·5% per year to/ from the labour force. It has to be stressed, though, that the relatively low migration rates do not necessarily imply a small impact of migration on, for example, economic growth. It may be the case, as suggested by BLANCHARD and KATZ, 1992, that the qualitative effects of migration (for example, in terms of the quality of the labour force, or spillover effects) may still be quite substantial.

Table 1 gives summary statistics for the variables employed in the study. In addition to the sample means, the table includes means for four groups of regions ranked from high to low depending on the level of GDP per capita. As is evident from the table, there are important differences between these groupings. At the high end we find many heavily urbanized regions, characterized by low unemployment, high levels of R&D and relatively high wages. At the opposite extreme – those with low GDP per capita – we find a number of agricultural regions with low population density, high unemployment and relatively low wages. Hence, as shown in Fig. 2, the 'poor' regions – those with low GDP per capita – also face the most serious unemployment problems, and vice versa. Another 'stylized fact' that comes out very clearly in the data is the positive relationship between GDP per capita and R&D (Fig. 3). Indeed, R&D efforts in the poor regions are very close to zero while, in some advanced regions, up to 2·5% of the business labour force is made up of R&D personnel.

The evidence considered so far indicates a strong polarization between regions with high and low levels of GDP per capita (or rich and poor regions). There are, however, some tendencies that qualify this pattern, and these are worth briefly mentioning. First, it should be noted that GDP per capita actually grows faster in

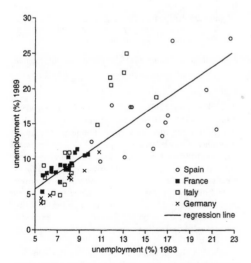

Fig. 1. The persistence of unemployment levels across European regions

Table 1. *Summary statistics for 64 European regions*

| Variable | Regional group (quartiles) means | | | | Total sample | |
	1st (high) quartile	2nd quartile	3rd quartile	4th (low) quartile	Mean	Standard deviation
GQ	0·0186	0·0182	0·020	0·022	0·0196	0·0066
GE	0·0079	0·0051	0·008	0·012	0·0082	0·0097
GN	0·0072	0·0056	0·010	0·016	0·0098	0·0093
Q	15·510	12·685	10·871	7·953	11·755	3·089
Wage[1]	23·993	23·066	20·871	19·669	21·713	2·441
RDE	1·013	0·548	0·338	0·081	0·495	0·588
PA	0·571	0·162	0·116	0·150	0·250	0·408
UE	0·070	0·075	0·107	0·144	0·099	0·042
MIR	−0·00053	0·00084	0·00096	−0·00187	−0·00015	0·0039
AGR	0·057	0·094	0·129	0·227	0·127	0·086
IND	0·361	0·361	0·334	0·267	0·331	0·073
SER	0·582	0·545	0·537	0·505	0·542	0·076

Note: 1. Results for the *Wage* variable exclude observations for France, as French wage data was unavailable.

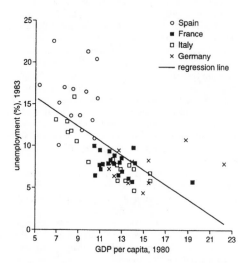

Fig. 2. *Unemployment and GDP per capita across European regions*

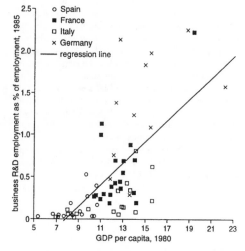

Fig. 3. *Innovation and GDP per capita across European regions*

the poor regions than in the others, although the difference is not large. Employment grows faster too, but so does the labour supply, so on balance unemployment in the poor regions is on the increase. Second, migration flows are not mainly from poor regions to rich ones, as one might expect. Rather it is the regions in the middle – those with close to average GDP per capita – that attract most migration.

EXPLORING THE RELATIONSHIP BETWEEN TECHNOLOGY, GROWTH AND EMPLOYMENT

Regions may benefit from technology in two different ways. First, regions may benefit from innovation,

proxied by R&D efforts, which is assumed to lead to higher growth in the region of origin. Hence, technology is not regarded as a pure 'public good', as in the traditional neoclassical perspective. Second, regions may benefit from diffusion; backward regions have a lot to learn by imitating the more advanced technologies already in use elsewhere. As in most of the literature on technology gaps, we use the distance in GDP per capita between the region in question and that of the frontier region as a proxy for the potential for imitation (i.e. we include the log of initial GDP per capita in the equation for growth).

Whether this potential is exploited or not depends on a number of factors. Although R&D is taken here as a measure of innovative efforts, it is also important for imitation, since a certain level of R&D is a pre-condition for successful imitation in many cases (COHEN and LEVINTHAL, 1989). Another factor that has been identified in the literature is investment in physical capital. However, recent theoretical work (ROMER, 1990; GROSSMAN and HELPMAN, 1991) has disputed the explanatory value of investment on the grounds that it is an effect, and not a cause, of economic growth. In a previous paper (FAGERBERG and VERSPAGEN, 1996) we showed that differences across European regions in investment activity did not contribute to the explanation of differences in growth of GDP per capita. The same was shown to be the case for regional support from the European Union.[7] We do not repeat these exercises here, partly because this would not add much to existing knowledge in this area, and partly because doing so would have implied a considerable reduction in the size of the sample (since these additional variables are not available for all regions).

We extend our previous analysis in two ways. First, we take into account the suggestion from the literature on regional economics that migration may be a source of convergence in GDP per capita in its own right (BARRO and SALA-I-MARTIN, 1991). Assume, for the purpose of illustration, that migrants are not economically active. Then, if people leave regions with low levels of GDP per capita and join those with high levels, GDP per capita will increase in the former and decrease in the latter, i.e. convergence in GDP per capita will occur. However, if migrants are very productive people, perhaps because they are better educated and/or more innovative than others, this might be different. Evidence from the USA and Japan seems to indicate that the latter may be closer to the truth than the former (BARRO and SALA-I-MARTIN, 1991, 1992).

Second, following some of the recent literature on economic geography (KRUGMAN, 1991, among others), we allow for the possibility that scale economies may result in higher growth in areas with high population density (so-called agglomeration). Some preliminary work on US data seems to support this suggestion (CICCONE and HALL, 1996). As in our previous work, we also include a structural variable, the share of agriculture in GDP, which is assumed to act as a constraint on productivity growth (because of the limited scope for technological progress and growth in agriculture). We also considered other structural variables: the shares of industry and services in GDP (*IND*, *SER*); and the *STRUC* variable suggested by BARRO and SALA-I-MARTIN (1991, 1992).[8] Basically, the latter is a synthetic measure of the economic structure of the region, with the relative size of each sector weighted by the average growth of that sector for the EU as a whole. If we apply a small open economy perspective to European regions, then this variable may be interpreted as reflecting the growth of external

demand for a region's products. However, since – as might be expected – these structural variables turned out to be closely correlated, we chose to include only one of them (*AGR*). The equation for growth, then, is the following:

$$GQ_i = c_1 + \alpha_1 \log(Q_i) + \alpha_2 RDE_i + \alpha_3 PA_i + \alpha_4 AGR_i + \beta_1 MIR_i \quad (1)$$

Although migration may play a role in the growth process, there is also ample evidence of a feedback from growth on migration. For instance, potential migrants take job availability into account when they make their decisions, and job growth depends on economic growth. Other variables that have been identified in the literature as important for migration flows include unemployment, wage-levels and population density (BARRO and SALA-I-MARTIN, 1991, 1992; BLANCHARD and KATZ, 1992; NEVEN and GOUYETTE, 1995). In short, people are assumed to migrate from areas with high unemployment, low wages and high population density (congestion problems) to areas where job opportunities and pay are better and living conditions more pleasant. The evidence concerning the impact of these factors is somewhat contradictory, though. BLANCHARD and KATZ, 1992, in a very thorough study based on US data, point to differences in unemployment, rather than wages, as the main impetus to migration. NEVEN and GOUYETTE, 1995, reach the opposite conclusion in the case of Europe, but their sample was limited to two countries only (UK and Italy). BARRO and SALA-I-MARTIN (1991, 1992) do not include unemployment as a possible source of migration. They conclude that 'the main results for Japan and the United States are similar: people move away from highly populated areas and into high-income areas' (1992, p. 339).

This leads us to use the following equation for migration:

$$MIR_i = c_2 + \gamma_1 PA_i + \gamma_2 RW_i + \gamma_3 UE_i + \beta_2 GE_i \quad (2)$$

RW – relative wages – is the (log of) the wage level in the region divided by the average wage level in the country to which the region belongs.[9] Since cross-country migration flows are not included in our migration figures, it was deemed natural to adjust the wage variable by taking out the part of the total variance that refers to cross-country differences in wage levels.

However, we are interested not only in the relationship between growth of GDP per capita and migration behaviour, but also in the outcome for employment. We therefore include a separate equation for employment growth. While it seems reasonable to model migration behaviour from the standpoint of the individual job-seeker, employment growth is, to a much larger extent, the result of decisions by firms. From this perspective, low wages should, *ceteris paribus*, be considered advantageous for job creation. Unemployment, on the other hand, may have a dual impact. On the one hand it signals availability of labour; on the other it suggests a state of economic depression that may not be so good for business after all (BLANCHARD and KATZ, 1992). A high population density may be good for employment growth, since it attracts firms and industries for whom proximity is an important competitive factor, and allows for a deeper specialization of labour. Higher overall growth (GDP per capita) should, *ceteris paribus*, be expected to be good for employment. Finally, we take into account the fact that European agriculture was under severe pressure during the 1980s, and that this may have affected employment growth in agricultural regions negatively. The equation we use is:

$$GE_i = c_3 + \delta_1 UE_i + \delta_2 RW_i + \delta_3 AGR_i + \delta_4 PA_i + \beta_3 GQ_i$$
$$(3)$$

As is customary in work on pooled samples, we estimate the above regressions including country-dummies.[10] This implies that we do not try to explain why, say, all Spanish regions grow faster than all German ones, but focus on growth differences between regions within countries. Thus, to the extent that there are important differences between these countries at the country level (such as growth of overall demand, for instance), these will be accounted for by the dummies. To avoid simultaneous equation bias, we estimate equations (1)–(2) using a 2SLS (instrumental variables) procedure, using all the exogenous variables included in the three equations, plus *IND* and *STRUC* as instruments.[11] The results of the estimations of these equations are reported in Table 2. Basically, the results confirm many of our priors. Both the scope for imitation and R&D turn up as important for growth. Migration is found to have a strong, positive impact on GDP per capita growth, consistent with previous findings. A high share of agriculture in GDP acts as a constraint on growth, as expected. However, there is not much support in these data for the agglomeration hypothesis. In fact, population density has a negative sign (although it is not significant).

The estimates for the migration equation confirm the hypothesis that people migrate from regions with high unemployment to areas where job opportunities are better (employment growth). The other two variables, relative wages and population density, both have the expected signs, but neither of them is significant. Hence, as in the study by BLANCHARD and KATZ, 1992, on US data, unemployment appears to be more important than relative wages in stimulating migration. Thus, our results do not confirm those reported by NEVEN and GOUYETTE, 1995, for a smaller sample (two EU countries).

Employment growth responds positively to growth in demand (GDP per capita), and negatively to high relative wages. The assumed negative effect on employment of agriculture is also confirmed. Population density has a positive effect, as suggested, but this effect is not very significant. Also unemployment failed to have a significant impact on employment growth, perhaps because the two mechanisms mentioned above counteract one another.

By solving the equations (1)–(3) for the endogenous variables, using the estimates from Table 2 above, we may get a better grasp of what explains the differences in growth and employment across European regions. These reduced-form equations may then be used to decompose predicted growth in GDP per capita and employment into its various components (i.e. our exogenous variables). The reduced form equations are reported in Table 3, while Table 4 gives the decomposition of the growth rates into the different effects.[12] The first column (mean) in Table 4 shows how the model explains the growth of GDP per capita for an 'average' European region (defined as having mean values of all variables). Both the potential for catch-up and R&D efforts emerge as important for growth, as do the economic structure (share of agriculture in GDP) and the level of unemployment. There is also a sizeable constant term (including country dummies) which we will have more to say about below.

More interesting, perhaps, is how this model explains the differences in GDP per capita growth between

Table 2. Estimation results[1]

Dependent variable	Adjusted R^2	n	Endogenous variables			Exogenous variables					
			GQ	MIR	GE	log(Q)	RDE	AGR	UE	PA	RW
GQ	0·31	64		0·96		−0·015	0·008	−0·027		−0·0014	
t-values				2·51**[2]		2·39**	2·80***	2·06**		0·28	
MIR	0·38	64			0·388				−0·07	−0·0014	0·0024
t-values					5·15***				5·17***	0·56	0·44
GE	0·71	64	0·624					−0·060	−0·03	0·0031	−0·057
t-values			3·49***					4·00***	0·83	1·19	4·00***

Notes: 1. Estimated by instrument variables (2SLS) with all exogenous variables and *IND* and *STRUC* as instruments.
    2. Two and three stars denote significance at a 5% or 1% level in a two-tailed *t*-test, respectively, using heteroscedasticity consistent standard errors. Country dummies are not explicitly documented.

Table 3. *Reduced form equations for growth of GDP per capita and growth of employment*

Dependent variable	Exogenous variables									
	log(Q)	RDE	AGR	UE	PA	RW	DIT	DFR	DES	constant
GQ	−0·0195	0·0102	−0·0643	−0·10	−0·0021	−0·0247	0·0165	0·0044	0·0231	0·0707
GE	−0·0122	0·0063	−0·1001	−0·09	0·0018	−0·0724	0·0081	−0·0015	0·0284	0·0487

Table 4. *Why growth rates of GDP per capita and employment differ (%)*

	GDP per capita		Employment	
	Mean (1)	Low–high (2)	Mean (1)	Low–high (2)
Catch-up	1·3	1·3	0·8	0·8
R&D	0·5	−0·9	0·3	−0·6
Population density	−0·1	0·1	0·0	−0·1
Structure	−0·8	−1·1	−1·3	−1·7
Unemployment	−1·0	−0·7	−0·9	−0·7
Wages	0·0	0·3	0·0	0·9
Constant	1·0		1·1	
Country specific	1·1	1·4	0·8	1·9
Total of above	*2·1*	*0·3*	*0·9*	*0·5*
Actual	2·0	0·3	0·8	0·4

Notes: 1. Decomposition of the growth rates of an 'average' region in our sample (point of gravity of the regression).
2. Decomposition of the difference in growth rates between 'rich' and 'poor' regions in our sample.

rich and poor regions. This is illustrated in the second column of Table 4 (low–high). Catch-up emerges as the most important factor for the poor regions, but this advantage is to a large extent eroded by the much higher R&D efforts in the rich regions. The performance of the poor regions is also significantly negatively affected by their industrial structure (characterized by a large agricultural sector) and high levels of unemployment. Finally, the growth of the poor regions is positively affected by country specific factors.

Regarding the latter, it can be shown that the country-specific factors partly responsible for the difference in GDP per capita growth between poor and rich regions all relate to one country (or dummy variable), i.e. Spain. This is not necessarily so surprising, since most of the poor regions in our sample are Spanish. It should be noted, also, that the very inclusion of country-specific factors in the regressions implies that the differences in, say, growth of GDP per capita between Spain and other countries will be explained by these dummies and not by the other variables included in the regressions. Thus, what this result tells us is simply that, on average, all Spanish regions grew faster than regions from other countries. Why this is so we do not know. But is tempting to suggest that catching up (between Spain and more advanced countries such as Germany) during the 1980s, as well as the entry of Spain into the European Community, may

have been factors in this. At least, the potential for catch-up was substantial. In fact, in 1980 GDP per capita in Spain was only 60% of that in Germany.

The third and fourth columns in Table 4 give similar predictions for employment growth. In general, the estimation results show that what is good for GDP per capita growth tends to be good for employment growth as well. However, catch-up and R&D have a smaller impact on differences in employment growth than on differences in growth of GDP per capita. Moreover, although relative wages do not matter much for growth, this variable has a sizeable impact on employment. This favours employment growth in the poorer regions. Also, an unfavourable industrial structure (i.e. a large agricultural sector) is even more damaging for employment growth than for growth of GDP per capita. The table also reveals that employment actually grows faster in poor regions. However, this is more than outweighed by more rapid growth of the labour supply there (see Table 1). As a result, differences in unemployment levels between poor and rich regions tend to increase, rather than the other way around.

CONCLUSIONS

This paper has tried to explore the relationship between technology, growth and employment growth across European regions. We have been motivated by the fact, laid out in the second section of this paper, that levels of GDP per capita and unemployment seem to be inversely related, i.e. that poor regions also tend to have high unemployment, and vice versa. Another source of inspiration has been our previous finding (FAGERBERG and VERSPAGEN, 1996) that unemployment seems to affect economic growth negatively. Taken together these findings suggest the possibility of a 'high unemployment–low GDP per capita trap' in Europe. Arguably, this may have strong implications for European 'cohesion'.

The explanation offered by the model for the negative correlation between growth and unemployment, is that unemployment affects growth negatively through its negative impact on inward migration (and positive impact on outward migration). In fact, net inward migration was found to have a strong, positive impact on growth. Unemployment acts as a factor that limits net inward migration and, hence, growth.

Regarding the persistence of high rates of unemployment in regions with low GDP per capita, the explanation seems to be that although employment grows somewhat faster in poorer regions (a fact attributed by our model mainly to a large scope for catch-up and relatively low wages, in combination with country specific factors), it does not grow rapidly enough to keep up with the growth of labour supply, which is also higher in more backward regions. Hence, unemployment rates in backward regions tend to increase rather than the other way around.

What are the policy implications of this study? First, note that some of the traditional policy recipes, such as encouraging migration and reducing wages in areas with high unemployment, do not necessarily alleviate the problem of a 'high unemployment–low GDP per capita trap'. In our model, migration flows are assumed to have a symmetrical impact on growth, i.e. inward migration increases growth, while outward migration decreases it. The estimated impact is quite large, although the flows are rather small (compared, for instance, to the number of unemployed in high unemployment areas). Hence, increased migration would be likely to increase the differences in GDP per capita between rich and poor regions, while having only a relatively modest impact on the recorded levels of unemployment in poor regions.[13] A reduction in wages, on the other hand, might have a more substantial effect on unemployment. But, in our model, this reduction in unemployment in the poor regions (due to a lowering of wages there) will occur at the expense of the workers in rich regions. The explanation is again one of symmetry, reduced relative wages – and more jobs – in the poor regions *ceteris paribus* transmits itself into increased relative wages in rich regions and, hence, fewer jobs in the latter. Thus, increased inequality between workers in poor and rich regions – through a widening of the difference in wage levels – will not cure the present high level of unemployment in the European Union, but it may contribute to a different regional distribution of unemployment. Whether this is an acceptable policy option or not is not for us to decide. However, it may be difficult to combine such a policy with the current aim in the EU to create a truly common European labour market.

Fortunately, our analysis indicates that there are other policy options that may have a more promising impact. First, encouraging R&D in backward regions appears crucial. Today, R&D is very unevenly distributed across Europe, with little or no R&D in most poor regions. However, without well-developed R&D capabilities, backward regions will find it increasingly difficult to exploit the potential for learning offered by more advanced technology developed elsewhere. Moreover, in contrast to migration or relative wages, this is not a zero-sum game. Hence, an increase in R&D in, say, the poor regions will – according to our model (and much recent theorizing in this area) – lead to higher growth in poor areas without necessarily decreasing growth elsewhere. However, it needs to be stressed that

encouraging R&D in backward regions is not simply a matter of subsidizing these activities. R&D is typically an activity that can only be undertaken in the context of an adequate infrastructure, i.e. when sufficient high quality labour and supporting institutions such as higher education institutions are available. Policies aimed at R&D thus have an essential long-run and structural character, both in terms of implementation and effect.

Second, the findings presented here point to economic structure, i.e. the dominant role played by agriculture in many poor regions, as an important barrier to growth of employment and GDP per capita in backward regions. Thus, rather than conserve the existing economic structure by such means as the Common Agricultural Policy, policy should be aimed at changing it.

It is, however, pertinent to stress that these conclusions rest on a number of assumptions which, although defendable, are not always tested (or even testable). One main reason for this is lack of data. For instance, if (for some variable) data is available for a single year only, econometric testing is necessarily limited. Rather than following the common practice of ignoring important variables for which data are scarce, we have in this paper tried to do much with little. Without denying the limitations that this places on the generality of the analysis, we nevertheless hope that this paper may provide some useful inputs to the debate about EU policy and regional policy in particular.

Acknowledgements – Financial support from European Union's Targeted Socio-economic Research Programme is gratefully acknowledged, as is support from the Norwegian Research Council. Bart Verspagen's research has been made possible by a fellowship of the Royal Netherlands Academy of Arts and Sciences.

NOTES

1. Note that a similar, though not identical, process can be shown to have taken place in the US and Japan (BARRO and SALA-I-MARTIN, 1992). This suggests that the factors responsible for these developments may be rather general in nature, rather than country or region specific. This is not inconsistent with the perspective we apply here, but we do not attempt to explain developments outside Europe.
2. DUNFORD, 1996, provides additional evidence on the relationship between GDP per capita and unemployment across European regions.
3. In the REGIO database, regions are identified in the NUTS-scheme. We use both NUTS 2-digit and 3-digit level regions, depending on data availability and the country. A listing of regions is in the Appendix table.
4. The only variable in this latter group that reflects change is the growth of labour supply (*GN*). This variable, it may be noted, is not included in any of the models/ regressions presented later, but used to illustrate the joint

impact of growth in the demand for and supply of labour on unemployment.

5. GDP per capita is closely related to income per head. This is why we sometimes denote regions with low GDP per capita as 'poor' and regions with high GDP per capita as 'rich'. We use national price indices and purchasing power parities to the Ecu, because region-specific data for these variables are lacking.

6. Unemployment, employment and the labour force data in the EUROSTAT REGIO database generally are not available for years before 1983, so we are forced to use the 1983 value as the initial year.

7. This applies to support through the so-called European Regional Development Fund, which is the main source for regional support at the EU level. Loans from the European Investment Bank (and supporting schemes), though much smaller in size, were found to have a more positive impact, however.

8. This is defined as $\Sigma_j \sigma_{ij} \gamma_j$, where γ_j is the European wide growth rate of GDP in sector j (agriculture, industry or services), and σ_{ij} is the share of sector j in GDP in region i.

9. Since we lacked wage data for France, we estimated these data on the basis of a linear regression of RW on a similarly constructed variable for GDP per capita for the other countries in our sample.

10. Technically speaking, we have three country dummies and a common constant term, which amounts to the same thing.

11. We cannot include SER, since SER, IND and AGR sum to one.

12. In order to quantify the effect of catching-up, we substituted the log of GDP per capita by a similar variable, but expressed relative to GDP per capita in the 'richest' region in the sample. At the same time, we add the log of GDP per capita in the 'richest' region in the sample multiplied by the catching-up coefficient to the constant term, thus leaving the statistical and arithmetical characteristics of the equation unchanged.

13. If the impact is not symmetrical, for instance because inward migration has a larger quantitative effect than outward migration, migration may also have an impact on the average growth rate of GDP per capita. However, as long as this does not change the qualitative impact of migration flows, one would still expect migration to drag down growth in poor regions (although less than in the case of symmetrical effects).

APPENDIX

Regions used in the regression analysis

Number	NUTS code	Country	Region
1	r11	Germany	Baden-Wuerttemberg
2	r12	Germany	Bayern
3	r13	Germany	Berlin
4	r15	Germany	Bremen
5	r16	Germany	Hamburg
6	r17	Germany	Hessen
7	r19	Germany	Niedersachsen
8	r1a	Germany	Nordrhein-Westfalen
9	r1b	Germany	Rheinland-Pfalz
10	r1c	Germany	Saarland
11	r1f	Germany	Schleswig-Holstein
12	r311	Italy	Piemonte
13	r313	Italy	Liguria
14	r32	Italy	Lombardia
15	r331	Italy	Trentino-Alto Adige
16	r332	Italy	Veneto
17	r333	Italy	Friuli-Venez. Giulia
18	r34	Italy	Emilia-Romagna
19	r351	Italy	Toscana
20	r352	Italy	Umbria
21	r353	Italy	Marche
22	r36	Italy	Lazio
23	r37	Italy	Abruzzo-Molise
24	r38	Italy	Campania
25	r391	Italy	Puglia
26	r392	Italy	Basilicata
27	r393	Italy	Calabria
28	r3a	Italy	Sicilia
29	r3b	Italy	Sardegna
30	r21	France	Ile de France
31	r221	France	Champagne
32	r222	France	Picardie
33	r223	France	Haute Normandie
34	r224	France	Centre
35	r225	France	Basse Normandie
36	r226	France	Bourgogne
37	r23	France	Nord-Pas-de Calais
38	r241	France	Lorraine
39	r242	France	Alsace
40	r243	France	Franche-Comté
41	r251	France	Pays de la Loire
42	r252	France	Bretagne
43	r253	France	Poitou-Charentes
44	r261	France	Aquitaine
45	r262	France	Midi-Pyrénées
46	r263	France	Limousin
47	r271	France	Rhône-Alpes
48	r272	France	Auvergne
49	r281	France	Languedoc-Roussillon
50	rb11	Spain	Galicia
51	rb12	Spain	Principado de Asturias
52	rb13	Spain	Cantabria
53	rb21	Spain	Pais Vasco
54	rb22	Spain	Comunidad Foral de Navarra
55	rb23	Spain	La Rioja
56	rb3	Spain	Comunidad de Madrid
57	rb41	Spain	Castilla y León
58	rb42	Spain	Castilla-la Mancha
59	rb43	Spain	Extremadura
60	rb51	Spain	Cataluña
61	rb52	Spain	Comunidad Valenciana
62	rb53	Spain	Islas Baleares
63	rb61	Spain	Andalucia
64	rb62	Spain	Región de Murcia

REFERENCES

BARRO R. J. and SALA-I-MARTIN X. (1991) Convergence across states and regions, *Brookings Pap. Econ. Activity*, No. 1, pp. 107–82.

BARRO R. J. and SALA-I-MARTIN X. (1992) Regional growth and migration: a Japan-United States comparison, *J. Jap. & Int. Econ.* **6,** 312–46.

BEGG I. and MAYES D. (1993) Cohesion in the European Community: a key imperative for the 1990s?, *Reg. Sci. & Urban Econ.* **23,** 427–48.

BLANCHARD O. J. and KATZ L. F. (1992) Regional evolutions, *Brookings Pap. Econ. Activity*, No. 1, pp. 1–70.

CANIËLS M. C. J. (1996) Regional differences in technology, theory and empirics, MERIT research memorandum 96-009, University of Maastricht, Maastricht.

CICCONE A. and HALL R. E. (1996) Productivity and the density of economic activity, *Am. Econ. Rev.* **86,** 54–70.

COHEN W. M. and LEVINTHAL D. A. (1989) Innovation and learning: the two faces of R&D, *Econ. J.* **99,** 569–96.

DUNFORD M. (1996) Disparities in employment, productivity and output in the EU: the roles of labour market governance and welfare regimes, *Reg. Studies* **30,** 339–57.

FAGERBERG J. (1987) A technology gap approach to why growth rates differ, *Research Policy* **16,** 87–99.

FAGERBERG J. (1988) Why growth rates differ, in DOSI G., FREEMAN C., NELSON R., SILVERBERG G. and SOETE L. (Eds) *Technical Change and Economic Theory*, pp. 432–57. Pinter, London.

FAGERBERG J. (1994) Technology and international differences in growth rates, *J. Econ. Lit.* **32,** 1,147–75.

FAGERBERG J. and VERSPAGEN B. (1996) Heading for divergence? Regional growth in Europe reconsidered, *J. Common Mkt. Studies* **34,** 431–48.

GROSSMAN G. M. and HELPMAN E. (1991) *Innovation and Growth in the Global Economy.* MIT Press, Cambridge, MA.

KRUGMAN P. (1991) *Economic Geography and Trade.* MIT Press, Cambridge, MA/London.

NEVEN D. and GOUYETTE C. (1995) Regional convergence in the European Community, *J. Common Mkt. Studies* **33,** 47–65.

ROMER P. (1990) Endogenous technological change, *J. Pol. Econ.* **98,** S71–S102.

SALA-I-MARTIN X. (1996) Regional cohesion: evidence and theories of regional growth and convergence, *Europ. Econ. Rev.* **40,** 1,325–52.

SOLOW R. M. (1956) A contribution to the theory of economic growth, *Quart. J. Econ.* **70,** 65–94.

VERSPAGEN B. (1991) A new empirical approach to catching up and falling behind, *Struct. Change & Econ. Dynamics* **2,** 359–80.

[6]

VISION AND FACT

A CRITICAL ESSAY ON THE GROWTH LITERATURE

Jan Fagerberg

INTRODUCTION

Many people think about growth theory as complicated mathematics. Others identify it with complex statistics. And it is true; growth theory is about both of these things. But first and foremost, I will argue, growth theory is about *vision*. It is concerned with questions such as these: Where are we heading, and why? What are the options we have to influence the direction? Which actions are needed to arrive at the preferred state? Thus growth theory is by its very nature deeply political.[1]

To provide answers to such questions, growth theory has to be based on a clear understanding of what the drivers of growth are. It is only natural that as capitalism has progressed and changed, so have the perceptions in the economic profession about what drives growth. From the Industrial Revolution onward, the main driver of growth was considered to be *mechanization,* that is, the substitution of machinery for human labor. This led in many quarters to a focus on how sufficient funds for investment in further mechanization could be generated, the division of total income into wages and profits, and the transmission of these sources of income into consumption and saving and investment. The prominent role that some economists attach to income policies is often based on this perspective. However, more recently, growth theorists have come to recognize the increasing role of knowledge, or the "human factor," in growth, and this has led to an accelerating focus among growth theorists and practitioners on

299

understanding the institutions and organizations in capitalism that produce and transmit knowledge, including the role that public policy may play. This chapter traces these changes in our understanding of growth and the sources of these changes as emphasis has shifted from a focus on the availability of financial capital to the quality of human capital.

RETROSPECT

The political nature of growth theory became abundantly clear as soon as the theory began to take shape two centuries ago, when writers such as Adam Smith and David Ricardo tried to convince people that stagnant growth and generally poor living conditions were not at all necessary, if only institutions and policies were geared toward allowing the capitalist machine to work at full speed. They argued forcefully that changes in institutions and policies, although detrimental to the narrow interests of some stakeholders in the existing system, would be enormously beneficial to society as a whole. This "free market" optimism has been a central ingredient in many economists' basic beliefs ever since.

Not all writers on growth were equally cheerful about the long-run outcome of free market capitalism, however. For instance, writers such as Thomas Malthus and Karl Marx both held that an unregulated capitalist market system was doomed to stagnation, crises, and possibly collapse, though for different reasons. Although mainstream (orthodox) economists generally rejected such ideas as faulty, economic developments in the first part of this century actually seemed to confirm the crisis-ridden character of capitalism. The view that capitalist growth if left to itself was not sustainable gained credibility as the crisis deepened and unemployment soared during the Great Depression of the 1930s. The central advocate of this view in the 1930s was of course John Maynard Keynes, who emphasized the importance of demand and the essential role of the government in managing the economy. His analysis—which was largely confined to the short run—was extended to the long run by Evsey Domar and Roy Harrod, among others, in the so-called post-Keynesian growth theory.[2] These theories showed that long-run growth with full

employment was indeed possible but depended on extensive intervention by the government (especially with respect to income distribution). By the end of the Second World War the Keynesian view of
the need for an active government had become widely shared among
policymakers and stakeholders in the Western world.

THE RETURN OF ORTHODOXY

The Keynesian dominance of growth theory did not last long.
There were several reasons for this. First, the conclusions of the
Keynesian and post-Keynesian theories were in conflict with what
most economists had been teaching since the days of Adam Smith,
that is, that capitalism is a self-regulating system that performs
best when interference in markets is at a minimum. For many economists, acceptance of this belief was (and in many quarters still is)
the most important criterion for being a member of the profession.
Second, the times were changing. The 1930s had produced depression and unemployment. Now, in the 1950s, the economies of the
West were running at full speed. Rather than economic misery, the
real threat to Western societies was generally conceived by many
observers, not just most economists, to be the expansion of the
state-led systems in Eastern Europe and Asia (the Soviet Union in
particular). An economic theory that advocated extensive state
intervention in the economy must have looked odd from such a
perspective.

   Whatever the reason, several orthodox economists started to
search for a new growth theory. The so-called neoclassical growth
theory developed by the Nobel laureate Robert Solow and others
in the 1950s proposed that long-run growth with full employment
was indeed possible as long as market forces were allowed to operate freely. However, the assumptions behind this conclusion were
severe. The theory rested on the idea of "perfect competition,"
and on an economy with many competing firms, each of them too
small to have a real impact on the market. In this idealized economy, economies of scale were ruled out by assumption, since this
was believed to imply that large firms would have lower unit costs
than smaller firms do and, hence, would be able to drive the latter
out of the market. Thus constant returns to scale were imposed—a
1 percent increase in all inputs yields exactly 1 percent growth in

output. Technology was regarded as an exogenous force, a "public good," readily available to everyone free of charge. By *exogenous,* economists meant that advances in technology were created outside the economic system that they were describing. The required assumption was that business exploited these technological advances but was not truly responsible for creating them. Investments by firms in the creation of new technology were thus also ruled out as a criterion of growth, since such investment would carry no particular financial reward for the firm that undertook it.

In such an economy, the only way for a firm or country to increase its productivity relative to its competitors would be to increase the amount of capital per worker, which is to say, to mechanize. But neoclassical economists also assumed that the rewards of such substitution of capital for labor gradually diminish as the amount of capital per worker increases. For a given level of technology, it was presumed that there exists a limit beyond which accumulation of capital per worker will not be profitable. When an economy has reached this limit, the amount of capital per worker has reached its "steady state" (equilibrium), and labor productivity will be constant (unless technology advances exogenously). Or, to put it differently, from this perspective the only source of long-run productivity growth is exogenous technological advance—that is, through discovery and invention that is purported to be separate from the natural workings of the economy.

As long as we accept these assumptions, this neoclassical theory leads to an important prediction when applied to the global economy. Countries that differ in terms of initial productivity levels will converge toward the same level of productivity and the same rate of productivity growth. If countries differ also in other influential respects, such as the growth of population or the propensity to save, convergence toward the same rate of growth of productivity will still be achieved, but long-run productivity levels will differ. In the literature, the latter is often called "conditional convergence."

Hence, the neoclassical growth theory developed by Robert Solow and others in the 1950s implied a liberal and optimistic view for global economic development. As long as market forces were allowed to operate freely, and other factors did not differ too much, everyone would be equally well off in the long run.

GROWTH ACCOUNTING

Although highly abstract and based on very strong assumptions, the neoclassical theory of growth was heartily welcomed by empirical growth analysts at the time, who felt that it might give theoretical backing to their attempts to calculate the contribution of increased use of labor and capital to the growth of GDP and productivity. This was so because, according to the theory, the price of any factor in production will reflect the contribution to GDP from using one more unit of it to produce goods and services (marginalism). Hence, following this, one could simply use the observed prices of labor and of capital (wages and profits) to calculate the contribution from increased use of labor and capital to growth of GDP. This practice came to be known as "growth accounting."[3] In the 1950s it was applied to historical data in the United States by Moses Abramovitz and others and in the 1960s and later to selected OECD countries by Edward Denison. Over the years this methodology has also been applied to many individual countries.

In the absence of exogenous technological progress, the contributions from growth of labor and capital should theoretically add up to the total growth in the economy. In practice, the first exercises carried out in this area showed that only a small part of actual growth could be attributed to growth of labor and capital. If there is more growth than what can be accounted for by increased use of labor and higher capital expenditures, the theory suggests that this is the contribution from exogenous technological progress and perhaps some other unknown factors. In fact, when the empiricists gathered their data and did their analyses, up to 80 percent of annual rates of growth remained unexplained by inputs of labor and capital.

That the lion's share of actual growth had to be explained by exogenous technological progress and other unidentified sources was something that left many economists skeptical. Various remedies were considered to improve on this rather odd and even embarrassing result. The first was to adjust the factors themselves by taking into account the changes in quality and composition of both capital and labor. For instance, newer vintages of capital, embodying the most recent technologies, were assumed to be more efficient than previous ones. However, though useful for accounting purposes, this did not really provide an explanation of why new vintages of capital were more productive than previous ones. Hence, to some extent this practice boiled down to no more than building the unexplained part of actual growth (exogenous technological progress and so forth) into the factors themselves. As for labor, its quality was assumed to increase with higher educational levels, the economic effect of which was normally calculated by observing the wage gaps between workers with different educational attainments.

A second general approach was to attempt to take into account entirely different factors that might directly affect growth, such as economies of scale, investments in R&D, structural change, and differences in the scope for imitation of best-practice technology. When the contribution to growth from these factors was added, a much larger part of actual growth was explained. There is one problem, however. The apparent influence of some of these additional factors actually contradicts the assumptions of the theory on which the analysis was based. For instance, as shown earlier, the theory explicitly assumes no economies of scale and does not really allow for R&D in firms. But if such additional factors as economies of scale and R&D are indeed important drivers of economic growth, and the available evidence suggests that they are, what you may need is a new theory. In other words, to make growth accounting work, so many new factors had to be taken into account that the underlying theory itself was called into question.

In fact, Richard Nelson pointed out the limitations of growth accounting long ago.[4] He argued that growth accounting is not a tested theory of growth. Rather, he argued, it is merely a description of a growth process that is based on certain assumptions, the validity of which have generally not been proven or even tested. It is important to keep these inadequacies in mind when assessing applications of this methodology. Consider, for instance, Alwyn Young's recent work on the East Asian countries, which was widely cited in the media.[5] Using growth accounting, he claims that accumulation of capital and labor account almost entirely for why these economies grew so rapidly. In other words, there was little technological progress in these countries, implying that whatever they did to speed up technological change, it cannot have been of much importance. However, such claims rest on a number of assumptions that do not necessarily hold in these countries. Were there no large firms with market power? Were there no economies of scale? Was technology available to everyone free of charge? Without affirmative and unambiguous answers to such questions, such growth accounting exercises cannot be used to draw simple conclusions about what drives growth. As Robert Lucas pointed out in reference to Young's findings, just observing the fact that input and output growth tend to go hand in hand explains nothing.[6] It merely shows that labor and capital inputs rise as GDP grows, but it does not necessarily assign causality. Arguably, any theory of growth would be consistent with observations of this sort.

With hindsight, the empiricists' attempt to base their work on the neoclassical theory of economic growth was less successful than initially conceived. Perhaps what the empiricists failed to recognize was that the theory was not at all geared toward the real world, but toward a largely artificial world of so-called perfect competition, in which many of the growth-enhancing factors in the real economy had been eliminated by assumption. For the theoreticians this did the trick, since in this way they were able to demonstrate that full employment was consistent with a market-oriented system of regulation. They did so at a high cost, however, because in contrast to the already existing post-Keynesian models of economic growth, the neoclassical model was unable to explain how the economy generates long-run growth in GDP per capita. In fact, the only type of growth that the model could truly explain was transitional in character (on the path toward long-run equilibrium) and the result of the substitution of capital for labor (that is, mechanization). In the long run, this type of growth was bound to cease as returns diminished. Once equilibrium was reached, there was no more growth to be had, except by exogenous technological advance. Such growth was simply "manna from heaven" to economists, over which there could be little control.

ALTERNATIVE PERSPECTIVES

I have used much space to explain how modern (neoclassical) growth theory and its empirical applications developed from the 1950s onward. The reason I did so is that it dominated the economic thinking about growth for a long time. Indeed this perspective is still highly influential, although there is growing controversy about it in the profession. This is not to say that the neoclassical views were the only ideas about growth around at the time. For instance, alternatives to the neoclassical interpretations of events had for a long time been advocated by a diverse group of historically oriented economists and economically oriented historians. For lack of a better word, I will classify these economists and historians as *evolutionaries.*[7]

I have chosen this word to signal the importance that these people attached to the study of economic evolution of actual, real-world economies. In particular, they were concerned with the relationship between technological advances and the workings of the economy. Technology to these analysts did not simply arise freely as "manna from heaven," but was the direct consequence of the interaction between business, institutions, and ideas. Rather than exogenous, it was—at least to some extent—considered *endogenous.*

The central contributor here was the Austrian-American economist Joseph Schumpeter.[8] In contrast to the traditional emphasis in economics on capital accumulation, Schumpeter focused on innovation in firms. To him, it was the driving force behind economic growth.[9] Essentially, he saw innovation as "new combinations" of existing pieces of knowledge, whether drawn from science, engineering, market research, organizational experience, or other sources, but always with a view toward commercial application. His concept of innovation is broad and goes beyond the mere invention of a new product or process. Innovative firms are assumed to benefit economically due to the temporary monopoly they get from the innovations they make. If you make a new successful product, you will profit until others learn to imitate and compete with it in the market. Eventually the knowledge embodied in innovations will diffuse to other firms and industries, and this will fuel further growth.

While Schumpeter particularly focused on deliberate and direct innovation strategies by firms, other writers in this tradition, such as Nicholas Kaldor,[10] Bengt Åke Lundvall,[11] and Nathan Rosenberg,[12] emphasized the importance of learning within firms and on plant floors as the source of technological progress and economic growth. Such learning occurs because people in their daily life, particularly at work, experience problems and—upon reflection—come up with new and improved solutions that increase productivity. These may originate in production, through investments and the subsequent application of new machinery, as the result of interaction with customers or suppliers, or through organized links with other firms or organizations. Learning may also give rise to organized R&D of the type emphasized by Schumpeter, to some extent blurring the traditional distinction between innovation and diffusion of technology. Hence, in this literature, learning is increasingly analyzed as an interactive process, with feedback to and from organized R&D whether in the private or public sector. This has recently led researchers in this area to view a country's innovation and learning performance as an entire system, focusing not only on the individual institutions and organizations that take part in innovation and learning but also on their mutual interaction. The concept "national system of innovation," used in several recent studies, reflects this perspective.[13]

The economic historian Alexander Gerschenkron pioneered the study of the international aspects of this process of innovation and learning. Some countries are at the technological frontier, he pointed out, while others lag behind. Although the technological gap between a frontier country and a laggard represents "a great promise" for the latter to catch up, there are also various problems that may prevent backward countries from reaping the potential benefits. Gerschenkron suggested that if one country succeeds in embarking on an innovation-driven growth path, others might find it increasingly difficult to catch up, and that they would have to compensate for this by developing new institutions, organizations, and policies that support industry. His favorite example was Germany's attempt to catch up with Britain a century ago. When Britain industrialized, technology was relatively labor intensive and small-scale. But in the course of time technology became much more capital and scale intensive, so when Germany entered the scene, the conditions for entry had changed considerably. Germany had to develop new institutional instruments for overcoming these obstacles, above all in the financial sector, "instruments for which there was little or no counterpart in an established industrial country."[14] He held these experiences to be valid also for other technologically lagging countries.

Moses Abramovitz,[15] arguing along similar lines, used the concepts "technological congruence" and "social capability" to characterize the situation that lagging countries face. The first concept refers to the degree to which leader and follower country characteristics are congruent in areas such as market size, the availability of labor, natural resources, and so forth. The second points to the various efforts and capabilities that backward countries have to develop in order to catch up, such as improving education, infrastructure, and technological capabilities (such as R&D facilities) in general. He explains the successful catch-up of Western Europe vis à vis the United States in the post–World War II period as the result of both increasing technological congruence and improved social capabilities. As an example of the former, he mentions how European economic integration led to the creation of larger and more homogenous markets in Europe, facilitating the transfer of scale-intensive technologies initially developed for U.S. conditions. Regarding the latter, he points among other things to such factors as the general increases in educational levels and the rise in the share of resources devoted to public and private sector R&D. In a similar vein, the failure of many so-called developing countries to exploit the same opportunities is commonly explained with reference to lack of technological congruence and missing social capabilities, such as inadequate education.

In some respects, these alternatives to neoclassical growth theory paint a much bleaker picture of the prospects for catch-up. Catch-up is not something that can be expected to occur only by allowing market forces to unfold; it requires a lot of effort and institution building on the part of the backward country. One main reason for this is that technology is viewed differently than in the standard neoclassical approach. Rather than something that exists in the public domain and can be exploited by anybody everywhere free of charge (the public good assumption), technological competence, whether created through learning or organized R&D, is commonly seen as deeply rooted in the specific capabilities of private firms and their networks and environments, including in many cases parts of the public sector.

The Convergence Controversy

For a long time, empirical work on economic growth was dominated by measurement (attempts to measure productivity in different countries, sectors, and industries) and growth-accounting exercises. However, as the empirical research agenda shifted from description toward the understanding and explanation of differences in growth rates between countries, researchers started to supplement this descriptive work with econometric techniques (such as multivariate regression) using cross-country datasets with the purpose of distinguishing between the potential for catch-up and the various factors that determine to what extent this potential is actually exploited.[16] The potential for catch-up was normally measured by the gap in productivity (or GDP per capita) between the country in question and the economically leading country of the sample (normally the United States). Other cross-country variables that were taken into account included differences across countries in rates of investment, educational attainment, R&D and innovation performance, openness to trade and competition, and size of government.

Initially, most studies were confined to the developed market economies for which data were most easily forthcoming (the OECD countries). It was shown that among these countries, a process of catching up had taken place from the 1950s onward, that is, that the initially poorest countries in the area had grown much faster per capita than the economically leading country, the United States. Moreover, the differences in GDP per capita had steadily been reduced between the OECD countries, suggesting a tendency toward convergence to a common level of GDP per capita for the area as a whole. It was also shown that these tendencies toward catch-up and convergence were much stronger when other conditioning variables were taken into account, indicating that the potential for catch-up and convergence was larger than what was actually realized. Many variables were found to contribute to this process, including—notably—investment, education, and R&D and innovation performance.[17]

Although several of these studies were inspired by evolutionary views on technology and catch-up, the results could also be interpreted as supportive of the basic neoclassical growth theory, since convergence to a common level of productivity was indeed found to take place. However, this evidence turned out to be more controversial than initially conceived. For instance, Bradford De Long pointed out in 1988 that the sample of OECD countries might be biased, since it consisted mainly of the countries in the global economy that had done reasonably well after the end of World War II.[18] He also presented some preliminary evidence suggesting that a similar tendency toward convergence could not be established for a more balanced sample. This suggested that larger samples than just the countries of the OECD area were required. This was made possible by the construction of new and larger datasets that were made available toward the end of the 1980s.[19]

Inspired by the work by Abramovitz and others on technology gaps and growth, William Baumol and co-authors applied regression models of the type just discussed to cross-country samples including up to a hundred countries or more.[20] The conclusion of this work was that although a tendency toward convergence could perhaps be established for the OECD countries in the postwar period, and may be extending to some other countries as well, it does not hold for the world as a whole. In fact, many poor countries fail more or less completely to exploit the potential for catch-up, something that obviously does not conform to the predictions of the traditional neoclassical theory. But the new evidence confirmed the finding of a considerable potential for catch-up by poorer countries, which, however, is not fully exploited due to lack of "social capability" and other factors.

Hence the evidence pointed toward a quite complex picture, with groups of countries with certain common characteristics performing differently in terms of rates of growth and convergence. One interpretation of this evidence was that there existed a multitude of different "convergence clubs."[21] For instance, the member countries of the OECD are often pointed to as an example of such a club, as in the opposite sense are the countries in Africa. How should this be explained? Would it be possible to explain this diversity within a common theoretical framework, though necessarily more complex than the neoclassical one that had dominated up to this point? This was the challenge confronting growth theorists toward the end of the 1980s.

THE NEW ORTHODOX THEORY

Some neoclassical economists recognized the problems of traditional growth theory and its empirical applications in explaining the observed patterns of long-run growth in the world economy, as well as the emergence of other, competing approaches. This led eventually to a search among neoclassical theorists for new models of growth. What they wanted was a formal model that continued to be based on the orthodox vision of the economy as a set of rational agents determined to maximize their economic utility (and endowed with perfect information and foresight). But they wanted a model that yielded predictions empirically consistent with what was actually observed.

The central contributor here has been Paul Romer. There were in particular two aspects of the old neoclassical theory of economic growth on which he wanted to improve. First, he wanted a theory (or "model") that could explain long-run growth without having to rely on the assumption that technological progress was essentially exogenous. Hence, he wished to endogenize technological progress. For this reason the theories that he helped to create are sometimes called "endogenous growth theories." These theories are also sometimes dubbed "new growth" theories, which is, of course, not very informative and—as time goes by—not very accurate either. Much of this thinking was anticipated by earlier growth economists, if in less formally mathematical ways.

Second, Romer wanted his model to yield predictions that were consistent with the diversity of growth patterns that empirical research had found to exist. In particular, he wanted to be able to explain why the poor countries did not catch up with the rich ones, but continued to stay poor (at least in relative terms).

In so doing, he encountered the problem that we have already discussed at some length, namely that within the usual neoclassical framework (and abstracting from exogenous technological progress) there is no incentive to further accumulation of capital per worker and, hence, no productivity growth in the long run. This result follows from two basic theoretical assumptions, so-called decreasing returns to capital-labor substitution and constant returns to scale. The first postulates that the profitability of new investments will decline as capital grows large relative to labor, the second that the growth of the economy will be independent of its size. However, if you dispense with the latter and instead allow for increasing returns to scale (as had been previously suggested by Nicholas Kaldor, among others, back in the 1950s), the long-run outlook for the economy may be quite different. In this case, the returns to further investments may continue to stay high, because the negative impact on profitability and growth by continuing accumulation of capital per worker may be counteracted by the positive scale-effect (which implies that all factors become more productive as the economy grows larger). The reason why orthodox theorists avoided this option for so long was probably that it was believed to be in conflict with their vision of a self-regulating market, since under such conditions, large firms would be more efficient than smaller ones.[22] In the long run, this might lead to some kind of monopoly. In such a situation, neoclassical theory would actually justify extensive intervention in the economy by the government, in contrast to what economists generally held to be the preferred public policy stance.

However, Romer showed that there was an easy way out of this, and that was to assume increasing returns to scale at the level of the country or industry rather than at the firm. The idea behind this assumption was a simple one—suggested by among others Kenneth Arrow and Kaldor two decades earlier—that the use of new forms of capital equipment leads to learning that may improve new generations of machinery. The beneficiaries of this learning will be the users of the new generations of capital equipment. The firm in which such learning occurs will also benefit, but not more than other users of the new equipment. Hence, the learning process will leave the relative competitive position of firms unchanged, and will—therefore—not induce changes in their behavior vis à vis each other. Firms continue to operate as if they were living within a world characterized by "perfect competition."[23]

At the aggregate level, however, the consequences are different from those of the traditional Solow model. As pointed out, all firms in a country are assumed to benefit collectively from the learning that goes on, in the form of new and more productive machinery. The ever-increasing productivity of new generations of capital, caused by learning, checks the tendency toward decreasing returns to capital accumulation that would otherwise have led productivity growth to slow down and eventually—in the absence of exogenous technological progress—to cease altogether.

Hence, because of learning, capitalists will continue to find it profitable to invest in new machines. As a consequence growth can be sustained into the long run, according to this model, even after equilibrium has been reached. This also implies that the forces in the traditional Solow model that were assumed to lead to convergence between rich and poor countries are no longer operative, because there is no longer an inherent tendency for capital accumulation to slow down as the amount of capital per worker increases. Hence, rich countries may grow as fast as the poor ones, consistent with the apparent lack of convergence in the global economy.

To some extent this model attained its objectives. But it had a major disadvantage. It did not allow for technological progress to be caused by organized R&D within firms. Obviously, in a world where a firm cannot accrue unique benefits to itself by investing in R&D, there will be no investment in R&D. To allow for technological progress to be caused by R&D, firms investing in R&D must—at least on average—receive an adequate return on these investments, as empirical research indeed suggests that they do.[24]

But what is the economic mechanism generating such returns? The great bulk of R&D investments are typically made early in the life of a product, often before it enters the market, and—in the case of success—paid back over the product's lifetime by keeping prices well above production cost. This implies, however, that the innovating firms have sufficient market power to keep prices at that level, in contrast to what is assumed to be the case in "perfect competition," where no firms have pricing power. Joseph Schumpeter, to repeat, had explained this as the result of the temporary monopoly that innovating firms get on the innovations they make, which might be related to legal forms of protection (patents and copyrights), but also—and perhaps more commonly—to the fact that imitation in many cases is difficult, time-consuming, and costly.

Based partly on these ideas, Paul Romer suggested an alternative theory in which both economies of scale and imperfect competition are assumed.[25] In contrast to the previous model, in which technological progress was considered as an unintended side effect of normal economic activity (a "positive externality"), the alternative approach proposes that innovation is the outcome of efforts by firms that do have sufficient market power to prevent the immediate and costless diffusion of their innovations to other firms and countries.

Romer's point, however, is that these R&D-based innovations have benefits beyond the individual firm. Every innovation, he argues, has two aspects. The first is specific and relates to a new product or process that may be protected by patents, trademarks, secrecy, or other means. The other aspect is general, not secret, and contributes to the advance of scientific and technological knowledge in society as a whole. This second aspect improves the capability to produce new innovations in the future. It is this continuous improvement in our capability to innovate that in this framework prevents decreasing returns on investments in R&D or other innovative activities.

Hence, in this second approach, long-run economic growth is explained through the interplay of imperfect competition, which enables companies to make profits from their R&D investment, and spillovers from these R&D investments to the general level of knowledge in society—and hence to our capability to produce innovations in the future. The main difference between this framework and Romer's previous one is that in this case it is the resources devoted to R&D—and the factors that influence the allocation of resources to this purpose—that determine economic growth, not capital accumulation in the traditional sense.

These new theories have interesting implications for policy. In the old neoclassical framework, where productivity growth in the long run depended only on exogenous technological progress, policy by definition could not have a long-run impact. In these new models this is no longer so. Policies that influence the propensities to invest in physical capital (the first type of model) or R&D and innovation (the second one) may raise growth permanently. Hence, as pointed out by Robert Lucas, from this perspective it is quite easy to conceive situations in which intervention by the government in the economy might have a significant, positive effect for the long-run performance of an economy.[26] However, it is difficult within such a framework to draw very firm conclusions on the use of specific policy instruments, since the appropriateness of these will depend on the characteristics of the country in question. These characteristics include country size, industrial structure, the skills of the labor force, and the country's relations with the global economy.[27]

One of the more controversial predictions from theories assuming economies of scale is that large countries, simply because of their size, tend to have faster technological progress and growth than other countries. Another is that as the economy grows larger, the rate of growth should be expected to increase. These "scale effects" imply that there are large potential benefits from economic integration (or "openness"). Moreover, if there is one economic activity characterized by economies of scale in the form of extensive spillovers between firms (say, R&D-intensive industry), and another that is not (say, traditional industry), the theory suggests that large countries tend to specialize in the former and small countries in the latter. If true, this implies that countries of different sizes may find themselves in quite different situations and would thus be inclined to choose quite different policy responses.

THE EVIDENCE

These theoretical advances led to a surge of empirical investigation. As the new theory differs from the old one in important respects, one might perhaps have expected that a new type of empirical work would have developed, focusing on new issues, using new data, and applying new methods. This, however, has generally not been the case, or at least not until very recently. An exception to this trend is the attempt by Charles Jones to test for the existence of "scale effects" on growth, especially that growth should be expected to increase through time as the economy becomes wealthier (and the investments in physical capital and/or R&D grow larger).[28] He finds little evidence of such "scale effects," raising doubts about the validity of formal models of this type and some of the predictions they give rise to.

What most applied researchers in this area have done is to follow the tradition of applying regression models to cross-country datasets. Ross Levine and David Renelt have summarized much of this work. What they did was to test the various factors that have been emphasized in the empirical literature in a systematic way in order to establish how robust the findings are.[29] The principal finding of Levine and Renelt was that the most robust relationship is between growth and investment. Some empirical support was also found that suggested there was a degree of catch-up on the part of lagging countries and also that educational effort influenced growth. All other explanatory variables were found to be fragile, including a large number of policy variables, openness to trade or competition from abroad, and political factors (such as democracy and political stability).[30]

But I will argue that there is not very much to learn from this new generation of empirical research. That investment is correlated with growth should come as no surprise. Indeed, this is something that would be consistent with most theories in this area, including those that consider investment as endogenous to the growth process, as some available evidence on time series data seems to suggest.[31] In other words, growth itself induces investment. The study by Levine and Renelt also fails to include R&D and innovation, and thus throws little light on the mechanisms highlighted by the most recent generation of growth theories.

Where the results from the empirical literature are useful is that they urge us to use some caution when assessing the impact of policy on growth. This lesson is especially relevant for those who believe that a so-called correct set of macroeconomic policies in combination with trade liberalization and deregulation are enough to foster development and growth. The World Bank, for example, makes such an argument.[32] In fact, as pointed out earlier, there is very little scholarly support for such an interpretation of events. On the contrary, it is clear that the governments in the most successful "catching-up" countries in the post–World War II period have all intervened extensively in the markets through various types of proactive policies.[33] Although the chosen policies may have differed from one country to another, they have by and large performed the same function. They generally increased the share of national resources devoted to growth and steered these resources to the technologically most progressive parts of the economy. This is a recipe for high growth that would be consistent with several versions in the most recent generation of growth theory.

Another relevant strand of research attempts to measure private and social returns on R&D and innovation. This type of work has been undertaken for a long time, independently of the developments in growth theory, but has attracted a growing interest due to the recent changes in formal theorizing. Generally, these empirical exercises tend to find high private returns on investments in R&D, about twice as high as for other types of investment.[34] This, of course, runs counter to traditional neoclassical perspectives on investment, according to which returns on different types of investments should be equalized. Hence one of the central issues in this area, which we will not venture into here, has been how these high private returns can be explained. High as these private returns may be, social returns are commonly found to be even higher, indicating important positive spillovers from R&D, especially when conducted in private firms. These findings suggest that from a social point of view, substantial underinvestment in (private sector) R&D is taking place, and that is an area where governmental intervention might be justified.

Recently, there have been some attempts to address these issues from a perspective that draws more explicitly on the advances in the growth literature. Central questions are: (a) to what extent the diffusion of new technology from one firm to the next is influenced by geographical, institutional, and cultural boundaries; (b) whether country size matters for the degree of success in innovation (as suggested by some recent theorizing); and (c) what the most efficient carriers of technology diffusion are. In fact, new technology may diffuse in many different ways—embodied in goods or services that make use of new technology, through foreign direct investments by multinational firms, or by imitative activities by domestic firms. There is some theoretical backing for all of these but there has until recently been little if any evidence on their relative importance.

Although research in this area is still in an early stage, the available evidence seems to indicate that diffusion of technology (knowledge spillover) is hampered by distance and is generally easier and quicker within than across country borders.[35] There is also some statistical evidence suggesting that returns to R&D investment may be higher in large countries, consistent with what the new growth theories predict.[36] On the last question—which carrier of technology is the most efficient—there is especially little evidence. For instance, some recent research suggests that R&D embodied in imports of goods and services is a very efficient way of transmitting new technology.[37] However, others, using essentially the same type of indicator, fail to reproduce these results.[38]

The picture that emerges is that innovation and diffusion of technology play an essential part in economic growth. Furthermore, the available evidence indicates that, from a social point of view, there is considerable underinvestment in innovation. This means that if firms could be induced to undertake more R&D, growth and welfare would be higher. Contrary to the assumption in exogenous technology models, the diffusion of technology is a difficult and costly process that requires a lot of effort. Moreover, the research shows that "national factors" still have an important role to play for diffusion processes. In fact, several recent studies indicate that there exist persistent differences across countries in their capacity to absorb new technology and that this can only partly be explained by differences in market size, investment in education, and other easily measurable factors.[39] This points to the potential importance of factors such as culture, language, and institutions. These are not easy to quantify, but nevertheless deserve serious attention.

CONCLUSION

What the various perspectives on growth discussed in this chapter have in common are two basic elements: *a view on what drives growth* and *what form of regulatory mechanisms may be necessary to stimulate further growth.*

Concerning the factors that drive growth, the dominant view has over the years largely identified the accumulation of capital as primary. This was the view of the classical political economists, including Karl Marx, post-Keynesian growth theorists such as Sir Roy Harrod or Evsey Domar, or Nicholas Kaldor for that matter, and—at least until very recently—all neoclassical theorists, including Robert Solow and Kenneth Arrow. From a historical point of view, it is not difficult to understand why this view emerged as the dominant one. Clearly, during the so-called Industrial Revolution and the period that followed, the capital accumulation involved with mechanization was a vital ingredient.

It is perhaps less evident why this view should have dominated economists' perceptions of the world for so long. In my view, the great achievement of Joseph Schumpeter (although he was not without forerunners) was to break with this one-sided view and bring to the economists' attention a totally different argument about what drives growth, focusing on qualitative (that is, innovation) rather than quantitative change. With hindsight, it was probably no coincidence that Schumpeter's own professional career ran parallel with the rise of science-based industry, organized corporate R&D, and the development of various types of institutions and organizations relating to this process. It testifies to his qualities as an analyst of contemporary developments that he was able to grasp the full impact of these tendencies at such an early stage. In fact, it took a long time for science-based industry and organized R&D to acquire the prominence it has today. Although pioneered in Germany at the turn of the century, it was only during the Second World War and the cold war that followed that these developments took off, and then primarily in the United States.

While most writers on growth initially shared a common perception of what drove growth, this was not the case for state regulation. Since the beginning, discussions of regulation have been dominated by adherents of two diametrically opposite positions— laissez-faire capitalism and state planning (or very extensive intervention). Among the classical political economists, who all saw the economy from the mechanization perspective, some, such as Adam Smith and David Ricardo, were liberal free marketers, while Karl Marx believed that laissez-faire was doomed to collapse, and had to be replaced by state planning. In the first half of this century, the view that a capitalist order ruled by free markets was basically unstable gained prominence as the crisis of the interwar period deepened, and led to the formulation of (the so-called post-Keynesian) growth theories advocating extensive state intervention in the economy. However, under the impact of the postwar boom and the cold war that followed, the nineteenth-century liberal view again got the upper hand, as reflected in the neoclassical model of economic growth developed by Robert Solow and others.

In my view, the main problem with the traditional neoclassical growth theory was that it was based on an outdated understanding of what drives growth and how the capitalist system, including its institutions, works. It simply did not have any useful advice for policy-makers who were concerned about the real workings of the economy. This is the reason why the works of Joseph Schumpeter and other economists with insights into how innovation and learning are shaped by—and shape—the economy started to gain prominence again from the 1960s onward, mainly through the writings of applied economists such as Christopher Freeman.[40] Although Schumpeter himself was a devoted free market liberal, much of the work that based itself on his ideas came to focus on limitations to the working of markets, particularly with respect to innovation and diffusion of technology, and what the government—in countries at different levels of development—might do to improve the economy in this respect.

What has happened in the area of theorizing in the last decade is that this agenda has been taken over by formal theorists. This has led to the creation of more complex models, incorporating technology and innovation, that arguably explain growth in a better way than before. These models are also more open in the sense that many different outcomes are possible, depending on what the key assumptions are. They also allow for more room for public policy. These new theories have, in turn, led to a new agenda for empirical research that is both more meaningful and more interesting than what we had before. However, the most important contribution that empirical work can make to theoretical work is not to test for the "truth" of these formal relationships but to improve the assumptions that theoreticians make use of.

While formal modeling in this area has greatly improved, other basic neoclassical features have been retained, including the idea of a "representative agent" that neoclassical theorists use when they construct their models. This implies that all agents (buyers and sellers) in the economy are treated as identical. In addition they are assumed to be "rational," to maximize their self-interest, and to be endowed with "perfect information." This necessarily runs counter to one of the most basic arguments of evolutionary reasoning—that economic agents are heterogeneous, and that it is this very difference that creates diversity and drives innovation. This is an area where more empirical work is needed, and one that potentially could be of great importance for formal theorizing.

However, to be able to respond to this challenge, empirical researchers have to go beyond approaches that essentially consist of filtering out heterogeneity. Arguably, to get a firm grasp on heterogeneity, one will need more case-oriented research of the type undertaken in many other disciplines, and frequently used by many of the grand economic masters of the past, including Adam Smith, Karl Marx, Alfred Marshall, and Joseph Schumpeter.[41]

1. See also my earlier paper, "Technology, Growth, and Policy: Theory, Evidence, and Interpretation," *Nordic Journal of Political Economy* 25, no. 1 (1999): 5–14.

2. For an overview see Luigi Pasinetti, *Growth and Income Distribution* (Cambridge: Cambridge University Press, 1974).

3. See Moses Abramovitz, "Resources and Output Trends in the United States since 1870," *American Economic Review* 46, no. 2 (May 1956): 5–23; and Edward F. Denison, *Why Growth Rates Differ: Post-War Experience in Nine Western Countries* (Washington, D.C.: Brookings Institution Press, 1967). A good overview of the research in this area is to be found in Angus Maddison, "Growth and Slowdown in Advanced Capitalist Economies: Techniques of Quantitative Assessment," *Journal of Economic Literature* 25, no. 2 (June 1987): 649–98.

4. Richard R. Nelson, "Aggregate Production Functions and Medium-Range Growth Projections," *American Economic Review* 54, no. 5 (September 1964): 575–606.

5. Alwyn Young, "The Tyranny of Numbers: Confronting the Statistical Realities of the East Asian Growth Experience," *Quarterly Journal of Economics* 110, no. 3 (August 1995): 641–80.

6. Robert E. Lucas, "Making a Miracle," *Econometrica* 61, no. 2 (March 1993): 251–72.

7. Hence, I use the notion *evolutionary* in a broad sense. In a more narrow sense the notion is also used to characterize a specific class of formal economic models inspired by the use of evolutionary models in biology. As in biology, these economic models operate with a set of competing "species," which in economics might be firms or technologies or both, and a selection environment that sets the rules for their survival and growth. The central reference here is Richard R. Nelson and Sidney G. Winter, *An Evolutionary Theory of Economic Change* (Cambridge, Mass.: Harvard University Press, 1982). For an overview and discussion of work in this area see Esben Sloth Andersen, *Evolutionary Economics: Post-Schumpeterian Contributions* (London: Pinter, 1994).

8. It is worth mentioning that the emphasis on historical analysis and technological change was quite widespread among German economists around the beginning of the twentieth century, particularly among the adherents of the so-called historical school, and that Schumpeter—although he never regarded himself as belonging to any school—was probably influenced by this. For his own view on the "historical school" in Germany and the controversies that followed in its wake, see Joseph Schumpeter, *History of Economic Analysis* (New York: Oxford University Press, 1954), Part IV, Chapter 4, Section 2.

9. Joseph Schumpeter, *The Theory of Economic Development* (Cambridge, Mass.: Harvard University Press, 1934; first German edition, 1911).

10. Nicholas Kaldor, "A Model of Economic Growth," *Economic Journal* 67 (December 1957): 591–624; Nicholas Kaldor, *Strategic Factors in Economic Development* (Ithaca, N.Y.: State School of Industrial and Labor Relations, Cornell University, 1967). Similar ideas, though in a more neoclassical framework, were proposed by Kenneth Arrow, "The Economic Implications of Learning by Doing," *Review of Economic Studies* 29, no. 3 (June 1962): 155–73.

11. Bengt Åke Lundvall, "Innovation as an Interactive Process: From User-Producer Interaction to the National System of Innovation," in Giovanni Dosi and others, *Technical Change and Economic Theory* (London: Pinter, 1988), pp. 349–69.

12. Nathan Rosenberg, "Learning by Using," in Nathan Rosenberg, *Inside the Black Box: Technology and Economics* (Cambridge: Cambridge University Press, 1982), pp. 120–40.

13. See Bengt Åke Lundvall, ed., *National Systems of Innovation: Towards a Theory of Innovation and Interactive Learning* (London: Pinter, 1992); Richard R. Nelson, ed., *National Innovation Systems: A Comparative Analysis* (Oxford, England: Oxford University Press, 1993); Charles Edquist, ed., *Systems of Innovation: Technologies, Institutions, and Organizations* (London: Pinter, 1997); Christopher Freeman, "The National System of Innovation in Historical Perspective," *Cambridge Journal of Economics* 19, no. 1 (1995): 5–24.

14. Alexander Gerschenkron, *Economic Backwardness in Historical Perspective* (Cambridge, Mass.: Belknap Press, 1962), p. 7.

15. Moses Abramovitz, "The Origins of the Post-War Catch-Up and Convergence Boom," in Jan Fagerberg, Bart Verspagen, and Nick von Tunzelman, eds., *The Dynamics of Technology, Trade, and Growth* (Aldershot, England: Elgar, 1994), pp. 21–52.

16. The pioneer in much of this was John Cornwall, who regressed variables assumed to reflect the scope for catch-up, investment, and endogenous technological progress (the so-called Verdoorn law) on GDP growth for a sample of OECD countries. See John Cornwall, "Diffusion, Convergence, and Kaldor's Law," *Economic Journal* 86 (June 1976): 307–14. Since then many studies of this type, including the scope for catch-up and some other conditioning variables as determinants of GDP and productivity growth, have been published. For overviews of this literature see Jan Fagerberg, "Technology and International Differences in Growth Rates," *Journal of Economic Literature* 32, no. 3 (September 1994): 1147–75; Jonathan Temple, "The New Growth Evidence," *Journal of Economic Literature* 37, no. 2 (March 1999): 112–56. In the more recent literature, such regression models have for some reason been dubbed "Barro-regressions" after Robert Barro, an economist who did not pioneer this type of research but picked it up at a rather late stage.

17. Although relevant, many applied studies did not include R&D or innovation performance, often with reference to lack of data (although this was not always entirely justified). For an exception to this trend see Jan Fagerberg, "A Technology Gap Approach to Why Growth Rates Differ," *Research Policy* 16, nos. 2–4 (August 1987): 87–99.

18. Bradford De Long, "Productivity Growth, Convergence, and Welfare," *American Economic Review* 78, no. 5 (December 1988): 1138–54.

19. Robert Summers and Alan Heston, "The Penn World Table (Mark 5): An Expanded Set of International Comparisons, 1950–1988," *Quarterly Journal of Economics* 106, no. 2 (May 1991): 327–68.

20. William J. Baumol, Sue Anne Batey Blackman, and Edward N. Wolff, *Productivity and American Leadership: The Long View* (Cambridge, Mass.: MIT Press, 1989).

21. Baumol, Blackman, and Wolff, *Productivity and American Leadership.*

22. Another reason might be that growth models assuming economies of scale may fail to produce a stable equilibrium. In fact, such models may easily, depending on the parameterization, predict explosive growth or, alternatively, no growth at all in the long run.

23. See Paul M. Romer, "Increasing Returns and Long-Run Growth," *Journal of Political Economy* 94, no. 5 (October 1986): 1002–37.

24. See the survey by Zvi Griliches, "The Search for R&D Spillovers," *Scandinavian Journal of Economics* 94, supplement (1992): S29–47.

25. Paul M. Romer, "Endogenous Technological Change," *Journal of Political Economy* 98, no. 5 (October 1990): S71–102. Models along similar lines were also suggested by a number of other authors. See for instance Pierre Aghion and Peter Howitt, "A Model of Growth through Creative Destruction," *Econometrica* 60, no. 2 (March 1992): 323–51; and Gene M. Grossman and Elhanan Helpman, *Innovation and Growth in the Global Economy* (Cambridge, Mass.: MIT Press, 1991).

26. Robert E. Lucas, "On the Mechanisms of Economic Development," *Journal of Monetary Economics* 22, no. 1 (July 1988): 3–42.

27. See Grossman and Helpman, *Innovation and Growth in the Global Economy*.

28. Charles I. Jones, "Time Series Tests of Endogenous Growth Models," *Quarterly Journal of Economics* 110, no. 4 (1995): 495–525; Charles I. Jones, "R&D-Based Models of Economic Growth," *Journal of Political Economy* 103, no. 2 (1995): 759–84. See also the overview and discussion of this issue in Temple, "The New Growth Evidence."

29. The method consists of selecting a set of basic variables, which are always included in the regression. Other possible variables are included one by one and the sensitivity of the result is then tested by including up to three other variables drawn from a large pool of possible explanatory factors. If the variable is always significant, the relationship is termed "robust." If it is insignificant in at least one case it is considered "fragile." See Ross Levine and David Renelt, "A Sensitivity Analysis of Cross-Country Growth Regressions," *American Economic Review* 82, no. 4 (September 1992): 942–63.

30. In a later study by Robert King and Ross Levine, the level of financial development of the country was added to the list of robust variables. See Robert King and Ross Levine, "Finance and Growth: Schumpeter Might Be Right?" *Quarterly Journal of Economics* 108, no. 3 (August 1993): 717–37.

31. Christopher D. Carrol and David N. Weil, "Saving and Growth: A Reinterpretation," *NBER Working Paper* no. 4470 (Cambridge, Mass.: National Bureau of Economic Research, 1993).

32. World Bank, *The East Asian Miracle: Economic Growth and Public Policy* (New York: Oxford University Press, 1993). In this report the bank argues that 60–90 percent of productivity growth of the so-called high-performing Asian economies can be explained by accumulation and thus that other "unconventional" factors were of relatively little importance. However, I have shown elsewhere (Aadne Cappelen and Jan Fagerberg, "East Asian Growth: A Critical Assessment," *Forum for Development Studies* no. 2 [1995]: 175–95) that this conclusion is not warranted. In fact, the models applied by the World Bank predict very poorly for the fast-growing countries of Asia! For a critical assessment of the World Bank's view see also Dani Rodrik, "King Kong Meets Godzilla: The World Bank and the East Asian Miracle," in Albert Fishlow and others, eds., *Miracle or Design? Lessons*

from the East Asian Experience, policy essay no. 11 (Washington, D.C.: Overseas Development Council, 1994), pp. 13–53.

33. See, for instance, Robert Wade, *Governing the Market: Economic Theory and the Role of Government in East Asian Industrialization* (Princeton, N.J.: Princeton University Press, 1990).

34. See the survey by Griliches, "The Search for R&D Spillovers."

35. See Adam B. Jaffe, "Real Effects of Academic Research," *American Economic Review* 79, no. 5 (December 1989): 957–70; Adam B. Jaffe, Manuel Trajtenberg, and Rebecca Henderson, "Geographic Localization of Knowledge Spillovers as Evidenced by Patent Citations," *Quarterly Journal of Economics* 108, no. 3 (August 1993): 557–98; Per B. Maurseth and Bart Verspagen, "Europe: One or Several Systems of Innovation," in Jan Fagerberg, Paolo Guerrieri, and Bart Verspagen, eds., *The Economic Challenge for Europe: Adapting to Innovation-Based Growth* (Aldershot, England: Elgar, 1999), pp. 149–74.

36. See David T. Coe and Elhanan Helpman, "International R&D Spillovers," *European Economic Review* 39, no. 5 (May 1995): 859–87.

37. The conclusion, then, would be that foreign R&D embodied in imports is the primary source of growth in most countries, particularly the developing ones, and that openness to trade is what is required if a country is going to benefit from the global process of innovation and diffusion. See Coe and Helpman, "International R&D Spillovers," and David T. Coe, Elhanan Helpman, and Alexander Hoffmaister, "North-South R&D Spillovers," *Economic Journal* 107 (January 1997): 134–49.

38. Maury Gittleman and Edward N. Wolff, "R&D Activity and Cross-Country Growth Comparisons," *Cambridge Journal of Economics* 19, no. 2 (March 1995): 189–207.

39. See Gittleman and Wolff, "R&D Activity and Cross-Country Growth Comparisons"; Jonathon Eaton and Samuel Kortum, "Trade in Ideas— Patenting and Productivity in the OECD," *Journal of International Economics* 40, nos. 1–2 (1996): 251–78; Jonathon Eaton, Eva Gutierrez, and Samuel Kortum, "European Technology Policy," *Economic Policy* no. 27 (October 1998): 405–38. Bart Verspagen argues that failure to take into account such differences in absorptive capacity across countries may in fact explain some of the conflicting evidence reported in the literature on the importance of other carriers of technology diffusion. See Bart Verspagen, "Estimating International Technology Spillovers Using Technology Flow Matrices," *Weltwirtschaftliches Archiv* 133, no. 2 (1997): 226–48.

40. See Christopher Freeman, *The Economics of Industrial Innovation,* (Harmondsworth, England: Penguin Books, 1974).

41. This does not, of course, invalidate the use of other methods that are currently in more use in economics. Arguably, empirical work will need to proceed at several levels, not in isolation, but in interaction.

PART II

TECHNOLOGY, TRADE AND STRUCTURAL CHANGE

[7]

Structural changes in international trade: who gains, who loses?

Jan Fagerberg

1 Introduction

Structural changes in international trade, and their consequences for different countries, have for a long time been the focus of interest of applied international economics. Relatively sophisticated methods have been developed to measure the effects on export performance of changes in the commodity and country composition of international trade.[1] But even so, it seems fair to say that much of this work has been of a purely descriptive character. The questions of why the commodity composition of international trade changes, how systematic these changes are, and why they turn out to have quite different consequences for different types of countries have received far less attention.

This paper focuses on these questions from a Schumpeterian perspective, emphasizing the role of international trade as the medium for the diffusion of technology and 'catch-up' processes between countries with different levels of economic and technological development. The next section outlines this theoretical perspective in more detail and analyses the structural changes in OECD trade between 1961 and 1983 from that angle. The data are then used to decompose the export performance of 18 OECD countries on the OECD market into effects of *structural changes in OECD trade, the ability to adapt the export structure* to these changes, and the *ability to compete for market shares within individual commodity groups*. In the final section of the paper, various economic, institutional and technological factors influencing these different aspects of export performance are discussed and tested.

2 Structural changes in OECD trade 1961–83

A theoretical perspective on structural change may be found in the works of Schumpeter (1934, 1939, 1947). According to his view, innovations tend to cluster in certain firms and industries, normally within the science-based and R&D-intensive sectors, from which they diffuse to other firms and industries. Since new products and technologies both fulfil new needs and substitute for older products and technologies, production and trade in new products and technologies tend to grow faster than for other products, causing the structure of production and trade to change. But even if Schumpeter's main work, *Business Cycles* (1939), was built on a careful study of the three most important capitalist countries of his time (the United States, the United Kingdom and Germany), Schumpeter did not analyse the international dimension of diffusion.

However, this extension was, as pointed out by Giersch (1981), very natural, and during the 1960s several authors (Posner (1961), Vernon (1966), Hirsch (1967) and others) began to use Schumpeterian concepts in studies of international trade. Generally, what these authors did was to add a spatial dimension to Schumpeter's theory, by assuming that innovations not only cluster in certain firms and industries, but that these firms and industries are located in certain countries (technological leaders), from which innovations diffuse to firms and industries in other countries through trade and other means of knowledge transfer.

Following this perspective, we should expect the fastest growing commodities in OECD trade in the post-war period to be relatively 'new' compared to other commodities and to originate in science-based, R&D-intensive industries or sectors of the economy. To test this, we have constructed a database on OECD trade for selected years from 1961 to 1983, consisting of all OECD countries for which data were available and disaggregated into 41 commodity groups.[2] Great care was taken to ensure that R&D-intensive products and products based on important, commercially successful innovations in the not-too-distant past were specified as separate products. More mature products,[3] on the other hand, such as raw materials, semi-finished products and a number of rather unsophisticated manufactures, were treated in a more aggregative way. Furthermore, in order to ensure that the data were comparable both across countries and over time, we had to take into account the fact that countries, mainly for industrial security reasons, have differing practices with regard to reporting data, and that the international trade classification (SITC) changes during the period of observation. This also put limitations on the level of aggregation.[4]

Like most trade studies, this study uses value data (OECD Trade Series C), the only type of data available on a sufficiently disaggregated level. It is often suggested that it would be preferable to use volume data instead of value data, but this is, as pointed out by Rotschild (1985), not always the case. There are two reasons for this. First, value data reflect better than volume data the effects of changes in export performance on the balance of trade. Second, volume data are problematic in cases where substantial technological changes occur, and become, for the very same reason, less reliable when the time span under consideration grows.

The classification of products according to R&D intensity (expenditures on R&D as a share in output or sales) was based on other studies, especially Kelly (1977), Aho and Rosen (1980) and OECD (1985). While the two earlier studies were based on US data only, the last one uses data for a group of OECD countries. However, with a few exceptions, these studies end up with rather similar rankings of commodities according to R&D intensity.[5] It should be noted, though, that a few products that were classified as R&D intensive in the two earlier studies, do not fulfil the requirements according to the last study. Even if this cannot be established with absolute certainty, it is probable that this difference refers as much to the difference in time span as to the difference in methodology between the two earlier and the last study. In our classification, the relevant products are typewriters and other (non-electronic) office machines, consumer electronics and road motor vehicles, products that, all other differences notwithstanding, have in common that by the 1970s they had entered the mature phase. Thus, we have chosen to regard these products as R&D intensive prior to, but not since, 1973.

Tables 1 and 2 rank growth of OECD imports by commodity in the periods 1961–73 and 1973–83, respectively, from highest growth to lowest growth. R&D-intensive commodities are marked with an 'H'.

The fastest-growing commodities in OECD trade between 1961 and 1973 may roughly be divided into three groups. First, a group of R&D-intensive commodities related to relatively recent innovations in *electronics* (semiconductors, computers, telecommunications, consumer electronics and scientific instruments). Second, some R&D-intensive *chemicals* related to innovations in the interwar and post-war periods (plastics – synthetic fibres – and pharmaceuticals). Third, commodities related to the diffusion of the lifestyle and pattern of consumption that developed in the United States in the first half of this century ('*the American way of life*') and to the rapid growth in private consumption in this period (cars, electrical household equipment, consumer electronics (already mentioned), clothing and furniture). A common characteristic of the two latter commodities in this period is the introduction of new materials in the process of production (synthetic fibres and light metals).

Booming oil prices during the 1970s caused high growth in OECD trade in oil and gas and other energy-intensive products between 1973 and 1983. But *electronics and to some degree chemicals continued to be strong growth sectors in OECD trade*. It should be noted, though, that the rate of growth in consumer electronics, now in its mature phase, declined markedly both in absolute terms and compared with other commodities. The same is true for non-electronic office machines, cars and electrical household equipment. What happened, probably, is that many commodities, especially those linked to the diffusion of 'the American way of life', during the 1970s entered the mature phase. However, the Schumpeterian suggestion, that R&D-intensive commodities linked to relatively recent innovations grow much faster than other commodities, holds good in both periods (see Table 3).

In summary, this section shows that OECD trade during the 1960s and 1970s underwent radical structural changes. Generally, commodities from R&D-intensive industries based on relatively recent innovations increased their share of OECD trade at the expense of raw materials, semi-finished products and mature manufactured products. In the following, we are going to discuss the relation between these changes and the export performance of different OECD countries during this period.

3 Structural change and export performance

Export performance is normally measured through changes in market shares. A country's share of the world market may change for different reasons.

First, the market shares for individual commodities on the world market may change. This is often referred to as changes caused by competitiveness, even if it may be objected that this implies a rather narrow view on what competitiveness is all about.

Second, the total market share may change even if market shares for individual commodities remain constant, because structural changes in international trade affect countries differently depending on their specialization patterns. Such changes in the total market share of a country are often referred to as changes caused by structural change or commodity composition.

Table 1   Growth of OECD imports, 1961–73 (yearly average value, %)

Rank	R&D	Commodity	Growth Rate
1		Furniture (39)	26.54
2	H	Consumer electronics (31)	24.87
3	H	Semiconductors (28)	23.77
4	H	Road motor vehicles (34)	23.18
5		Clothing (40)	22.40
6	H	Computers and peripherals (27)	21.15
7	H	Typewriters and office machines (26)	21.14
8	H	Plastic materials (20)	21.07
9	H	Telecommunications (29)	19.08
10	H	Scientific instruments, photographic supplies, watches and clocks (33)	18.84
11	H	Pharmaceuticals (18)	18.83
12		Organic chemicals (15)	18.43
13		Domestic electrical equipment (32)	18.41
14		Pumps and centrifuges (25)	18.33
15		Other engineering products (37)	18.33
16	H	Power-generating machinery (22)	17.92
17	H	Machinery for production and distribution of electricity (30)	17.72
18		Feeding-stuff for animals (5)	17.06
19		Heating and cooling equipment (24)	16.92
20		Other industrial products (41)	16.45
21		Manufactures of metal (38)	16.44
22		Oil and gas (14)	15.86
23		Dyestuffs, colouring materials (17)	15.82
24		Fish and fish preparations (3)	14.98
25		Other chemicals (21)	14.90
26		Wood and wood manufactures (7)	14.71
27		Animals, meat and meat preparations (1)	14.65
28		Aluminium (12)	14.05
29		Iron, steel and ferro alloys (11)	14.04
30	H	Aircraft (35)	13.67
31	H	Inorganic chemicals (16)	13.66
32		Ships and boats (incl. oil rigs) (36)	13.52
33		Machinery for special industries or processes (23)	13.32
34		Pulp and paper (8)	11.19
35		Other products based on natural resources (13)	11.06
36		Skins and leather manufactures (6)	10.95
37		Dairy products and eggs (2)	10.76
38		Cereals and cereal preparations (4)	10.32
39		Fertilizers (19)	10.27
40		Iron ore (10)	9.92
41		Textiles (9)	9.82

In comparison:
All commodities: 14.49.

Table 2   Growth of OECD imports, 1973–83 (yearly average value, %)

Rank	R&D	Commodity	Growth Rate
1	H	Computers and peripherals (27)	21.30
2		Oil and gas (14)	19.72
3	H	Semiconductors (28)	15.64
4	H	Aircraft (35)	15.36
5		Organic chemicals (15)	14.78
6		Aluminium (12)	14.57
7	H	Telecommunications (29)	14.31
8		Other chemicals (21)	13.88
9	H	Scientific instruments, photographic supplies, watches and clocks (33)	13.14
10		Other industrial products (41)	13.04
11	H	Plastic materials (20)	12.94
12		Furniture (39)	12.63
13		Fertilizers (19)	12.55
14		Clothing (40)	12.44
15		Road motor vehicles (34)	12.32
16	H	Pharmaceuticals (18)	12.10
17	H	Machinery for production and distribution of electricity (30)	11.91
18	H	Inorganic chemicals (16)	11.80
19	H	Power-generating machinery (22)	11.52
20		Consumer electronics (31)	11.36
21		Fish and fish preparations (3)	11.31
22		Pumps and centrifuges (25)	11.06
23		Domestic electrical equipment (32)	10.86
24		Pulp and paper (8)	10.16
25		Manufactures of metal (38)	9.65
26		Dairy products and eggs (2)	9.47
27		Dyestuffs, colouring materials (17)	9.17
28		Other engineering products (37)	9.06
29		Other products based on natural resources (13)	8.18
30		Heating and cooling equipment (24)	8.09
31		Feeding-stuff for animals (5)	8.08
32		Machinery for special industries or processes (23)	7.39
33		Iron, steel and ferro alloys (11)	6.35
34		Skins and leather manufactures (6)	5.96
35		Cereals and cereal preparations (4)	5.32
36		Textiles (9)	5.16
37		Iron ore (10)	4.64
38		Wood and wood manufactures (7)	4.33
39		Animals, meat and meat preparations (1)	4.17
40		Ships and boats (incl. oil rigs) (36)	3.85
41		Typewriters and office machines (26)	0.38

In comparison:
All commodities: 11.43.

Table 3   Test of differences in growth rates between R&D-intensive commodities and other commodities

	1961–73		1973–83	
	R&D	REST	R&D	REST
Number	13	28	10	31
Growth	19.1	15.0	14.0	9.4
F-test (1, 39)	13, 27		11.03	
	(*)		(*)	

* denotes significance of F-test at the 1% level.

Third, changes in the export structure of a country may increase or decrease a country's market share on the world market depending on how well these changes correspond to the changes in world trade. This may be referred to as changes in the market share caused by a country's ability to adapt its export structure to changes in the composition of world trade.

In the following, we will calculate the importance of these three effects. The method is a version of the so-called 'constant market shares analysis' (CMS), which, however, differs from the version commonly used, that of Leamer and Stern (1970), in several respects.[6] Contrary to Leamer and Stern, we are concerned with the change in the market share for exports, not export growth, and, since the purpose of the investigation is the consequences of long-run changes in the commodity composition of OECD trade, we do not calculate separate 'commodity composition' and 'country composition' effects. Furthermore, we allow for a separate 'adaptability' effect, an effect which Leamer and Stern include in the other effects in a rather arbitrary way. The following symbols will be used:

X_i = country A's export of commodity i;
M_i = the market's import of commodity i;
a_i = country A's market share for commodity i;
b_i = commodity i's share of the market;
m = country A's market share for all commodities;

so that:

$$a_i = \frac{X_i}{M_i} \tag{1}$$

$$b_i = \frac{M_i}{\sum_i M_i} \tag{2}$$

$$m = \frac{\sum_i X_i}{\sum_i M_i} \tag{3}$$

By substituting (1) – (2) in (3) :

$$m = \frac{\sum_i \left(\frac{X_i}{M_i} \cdot M_i\right)}{\sum_i M_i} = \sum_i \left[\frac{X_i}{M_i} \cdot \frac{M_i}{(\sum_i M_i)}\right]$$

$$m = \sum_i a_i b_i$$

(4)

Let superscript (0, 1) denote two points in time:

$$m^0 = \sum_i a_i^0 b_i^0 \tag{5}$$

$$m^1 = \sum_i a_i^1 b_i^1 \tag{6}$$

By subtraction of (5) from (6) (Δ denotes difference):

$$\Delta m = \sum_i a_i^1 b_i^1 - \sum_i a_i^0 b_i^0$$

$$\Delta m = \sum_i (a_i^0 + \Delta a_i)(b_i^0 + \Delta b_i) - \sum_i a_i^0 b_i^0$$

$$\Delta m = \sum_i (\Delta a_i\, b_i^0 + \Delta b_i\, a_i^0 + \Delta a_i\, \Delta b_i)$$

$$\Delta m = \underset{\text{(I)}}{\sum_i \Delta a_i\, b_i^0} + \underset{\text{(II)}}{\sum_i \Delta b_i\, a_i^0} + \underset{\text{(III)}}{\sum_i \Delta a_i\, \Delta b_i}$$

(7)

The first effect (I) is the changes in market shares for individual products weighted by the commodity composition of the market in the initial year (*market share effect*), while the second (II) is the changes in the commodity composition of the market weighted by the country's market shares in the initial year (*commodity composition effect*). The third effect (III) is the product of the changes in the market shares for individual products and the changes in the commodity composition of the market. This effect shows the degree of correlation between the changes in market shares and the changes in the composition of the market, and we will therefore label it the *adaptability effect*.[7] The interpretation of the latter effect may be understood quite intuitively, but we will nevertheless give the following proof.

Lemma: The adaptability effect measures the correlation (covariance (cov)) between the changes in the market shares for individual products and the commodity composition of the market (number of commodities: $i = 1, \ldots, n$).

Proof :

$$\text{Cov}(\Delta a, \Delta b) = \frac{1}{n} \sum_i \left[\Delta a_i - \left(\frac{\sum_i \Delta a_i}{n}\right)\right]\left[\Delta b_i - \left(\frac{\sum_i \Delta b_i}{n}\right)\right] \tag{8}$$

$$\text{Cov} = \frac{1}{n} \sum_i \left[\Delta a_i - \left(\frac{\sum_i \Delta a_i}{n} \right) \right] \Delta b_i \quad \text{(since } \sum_i \Delta b_i = 0\text{)}$$

$$\text{Cov} = \frac{1}{n} \sum_i \Delta a_i \, \Delta b_i - \frac{1}{n} \sum_i \left[\left(\frac{\sum_i \Delta a_i}{n} \right) \Delta b_i \right]$$

$$\text{Cov} = \frac{1}{n} \sum_i \Delta a_i \, \Delta b_i - \frac{1}{n} \left(\frac{\sum_i \Delta a_i}{n} \right) \left(\sum_i \Delta b_i \right)$$

$$n \cdot \text{Cov} = \sum_i \Delta a_i \, \Delta b_i \qquad\qquad (9)$$

The calculations were carried out for 18 OECD countries and the periods 1961–73 and 1973–83, using 1961 (for 1961–73) and 1973 (for 1973–83) as base years. As in the previous section, the data were taken from OECD Trade Series C.[8] The commodity breakdown is the same as earlier, but we chose to exclude oil and gas from the calculations, because otherwise the calculations for the post-1973 period would have been totally dominated by the growth in oil prices. The results are given in Tables 4 and 5.

Generally, structural changes in OECD trade had quite important consequences for the export performance of the OECD countries. The commodity composition effect was especially important for some of the most industrialized countries of the sample,[9]

Table 4   Decomposition of changes in market shares, 1961–73

Country	Commodity Composition	Market Shares	Adaptation	Total
USA	3.51	−18.58	−1.06	−16.13
Japan	22.11	61.11	33.99	117.21
Germany	27.31	6.49	−11.58	22.22
France	8.45	35.92	−8.16	36.21
UK	19.79	−17.60	−18.32	−16.13
Italy	19.24	16.23	−7.94	27.54
Canada	−16.20	−7.32	16.38	−7.14
Austria	4.84	−6.16	−3.90	−5.21
Belgium	1.22	29.42	−0.60	30.08
Denmark	5.75	−15.72	−3.25	−13.21
Netherlands	−1.16	39.51	−5.85	32.51
Norway	−6.79	14.03	−0.18	7.06
Sweden	7.70	−1.03	−3.11	3.56
Switzerland	19.23	−4.64	−12.29	2.29
Finland	−11.76	−16.23	4.38	−23.60
Ireland	−2.42	1.45	−2.39	−3.36
Portugal	−11.33	68.09	3.30	53.46
Spain	−19.06	52.68	8.93	42.54

Table 5   Decomposition of changes in market shares, 1973–83

Country	Commodity Composition	Market Shares	Adaptation	Total
USA	4.18	−8.49	0.86	−3.46
Japan	9.68	42.25	8.63	60.55
Germany	5.36	−11.82	−1.62	−8.09
France	−0.28	−8.34	−1.16	−9.78
UK	4.12	−9.90	−0.93	−6.72
Italy	6.90	15.49	−6.81	15.57
Canada	1.16	3.77	−1.66	3.26
Austria	−4.79	19.54	−1.51	13.24
Belgium	−2.17	−15.89	−0.66	−18.72
Denmark	−8.53	4.01	−4.79	−9.31
Netherlands	−2.95	−2.22	0.96	−4.21
Norway	−3.43	−25.56	1.73	−27.25
Sweden	−1.50	−13.49	−2.44	−17.43
Switzerland	7.14	2.76	−5.16	4.74
Finland	−8.10	2.54	−1.24	6.79
Ireland	−9.08	39.64	16.38	46.94
Portugal	−6.16	8.50	1.41	3.74
Spain	−1.88	25.83	0.92	24.87

for which it contributed positively, and for some of the least industrialized countries of the sample, for which it contributed negatively. It did also contribute negatively for some industrialized countries with a relatively mature industrial structure dominated by production of raw materials and semi-finished goods.

However, even if the commodity composition effect was important, and in some cases decisive, for most countries the market share effect mattered most. The general picture was that Japan, joined by some of the least industrialized countries of the sample, won market shares within individual commodity groups at the expense of some of the more industrialized ones. The adaptability effect was generally of less importance than the other effects. But it was nonetheless quite important in some cases, especially for Japan and some of the least industrialized countries of the sample, for which it contributed positively. In general, for the least industrialized countries, negative commodity composition effects tended to be outweighed by positive market share and adaptability effects.

After 1973, the commodity composition and adaptability effects became somewhat less important compared with the market share effect, but the general picture was the same in both periods.

As noted, the calculations were carried out using export data for individual countries and import data for the OECD area as a whole. Since data on exports and imports as, for instance, country A's exports of commodity *i* to country B and country B's imports of commodity *i* from country A, generally differ, the resulting calculations will not be totally consistent. Alternatively, we could have constructed the export data for individual countries to the OECD from the imports of all other OECD countries. This would have given consistent, but not necessarily more reliable, results. However, to test the results for the way data were handled, we repeated the calculations on a database constructed from import data only. The results were not qualitatively different from the ones presented here, and are therefore not reported.

4 Explaining effects of structural change

What remains to be examined is to what degree these effects can be explained with reference to technological, economic and institutional factors that differ between countries. In section 2 of this paper it was postulated, and subsequently verified, that demand generally grows faster for new products and technologies originating in R&D-intensive industries and firms. Thus, following this (Schumpeterian) perspective, we should expect structural changes in international trade to be more favourable for countries with a high level of innovative activity and R&D than for other countries.

Vernon (1966), building on earlier work by Linder (1961), has developed this argument further by relating innovation to various economic aspects, such as the level of income in the country and the size of the market. A high level of income in a country, it is argued, implies a sophisticated demand structure, which in turn is assumed to feed back to the structure of production, giving the country a comparative advantage in 'new' sophisticated goods. Furthermore, Vernon argues that since many such goods are produced under conditions of economics of scale, countries with access to large domestic markets should also be more likely to develop a comparative advantage in such goods than other countries. Thus, following these arguments, structural changes in international trade should be expected to affect countries with high levels of income and access to large domestic markets favourably.

However, even if structural changes in world trade in general favour countries with a high economic and technological level of development, it does not follow that these countries also are best placed when it comes to competing for market shares within individual commodity groups or adapting their export structure to the changing composition of demand. On the contrary, it is often suggested (Posner 1961, Gerschenkron 1962 and others) that countries on a comparatively low level of economic and technological development for various reasons are better placed in this respect (the 'latecomer' hypothesis). Following this argument, latecomers have the opportunity of building up new competitive export sectors, and increasing market shares within individual commodity groups, by imitating technologies developed elsewhere and by exploiting cost advantages. If correct, we should expect a negative relation between the level of economic and technological development and the adaptability and market share effects. But, as pointed out by several writers (Cornwall 1976; Abramowitz 1979), building new production capacity and skills is not costless. Following this, we should expect a positive relation between the adaptation and market share effects and the mobilization of resources for growth and structural change, such as investments in production capacity and increases in the level of skills and innovative efforts.

Olson (1982) has developed the 'latecomer' hypothesis further by extending it to the institutional setting. According to this argument, institutional stability favours the development of narrowly based interest groups, groups which oppose, often with some success, structural changes that affect their members negatively, even if these changes would have increased social efficiency and income in the country. If correct, we should expect a negative relation between the adaptability effect and institutional stability. Another view, put forward by Katzenstein (1985) and others, relates differences in institutional flexibility towards structural change to differences in size. Small countries, it is argued, are because of their vulnerability forced to be more adaptive to changes in the international environment than large countries.

In the following, we are going to test the hypotheses outlined above. What we will do is to regress the effects calculated in the previous section on proxy variables related to hypotheses under test, using ordinary least squares. Since Japan is known to be a special case, the hypotheses are tested both with and without a dummy for Japan. If the sign of the estimated coefficient is the opposite of what should be expected, or not significantly different from zero in a two-tailed test, the hypothesis is rejected, otherwise not. Thus, the test should only be regarded as an attempt to discriminate between hypotheses that are supported by the data, and hypotheses that are not.

A major problem in the test was to find reliable indicators for the explanatory factors discussed above, especially those related to technology. For the level of technological development, we used two indicators: civil R&D as a percentage of gross national product (R&D) and a patent based measure (Patenting). The problems of comparing patenting across countries are discussed elsewhere (Soete 1981; Fagerberg 1987). Suffice it to say that these problems are reduced as far as possible by using patents filed abroad only (external patents),[10] and by adjusting for differences in size and degree of outwardness between countries. For growth in innovative effort, we had to rely on growth in external patenting only, because annual R&D statistics were not available for the majority of countries and time spans. For the level of economic development, we used GDP per capita in constant 1980 US dollars (GDP per cap.), and for size the number of inhabitants (Population). Since capital data were not available for all countries, we used gross investments as a share of GDP (Investments) as a proxy for growth in productive capacity. Furthermore, we included growth in relative unit labour costs and growth in relative export unit values in the investigation, to capture the familiar assumed negative effect of increasing costs or prices on market shares for individual products.[11] For institutional stability (Stability), we used an index borrowed from Choi (1983) which reflects the number of years since the consolidation of 'modern leadership'/beginning of economic modernization, adjusted for 'disruptions'. The results are listed in Tables 6 and 7.

The results support the hypothesis of a positive relation between the commodity composition effect and innovative effort measured through patents or R&D, while there is less support for the hypothesis of a positive relation between the commodity composition effect and the level of income measured through GDP per capita, even if it cannot be rejected on a 20% level of significance. Thus, the results seem to lend more support to Schumpeterian views on structural change, emphasizing the importance of innovative effort, than to the demand-led view on structural change advocated by Linder and Vernon. But there is some support, especially after 1973, for the hypothesis of a positive relation between the commodity composition effect and the possibilities of realizing economies of scale through a large domestic market.

Table 6   Regression results

	Level or Share Variables						Growth Variables		
	Stability	R&D	Patenting	GDP per cap.	Population	Investment	Patenting	Rel. export values	Rel. unit labour cost
No. of observations	16	18	17	18	18	18	17	17	15
Commodity effect (1)		13.71 (3.02) *	7.39 (2.87) **	1.61 (1.38)	4.51 (1.80) ***				
Commodity effect (2)		6.06 (3.26) *	3.11 (2.45) **	0.51 (1.22)	3.37 (4.42) *				
Market share effect (1)		−6.61 (−0.58)	−6.74 (−1.18)	−5.91 (−2.90) *		2.22 (1.21)	2.12 (1.44)	−4.03 (−0.78)	9.29 (2.66) **
Market share effect (2)		−10.79 (−1.47)	−6.68 (−1.42)	−3.44 (−2.99) *		1.80 (1.66)	2.89 (1.94) ***	−3.28 (−1.36)	−1.63 (−0.63)
Adaptation effect (1)	−0.35 (−2.09) ***	−4.38 (−0.93)	−3.91 (−1.48)	−1.43 (−1.44)	1.26 (0.54)	1.39 (1.93) ***	2.25 (4.81) *		
Adaptation effect (2)	−0.12 (−1.47)	1.04 (−0.48)	−2.38 (−1.90) ***	−0.67 (−1.83) ***	−0.31 (−0.30)	0.68 (2.44) **	0.40 (0.89)		

Notes:
The numbers in brackets below the estimates are *t*-statistics.
One star denotes significance of test at the 1% level, two stars at the 5% level and three stars at the 10% level in a two-tailed test.

Table 7   Regression results (with Japan dummy)

	Level or Share Variables						Growth Variables		
	Stability	R&D	Patenting	GDP per cap.	Population	Investment	Patenting	Rel. export values	Rel. unit labour cost
No. of observations	16	18	17	18	18	18	17	17	15
Commodity effect (1)		12.73 (2.77) **	7.48 (3.10) *	1.97 (1.77) ***	3.69 (1.37)				6.85 (2.09) ***
Commodity effect (2)		5.24 (2.78) **	2.77 (2.33) **	0.59 (1.55)	3.03 (3.73) *				0.45 (0.22)
Market share effect (1)		-10.92 (-1.02)	-6.49 (-1.31)	-5.31 (-2.70) **		0.44 (0.19)	-1.44 (-0.59)	2.66 (0.48)	
Market share effect (2)		-17.18 (-2.99) *	-8.41 (-2.17) **	-3.21 (-3.20) *		0.74 (0.61)	1.72 (1.08)	-1.92 (-0.84)	
Adaptation effect (1)	-0.09 (-0.59)	-7.48 (-2.60) **	-3.73 (-2.21) **	-0.88 (-1.24)	-2.20 (-1.05)	-0.02 (-0.02)	1.50 (1.84) ***		
Adaptation effect (2)	-0.07 (-0.73)	-2.32 (-1.12)	-2.79 (-2.52) **	-0.61 (-1.79)	-1.06 (-1.05)	0.56 (1.67)	0.08 (0.17)		

Notes:
The numbers in brackets below the estimates are *t*-statistics.
One star denotes significance of test at the 1% level, two stars at the 5% level and three stars at the 10% level in a two-tailed test.

Regarding the growth of market shares within individual commodity groups, the results support the latecomer hypothesis of a negative relation between the market share effect and the level of economic development, more so than in the case of the related hypothesis of a negative relation between the market share effect and the level of technological development.[12] Growth in relative prices or costs does not seem to influence market shares in individual commodity groups, except for costs in the first period, and then with the opposite sign to what should be expected.[13] There is not much support for the hypotheses of a positive relation between the market share effect and efforts such as investments and patent growth (especially not when a dummy for Japan is introduced).

At a first glance, the most significant factor affecting adaptability seems to be investments, but this result vanishes when a dummy for Japan is introduced. However, there is some support for the latecomer hypothesis of a negative relation between adaptability and the level of economic and technological development, especially when patenting is used as the independent variable and a dummy for Japan is included. The correlation between adaptability and growth in patents is positive, as expected, but significant in the first period only. Furthermore, in Table 6, the estimated correlation coefficients between adaptation and stability are negative in both periods, as Olson suggests, and significantly different from zero at the 10 and 20% level, respectively. But when a dummy for Japan is introduced, the estimated coefficients are no longer statistically different from zero. Furthermore, contrary to what is sometimes suggested, there does not seem to be any relation whatsoever between adaptability and differences in size between countries.

5   Concluding remarks

This paper shows that the structure of OECD trade between 1961 and 1983 changed quite radically. The main source of these changes was the creation and subsequent diffusion of new products and technologies originating in R&D-intensive industries and firms. These changes favoured countries with a high level of institutionalized innovative activity, measured through R&D or patent statistics. However, this process did at the same time favour countries at a lower level of economic and technological development, by allowing them to catch up and increase market shares through structural change (adaptation), imitation of technologies developed elsewhere and exploitation of cost advantages. In general, the latter type of effects outweighed the former. The structural changes in OECD trade in this period were least favourable for countries with high levels of income and costs, but with low levels of innovative activity.

Appendix

Sources
Trade statistics:
OECD Trade Series C and national sources (Finland and Japan, 1961)

Real GDP per capita (1980 market prices in US dollars):
IMF International Financial Statistics

External patent applications:
OECD/STIIU Data Bank and World International Property Organization (WIPO): Industrial Property Statistics

The R&D data are estimates based on the following sources:
OECD Science and Technology Indicators, Basic Statistical Series (Vol. B, 1982 and Recent Results 1984), UNESCO Statistical Yearbook and various UNESCO surveys on resources devoted to R&D.

Military R&D expenditures were, following the OECD, assumed to be negligible in all countries except the United States, France, Germany, Sweden and the United Kingdom. The R&D data for these countries were adjusted downward according to OECD estimates. The estimates were taken from *OECD (1983), Directorate for Science, Technology and Industry: The Problems of Estimating Defence and Civil GERD in Selected OECD Member Countries (DSTI/SPR/83-2)*. For other countries, civil and total R&D as a percentage of GDP were assumed to be identical.

Data on population and export shares in GDP were taken from:
OECD Historical Statistics 1960–1983, *OECD National Accounts* (various editions), *IMF Supplement on Output Statistics*, *UN Monthly Bulletin of Statistics* (various editions) and *Statistical Yearbook of the Republic of China 1984*.

Growth in relative unit labour costs:
IMF Financial Statistics

Growth in relative export unit values:
UN International Trade Statistics Yearbook

Methods
Growth rates are calculated as geometric averages for the periods 1960–73 and 1970–83, or the nearest period for which data exist. Levels and shares are calculated as arithmetic averages for the periods 1960–73 and 1974–83, or the nearest period for which data exist.

Table A1   Classification of products

		SITC. Rev. 1	SITC. Rev. 2
101	*Products based on natural resources*		
1	Animals, meat, and meat preparations	00, 01, 091.3, 411.3	00, 01, 091.3, 411.3
2	Dairy products and eggs	02	02
3	Fish and fish preparations	03, 411.1	03, 411.1
4	Cereals and cereal preparations	04	04
5	Feeding-stuff for animals	08	08
6	Skins and leather manufactures	21, 61	21, 61
7	Wood and wood manufactures	24, 63	24, 63
8	Pulp and paper	25, 64	25, 64
9	Textiles	26, 65	26, 65
10	Iron ore	281	281
11	Iron, steel and ferro alloys	67	67
12	Aluminium	684	684
13	Other products based on natural resources	05, 06, 07, 091.4, 099, 11, 12, 22, 23, 27, 282, 283, 284, 285, 286, 29, 32, 35, 42, 43, 62, 66, 681, 682, 683, 685, 686, 687, 688, 689	05, 06, 07, 091.4, 098, 11, 12, 22, 23, 27, 282, 286, 287 (−:32), 288, 289, 29, 32, 35, 42, 43, 62, 66, 681, 682, 683, 685, 686, 687, 688, 689, 699.9
102	*Oil and Gas*		
14	Oil and gas	33, 34	33 (−:5.2), 34
103	*Chemicals*		
15	Organic chemicals	512	51
16	Inorganic chemicals	513, 514	522, 523, 287.32
17	Dyestuffs, colouring materials	53	53
18	Pharmaceuticals	54	54
19	Fertilizers	56	56
20	Plastic materials	581.1:2	582, 583, 893.91:2
21	Other chemicals	515, 52, 55, 57, 581.3:9, 59	335.2, 524, 55, 57, 584, 585, 59, 894.63, 899.39, 951.66
104	*Engineering, electronics and transport equipment*		
22	Power-generating machinery	711	711, 712, 713, 714, 718

Table A1 (cont.)

		SITC. Rev. 1	SITC. Rev. 2
23	Machinery for special industries or processes	712, 715, 717, 718, 719.3:5:8	72, 73 (–:7.32), 744, 745.1
24	Heating and cooling equipment	719.1	741 (–:31)
25	Pumps and centrifuges	719.2	742, 743
26	Typewriters and office machines	714.1:9	751.1:81:88, 759.11:15
27	Computers and peripherals	714.2:3	751.2, 752, 759.9
28	Semiconductors	729.3	776
29	Telecommunications	724.9	764 (–:99)
30	Machinery for production and distribution of electricity	722, 723, 729.9	771, 772, 716, 773, 778.8 (–:5), 737.32, 741.31
31	Consumer electronics	724.1:2, 891.1	761, 762, 763, 764.99
32	Domestic electrical equipment	725	775
33	Scientific instruments, photographic supplies, watches and clocks	726, 729.5:7, 861, 862, 864	751.82, 759.19, 774, 778.85, 87, 88 (–:3)
34	Road motor vehicles	732	78 (–:5(–:1:39))
35	Aircraft	734	792 (–:83)
36	Ships and boats (incl. oil rigs)	735	793
37	Other engineering products	719.6:7:9, 729.1:2: 4:6, 731, 733	745.2, 749, 778 (–:8), 785.2:31, 786, 791
105	*Traditional industrial products*		
38	Manufactures of metal	69, 719.4, 812.1:3	69 (–:9.9), 812.1
39	Furniture	82	82
40	Clothing	84	655.3, 658.98, 84 (–:8.21)
41	Industrial products	812.2:4, 83, 85, 863 891.2:4:8:9, 892, 893, 894, 895, 896, 897, 899, 9	792.83, 812.2:4, 83, 848.21, 851, 883, 892, 893 (–:91:92), 894 (–:63), 895, 896, 897, 898, 899.1:3 (–:9) :4:6:7:8:9, 9
106	*Sum of all products*		
42	Sum of all products		

Notes:
1. The abbreviations should be read as the following examples show:
   891.l:3 should be read as 891.1 + 891.3.
   899.3 (–:9) should be read as 899.3 – 899.39.
2. Commodity no. 14 (oil and gas) was not included in the calculations.

Table A2   Data used in regressions

Patents	R&D	Investment	GDP per cap.	RUV[a]	RULC[b]	Patent growth	Population
10291.80	1.71	18.12	9.93	−0.90	−3.18	3.47	198.71
4373.65	1.82	17.94	12.23	2.01	1.35	−5.38	222.59
1569.83	1.61	32.61	4.92	−3.34	2.08	18.22	99.92
2117.26	2.11	31.36	8.32	−2.59	−2.04	0.40	114.92
5292.36	1.63	24.89	8.05	−3.09	2.04	3.47	59.29
3182.67	2.21	21.14	11.10	−4.75	−0.62	−7.50	61.33
3127.67	1.54	22.68	7.21	−0.18	−0.79	4.07	49.55
1725.23	1.57	21.98	10.40	−1.38	−0.60	−5.58	53.28
2842.43	1.64	18.34	7.21	−0.94	−2.28	0.98	54.93
1323.77	1.76	18.40	8.86	1.91	2.77	−6.58	55.90
1086.82	0.78	21.28	4.40	−1.60	1.20	3.86	52.67
676.67	0.91	19.68	6.11	−0.03	1.02	−3.66	56.13
1075.52	1.15	21.91	7.94	−1.36	−0.87	4.62	20.41
716.69	1.15	22.46	10.84	0.90	1.05	−4.70	23.55
1598.29	0.48	26.71	5.71	−1.25	0.73	3.92	7.32
1082.27	1.02	25.44	8.59	−1.71	−0.25	−5.60	7.51
912.69	1.20	21.64	6.78	−0.75	−0.15	1.40	9.58
430.63	1.37	20.46	9.79	−1.10	−3.29	−6.98	9.83
1630.79	0.73	23.78	8.89	0.06	−0.19	4.14	4.84
1269.69	1.01	19.94	11.22	−1.77	−1.73	−4.64	5.10
2101.80	1.91	25.00	7.76	−0.37	1.88	0.82	12.60
1202.29	1.95	20.22	10.36	1.22	−1.01	−6.44	13.94
653.86	0.91	28.38	8.59	−0.50	1.61	3.01	3.79
575.65	1.32	30.06	12.36	2.38	2.15	−6.64	4.06
4997.68	1.03	23.40	10.32	0.20	−0.05	3.26	7.87
3104.83	1.78	20.04	13.03	−0.46	−2.25	−5.86	8.28
11868.32	2.35	27.96	13.00	1.57	0.83	3.43	6.06
7287.42	2.34	23.06	15.35	0.75	1.49	−8.02	6.34
810.43	0.56	26.45	6.48	−0.13	−0.59	9.27	4.61
1184.37	1.09	26.28	9.33	1.60	0.32	4.08	4.75
204.55	0.62	20.47	3.58	0.18	na	9.44	2.90
163.88	0.80	26.34	4.84	−0.29	na	−4.26	3.31
na	0.29	23.97	1.39	na	na	na	9.10
na	0.31	27.70	2.18	na	na	na	9.80
347.01	0.20	21.16	3.44	0.77	na	6.18	32.85
253.96	0.37	20.76	4.98	−2.30	na	−5.22	36.78

Notes:
[a] Growth in relative unit export values.
[b] Growth in relative unit labour costs.

For the order of countries, see Table 5. (The first observation is the United States in the first period, the second the United States in the second period, the third Japan in the first period and so on.)

The Choi index of institutional stability (same order as above, one observation per country): 76.54, 20.82, 46.07, 43.56, 90.08, 43.60, 65.26, 35.95, 61.19, 57.60, 63.21, 56.94, 59.90, 63.24, 40.26, 37.34, na, na.

Notes

1. For overviews, see Leamer and Stern (1970) and Fagerberg and Sollie (1987).
2. The database used in the study was constructed jointly by Bent Dalum, University of Aalborg, and the author. The calculations were carried out by Leif Seerup at the University of Aalborg Data Center.
3. By mature products we mean products where both product characteristics and production technology are fairly standardized.
4. See Table A1 in the appendix for further details regarding the commodity classification.
5. Pavitt (1982) has developed an entirely different approach to ranking according to technology intensity. Instead of ranking commodities according to R&D intensity, he proposes to rank them according to the importance of technological competition, measured through the statistical significance of the correlation between per capita exports and per capita US patents for different countries within the same commodity group. This method has the disadvantage that it does not allow for the inclusion of the United States in the investigation. However, the results are not very different from the OECD study, with the exception that Pavitt includes a larger part of the engineering sector (and excludes aircraft) from the list of technology-intensive products (the 'upper third' in Pavitt's ranking).
6. For a more comprehensive discussion of different versions of the CMS method, the reader is referred to Fagerberg and Sollie (1987).
7. The original version of the CMS method, developed by Tyszynski (1951), contained only two effects, the commodity composition effect and a residual which he attributed to 'competitiveness'. Baldwin (1958) and Spiegelglas (1959) did independently point out that if Laspeyres indices are used throughout the calculation, a third 'interaction effect' necessarily appears, but they did not attribute any economic significance to it. In his review of the method, Richardson (1971) pointed out the economic significance of this effect, and suggested that it should be viewed as 'a second measure of competitiveness'. However, this suggestion seems largely to have been ignored.
8. Since the OECD tapes lack export data for Finland and Japan in 1961, exports from these countries to the OECD in 1961 were constructed using the other OECD countries' imports from Finland and Japan and national sources.
9. It was, surprisingly perhaps, less positive for the United States than for many other industrialized countries. However, the explanation is fairly simple. The United States is specialized in *both* R&D-intensive (high-growth) products and agricultural (low-growth) products.
10. External patents for country *i* are defined as the total number of patent applications from residents in country *i* in all countries that report patents to WIPO (the World Intellectual Property Organization) less patent applications from residents of country *i* in that country.
11. See, for instance, Leamer and Stern (1970, ch. 2), and Thirlwall (1980, chs 8–9).
12. It should be noted, though, that after 1973, and with a dummy for Japan included, the estimated correlation coefficients between the market share effect and R&D and Patenting turn up with the expected negative signs, significantly different from zero at a 1 and 5% level respectively.
13. It should be noted, however, that since market shares in this case are measured in value, a negative relation between growth in relative prices or costs should only be expected if the elasticity of export volume with respect to relative prices is greater (more negative) than –1.

References

Abramowitz, M. (1979) 'Rapid Growth Potential and Its Realization: The Experience of Capitalist Economies in the Postwar Period', in Malinvaud, E. (ed.), *Economic Growth and Resources*, London: Macmillan

Aho, M.C. and H.F. Rosen (1980) *Trends in Technology Intensive Trade: With Special Reference to US Competitiveness*, US Department of Labor

Baldwin, R.E. (1958) 'The Commodity Composition of World Trade: Selected Industrial Countries 1900–1954', *Review of Economics and Statistics*, 40, 50–71

Choi, K. (1983) *Theories of Comparative Growth*, Ames: Iowa State University Press

Cornwall, J. (1976) 'Diffusion, Convergence and Kaldor's Law', *Economic Journal*, 85, 307–14

Fagerberg, J. (1987) 'A Technology Gap Approach to Why Growth Rates Differ', *Research Policy*, 16, 87–99

Fagerberg, J. and G. Sollie (1987) 'The Method of Constant-market-shares Analysis Reconsidered', *Applied Economics*, 19, 1571–83

Gerschenkron, A. (1962) *Economic Backwardness in Historical Perspective*, Cambridge, MA: Belknap Press

Giersch, H. (1981) 'Aspects of Growth, Structural Changes, and Employment – A Schumpeterian Perspective', in Giersch, H. (ed.), *Macroeconomic Policies for Growth and Stability*, Tubingen: J.C.B. Mohr

Hirsch, S. (1967) *Location of Industry and International Competitiveness*, Oxford: Clarendon Press

Katzenstein, P. (1985) *Small States in World Markets*, Ithaca: Cornell University Press

Kelly, R. (1977) *The Impact of Technological Innovation on International Trade Patterns*, US Department of Commerce

Leamer, E. and R. Stern (1970) *Quantitative International Economics*, Chicago: Aldine Publishing Company

Linder, S.B. (1961) *An Essay on Trade and Transformation*, Uppsala: Almquist & Wiksell

OECD (1985) *Trade in High Technology Products: An Initial Contribution to the Statistical Analysis of Trade Patterns in High Technology Products*, DSTI/SPR/84/66 (1st Revision)

Olson, M. (1982) *The Rise and Decline of Nations*, New Haven: Yale University Press

Pavitt, K. (1982) 'R&D, Patenting and Innovative Activities – A Statistical Exploration', *Research Policy*, 11, 33–51

Posner, M.V. (1961) 'International Trade and Technical Change', Oxford Economic Papers, 13, 323–41

Richardson, J.D. (1971) 'Constant Market Shares Analysis of Export Growth', *Journal of International Economics*, 1, 227–39

Rotschild, K.W. (1985) 'Exports, Growth and Catching-up: Some Remarks and Crude Calculations', *Weltwirtschaftliches Archiv*, 121, 304–14

Schumpeter, J. (1934) *The Theory of Economic Development*, Cambridge: Harvard University Press

Schumpeter, J. (1939) *Business Cycles I–II*, New York: McGraw-Hill

Schumpeter, J. (1947) *Capitalism, Socialism and Democracy*, London: Unwin

Soete, L. (1981) 'A General Test of Technological Gap Trade Theory', *Weltwirtschaftliches Archiv*, 117, 638–60

Spiegelglas, S. (1959) 'World Exports of Manufactures, 1956 vs. 1937', *The Manchester School*, 27, 111–39

Thirlwall, A.P. (1980) *Balance-of-Payments Theory and the United Kingdom Experience*, London: Macmillan

Tyszynski, H. (1951) 'World Trade in Manufactured Commodities, 1899–1950', *The Manchester School*, 19, 272–304

Vernon, R. (1966) 'International Investment and International Trade in the Product Cycle', *Quarterly Journal of Economics*, 80, 190–207

Applied Economics, 1987, **19**, 1571–1583

The method of constant market shares analysis reconsidered

JAN FAGERBERG and GUNNAR SOLLIE

Norwegian Institute of International Affairs, PO Box 8159, Dep. 0033, Oslo 1 and *The Price Directorate, PO Box 8132, Dep. 0033, Oslo 1, Norway*

Constant market shares (CMS) analyses are frequently used in applied studies of export development. This paper reviews the development of the method and argues that it can be considerably improved. A new version of the method is developed which, in addition to the familiar CMS effects, also allows for the calculation of effects reflecting the ability of each country to adapt its export structure to the changes in the commodity and country composition of world imports. The method is applied to a sample of 20 OECD countries for the period 1961–83.

I. INTRODUCTION

In the 1950s several studies appeared focusing on structural changes in world trade and production and the consequences of these changes for the export performance and growth of individual countries. One of the earliest contributors, Tyszynski (1951), gave the following outline of the perspective underlying much of this work:

> Over the last hundred years, or so, the gradual industrialization of different areas of the world has led to significant changes in the nature of the demand for exports of manufactured commodities. It is a well established proposition that industrial equipment and modern means of transport considerably gained in relative importance at the expense of a number of consumer goods, notably textiles. It is also well known that, in the course of time, the old manufacturing nations exhibited greatly varying degrees of adaptability to this process. It was the purpose of this investigation to give a clearer picture of these changes in world demand for exports and in the competitive position of the leading manufacturing nations of the world.

To find out to what degree the changes in the market shares of different countries on the world market could be explained by the initial commodity composition of each country's exports, he calculated what the aggregate market share of a country on the world market would have been if its market shares in individual commodity groups had remained constant. He referred to the difference between this hypothetical market share and the initial share as change in the market

0003–6846/87 $03.00 + .12 © *1987 Chapman and Hall Ltd.* 1571 share caused by structural changes in world trade. The residual – the difference between the final and the hypothetical market share – was referred to as change caused by changes in competitiveness. This method is what later became known as 'constant market shares analysis'.

Calculations of the type carried out by Tyszynski soon became popular in applied international economics.[1] A detailed discussion of the method and its possible applications was given by Leamer and Stern (1970) in their influential book on quantitative international economics. They also proposed a new version of the method which has been used in a number of studies.[2] Even if at first glance it does not appear to be the case,[3] they in fact followed Tyszynski to a considerable extent by calculating Tyszynski's 'structural' effect, which they labelled commodity composition effect, and a competitiveness effect which they, as Tyszynski, calculated as a residual. They did, however, add one 'intermediate' effect, the effect of the market distribution of a country's exports. The idea behind this was that since the imports of different countries grow at different rates, the geographical distribution of a country's exports may also affect the export growth of the country.

While it was found to be a useful tool by Leamer and Stern, a much more critical evaluation of the method was given by Richardson (1971). He pointed out that Leamer and Stern's commodity composition and market distribution effects are interdependent, i.e. that the order in which they are calculated matters,[4] and that the values and signs of the various effects may change if the final, instead of the initial, year of the period under consideration is used as base year. However, this criticism (which is assumed basically correct, though not exhaustive) does not seem to have reduced the popularity of the method in empirical studies of export performance.

The purpose of this paper is to develop a new version of the method which avoids the problems and weaknesses outlined above. The main arguments are that the CMS method can be considerably improved in theoretical consistency as well as in empirical applicability if initial years' weights (Laspeyres indices) are used throughout the calculations, and the economic interpretation of the residual terms is made explicit (instead of including them in an arbitrary way in some of the other effects). As a consequence, five effects instead of Leamer and Stern's three are obtained, where the two additional effects reflect a country's ability to adapt its export structure to the changes in the commodity and market composition of world imports, respectively. These additional effects may in some cases be quite important, as shown in the fourth section where the method developed in this paper is applied to a sample of 20 OECD countries for the period 1961–83.

[1] The second to apply the method was Svennilson (1954). Among the early contributors to the development of the method and its application were Baldwin (1958) and Spiegelglas (1959).

[2] Bowen and Pelzman (1984), Ferreira and Rayment (1984), Horwitz (1984) and Utne (1984) just to mention a few, relatively recent examples.

[3] The reason why it does not appear to be the case is that Leamer and Stern calculated effects influencing the growth of exports, not the growth of the market share, as Tyszynski did. This difference, however, is not essential, and the method proposed by Leamer and Stern may easily be converted into a 'market share' version. (A note showing this is available on request from the authors.) The only difference between an 'export growth' and a 'market share' version of the Leamer and Stern method is that the effect of the general rise in world demand disappears when changes in exports are normalized to changes in market shares.

[4] This was mentioned already, in fact, by Leamer and Stern themselves.

II. THE 'SEVERAL COMMODITIES/ONE MARKET' CASE

The main purpose of this section is to show that Tyszynski's residual effect, which he referred to as caused by changes in competitiveness, can be split into two separate effects, both with a clear-cut economic interpretation.

The following symbols will be used:

n = number of commodities;

$0, t$ = subscripts which refer to the initial year and to the final year of the comparison, respectively;

X_i^{kl} = country k's exports of commodity i to country l;

B_i^l = country l's imports of commodity i;

M^{kl} = market share of country k (macro share of country k) in country l's imports;

$$M^{kl} = \sum_i X_i^{kl} / \sum_i B_i^l;$$

$\mathbf{a}^{kl}$ = market shares, by commodity, of country k (micro shares of country k) in country l's imports; row vector of dimension n; $\mathbf{a}^{kl} = (a_1^{kl}, \ldots, a_n^{kl})$, where $a_i^{kl} = X_i^{kl}/B_i^l$,

$\mathbf{b}^l$ = commodity shares of country l's imports; column vector of dimension n; $\mathbf{b}^l = (b_1^l, \ldots, b_n^l)'$, where $b_i^l = B_i^l / \sum_i B_i^l$ and $'$ denotes transposition.

The macro share of country k (M^{kl}) may be written as the inner product of the vector of its micro shares ($\mathbf{a}^{kl}$) and the vector of commodity shares of country l's imports ($\mathbf{b}^l$):

$$M^{kl} = \mathbf{a}^{kl}\mathbf{b}^l \tag{1}$$

The change in M^{kl} between time 0 and time t is

$$\Delta M^{kl} = M_t^{kl} - M_0^{kl}. \tag{2}$$

Tyszynski calculated the effect of changes in the commodity shares of the market ($\mathbf{b}_t^l - \mathbf{b}_0^l$), using the micro shares of the initial year ($\mathbf{a}_0^{kl}$) as weights, and a competitiveness residual. Regarding the last term, he explicitly assumed that it represented a measure of changes in the micro shares. However, as pointed out by Baldwin (1958) and Spiegelglas (1959), this is the case only as long as some kind of mix of initial and final year weights (Laspeyres and Paasche indices) are used in the calculations. In other words, if the first effect is calculated by using initial-year weights, then the second effect must necessarily be calculated by using final-year weights, if the sum of the two effects is going to be equal to the change in the macro share. If either Laspeyres or Paasche indices are used throughout the calculations, a third (residual) term necessarily appears,[5] as shown below (Laspeyres indices or initial year weights are used):

$$\Delta M^{kl} = \Delta M_\mathbf{a}^{kl} + \Delta M_\mathbf{b}^{kl} + \Delta M_{\mathbf{ab}}^{kl} \tag{3}$$

The first of these terms ($\Delta M_\mathbf{a}^{kl}$) is the effect of changes in the micro shares (market share effect), while the second ($\Delta M_\mathbf{b}^{kl}$) is the familiar commodity composition effect calculated by Tyszynski.

[5]That is, neither the Laspeyres nor the Paasche index passes the 'factor reversal test': cf. Allen (1975) or any standard textbook on index theory.

The third (residual) term (ΔM_{ab}^{kl}) is the inner product of a vector of changes in micro shares and a vector of changes in commodity shares.

$$\Delta M_a^{kl} = (a_t^{kl} - a_0^{kl})b_0^l \tag{4}$$

$$\Delta M_b^{kl} = a_0^{kl}(b_t^l - b_0^l) \tag{5}$$

$$\Delta M_{ab}^{kl} = (a_t^{kl} - a_0^{kl})(b_t^l - b_0^l) \tag{6}$$

Does this residual have any economic meaning?[6] In the opinion of the present authors it does, because its sign and value depends on the correlation between the changes in the micro shares of the country and the changes in the commodity composition of the market. A formal proof of this statement is given below. For the sake of simplicity, the superscripts are omitted in the proof:

$$\Delta M_{ab} = (a_t - a_0)(b_t - b_0) \tag{7}$$

The correlation coefficient between the changes in micro shares and the changes in commodity shares, r_{ab}, is defined by

$$r_{ab} = \frac{(a_t - a_0 - \bar{a}_t + \bar{a}_0)(b_t - b_0 - \bar{b}_t + \bar{b}_0)}{\|a_t - a_0 - \bar{a}_t + \bar{a}_0\| \, \|b_t - b_0 - \bar{b}_t + \bar{b}_0\|} \tag{8}$$

The symbol $\| \ \|$ denotes vector norm, while $\bar{a}_t$, $\bar{a}_0$, $\bar{b}_t$ and $\bar{b}_0$ are vectors of means, defined by

$$\bar{a}_t = (1/n)a_t ee' \tag{9}$$

$$\bar{a}_0 = (1/n)a_0 ee' \tag{10}$$

$$\bar{b}_t = (1/n)e \tag{11}$$

$$\bar{b}_0 = (1/n)e \tag{12}$$

where e is a column vector of ones and ' denotes transposition. It follows from Equations 8–12 that

$$\|a_t - a_0 - \bar{a}_t + \bar{a}_0\| \, \|b_t - b_0\| r_{ab} = (a_t - a_0 - (1/n)a_t ee' + (1/n)a_0 ee')(b_t - b_0) \tag{13}$$

By rearranging:

$$\|a_t - \bar{a}_0 - \bar{a}_t + a_0\| \, \|b_t - b_0\| r_{ab} = (a_t - a_0)(b_t - b_0) - (1/n)(a_t - a_0)ee'(b_t - b_0) \tag{14}$$

Since the sum of the commodity shares is always equal to one, it follows that

$$e'(b_t - b_0) = 0 \tag{15}$$

Substituting Equation 15 into Equation 14 gives

$$\|a_t - a_0 - \bar{a}_t + \bar{a}_0\| \, \|b_t - b_0\| r_{ab} = (a_t - a_0)(b_t - b_0) \tag{16}$$

By substituting Equation 16 into Equation 7, the residual can be expressed as the product of the correlation coefficient between the changes in micro shares and the changes in commodity

---

[6] Both Baldwin (1958) and Spiegelglas (1959) mention that a third 'interaction' effect exists, but they do not discuss its interpretation.

shares, and two terms which are necessarily non-negative. The first of these terms is a measure of the spread of the changes in micro shares, while the second is a measure of the changes in commodity shares (superscripts are reintroduced):

$$\Delta M_{ab}^{kl} = \| \mathbf{a}_t^{kl} - \mathbf{a}_0^{kl} - \bar{\mathbf{a}}_t^{kl} + \bar{\mathbf{a}}_0^{kl} \| \; \| \mathbf{b}_t^l - \mathbf{b}_0^l \| r_{ab}^{kl} \tag{17}$$

Thus, this third effect indicates to what degree a country has succeeded in adapting the commodity composition of its exports to the changes in the commodity composition of the market.[7] It was therefore decided to label it the commodity adaptation effect. However, a zero commodity adaptation effect does not indicate that no adaptation takes place, but that the country transforms – or adapts – its export structure at exactly the same rate as the average of all countries exporting to the market in question. Thus, a more correct name would be 'relative adaptation effect', but for convenience the term 'relative' is dropped.

III. THE 'SEVERAL COMMODITIES/SEVERAL MARKETS' CASE

The interpretation of the third (residual) term in the 'several commodities/one market' case is quite simple and may to some extent be understood intuitively. In this section the analysis is extended to the more complicated 'several commodities/several markets' case. As in the previous case Laspeyres indices are used throughout the calculations.

The following symbols will be used:

s = number of countries,

M^k = market share of country k in world imports; $M^k = \sum_l \sum_i X_i^{kl} \bigg/ \sum_l \sum_i B_i^l$,

$\mathbf{m}^k$ = macro shares of country k in world imports; row vector of dimension s; $\mathbf{m}^k$
$\quad\quad = (M^{k1}, \ldots, M^{ks})$,

$\mathbf{c}$ = country shares of world imports; column vector of dimension s; $\mathbf{c} = (c^1, \ldots, c^s)'$,

where $c^l = \sum_i B_i^l \bigg/ \sum_l \sum_i B_i^l$ and ' denotes transposition.

g^l = rate of growth of country l's imports, $l = 1, \ldots, s$.

The market share of country k in world imports (M^k) may be written as the inner product of the vector of its macro shares ($\mathbf{m}^k$) and the vector of country shares of world imports ($\mathbf{c}$):

$$M^k = \mathbf{m}^k \mathbf{c} \tag{18}$$

The change in M^k between time 0 and time t is

$$\Delta M^k = M_t^k - M_0^k \tag{19}$$

[7]Another measure of this is of course the correlation coefficient r_{ab}^{kl} itself. However, this coefficient may be quite high, even in cases where the changes in micro shares are quite uniform and the commodity composition of the market does not change much, i.e. when adaptation is of minor economic importance. The commodity adaptation effect, on the other hand, which is the product of the correlation coefficient, the spread in the changes in micro shares, and the degree of change in the commodity composition of the market, would in such cases be quite low. Thus, the commodity adaptation effect is an economically more meaningful measure than the pure correlation coefficient.

The change in the market share (ΔM^k) may be split into three effects

$$\Delta M^k = \Delta M^k_m + \Delta M^k_c + \Delta M^k_{mc} \tag{20}$$

where

$$\Delta M^k_m = (\mathbf{m}^k_t - \mathbf{m}^k_0)\mathbf{c}_0 \tag{21}$$

$$\Delta M^k_c = \mathbf{m}^k_0 (\mathbf{c}_t - \mathbf{c}_0) \tag{22}$$

$$\Delta M^k_{mc} = (\mathbf{m}^k_t - \mathbf{m}^k_0)(\mathbf{c}_t - \mathbf{c}_0) \tag{23}$$

The first effect is the changes in the macro shares weighted by initial year country shares, while the second effect is the changes in the country shares weighted by initial year macro shares. Thus, the second effect measures the effect on the market share of a country in the world market of changes in the composition of the market. It was therefore decided to label it the market composition effect. The third effect can be interpreted as the degree of success of the country in adapting the market composition of its exports to the changes in the country composition of world imports. Therefore, following the argument of the previous section, it was decided to label it market adaptation effect. Since the proof is analogous to the previous section, the result of the proof is simply stated here. Let r^k_{mc} be the correlation coefficient between the changes in macro shares and the changes in country shares, and let $\bar{\mathbf{m}}^k_0$ and $\bar{\mathbf{m}}^k_t$ be vectors of means, then

$$\Delta M^k_{mc} = \| \mathbf{m}^k_t - \mathbf{m}^k_0 - \bar{\mathbf{m}}^k_t + \bar{\mathbf{m}}^k_0 \| \, \| \mathbf{c}_t - \mathbf{c}_0 \| r^k_{mc} \tag{24}$$

By taking into account Equations 2–6 and the definition of $\mathbf{m}^k$, ΔM^k_m may be written as the sum of three effects:

$$\Delta M^k_m = \Delta M^k_a + \Delta M^k_b + \Delta M^k_{ab} \tag{25}$$

$$\Delta M^k_a = \sum_l (\mathbf{a}^{kl}_t - \mathbf{a}^{kl}_0) \mathbf{b}^l_0 \mathbf{c}^l_0 \tag{26}$$

$$\Delta M^k_b = \sum_l \mathbf{a}^{kl}_0 (\mathbf{b}^l_t - \mathbf{b}^l_0) \mathbf{c}^l_0 \tag{27}$$

$$\Delta M^k_{ab} = \sum_l (\mathbf{a}^{kl}_t - \mathbf{a}^{kl}_0)(\mathbf{b}^l_t - \mathbf{b}^l_0) \mathbf{c}^l_0 \tag{28}$$

The first effect (ΔM^k_a) is the effect of changes in the micro shares of country k in each market weighted by the commodity composition of each market and the country composition of world imports in the initial year. Following the argument of the previous section, this is labelled the market share effect. By the same token, the second effect (ΔM^k_b) may be labelled the commodity composition effect and the third (ΔM^k_{ab}) the commodity adaptation effect. Since the proof and interpretation in the latter case is quite analogous to the previous cases, the result of the proof is simply stated here:

$$\Delta M^k_{ab} = \sum_l \| \mathbf{a}^{kl}_t - \mathbf{a}^{kl}_0 - \bar{\mathbf{a}}^{kl}_t + \bar{\mathbf{a}}^{kl}_0 \| \, \| \mathbf{b}^l_t - \mathbf{b}^l_0 \| r^{kl}_{ab} \mathbf{c}^l_0 \tag{29}$$

To sum up, the change in a country's market share in world imports may be split into five effects:

ΔM^k_a = the market share effect;
ΔM^k_b = the commodity composition effect;
ΔM^k_c = the market composition effect;
ΔM^k_{ab} = the commodity adaptation effect;
ΔM^k_{mc} = the market adaptation effect;

so that

$$\Delta M^k = \Delta M^k_a + \Delta M^k_b + \Delta M^k_c + \Delta M^k_{ab} + \Delta M^k_{mc} \tag{30}$$

There are two main differences between this and most previous works on the subject. First, Laspeyres indices were used throughout the calculations.[8] Lack of comparability due to differences in weighting procedures is thus avoided. As a consequence, in the general 'several commodities/several markets case' studied by Leamer and Stern, five effects instead of Leamer and Stern's three are obtained.[9] Second, formal proofs have been given of the economic interpretation of the two residual effects.

The interpretation of the residuals has some affinity to a point discussed by Richardson (1971). He pointed out that effects calculated with Laspeyres indices in general differ from effects calculated with Paasche indices, and since he held the choice of index to be relatively arbitrary, he proposed to test the sensitivity of the results by doing both. Richardson focused especially on the difference between Leamer and Stern's market share effects calculated with Laspeyres and Paasche indices, respectively, which in the present notation may be written as follows:

$$\text{SMC} = \sum_l \left[(a_t^{kl} - a_0^{kl})(b_t^l(1 + g^l) - b_0^l) \sum_i B_{i0}^l \right] \tag{31}$$

Without giving any formal proof of its interpretation, he labelled this difference 'a second measure of competitiveness' (SMC), and claimed that it would be positive if the country increased its market shares in rapidly growing commodities and markets (p. 236), otherwise not. Comparing Equation 31 with Equation 28 reveals that the signs of Richardson's 'second measure of competitiveness' and this paper's commodity adaptation effect are equal in all cases if, and only if, $g^l \equiv 0$, i.e. if there is no growth in imports. But normally the growth rates of imports will be positive, especially when value data are used. This implies that the sign of Equation 31 for practical purposes depends on the growth of market shares, not on whether these market shares grow especially fast in products or markets that grow faster than average.

---

[8] Reymert and Schulz (1985) also use (chained) Laspeyres indices, but contrary to this paper they hold that the residuals thus obtained have no interesting economic interpretation (p. 9).
[9] Brakman *et al* (1982) also use a CMS method which in addition to the familiar CMS effects contains two different 'interaction' effects. The first is Richardson's 'second measure of competitiveness', discussed below. Unfortunately, the paper does not discuss the economic interpretation of the various effects, and the references for further information are to two working papers in Dutch. It is not possible, therefore, to discuss their method in detail here. Suffice it to say that their method is rather different from the one developed in this paper, and that there is no exact correspondence between the effects of the two methods.

Richardson should be credited for his attempt to discuss the implications of using different indices in the calculations, but unfortunately his reasoning was not entirely correct.[10]

IV. EMPIRICAL RESULTS

To test the empirical relevance of the method, it was used to analyse the export performance of 20 OECD countries on the OECD market (defined as the total imports(value) of the 20 OECD countries) in the periods 1961–73 and 1973–83. For each country, the change in market share (macro share) on the OECD market was decomposed into the five effects discussed in the previous section, using Laspeyres indices or 'initial year weights' (1961 for 1961–73 and 1973 for 1973–83). Great care was taken in order to ensure that commodities characterized by high growth in production and trade were specified as separate commodities, since the results also depend on the commodity breakdown used in the calculations.[11] Furthermore, it was decided to exclude oil and gas from the calculations, because if included, the calculations for the post-1973 period would have been totally dominated by the growth in the relative price of oil and gas. The data[12] were taken from OECD Trade Series C, with the exception of Japan and Finland for 1961, where it was necessary to supplement the OECD data with data from national sources.

The results are given in Tables 1 and 2. The column to the right gives the total percentage change in the market share on the OECD market in the period under consideration. The other five columns add up to this total change. Changes in the structure of OECD trude turned out to be of great importance for the export performance of most OECD countries, especially prior to 1973. During this period (Table 1), the commodity composition effect was strongly positive for a group of relatively advanced industrial countries: Germany, Switzerland, Italy, the UK and the Netherlands, and strongly negative for the least developed countries of the sample: Ireland, Turkey, Greece, Finland, Spain and Portugal. The commodity composition effect contributed negatively to the export performance of Canada, Norway and Denmark during this period, all relatively developed countries with an export structure dominated by raw materials and semi-finished products. The results for the post-1973 period (Table 2) resemble the results from the preceding period, but the effects were in general smaller.

The market composition effect was generally less important than the commodity composition effect, especially prior to 1973. It turned out to be strongly negative for Ireland, and to a lesser degree also for the Nordic countries. After 1973 the market composition effect was of special importance (strongly positive) for Canada, Ireland and Japan.

Even if commodity and market composition effects were important, and in some cases decisive, for most countries the development of market shares within individual commodity

---

[10]He also wrongly states that his 'second measure of competitiveness' is the same as the Baldwin–Spiegelglas 'interaction effect'.

[11]The commodity classification used is given in the Appendix.

[12]As is well known, data on exports and imports are not directly comparable. For instance, the value of total intra-OECD trade is not the same according to exports and imports statistics. To assure consistency, only import data were used in the calculations. This implies that the export from country k to country l of commodity i is defined as the import of country l from country k of commodity i, or

$$X_i^{kl} = B_i^{lk}$$

Constant market shares analysis reconsidered

Table 1. *Export performance of 20 OECD countries on the OECD market, 1961–73*

	Commodity composition,	Market composition	Market share	Commodity adaptation	Market adaptation	Total
Canada	−28.51	1.17	−1.57	15.05	2.86	−11.00
USA	−0.44	0.81	−21.32	2.14	−2.03	−20.84
Japan	−5.69	3.61	58.12	40.69	1.58	98.31
Austria	−1.35	1.03	4.18	−1.07	−6.38	−3.60
Belgium	−7.74	3.14	12.26	6.71	4.07	18.44
Denmark	−11.10	−9.68	0.18	−0.32	−0.55	−21.48
Finland	−23.07	−6.16	3.21	7.25	−5.58	−24.34
France	1.38	4.31	24.51	−0.70	0.14	29.64
Germany	17.14	1.74	1.79	−9.11	0.60	12.17
Greece	−23.23	2.54	35.05	7.24	1.33	22.93
Ireland	−27.21	−19.66	20.54	2.16	5.82	−18.35
Italy	12.89	2.66	12.18	−6.22	4.11	25.62
Netherlands	6.05	1.74	17.13	−7.78	0.43	17.57
Norway	−13.76	−7.99	17.93	−2.93	−4.03	−10.78
Portugal	−21.13	−0.78	64.82	3.06	−11.48	34.49
Spain	−22.89	0.00	23.73	3.77	3.12	7.74
Sweden	−5.35	−5.96	1.99	−2.82	−2.67	−14.80
Switzerland	15.96	3.50	−8.89	−10.22	−3.78	−3.53
Turkey	−24.62	4.63	−16.15	8.16	−2.66	−30.63
UK	7.02	−4.22	−25.15	−8.56	1.69	−29.22

Table 2. *Export performance of 20 OECD countries on the OECD market, 1973–83*

	Commodity composition	Market composition	Market share	Commodity adaptation	Market adaptation	Total
Canada	−4.24	15.15	−8.69	−2.61	−2.17	−2.56
USA	3.63	1.35	−1.53	1.28	−0.15	4.59
Japan	3.77	10.32	41.01	6.18	4.87	66.14
Austria	−5.56	−2.40	16.80	0.78	−1.27	8.34
Belgium	−4.71	−3.31	−12.39	0.47	0.78	−19.15
Denmark	−9.09	−0.31	7.41	−2.13	−2.12	−6.22
Finland	−10.66	−2.03	9.54	1.47	−3.15	−4.83
France	−1.10	−3.63	−4.33	2.79	0.63	−5.65
Germany	1.24	−3.66	−6.78	0.07	0.52	−8.61
Greece	−10.41	−1.51	23.01	−5.41	−0.61	5.07
Ireland	−7.19	11.04	34.00	11.93	−3.45	46.33
Italy	1.62	−0.90	18.31	−7.45	−0.33	11.25
Netherlands	−1.99	−3.12	−7.38	1.45	0.31	−10.71
Norway	−7.77	−3.17	−10.44	0.26	−0.94	−22.05
Portugal	−4.31	2.24	9.03	−1.73	−3.92	1.32
Spain	−3.99	1.67	23.50	2.58	−2.32	21.45
Sweden	−5.14	−3.48	−11.21	−2.42	−0.18	−22.42
Switzerland	5.95	0.00	10.81	−4.13	−0.33	12.31
Turkey	−14.76	−1.37	13.27	−3.64	0.65	−5.85
UK	4.07	1.22	−10.35	−0.95	−1.25	−7.25

groups was the most important single factor. The general picture both before and after 1973 was that some of the least developed countries of the sample won market shares at the expense of some of the more developed ones. Prior to 1973, the five most important gainers were Portugal, Japan, Greece, France and Spain; after 1973 Japan, Ireland, Spain, Greece and Italy. Moving to the important losers, prior to 1973, there were only four: the UK, the USA, Turkey and Switzerland. After 1973, the five most important losers were Denmark, Sweden, Norway, the UK and Canada.

The calculations show that the adaptation effects in some cases were quite important, the single most important example being Japan before 1973, where approximately 40% of the increase in market shares was due to the commodity adaptation effect. During this period, commodity adaptation also contributed positively to the export performance of Canada, Turkey, Greece and Finland, and negatively for Switzerland, Germany, the UK, the Netherlands and Italy. Thus, there seems to be a tendency that countries with a positive commodity composition effect adapt less well than countries with a negative commodity composition effect, and vice versa. After 1973 the differences were smaller; Ireland and Japan may be mentioned on the positive side, Greece and Switzerland on the negative side. Market adaptation effects were in general less important, with Japan (on the positive side) and Finland and Portugal (on the negative side) as possible exceptions.

V. CONCLUDING REMARKS

The method of constant market shares analysis was developed by Tyszynski (1951) and others, and further elaborated by Leamer and Stern (1970), as a tool to study the relation between structural changes in world trade and the export performance of individual countries. However, both Tyszinski's and Leamer and Stern's versions of the method suffer from major weaknesses: An inconsistent use of indices, and an insufficient discussion of how the residuals in the calculations should be interpreted. As a consequence, doubts have been expressed – starting with Richardson (1971) – regarding the interpretation of the various effects and the usefulness of the method in general.

The method developed in this paper differs from most other works on the subject in at least two respects: Laspeyres indices are used consistently throughout the calculations, and proofs are given for the economic interpretation of the residuals. As a consequence, five effects instead of Leamer and Stern's three are obtained. The two additional effects were found to be measures of a country's ability to adapt its export structure to changes in the commodity and market composition of world imports, respectively. Thus, the method developed in this paper provides a solution to the problem originally posed but only partly solved by Tyszynski: to develop a method which gives a clear picture of the adaptability of different countries to changes in the patterns of world trade.

When applied to a sample of 20 industrial countries between 1961 and 1983, several interesting results emerged. First, the structural changes in OECD trade turned out to have been quite important for the export performance of most countries during the period under consideration. In general, the structural changes contributed positively to the export performance of the economically most advanced countries of the sample, and negatively to the export performance of the less developed ones. Second, differences in adaptability were in some cases quite important, especially for Japan, but also for a number of other countries. In general, the economically most advanced countries adapted less well than the others. Third, changes in market shares within individual commodity groups and markets turned out to be the single most important factor shaping the export performance of the OECD countries. The general picture was that some of the economically less developed countries of the sample won market shares at the expense of some of the more developed ones.

APPENDIX

Classification of products	SITC Rev. 1	SITC Rev. 2
(101) *Products based on natural resources*		
1. Animals, meat, and meat preparations	00, 01, 091.3, 411.3	00, 01, 091.3, 411.3
2. Dairy products and eggs	02	02
3. Fish and fish preparations	03, 411.1	03, 411.1
4. Cereals and cereal preparations	04	04
5. Feeding-stuff for animals	08	08
6. Skins and leather manufactures	21, 61	21, 61
7. Wood and wood manufactures	24, 63	24, 63
8. Pulp and paper	25, 64	25, 64
9. Textiles	26, 65	26, 65
10. Iron ore	281	281
11. Iron, steel and ferro alloys	67	67
12. Aluminum	684	684
13. Other products based on natural resources	05, 06, 07, 091.4, 099, 11, 12, 22, 23, 27, 282, 283, 284, 285, 286, 29, 32, 35, 42, 43, 62, 66, 681, 682, 683, 685, 686, 687, 688, 689	05, 06, 07, 091.4, 098, 11, 12, 22, 23, 27, 282, 286, 287(−:32), 288, 289, 29, 32, 35, 42, 43, 62, 66, 681, 682, 683, 685, 686, 687, 688, 689, 699.9
(102) *Oil and gas*		
14. Oil and gas	33, 34	33 (−:5.2), 34
(103) *Chemicals*		
15. Organic chemicals	512	51
16. Inorganic chemicals	513, 514	522, 523, 287.32
17. Dyestuffs, colouring materials	53	53
18. Pharmaceuticals	54	54
19. Fertilizers	56	56
20. Plastic materials	581.1:2	582, 583, 893.91:2
21. Other chemicals	515, 52, 55, 57, 581.3:9, 59	335.2, 524, 55, 57, 584, 585, 59, 894.63, 899.39, 951.66
(104) *Engineering, electronics and transport equipment*		
22. Power generating machinery	711	711, 712, 713, 714, 718

Classification of products	SITC Rev. 1	SITC Rev. 2
23. Machinery for special industries or processes	712, 715, 717, 718, 719.3:5:8	72, 73 (− :7.32) 744, 745.1
24. Heating and cooling equipment	719.1	741 (− :31)
25. Pumps and centrifuges	719.2	742, 743
26. Typewriters and office machines	714.1:9	751.1:81:88, 759.11:15
27. Computers and peripherals	714.2:3	751.2, 752, 759.9
28. Semiconductors	729.3	776
29. Telecommunications	724.9	764 (− :99)
30. Machinery for production and distribution of electricity	722, 723, 729.9	771, 772, 716, 773, 778.8 (− :5), 737.32, 741.31
31. Consumer electronics	724.1:2, 891.1	761, 762, 763, 764.99
32. Domestic electrical equipment	725	775
33. Scientific instruments photographic supplies, watches and clocks	726, 729.5:7, 861, 862, 864	751.82, 759.19, 774, 778.85, 87, 88 (− :3)
34. Road motor vehicles	732	78 (− :5 (− :1:39))
35. Aircraft	734	792 (− :83)
36. Ships and boats (incl. oil rigs)	735	793
37. Other engineering products	719.6:7:9, 729.1:2: 4:6, 731, 733	745.2, 749, 778 (− :8), 785.2:31, 786, 791
(105) *Traditional industrial products*		
38. Manufactures of metal	69, 719.4, 812.1:3	69 (− :9.9), 812.1
39. Furniture	82	82
40. Clothing	84	655.3, 658.98, 84 (− :8.21)
41. Industrial products	812.2:4, 83, 85, 863, 891, 2:4:8:9, 892, 893, 894, 895, 896, 897, 899, 9	792.83, 812.2:4, 83, 848.21, 851, 883, 892, 893 (− :91:92), 894 (− :63), 895, 896, 897, 898, 899.1:3 (− :9):4:6:7:8:9, 9
(106) *Sum of all products*		
42. Sum of all products		

The abbreviations should be read as the following examples show:

891.1:3 should be read as 891.1 + 891.3.
899.3 (− :9) should be read as 899.3 − 899.39.

Commodity no. 14 (oil and gas) was not included in the calculations.

ACKNOWLEDGEMENTS

The work presented in this paper started while the authors worked together at the Central Bureau of Statistics, Oslo in 1984–5. The empirical calculations were carried out later at the University Center of Aalborg as a part of a project on international competitiveness for which Fagerberg is responsible. Economic support from the Norwegian Research Council for Social Sciences and the Humanities (NAVF) is gratefully acknowledged. We are indebted to Bent

Dalum and Leif Seerup, University Center of Aalborg, for assistance in data work and calculations, and to Aadne Cappelen, Petter Frenger, and Anders Rygh Svendsen, all at the Central Bureau of Statistics, for valuable comments and suggestions at different stages of the development of this paper.

REFERENCES

Allen, R. G. D. (1975) *Index Numbers in Theory and Practice*, Macmillan, London.

Baldwin, R. E. (1958) The commodity composition of world trade: selected industrial countries 1900–1954, *Review of Economics and Statistics*, **40**, 50–71.

Bowen, H. P. and Pelzman, J. (1984) US export competitiveness: 1962–77, *Applied Economics*, **16**, 461–73.

Brakman, S., Jepma, C. J. and Kuipers, S. K. (1982) The deterioration of the Netherlands' export performance during the late 1970's, *De Economist*, **3**, 360–80.

Feirrara, M. P. and Rayment, P. (1984) Exports of manufactures from South European countries, *Journal of World Trade Law*, **18**, 235–51.

Horwitz, C. (1984) Export performance of the Nordic countries 1965–1982, in *Economic Growth in a Nordic Perspective* (Ed.) G. Eliasson *et al.*, DOR Sekretariet, Copenhagen/Helsinki/Stockholm/Bergen, 260–84.

Leamer, E. E. and Stern, R. M. (1970) *Quantative International Economics*, Aldine Publishing Co., Chicago.

Reymert, R. and Schultz, C. E. (1985) Eksport og markedsstruktur, Rapporter 85/5, Central Bureau of Statistics, Oslo.

Richardson, J. D. (1971) Constant-market-shares analysis of export growth, *Journal of International Economics*, **1**, 227–39.

Spiegelglas, S. (1959) World exports of manufactures, 1956 vs. 1937, *The Manchester School*, **27**, 111–39.

Svennilson, I. (1954) *Growth and Stagnation in the European Economy*, United Nations Economic Commission for Europe, United Nations Publications, Geneva.

Tyszynski, H. (1951) World trade in manufactured commodities, 1899–1950, *The Manchester School*, **19**, 272–304.

Utne, A. (1984) The EFTA countries' export performance for manufactured goods 1970–1982, Occasional Paper no. 7, EFTA, Geneva.

[9]

Diffusion, Structural Change and Intra-Regional Trade: The Case of the Nordic Countries 1961-1983[1]

Jan Fagerberg

2.1 INTRODUCTION

This paper focuses on the possibilities for small developed countries to take part in the international process of innovation and diffusion, with special emphasis on the experiences of the Nordic countries between 1961 and 1983.[2] It is often suggested that access to a large, advanced and homogeneous domestic market is an important factor facilitating both innovation and diffusion of technology, and that small countries, as a result of this, have significant competitive disadvantages in new products and technologies.[3] The next section discusses this view in more detail and considers to what extent producers in small countries may overcome such disadvantages by "extending" their domestic market to neighbouring countries (the "extended home market" hypothesis). The remaining part of the paper examines the development of Nordic trade patterns, with special emphasis on intra-Nordic trade, from this perspective.

[1]This is a revised version of a paper presented at the Symposium "R&D, Industrial Change and Economic Policy" in Karlstad 22-26 June 1987. The paper has benefitted from comments by three anonymous referees. The calculations presented in the paper were carried out with the assistance of Leif Seerup at the University of Aalborg Data Center, using a database on trade statistics constructed jointly by Bent Dalum, Institute of Production, University of Aalborg and the author from OECD sources. Financial support from the Joint Committee of the Nordic Social Science Research Councils (NOS-S) and the Norwegian Research Council for the Social Sciences and the Humanities (NAVF) is gratefully acknowledged.
[2]It should perhaps be stressed that the discussion in this paper confines itself to the relation between country size and innovation-diffusion, and that other aspects of "country size" will not be discussed. For instance, there is no treatment here of whether small countries gain more (or less) from trade than others, to what extent trade makes small countries more "vulnerable" than others or questions related to trade-policy. For a recent discussion of some of these issues within a game-theoretic approach, which, incidentally, also considers Nordic economic cooperation, see Dixit (1987).
[3]For a recent overview of the research on relations between technology and small-country disadvantages in trade, see Walsh (1987).

2.2   A SCHUMPETER-LINDER-VERNON APPROACH TO INTER-NATIONAL DIFFUSION OF TECHNOLOGY

According to Schumpeterian views of technological progress, innovations are not evenly distributed, either across the economic system, or over time. On the contrary, innovations tend to cluster in special parts or branches of the economy, located in special countries or regions, and the locus of innovation tends to change over time. Thus, each epoch[4] may be said to be characterized by *an economic centre - i.e. a set of fast-growing technological systems* - located to *a geographical (or spatial) centre*. Obviously, the United States (until recently at least) played this role in the post-war period.

The diffusion of new product and process innovations takes place along two dimensions, economically to other sectors of the economy, and geographically to other regions and countries (*geographical periphery*). The extent to which countries in the geographical periphery manage to take part in the international process of diffusion (or transfer of technology) by establishing domestic production, reducing import dependency and increasing exports, will be of crucial importance for the development of market shares (domestically and abroad) and, hence, for economic growth.

What, then are the conditions for countries with different sets of characteristics to exploit the possibilities offered by the international process of diffusion to establish new production and, hence, exports? As pointed out by Mansfield (1982, p.29), there has been relatively little research in this area. In fact, most diffusion studies have focused on process innovations or diffusion among users (not producers) of new products.[5] Probably, the most systematic attempts to cope with this issue are still those made by the so called "neotechnological" trade theorists in the 1960's (Posner, 1961; Vernon, 1966; Hufbauer, 1966; Hirsch, 1967; and others).

The seminal contribution by Linder (1961), though not focusing exclusively on diffusion aspects, provides a useful point of departure. According to Linder, a necessary condition for firms to engage in the production of new products is that they receive signals from their traditional markets, in most cases the domestic market, that this is a profitable way to go. As a result, producers should be expected to start production by selling to the domestic market, and later - if successful there - exploit the accumulated experiences from the domestic market to engage in exports. Consequently, learning[6] through domestic "user-producer" interaction (Lundvall, 1988) - enters as a crucial factor for the outcome of innovation and diffusion processes (and specialization patterns in international trade[7]). Thus, following this view, the quality, composition and - in the case of economies of scale - size of the domestic market should be expected to be important

---

[4]This is what Schumpeter labeled "long waves", but since we do not adhere to any mechanistic wave theory, we prefer to speak of epochs with certain common characteristics which strongly influence the diffusion of technology and trade.

[5]For recent overviews of diffusion theory and applied studies, see Davies (1979) and Stoneman (1983).

[6]On the importance of learning by "doing", "using", "interacting" etc. see Arrow (1962), Rosenberg (1982) and Lundvall (1988).

[7]One implication of Linder's view is that since demand affects the composition of both exports and imports, countries with similar demand structures should be expected to trade more extensively with each other. If the structure of demand reflects the level on income, this implies that countries at approximately the same level of income should be more inclined to trade with each other than countries at different levels of income. This hypothesis, which is sometimes referred to as *the* Linder view, has undergone extensive empirical testing, most of which is supportive (for a recent test on a large data set including 100 countries, see Kleiman and Kop, 1984). Though empirically supported, we hold this to be a too narrow interpretation of Linder's view. In essence, Linder's argument is an evolutionary one, that specialization patterns evolve through learning processes related to (historically given) structures which (though related to the level of income) also differ among countries at comparable levels off income. For an earlier attempt to analyse export specialization in producer goods from this (latter) perspective, see Andersen et al. (1981a,b).

factors influencing a country's ability to enter new production areas. Other complementary factors, such as a infrastructure, education and R&D facilities[8] could be added to this list.

Diffusion conditions do not only depend on factors related to the recipient country, but also on technological factors. Vernon (1966) was among the first to present a systematic theory which reflected both. Following Linder's arguments he assumes that most new products will be developed in the United States (because of the favourable demand conditions there).[9] However, in the course of time, product characteristics and technologies are assumed to become standardized ("mature"), price competition to become gradually more important, and capital-intensive, but less flexible, production methods (based on the exploitation of static economies of scale) to be introduced. As a consequence, diffusion (transfer of production) to other countries is assumed to take place, starting with diffusion from the United States (the innovating country) to other developed countries, and continuing with diffusion from the United States and other developed countries to less-developed, low-cost countries. Thus, following Vernon, small developed countries should be expected to have a comparative disadvantage both in the introductory phase (because of small domestic markets for new products) and in the late phase (because of increasing importance of economies of scale and low (wage) costs). Thus, to the extent that they succeed in increasing domestic production and exports through imitation, these gains should be expected to be of a transitory nature.

However, the product cycle theory, though relevant in many instances, is built on quite strong assumptions. As pointed out by Walker (1979), products do not always mature (or do so extremely slowly), and even when they do, the production methods may not.[10] In the words of Van Duijn (1983) the product life cycle may be "extended" because new innovations (or technological competition) take place. In such cases, the competitive position of the innovator often remains strong relative to imitators, and diffusion (or transfer of production) may be delayed or blocked entirely, depending on the character of the technologies, industries and markets involved. One case refers to industries characterized by rapid technological shifts and increasingly complex technologies, delivering to customers all over the world, as, for instance, the aircraft industry and the computer industry (Rosenberg, 1982; Porter, 1986; Dalum et al., 1988). These industries are characterized by increasing dynamic and static economies of scale and, consequently, increasing disadvantages for small firms or, which is often the same, firms from countries with small domestic markets. However, when large technological shifts occur, new possibilities of entry will emerge, provided that the entrants react early enough ("early movers"). Another case refers to industries which produce "tailor-made"-products for user-specific needs or differentiated products in small series for customers throughout the world, as, for instance, the scientific instruments industry (Dalum et al., 1988). Here small-country disadvantages are less pronounced. But to the extent that learning curves are steep (dynamic economies of scale), significant "early mover" advantages should be expected.

---

[8]The importance of education and R&D-faciliites for technology transfer is emphasized by a.o. Freeman (1982) and Mansfield et al. (1982).

[9]In contrast to Vernon, Hirsch (1967), though acknowledging the leading role of the United States in new technologies, holds that small developed countries may have a comparative advantage in the early phase, because static economies of scale are less manifest than in the later phases.

[10]Another shortcoming, pointed out by Vernon (1979), Caves (1982) and Mansfield (1982), is that the theory does not take the increasing importance of multinationals with world-wide activities (MNE's) sufficiently into account. According to these writers, if the innovator is a MNE, this may significantly shorten (or abolish altogether) the period when the innovating country exports the technology in question, since the MNE is free to locate production in other countries than the country of origin. However, as pointed out by Vernon (1979), this is probably more relevant for large countries than for small countries. Anyway, it is not a major problem in the present context, which focuses mainly on diffusion aspects (imitation).

Thus, even though small country disadvantages exist, they are not uniformly distributed, either across industries or over time. As pointed out by Walsh (1987), small countries may in many cases overcome such disadvantages by adopting adequate strategies, for instance by adopting an "early mover" strategy in selected areas, by supporting "user-producer"-interactions in areas where competent domestic users exist or by "extending" the domestic market to neighbouring countries. The latter should be expected to be easiest in cases where similarities in tastes, cultures, income levels, institutions and markets exist, and the level of protectionism is low. Thus, this hypothesis should be applicable to the Nordic countries.

2.3   DATA

The discussion which follows, draws on a database on OECD trade for selected years 1961-1983, including all the OECD countries for which data were available. The data were aggregated into 5 sectors (*Products based on natural resources, Oil and gas, Chemicals, Machinery* and *Traditional industrial products*) and 41 product groups (Chart 2.1). Great care was taken to ensure that research- and development-intensive products and products based on important, commercially successful innovations in the not too distant past were specified as separate products. More mature products, on the other hand, like raw materials, semi-finished products and a number of rather unsophisticated manufactures, were treated in a more aggregative way. Furthermore, in order to ensure that the data were comparable both across countries and over time, we had to take into account the fact that, mainly for industrial security reasons, countries have differing practices with regard to reporting data, and that the international trade classification (SITC) changed during the period of observation. This also put limitations on the level of aggregation.

Like most trade studies, this study uses value data (OECD Trade Series C), which was the only type of data available on a sufficiently disaggregated level. It is often suggested that it would be preferable to use volume data instead of value data, but this is not always the case. There are two reasons for this. First, value data reflect better than volume data the effects of changes in export performance on the balance of trade. Second, volume data are problematic in cases where substantial technological change occur and, for the same reason, become less reliable as the time span under consideration grows.

The classification of products according to research and development intensity (expenditures on research and development as a share of output or sales) was based on other studies, especially Kelly (1977), Aho and Rosen (1980) and OECD (1985). While the two earlier studies were based on United States data only, the last one uses data for a group of OECD countries. However, with a few exceptions, these studies end up with rather similar rankings of products on the basis of R&D intensity.[11] It should be noted, though, that a few products that were classified as research and development-intensive in the two earlier studies, do not fulfil the requirements laid down in the last study. Even if this cannot be established with absolute certainty, it is probable that this difference refers as much to the difference in time span as to the difference in methodology between the two earlier studies and the last one. In our classification, the relevant products are type-

---

[11]Pavitt (1982) has developed an entirely different approach to ranking on the basis of technology intensity. Instead of ranking commodities according to R&D intensity, he proposes ranking them according to the importance of technological competition measured in terms of the statistical significance of the correlation between per capita exports and per capita US patents for different countries within the same commodity group. This has the disadvantage that it does not allow for the inclusion of the US in the investigation. However, the results are not very different from the OECD study, with the exception that Pavitt includes a larger part of the engineering sector (and excludes aircraft) from the list of technology-intensive products (the "upper third" in Pavitt's ranking).

Chart   2.1   Classification of Products (see the Appendix for difinitions according to SITC Rev. 1 and 2).

101	**Products based on natural resources**
1	Animals, meat and meat preparations
2	Dairy products and eggs
3	Fish and fish preparations
4	Cereals and cereal preparations
5	Feeding-stuff for animals
6	Skins and leather manufactures
7	Wood and wood manufactures
8	Pulp and paper
9	Textiles
10	Iron ore
11	Iron, steel and ferro alloys
12	Aluminium
13	Other products based on natural resources
102	**Oil and gas**
14	Oil and gas
103	**Chemicals**
15	Organic chemicals
16*	Inorganic chemicals
17	Dyestuffs, coloring materials
18*	Pharmaceuticals
19	Fertilizers
20*	Plastics
21	Other chemicals
104	**Engineering, electronics and transport equipment**
22*	Power-generating machinery
23	Machinery for special industries or processes
24	Heating and cooling equipment
25	Pumps and centrifuges
26*	Typewriters and office machines
27*	Computers and peripherals
28*	Semiconductors
29*	Telecommunications
30*	Machinery for production and distribution of electricity
31*	Consumer electronics
32	Electrical household appliances
33*	Scientific instruments, photographic supplies, watches and clocks
34*	Road motor vehicles
35*	Aircraft
36	Ships and boats (incl. oil rigs)
37	Other engineering products
105	**Traditional industrial products**
38	Manufactures of metal
39	Furniture
40	Clothing
41	Industrial products n.e.c.

writers and other (non-electronical) office machines, consumer electronics and road motor vehicles, products which, all other differences notwithstanding, have in common that by the seventies they were approaching the mature phase. Thus, we have chosen to regard these products as R&D intensive prior to 1973 but not later. In Chart 2.1 research and development-intensive products are marked with an asterisk.

2.4   THE NORDIC COUNTRIES' PATTERNS OF PRODUCTION AND TRADE AROUND 1960

In the 1950s and 1960s the United States was the uncontested centre of the capitalist world; technologically and economically. In 1960 GDP per man-hour in the United States was about twice as high as in Western Europe (Maddison, 1982). New products and technologies originated as a rule in the United States, from which they diffused at different speeds to Western Europe, Japan and other countries through trade and other means of knowledge transfer.

Just as the United States was a highly productive centre in the OECD area, so was Sweden in the Nordic area, even though the differences between the Nordic countries were less pronounced. In 1960, GDP per man-hour in Sweden was about 50% higher than in Finland and Iceland. Compared to Sweden, Finland and Iceland in the 1950s were industrially poorly developed, in the same way as most countries in Western Europe were industrially poorly developed in comparison with the United States.

The low level of industrial development of the Nordic countries compared to the United States, and to some extent, also to other OECD countries, was clearly reflected in the specialization patterns of the Nordic countries on the OECD market. In 1961, three quarters of the Nordic countries' total exports to other OECD countries were made up of products based on natural resources, cf. Table 2.1. The percentages were highest for the less developed countries.[12] In the case of Iceland, 99.4% of its export to the other OECD countries[13] consisted of natural-resource based products (mainly fish and fishery products), while the share for Finland was 97.6% (forest products and pulp/paper). Also Norway and Denmark were highly specialized in natural-resource based products: for Norway the share was 83.9% (mainly metals, forest products and pulp/paper, and fish), and for Denmark 72.9% (agricultural products). Sweden too had a large share of natural-resource based products in 1961, 66.0% (metals, forest product and pulp/paper). However, Sweden also had a substantial export of more advanced products such as machinery and transport equipment (25.4% of the export to the other OECD countries in 1961).

The imports to the Nordic countries at the beginning of the 1960s were far more differentiated than the exports, reflecting the fact that the composition of demand was much more differentiated than the structure of production. Intra-Nordic trade also had a far larger share of industrial products than the exports to the other OECD countries. At the outset this was especially important for Sweden and Denmark, which, at that time, were industrially the most advanced of the Nordic countries. For instance, 50.0% of Sweden's and 35.6% of Denmark's exports to the Nordic countries in 1961 consisted of machinery and transport equipment, and in both cases the Nordic market absorbed approximately one third of total Swedish and Danish exports of these products. For some "new" products the share of the Nordic market of total exports was even larger. For instance, in 1961, the Nordic countries absorbed 44.4% of Swedish exports of pharmaceuticals, and 53.7% of Danish exports of consumer electronics.

---

[12]For a documentation of the country-specific data referred to in this and the following sections, see the supplementary tables (Vedlegg 2) in Fagerberg (1986).

[13]With "other OECD countries" we mean OECD less the Nordic countries. This notion will be used throughout this paper.

Table 2.1 The Commodity Composition of Nordic Trade 1961-1983, Value.

Nordic exports to the OECD (excl. Nordic countries)

	1961	1973[1]		1983[1]	
Products based on natural resources (101)	78.6	60.0	(60.4)	42.7	(55.5)
Oil and gas (102)	0.0	0.6		23.1	
Chemical products (103)	2.5	3.5	(3.5)	5.2	(6.8)
Machinery and transport equipment (104)	14.7	28.7	(28.9)	22.8	(29.6)
Traditional industrial products (105)	4.2	7.1	(7.1)	6.1	(7.9)
	100	100	(100)	100	100

Nordic imports from the OECD (excl. nordic countries)

	1961	1973[1]		1983[1]	
Products based on natural resources (101)	38.4	31.4	(33.3)	24.4	(27.4)
Oil and gas (102)	7.0	5.9		10.8	
Chemical products (103)	8.7	10.0	(10.6)	11.7	(13.1)
Machinery and transport equipment (104)	38.2	44.2	(47.0)	41.6	(46.6)
Traditional industrial products (105)	7.7	8.6	(9.1)	11.5	(12.9)
	100	100	(100)	100	(100)

Intra-Nordic trade

	1961	1973[1]		1983[1]	
Products based on natural resources (101)	44.9	40.0	(41.2)	34.0	(40.2)
Oil and gas (102)	1.8	3.0		15.4	
Chemical products (103)	8.1	7.8	(8.0)	8.9	(10.5)
Machinery and transport equipment (104)	36.0	33.0	(34.0)	26.5	(31.3)
Traditional industrial products (105)	9.3	16.3	(16.8)	15.2	(18.0)
	100	100	(100)	100	(100)

[1] The figures in brackets are excl. oil and gas

Source: OECD Trade Series C

2.5   DIFFUSION AND STRUCTURAL CHANGE 1961-1973: THE ROLE OF INTRA-NORDIC TRADE

Between 1961 and 1973, an extensive change in the traditional natural-resource based specialization pattern took place. The share of natural-resource based products in the Nordic countries' exports to the other OECD countries decreased from 78.6% to 60.0%, while the share of machinery and transport equipment doubled, from 14.7% to 28.7%. Except for Iceland, all the Nordic countries took part in this development, but the changes were especially marked for Denmark and Norway. The structure of the Nordic countries' imports and mutual trade, which at the outset were less natural-resource based, changed too, but less markedly than in the case of exports.

As discussed earlier, diffusion (transfer of production) may be facilitated if the level and growth of demand for the product in the markets familiar to the producer are high. The Nordic market had a favourable effect in this respect because the demand structure was relatively advanced, i.e. Nordic consumers had already adapted their consumption patterns to a large number of new products which had initially been introduced in the United States, and because demand grew at a steady rate. However, for successful diffusion to take place, local producers must be able to compete favourably with competitors from the innovating country and other "early imitators". This means that there must be local competitive advantages either in the form of tariffs or other trade restrictions, or in the form of norms on the demand side that the local producers are better placed to adapt to, or in the form of cost components (such as transport costs) that are lower for local producers. The Nordic market had several favourable features. First, all Nordic countries were members of EFTA, which means that they increasingly practiced free trade between themselves and towards other EFTA countries, but exercised some protection towards producers from the United States and the EEC. Second, common norms and mutually intelligible languages made it easy for Nordic producers to develop product variants which were considered attractive in the Nordic market. And thirdly, the geographical location of the Nordic countries (far away from the United States and the large European countries) provided an incentive to start local production in cases where transport costs were high.

To investigate the impact of intra-Nordic trade on the process of transfer of production from the more advanced OECD countries - primarily the United States - to the Nordic countries in this period, we shall consider more closely the development within ten selected product groups. These products have been chosen because they belong to the one third which increased most in OECD trade between 1961 and 1973 (Fagerberg, 1986), and because they (with one exception, electrical household appliances[14]) have a high research intensity. What we should expect, given the assumption of a positive relation between diffusion and intra-Nordic trade, is the following:

1) The Nordic market should be important for Nordic producers, i.e. a large share of total Nordic exports should go to other Nordic countries, especially at an early stage of the diffusion process.

2) Nordic producers should cover a small share of the Nordic market at the beginning of the diffusion process, but this share should soon start to increase.

3) Nordic market shares in the other OECD countries should initially be at a low level, but should after a while start to increase.

As is evident from tables 2.2-4, pharmaceuticals, plastics, telecommunications equipment, consumer electronics, electrical household appliances and motor vehicles follow a pattern which is quite close to the one predicted. For these products, the Nordic market was initially relatively important for Nordic producers, even though the Nordic producers had a relatively small share of the Nordic market. The Nordic producers' share of Nordic imports increased rapidly, however, and more so than the average for all products. For some products, the market shares in the OECD market decreased at an early stage, and then picked up again, whilst in other instances they increased from a low level as expected. A possible explanation of the former type of development is that it took Nordic producers some time to adapt to new technologies, and that during this period they lost market shares abroad.

Also for "scientific instruments" we find that the Nordic market received a relatively large share of total Nordic exports at the beginning of the 1960s, but the Nordic producers' share of total Nordic imports remained low. Internationally, however, their market share increased. A possible explanation for this may be the level of aggregation; this group contains both scientific instruments, photographic equipment and watches. If

---

[14]The group of electrical household appliances was chosen because it includes many typical "American Way of Life" products that diffused from the United States to the Nordic countries in this period.

Nordic exports are concentrated to one of these groups (scientific instruments, probably), this may explain the low market share in the Nordic market.

However, office machinery, computers and semi-conductors do not conform to the pattern suggested by the "extended home market" hypothesis. For semi-conductors the market shares both domestically and abroad remained close to zero. For computers, the market shares in the Nordic market as well as the OECD market declined steadily from the early/mid 1960s onwards. The latter type of development reflects the fact the Nordic producers gradually lost ground as mechanical and electromechanical solutions were replaced by electronic ones.[15]

Table 2.2 Intra-Nordic Trade as a Percentage of Total Nordic Exports (Selected Products, Value)

	1961	1965	1969	1973	1979	1983
Pharmaceuticals (18)	23.0	29.5	34.4	34.6	28.7	23.4
Plastics (20)	37.5	53.1	63.1	60.0	50.7	44.8
Office machinery (26)	13.4	16.8	11.8	17.6	13.7	14.6
Computers (27)	10.7	11.5	9.2	12.2	19.3	21.2
Semiconductors (28)	22.4	30.9	47.8	35.3	29.2	23.3
Telecommunications equipment (29)	24.6	31.2	25.0	27.2	22.0	19.3
Consumer electronics (31)	36.7	51.8	60.5	40.5	35.2	25.6
Scientific instruments (33)	21.5	22.0	20.4	18.9	15.6	14.8
Motor vehicles (34)	39.1	40.1	34.6	29.0	22.7	20.1
Electrical household appliances (32)	37.6	45.7	35.8	38.0	37.4	38.2
All products	18.2	22.3	24.5	25.1	23.0	20.4

Table 2.3 Intra-Nordic trade as a Percentage of Total Nordic Imports (Selected Products, Value)

	1961	1965	1969	1973	1979	1983
Pharmaceuticals (18)	13.3	15.7	18.3	20.3	21.7	21.4
Plastics (20)	11.3	17.8	21.3	25.3	26.4	26.4
Office machinery (26)	6.7	6.9	6.6	9.3	9.9	7.4
Computers (27)	11.7	16.9	7.8	7.2	7.8	7.5
Semiconductors (28)	0.9	1.2	3.4	1.8	2.1	2.5
Telecommunications equipment (29)	15.1	20.0	26.6	38.7	31.8	26.7
Consumer electronics (31)	8.8	26.2	25.0	27.5	18.4	10.0
Scientific instruments (33)	5.5	6.6	7.2	8.0	7.9	7.7
Motor vehicles (34)	10.5	11.0	16.2	19.4	16.9	16.0
Electrical household appliances (32)	13.4	28.9	33.8	38.6	33.2	35.7
All products	15.2	18.9	21.7	23.2	21.2	21.3

---

[15]The development (including export performance) of the Nordic electronic industries in this period is analysed in more detail in Dalum et al. (1988).

Table 2.4 Nordic Market Shares on the OECD Market (Selected Products, Value)[1]

	1961	1965	1969	1973	1979	1983
Pharmaceuticals (18)	3.7	3.3	3.1	3.1	4.4	5.3
Plastics (20)	2.9	2.6	2.0	1.9	2.8	3.0
Office machinery (26)	3.5	2.6	2.8	2.4	2.9	2.8
Computers (27)	9.7	8.4	6.2	3.5	3.3	2.5
Semiconductors (28)	0.3	0.3	0.2	0.1	0.2	0.2
Telecommunications equipment (29)	4.4	4.1	5.2	6.8	5.0	3.9
Consumer electronics (31)	1.3	1.4	0.9	2.6	1.9	1.4
Scientific instruments (33)	2.5	2.3	2.5	2.8	2.9	2.8
Motor vehicles (34)	2.7	2.4	1.9	2.6	2.6	2.7
Electrical household appliances (32)	3.3	5.3	8.6	7.9	5.5	4.8
All products	4.8	4.6	4.1	4.1	3.6	3.9

[1] Nordic exports to the OECD(excl. intra-nordic trade) as a percentage of the imports of other OECD countries.

Apart from Iceland, all the Nordic countries took part in the rapidly increasing intra-Nordic trade in advanced products. In most instances, all the Nordic countries increased their market shares in the Nordic market in all products. Typical areas where all the countries increased their market shares were telecommunications equipment, consumer electronics and electrical household appliances. Within telecommunications equipment, Sweden acquired a leading position in the Nordic market with a market share of 27.1% in 1973. Other products where Sweden attained a strong position were electrical household appliances (17.2%), motor vehicles (15.4%), plastics (14.5%) and consumer electronics (11.8%). Norway also achieved a strong position within some of the new commodity groups, especially electrical household appliances (12.4%) and consumer electronics (7.6%). Denmark attained a strong position among the Nordic countries within pharmaceuticals (10.3%) followed by Sweden (9.4%)

However, it was not only in the process of technology transfer from the United States and other developed countries to the Nordic countries that the Nordic market played an important role. Equally important, perhaps, was the role of the Nordic market as a medium for a reduction of the technological and economic differences within the Nordic area, between Sweden on the one hand and the other Nordic countries on the other. This proved to be especially important for Finland, which by the early 1960s was at a much earlier stage of industrial development than Norway and Denmark were. Through deliveries to the Nordic market, initially of relatively simple industrial products, such as clothing, but gradually also of more advanced products, a fundamental restructuring of Finnish production and foreign trade took place. Between 1961 and 1973, Finland's market share of clothing in the Nordic market rose from 0.5% to 16.1%. But also for the other Nordic countries, increased intra-Nordic trade in relatively traditional industrial products provided a stimulus to industrial development (for instance, within the furniture industry, to mention just one example).

2.6   POST 1973: NEW EXTERNAL CONDITIONS - NEW PROBLEMS

In the 1970s, the conditions that made the structural changes of the preceding decade in Nordic-OECD trade relationships and intra-Nordic trade possible, had changes in a number of respects. First, the technological differences both within the Nordic countries and between these countries and the most developed countries of the OECD area, were strongly reduced. A few main figures may serve as an illustration. Within the Nordic area: In 1960 GDP per man-hour in Sweden was 50% higher than in Finland - in 1970 25% higher. Between the Nordic countries and the United States: In 1960 GDP per man-hour in the United States was 64% higher than in Sweden - in 1970 only 27% higher. Further-more, during this period, the structural differences between Nordic exports and OECD trade were much reduced, even though natural-resource based products continued to play a more important role in Nordic exports than in OECD trade.

Second, the structure of OECD imports was changed. The major price increases on some raw materials, primarily oil, gas and some energy-intensive products, increased these products' share of OECD trade in value terms. Except for Norway, which at that time had just begun to produce oil on its continental shelf, this had a negative influence on the Nordic countries' market shares, terms of trade and external balances. Furthermore, some of the important "growth sectors" in OECD trade of the previous decade had now entered the phase where growth decreases relative to other products and price competition increases, especially from producers in the "newly industrialized countries" (the NICs). This was of special importance for the Nordic countries because, to a considerable extent, it was precisely in these sectors that the Nordic countries had increased production most markedly and gained market shares in the 1960s.

Third, the institutional structure of intra-Nordic trade and Nordic economic co-operation was changed. Denmark entered the EEC in 1972, while the other Nordic countries remained in EFTA. However, great caution should be shown when estimating the economic impact of this, since the other Nordic countries soon negotiated free trade agreements with the EEC.

Nevertheless, it is a striking fact that *after 1973, the trend towards increased intra-Nordic trade was broken*. The Nordic countries' share of Nordic imports fell from 23.2% to 21.3% between 1973 and 1983, most markedly in machinery, transport equipment, and traditional industrial products (Table 2.5). Within chemicals there was only a slight decrease, and no change for natural-resource based products, whilst the Nordic countries (e.g. Norway) - not surprisingly - increased their market share on the Nordic market for oil and gas. Thus, the decrease in intra-Nordic trade as a share of total Nordic imports was wholly cause by developments for manufacturing products.

Table 2.5 Intra-Nordic Trade as a Percentage of Total Nordic Imports (Main Products, Value)

	1961	1965	1969	1973	1979	1983
Products based on nat. resources (101)	15.7	19.4	24.4	25.9	26.0	25.7
Oil and gas (102)	3.0	5.5	6.9	7.5	9.5	17.7
Chemical products (103)	15.7	17.9	19.2	20.9	20.0	19.1
Machinery and transport equipment (104)	17.3	20.1	20.0	21.4	20.1	17.9
Traditional industrial products (105)	18.8	25.4	31.0	36.3	31.7	27.6
All products	15.3	18.9	21.7	23.2	21.2	21.3

If we study this development in more detail, we find that the decrease in intra-Nordic trade is concentrated to a few groups. First, it concerns consumer electronics where Nordic producers' share of the Nordic market share was dramatically reduced, from 27.5% in 1973 to 10.0% in 1983. Other groups where Nordic producers lost from 5 to 10% of the Nordic market between 1973 and 1983, are fertilizers, heating and cooling equipment, pumps and separators, telecommunications equipment, metal products and clothing.

Among the Nordic countries, Sweden, Denmark and Iceland were the main losers of market shares in the Nordic market throughout this period. For Sweden the decline was especially evident for machinery, in particular heating and cooling equipment, pumps and separators, telecommunications equipment, consumer electronics and motor vehicles, and for furniture. Denmark's loss in market shares was especially evident for ships, power machinery and engines, pumps and separators. For Iceland the decline took place in traditional raw-material based export products such as meat, fish and feeding stuff for animals. Norway's total share of the Nordic market held up well because of oil, but otherwise Norway lost market shares for a large number of industrial products, most markedly for fertilizers, consumer electronics, electrical household appliances and metal products. In contrast to the other countries, Finland continued to increase its market shares on the Nordic market for a large number of products, but for a mature group like clothing, Finland also lost market share (from 16.1% in 1973 to 10.6% in 1983).

Also in the OECD market the trend from the 1960s and the first part of the 1970s was broken. Up to 1973 (Table 2.6), the Nordic countries lost market shares for natural-resource based products in the OECD market. The market shares for oil and gas, chemical products and traditional industrial products changed little between 1961 and 1973, whereas the market shares for machinery and transport equipment increased. After 1973 this process was reversed: the market share for natural-resource based products remained stable, the market shares for chemical products and oil and gas increased, whereas the market shares for machinery and transport equipment and traditional industrial products decreased drastically.

In chemicals, what is most striking is the strong increase in the Nordic countries' market shares in the OECD market for pharmaceuticals and plastics. In pharmaceuticals, it was especially Sweden and Denmark that increased market shares, for plastics it was Norway that showed the strongest increase. For machinery and transport equipment, where the Nordic countries as a whole lost market shares in the OECD market between 1973 and 1983, the decline was especially marked in ships, telecommunications equipment, electrical household appliances, pumps and separators, and consumer electronics. Apart from Iceland (which had nothing to lose) and Finland (for one commodity: pumps and separators), all the Nordic countries lost market shares in the OECD market for these groups. The Nordic countries also lost market shares for traditional industrial products, especially clothing.

Even though the Nordic countries' total market share held up better in the OECD market than in the Nordic market between 1973 and 1983, *there are strong similarities between the developments in the two markets.* In both instances the Nordic countries' market shares fell markedly for machinery and traditional industrial products. To get an idea of what happened, it may be of some value to ask who actually won the market shares that the Nordic countries lost. To answer this, consider Table 2.7 below, which covers the OECD market as a whole, with Nordic imports included. The answer is fairly unambiguous. In products where the Nordic countries lost market shares, the other OECD countries as a group lost market shares as well during this period, whereas countries outside of the OECD area (NIC countries, developing countries) gained.[16] Furthermore, it may be shown that in relative terms (growth-rates), Nordic losses were generally larger than those of the group of other OECD countries.[17] Thus, the Nordic countries appear to have been especially vulnerable to the increasing competition from

---

[16]It may be noted that in contrast to the other OECD countries as a group, Japan gained market shares in the five machinery groups covered in Table.7. In absolute terms, the gains were largest for consumer electronics (where Japan's market share of the OECD market exceeded 50% in 1983) and telecommunications equipment. However, for metal products, furniture and clothing, Japan too lost market shares.

[17]This holds, whether Japan is included in the group of other OECD-countries or not (though much less pronounced in the latter case). for 6 of the 8 products covered by Table 2.7 (the exceptions are electrical household appliances and ships).

non-OECD countries (and to some extent Japan as well) in the seventies and early eighties.

Table 2.6 Nordic Market Shares on the OECD-market[1] (Main Products, Value)

	1961	1965	1969	1973	1979	1983
Products based on nat. resources (101)	6.3	6.1	5.5	5.4	5.2	5.4
Oil and gas (102)	0.0	0.1	0.1	0.2	2.2	4.0
Chemical products (103)	2.4	2.5	2.7	2.2	2.4	2.7
Machinery and transport equipment (104)	4.0	4.1	3.7	4.4	3.5	3.2
Traditional industrial products (105)	2.9	2.8	2.5	2.9	2.4	2.2
All products	4.8	4.6	4.1	4.1	3.6	3.9

[1]Nordic exports to the OECD countries (excl. intra Nordic trade) as a percentage of the imports of other OECD countries

Table 2.7 Shares of OECD Imports 1973-1983 (Selected Products, Value)[1]

	Nordic countries	Nordic countries	OECD excl. Nordic countries	Socialist countries	Rest of the world
	Level 1973	Change 73-83	Change 73-83	Change 73-83	Change 73-83
Pumps and separators (25)	10.0	-2.9	-4.6	+0.2	+7.3
Telecommunications equipment (29)	9.3	-4.3	-10.5	-0.2	+15.1
Consumer electronics (31)	4.2	-2.4	-4.5	-0.2	+8.6
Electrical household appliances (32)	8.5	-0.9	-11.7	+0.9	+11.2
Ships (36)	23.6	-1.2	-14.8	-3.1	+19.4
Metal products (38)	8.4	-1.9	-6.0	-0.6	+8.5
Furniture (39)	13.3	-1.7	-8.0	+0.2	+9.5
Clothing (40)	4.7	-2.1	-12.6	-1.2	+15.8
All products	5.6	-0.5	-4.6	+0.4	+5.9

[1] The change do not always add up because of lack of data for country of origin.

The tendency towards decreasing market shares for machinery was not limited to the Nordic and OECD markets, but characterized the Nordic countries' exports to the growing markets in NIC countries and developing countries as well. The Nordic countries' share of OECD's export to "the rest of the world" of machinery and transport equipment declined between 1973 and 1983 from 4.4% to 3.5%. Even though the market shares for the other main products increased or remained stable, the Nordic countries' total share of OECD exports to these markets decreased, from 3.6% in 1973 to 3.3% in 1983. Thus, with one partial exception - Finland[18] - the Nordic countries did not succeed in their attempts to find new markets for their manufacturing exports.

---

[18]Finland is in a special position because Finland's trade with the socialist countries has been regulated through agreements designed to ensure balanced trade.

2.7   CONCLUDING REMARKS

The example of the Nordic countries in the period 1961-1973 shows that small, natural-resource based economies are not necessarily "locked" in their traditional patterns of specialization. During this period Nordic producers managed to exploit the possibilities offered by the international process of innovation-diffusion to an extent that significantly changed their industrial structures and specialization patterns. In this process, intra-Nordic trade played an essential role, by providing an "extended home market" for firms that wanted to engage in production and exports of "new" products. This example points to the important role that intra-regional trade may play for small countries that want to catch up in technology and increase their manufacturing base.

However, the tendencies that gained strength in 1960's did not continue in the 1970's. When assessing this result, it should be taken into account that the pre-1973 period was a particularly favourable period for technology diffusion. Historical factors had created a large backlog of technologies which could be easily imitated provided that the necessary skills were available and demand conditions were sufficiently favourable. The Nordic countries cleverly exploited these opportunities to change the composition of production and exports and increase overall productivity and income levels. By the mid 1970's this backlog was much reduced, and the income and productivity levels of the Nordic countries approached those of the United States and other developed OECD countries. As a consequence, it now became more demanding to enter new areas of production. This tendency was strengthened by the fact that some of the most rapidly growing industries worldwide in the 1970's and 1980's, like the computer and aircraft industries, are characterized by increasing dynamic and static economies of scale that make it difficult for small firms, or firms with small domestic markets, to enter. Furthermore, many areas where the Nordic countries had increased production and exports during the 1960's were now approaching the mature phase, where demand slows down relative to other products and competition from low-cost producers in industrially less developed countries increases. The combined outcome of these factors was - as the preceding section shows - that the Nordic countries in the 1970's lost market shares in a number of areas both in the Nordic and the OECD markets.

Even though many of the changes of the 1970's were imposed upon the Nordic countries by the international economic environment, these changes did not necessarily imply that the Nordic market should cease to function as an "extended home market" for advanced Nordic products. Rather the implication was that since entrance into new areas had now become more demanding, closer cooperation between the Nordic countries in support of Nordic user-producer interaction in selected areas would be required. One successful example of this from the last decade is the cooperation between the Nordic countries on a system for mobile telecommunication (the NMT system), which resulted in rapidly growing market shares for Nordic firms in this area both in the Nordic and the OECD markets.[19] However, in general, the Nordic governments seem to have been unable or unwilling to increase their cooperation along these lines, and the result has been a gradual disintegration instead of a further strengthening of Nordic economic cooperation. It is beyond the scope of this paper to discuss the reasons for this, but different attitudes among the Nordic countries towards European economic and political integration are obviously an important factor.

---

[19] Among the companies that took advantage of these opportunities were Ericsson and NOKIA. This is a good example of how dependent many companies, even quite large and internationalized ones (as Ericsson and NOKIA), are on their "home markets" for successful product innovation. Another example from the same companies relates to the development of digital public switches (where Ericsson and NOKIA are among the few companies competing world wide), which in both cases were developed in joint ventures with, and with support from, the national governments /PTTs. See Dalum et al. (1988) for a more detailed account.

APPENDIX

Classification of products	Sitc. Rev. 1	Sitc. Rev. 2
101 Products based on natural resources		
1 Animals, meat and meat preparations	00, 01, 091.3, 411.3	00, 01, 091.3, 411.3
2 Dairy products and eggs	02	02
3 Fish and fish preparations	03, 411.1	03, 411.1
4 Cereals and cereal preparations	04	04
5 Feeding-stuff for animals	08	08
6 Skins and leather manufactures	21, 61	21, 61
7 Wood and wood manufactures	24, 63	24, 63
8 Pulp and paper	25, 64	25, 64
9 Textiles	26, 65	26, 65
10 Iron ore	281	281
11 Iron, steel and ferro alloys	67	67
12 Aluminium	684	684
13 Other products based on natural resources	05, 06, 07, 091.4, 099, 11, 12, 22, 23, 27, 282, 283, 284, 285, 286, 29, 32, 35, 42, 43, 62, 66, 681, 682, 683, 685, 686, 687, 688, 689	05, 06, 07, 091.4, 098, 11, 12, 22, 23, 27, 282, 286, 287(-:32), 288, 289, 29, 32, 35, 42, 43, 62, 66, 681, 682, 683, 685, 686, 687, 688, 689, 699.9
102 Oil and gas		
14 Oil and gas	33, 34	33(-:5.2), 34
103 Chemicals		
15 Organic chemicals	512	51
16 Inorganic chemicals	513, 514	522, 523, 287.32
17 Dyestuffs, coloring materials	53	53
18 Pharmaceuticals	54	54
19 Fertilizers	56	56
20 Plastic materials	581.1:2	582, 583, 893.91:2
21 Other chemicals	515, 52, 55, 57, 581.3:9, 59	335.2, 524, 55, 57, 584, 585, 59, 894.63, 899.39, 951.66
104 Engineering, electronics and transport equipment		
22 Power generating machinery	711	711, 712, 713, 714, 718
23 Machinery for special industries and processes	712, 715, 717, 718,	72, 73(-:7.32), 744, 719.3:5:8 745.1
24 Heating and cooling equipment	719.1	741(-:31)
25 Pumps and centrifuges	719.2	742, 743

26	Typewriters and office machines	714.1:9	751.1:81:88, 759.11:15
27	Computers and peripherals	714.2:3	751.2, 752, 759.9
28	Semiconductors	729.3	776
29	Telecommunications	724.9	764(-:99)
30	Machinery for production and distribution of electricity	722, 723, 729.9	771, 772, 716, 773, 778.8(-:5), 737.32, 741.31
31	Consumer electronics	724.1:2, 891.1	761, 762, 763, 764.99
32	Electrical household appliances	725	775
33	Scientific instruments, photographic supplies, watches and clocks	726, 729.5:7, 861, 862, 864	751.82, 759.19, 774, 778.85, 87, 88(-:3)
34	Motor vehicles	732	78(-:5(-:1:39))
35	Aircraft	734	792(-:83)
36	Ships and boats (incl. oil rigs)	735	793
37	Other engineering products	719.6:7:9, 729.1:2:4:6, 731, 733	745.2, 749, 778(-:8), 785.2:31, 786, 791
105	Traditional industrial products		
38	Manufactures of metal	69, 719.4, 812.1:3	69(-:9.9), 812.1
39	Furniture	82	82
40	Clothing	84	655.3, 658.98, 84(-:8.21)
41	Industrial products n.e.c.	812.2:4, 83, 85, 863, 891.2:4:8:9, 892, 893, 894, 895, 896, 897, 899, 9	812.2:4, 83, 848.21, 851, 883, 892, 893(-:91:92), 894(-:63) 895, 896, 897, 898, 899.1:3(-:9):4:6:7:8:9,9

Notes

1) The abbreviations should be read as the following examples show:

891.1:3 should be read as 891.1+891.3.
899.3(-:9) should be read as 899.3-899.39.

REFERENCES

Aho, M.C. and H.F. Rosen, 1980, *Trends in Technology Intensive Trade: With Special Reference to United States Competitiveness*, US Department of Labor.

Andersen, E.S., B. Dalum and G. Villumsen, 1981a, *International Specialization and the Home Market*, Aalborg University Press, Aalborg.

Andersen, E.S., B. Dalum and G. Villumsen, 1981b, The Importance of the Home Market for the Technological Development and the Export Specialization of Manufacturing Industry, in Freeman, C., ed., *Technological Innovation and National Economic Performance*, Aalborg University Press, Aalborg.

Arrow, K., 1962, The Economic Implications of Learning by Doing, *Review of Economic Studies*.

Caves, R.E., 1982, *Multinational Enterprise and Economic Analysis*, Cambridge University Press, Cambridge.

J. Fagerberg   35

Dalum, B., J. Fagerberg and U. Jørgensen, 1988, Small Countries in the World Market for Electronics - The Case of the Nordic Countries, in Freeman, C. et al., eds., *Small Countries Facing the Technological Revolution*, Frances Pinter, 1988.

Davies, S., 1979, *The Diffusion of Process Innovations*, Cambridge University Press, Cambridge.

Dixit, A., 1987, Issues of Strategic Trade Policy for Small Countries, *Scandinavian Journal of Economics*

Fagerberg, J., 1986, *Norden og strukturendringene på verdensmarkedet, En analyse av de nordiske lands handel med hverandre og de øvrige OECD-landen 1961-1983* (The Nordic Countries and the Structural Changes in the World Market. An Analysis of the Intra-Nordic Trade and Trade between the Nordic Countries and other OECD-countries 1961-1983), Rapport fra Statistisk Sentralbyrå 86/18, Statistisk Sentralbyrå, Oslo.

Freeman, C., 1982, *The Economics of Industrial Innovation* 2nd ed., Frances Pinter, London.

Hirsch, S., 1967, *Location of Industry and International Competitiveness*, Clarendon Press, Oxford.

Hufbauer G., 1966, *Synthetic Materials and the Theory of International Trade*, Harvard University, Cambridge, Mass.

Kelly, R., 1977, *The Impact of Technological Innovation on International Trade Patterns*, US Department of Commerce.

Kleiman, E. and Y. Kop, 1984, Who Trades with Whom - The Income Pattern of International Trade, *Weltwirtschaftliches Archiv*.

Linder, S.B., 1961, *An Essay on Trade and Transformation*, Almquist & Wiksell, Uppsala.

Lundvall, B.Å., 1988, Innovation as an Interactive Process - from User-Producer Interaction to the National System of Innovation, in Dosi, G. et al. , eds., *Technical Change and Economic Theory*, Frances Pinter, London.

Maddison, A., 1982, *Phases of Capitalist Development*, Oxford University Press, Oxford.

Mansfield, E., A. Romeo, M. Schwartz, D. Teece, S. Wagner and P. Brach, 1982, *Technology Transfer, Productivity, and Economic Policy*, Norton, New York.

OECD, 1985, *Trade in High Technology Products. An Initial Contribution to the Statistical Analysis of Trade Patterns in High Technology Products*, DSTI/SPR/84/66, 1st Revision.

Pavitt, K., 1982, R&D, Patenting and Innovative Activities - A Statistical Exploration, *Research Policy*

Porter, M., 1986, Changing Patterns of International Competition, *California Management Review*

Posner, M.V., 1961, International Trade and Technical Change, *Oxford Economic Papers*

Rosenberg, N., 1982, *Inside the Black Box: Technology and Economics*, Cambridge University Press, Cambridge.

Stoneman, P., 1983, *The Economic Analysis of Technological Change*, Oxford University Press, Oxford.

Van Duijn, J.J., 1983, *The Long Wave in Economic Life*, Allen & Unwin, London.

Vernon, R., 1966, International Investment and International Trade in the Product Cycle, *Quarterly Journal of Economics*

Vernon, R., 1979, The Product Cycle Hypothesis in a New International Environment, *Oxford Bulletin och Economics and Statistics*

Walker, W.B., 1979, *Industrial Innovation and International Trading Performance*, JAI Press, Greenwich

Walsh, W., 1987, *Technology, Competitiveness and the Special Problems of Small Countries*, OECD STI Review, Paris.

Small Open Economies in the World Market for Electronics: The Case of the Nordic Countries

Bent Dalum, Jan Fagerberg and Ulrik Jørgensen *

During past decades, the structures of world trade and production have undergone radical changes. Electronics have played a key role in this process, partly because electronic products have been among the fastest growing products in world trade and production, and partly because the introduction and use of electronics in other sectors of production have shaped the pace and direction of structural change there. To an increasing degree policy-makers and observers seem to hold that the ability to use electronics in the process of production and the degree of success in developing an indigenous electronics industry are of vital importance for national economic performance.

However, relatively few countries have succeeded in developing a strong, indigenous electronics industry. In the post-war period most product and process innovations in electronics were until recently carried out in the United States, in later years to some degree in Japan as well. As a consequence, these two countries now share the technological leadership in electronics, while the European countries to an increasing degree lag behind (Patel and Pavitt, 1987). This is especially true for the small European countries, which all are net importers of electronic products. Thus the question arises whether there exist significant small-country disadvantages in electronics, and if so, what the consequences for the future economic performance of the small countries are.

This paper focuses on these questions by means of a comparative analysis of the development of the electronic industries in four Nordic countries in the post-war period. The next section considers the relation between industry- and country-specific factors in electronics.[1] Following Freeman, Clark and Soete (1982) and others,[2] technological progress is analysed as a set of industry- and sector-specific trajectories that present countries which differ

*This paper draws on a more detailed comparative study developed for the Norwegian Technology History Project (Dalum, Fagerberg and Jørgensen, 1988). Earlier versions of the paper have been presented at a seminar at the University of Trondheim, Norway, 24 June 1986, organized by 'Samarbeidsgruppa for teknologi og samfunn', and at the IKE Workshop on Technological Change and the Competitiveness of Small Countries, Tannishus, Denmark, 18–21 August 1987. We want to thank the participants at these seminars, colleagues from the Norwegian Technology History Project, a group of industry experts and the editors of this book for constructive feedback.

114   B. Dalum, J. Fagerberg and U. Jørgensen

in terms of size, demand structure and other characteristics, with different opportunities. The outcome, however, does also depend on the behaviour of firms which, given the character of their environments and the opportunities in front of them, develop their own strategies (Freeman, 1982; Porter, 1980, 1985). In this paper, we attempt to analyse the development of the electronic industries in the four Nordic countries (sections 2–5) from this twin perspective. The final section summarizes the findings and considers some relevant policy issues.

1.   Technology, industry structure and national characteristics

What are the conditions of diffusion and entry in the electronic industries?

The classic theory of diffusion is the one outlined by Vernon (1966), according to which diffusion should be expected to take place in a mechanistic, predetermined fashion as the product moves through the three phases of the product life-cycle (introduction, growth and maturity). In this case, the diffusion process begins with diffusion from the technological leader country to other developed countries, characterized by a high level of demand for the product and a relatively high level of technical competence in production, and continues with diffusion to less-developed countries, characterized by cost advantages. However, as pointed out by, among others, Walker (1979), products do not always mature, and even if they do, the process of production may not. To put it in the words of van Duijn (1983), the product life-cycle may be 'extended' because new innovations (technological competition) take place.

With regard to differences in conditions for diffusion and entry across industries, a distinction should be made between industries which produce 'tailor-made products' or differentiated products in small series, where 'learning by doing' (or 'dynamic economies of scale'[3]) and 'user–producer relations' (Lundvall, 1985) are crucial, and industries which produce for mass markets, where the exploitation of static economies of scale enters as an important factor for competitiveness. Following Porter (1986), a distinction will also be made between industries where the conditions of competition are specific for each country or market ('multidomestic' industries), and industries where the conditions of competition are more or less the same all over the world ('global' industries). These distinctions partly overlap because production of 'tailor-made products' naturally takes place in 'multidomestic' industries, while products for the mass market, characterized by the existence of static economies of scale, are normally produced in 'global' industries. However, some industries which produce differentiated products in small series, may well be 'global' in Porter's sense, even if static economies of scale are relatively unimportant. On the basis of these criteria, a tentative classification of electronic industries may be made (Table 6.1).

Table 6.1 Classification of electronic industries

Scale	Industry	
	Multidomestic	Global
Mass markets	Telecommunications (moving towards global)	Semiconductors Computers Consumer electronics (mature phase)
Small-scale markets	Tailor-made instruments	Specialized instruments

Semiconductors[4]

Among the electronic industries, the semiconductor industry is probably the best example of a truly 'global' industry. Dynamic economies of scale have made it increasingly difficult for new firms, especially outside the technological leader countries, to enter the industry. Static economies of scale also gradually became more important. As a consequence, the semiconductor industry has become totally dominated by a relatively small number of large companies. The size of the American market for electronic components made it easier for American firms than for others to exploit the possibilities for economies of scale, and, as a consequence, American firms remained for a long time competitive in a broad range of electronic components in spite of high costs. Japanese firms have, thanks to a large domestic market for electronic components and massive investments, succeeded in conquering significant shares of the markets for semiconductors, mainly, but not exclusively, in the lower performance/price range. European firms have generally been less successful than their American and Japanese competitors.

Computers

The computer industry is also a 'global' industry in Porter's sense, even if the close connection between hardware and (often highly country- and user-specific) software adds a 'multidomestic' dimension to the industry, which especially European computer firms have been eager to exploit. In the early phases of the industry, US military demand was of utmost importance, and this gave US firms an initial technological lead. Other important customers were to be found in the public sector and in large financial and industrial corporations. It was natural, therefore, that the large, established office machinery firms (IBM, Remington, Rand, Burroughs, etc.) took steps although sometimes with hesitation to integrate computers in their product spectre.[5] Thanks to initial technological lead, static and dynamic economies of scale, and a continuous stream of new innovations, these firms have been among the dominant in the industry from its very beginning.

116   B. Dalum, J. Fagerberg and U. Jørgensen

However, radical changes in component technology have on several occasions provided firms with the opportunity of launching new and radically improved products, opportunities which by and large were first exploited by new firms, mostly but not exclusively American ones. For instance, the third largest computer firm today, Digital Equipment Corporation (DEC, founded in 1957), created itself a strong competitive advantage when it launched small, transistor-based computers for universities, public institutions and medium-sized firms at a point of time when the industry leaders were busy competing with each other in the mainframe market. In a similar way, when transistors were replaced by (increasingly large-scale) integrated circuits in the late 1960s, a 'swarm' of new computer firms emerged, exploiting the rapidly growing market for (networks of) relatively small computers (distributed data power). Among the most important examples are Data General, Hewlett Packard and, in Europe, Nixdorf and Norsk Data. The invention of the microprocessor (1971) strengthened this trend. In 1977 a new firm, Apple, exploited this invention in a product innovation: a small, cheap 'personal computer', a product which turned out to have a large commercial appeal, and was rapidly imitated (and improved) by IBM and many other firms.

Telecommunications[6]

Based on innovations in electrical technology in the previous century, the telecommunications industry was well established 100 years ago, and many present industry leaders, such as Siemens, AT & T and Ericsson, were already in the industry at that time. Strong national regulations and widely differing standards have given the industry a 'multidomestic' character, and most developed countries have a relatively well-developed, indigenous telecommunications industry. From the mid-1960s telecommunication firms began to take advantage of the developments in semiconductor and computer technology in their research and development efforts, and the last decade or so has witnessed the launch of digitalized public switches. The development costs were very large and, as a consequence, only a few firms are presently competitive in this area. This implies, of course, that the industry to an increasing degree is turning 'global'.[7] At present, efforts are concentrated on ISDN-networks—that is, the transmission of not only voice but also data, text, images, and so on, in one single network structure. Since these developments to an increasing degree require integration of telecommunication and computer technologies, a number of cooperation agreements between telecommunication and computer firms have been or are likely to be made.

Compared to the telephone area, radio communications have been an area where small firms, on the basis of accumulated experience (often from radio production) and domestic or regional opportunities, have managed to specialize and compete world-wide. Nationally or regionally based standards and regulations have given this area a 'multidomestic' character. However, the forthcoming pan-European (fully digitalized) mobile communications network may well trigger off an increasing concentration (and 'globalization') in this area in the near future (see also Ch. 9 below, by van Tulder).

Instruments[8]

We use electronic instruments in a wide sense, which implies that electronic equipment for measurement and control (in industry, government laboratories, etc.) as well as electromedical equipment, is included in this category.[9] In this industry, success depends to a large degree on the exploitation of local or specialized markets and user–producer relations. In some segments of the industry, notably instruments for industrial control and automation, firms typically specialize in tailor-made products. Such firms continue to be strongly tied to local markets and seldom export more than 50 per cent of their production. In other segments, firms produce specialized instruments in small series for customers throughout the world, and in these cases, exports may well be 80–90 per cent of production. Although most instrument firms are relatively small, with competitive advantages based on local market experiences, there are also some big multinationals active in this areas, such as Siemens and General Electric. At present, the most important challenge comes from recent developments in semiconductor technology, for example 'application-specific integrated circuits' (ASICs), which probably will favour firms with in-house know-how in this technology (mostly multinationals).

Consumer electronics

As in other parts of the electronics industry, a number of important product and process innovations have taken place during the half-century the consumer electronics industry has existed.[10] Still, the consumer electronics industry is probably the part of the electronics industry which conforms most accurately to the pattern described by Vernon. Production of consumer electronics started to diffuse to the Nordic and other countries in successive steps from the inter-war period onwards, starting with radios, and consumer electronics were for a long time the most important part of the electronics industry in many European countries. However, by the early 1970s most electronic consumer products had reached the mature phase of the product cycle, the industry did to an increasing degree turn 'global', and European producers came under increasing competitive pressure from Japan and low-cost producers in NIC-countries. As a consequence, in the United States and Europe there are now relatively few firms left in the consumer electronics industry. In Europe, among those left are companies like Philips and Thomson, that is multinationals able to exploit cost advantages world-wide.

118   B. Dalum, J. Fagerberg and U. Jørgensen

As the preceding discussion shows, conditions for diffusion vary across industries and between sectors of the same industry. However, what actually happens does also depend on country-specific conditions, as for instance the level of development, market access, the quality of demand, industrial and institutional structures, as well as firm behaviour and governmental policies. By relating sector- and country-specific conditions for diffusion to each other, some tentative hypotheses on the development of the Nordic electronic industries can be made.

The existence of significant static and dynamic economies of scale in the semiconductor industry on the one hand, and the very limited size of the Nordic domestic markets (and the large distance to the US market) on the other, make it less likely that Nordic producers should succeed in entering the mass market for semiconductors. The same holds to some extent for computers, but more for mainframes than for minis and micros, and more for hardware than for systems of hardware and application- or market-specific software.

On the other hand, where static economies of scale are less important, and domestic demand is quantitatively sufficient and of high quality, the conditions for diffusion or entry should be better. The development of the Nordic electronic instruments and telecommunications industries may have been facilitated by a protected domestic market and a relatively sophisticated demand structure. In a similar way, the relatively advanced demand structure in the Nordic countries in the 1950s and 1960s shaped by an egalitarian distribution of income and a rapidly rising standard of living, should be seen as a major factor facilitating the diffusion of production of consumer electronics in the premature phases of the product cycle. These advantages, of course, rapidly diminished as the industry matured and static economies of scale became more important.

2.   The case of Sweden

Compared to the other Nordic countries, Sweden was industrialized rather early. Industry became dominated by resource-based production (e.g. paper, metals, wood products) and heavy mechanical engineering (e.g. ships, cars, mining and forest machinery). The demand from the industrial sectors, the rapidly expanding public sector (public infrastructure and the welfare state) and the military (armed neutrality based on domestically developed and produced weapon systems) were all important factors behind the development of an indigenous electronics industry. This industry employs approximately 50,000 persons, or 5 per cent of total industrial employment. Telecommunications equipment accounts for approximately 50–60 per cent of total production and exports of electronics (Table 6.2). In 1985, one company, Ericsson dominated the industry, with 80–90 per cent of total exports and 75 per cent of total employment. The company is controlled by the Wallenberg group, which owns several large Swedish firms and financial institutions.

Table 6.2 Sweden: production and exports of electronics

Production	1961	1965	1969	1973	1979	1983		
Computers	24.7	18.8	21.8	17.1	20.3	19.8		
Components	0.6	0.5	0.5	0.7	1.3	2.3		
Telecommunications	51.1	62.4	61.5	60.8	58.9	59.2		
Consumer electronics	19.7	10.9	8.7	14.6	8.3	4.6		
Electromedical	2.4	2.6	3.1	3.1	6.0	4.9		
Other instruments	1.6	4.7	4.3	3.7	5.9	9.2		
Electronics	100	100	100	100	100	100		

Exports	1961	1965	1969	1973	1979	1983	1984	1985
Computers	48.1	37.1	33.1	23.0	27.8	34.4	32.1	33.3
Components	0.7	0.8	1.4	0.8	1.3	1.8	2.1	1.9
Telecommunications	41.1	48.6	51.7	55.9	51.2	46.7	48.7	48.1
Consumer electronics	2.2	2.9	3.3	10.0	7.5	4.8	5.7	4.7
Electromedical	5.5	5.8	5.2	5.2	5.4	4.6	4.1	4.3
Other instruments	2.4	4.8	5.3	5.0	6.8	7.6	7.3	7.7
Electronics	100	100	100	100	100	100	100	100

Export specialization	1961	1965	1969	1973	1979	1983	1984	1985
Computers	2.83	2.53	1.95	1.47	1.19	0.97	0.73	0.82
Components	0.08	0.08	0.12	0.06	0.13	0.12	0.10	0.12
Telecommunications	1.60	1.79	2.28	2.57	2.59	2.30	2.28	2.52
Consumer electronics	0.09	0.14	0.13	0.42	0.42	0.24	0.25	0.24
Electromedical	2.25	2.37	2.01	1.89	1.51	1.21	1.07	1.20
Other instruments	0.22	0.39	0.49	0.53	0.60	0.60	0.55	0.66
Electronics	1.12	1.14	1.10	1.16	1.16	0.93	0.79	0.91

For definitions and sources, see Appendix to this chapter

Telecommunications: the Ericsson story[11]

Founded in 1876, Ericsson was already active in the international markets for telephone exchanges and networks in the last century. During the inter-war period, the company did not manage to stay technologically competitive, and only a rescue operation by the Wallenberg family prevented it from being taken over by one of its most fierce competitors, ITT. The company, to some degree favoured by Swedish neutrality in the Second World War, was in the late 1940s able to launch public exchanges based on its own cross bar technology. However, Ericsson faced great troubles in penetrating the markets in other developed countries, and for a long time concentrated most of its efforts on markets in the Third World, especially Latin America and the Middle East. As a consequence, in most of the post-war period, 50–60

120   B. Dalum, J. Fagerberg and U. Jørgensen

per cent of Swedish exports of telecommunications have gone to non-OECD countries.

Even though Ericsson's own research efforts, supplemented by know-how obtained elsewhere (especially from the Bell Labs), have been of vital importance, the collaboration with the Swedish PTT should be counted as a decisive factor in the creation of the company's present competitive advantage.[12] In 1970 the two parties formed a fifty–fifty development company, Ellemtel, to develop a digital public switching system. The result, the Axe system, has since the late 1970s been the core technology of Ericsson, and the main factor behind its present position as one of the industry leaders. Recently, Ericsson has tried to strengthen its position in 'First World' markets through acquisitions and joint ventures, the most recent example being the acquisition of the French company CGCT (1987).

Another important area for Ericsson is radio communications, especially mobile communications for cars ('cellular networks'). In this case, an important institutional event was the establishment in 1981 of the Nordic Mobile Telephone system (NMT) based on standards developed in cooperation between the Nordic PTTs. According to one source, there are now 300,000 subscribers to the NMT system, which amounts to approximately one-fourth of all subscribers world-wide to such systems ('Ericsson Connexion', No. 10, August 1987). Ericsson is now reported to have 45 per cent of the world market for switches for cellular networks (based on the AXE system).

However, the EC plans of a fully digitalized pan-European network, to operate by the early 1990s, threaten the present competitive advantages of Nordic firms (based on accumulated experiences from the NMT system). New standards will be established, and the development costs for the new generation of technology will be very high. Currently, a number of joint ventures is underway to prepare for the coming competition. Three European groups are already established, one of them includes Ericsson.[13]

Computers[14]

Country size left apart, Sweden in the early 1960s had many of the characteristics normally deemed necessary for the development of an indigenous computer industry: a high share of national resources devoted to R & D a strong priority for indigenously developed weapon systems, and a large domestic manufacturer of office and calculating machinery, (later named) Facit. The latter is reflected in the statistics (see, Table 6.2), according to which, in the early 1960s, approximately one-fourth of total production and one-half of total exports in the Swedish electronics industry consisted of 'computers'. Although this was not computers in the modern sense, but mechanical and electromechanical devices (calculators), it represented a possible base for diversification into computers, as the history of the computer industry has shown.

As should be expected, perhaps, Swedish researchers were among the earliest in Europe to construct valve-based computers (BESK, 1953). Even though university needs triggered off the project, military demand turned out to be crucial for its accomplishment. However, new orders were not forthcoming, and the research team (the BESK group) joined the Facit company, which at that time did not give high priority to computers. As a consequence, later military orders went to IBM, which came to dominate the Swedish market. This dominance was, ironically enough, enforced by contemporary governmental procurement policies, which favoured IBM.[15] However, the construction of the Viggen fighter gave birth to another computer firm, Datasaab, which with some success competed with IBM in the mainframe market in the late 1960s.

During the 1970s the Swedish computer industry suffered heavy losses and the government was involved in a series of rescue operations and restructuring efforts.[16] Finally, in 1981–2 what was left of Facit's and Datasaab's activities was taken over by Ericsson, and merged into a new company, Ericsson Information Systems (EIS).[17] The purpose was to strengthen Ericsson's capabilities in the converging technologies of computers, office machinery and telecommunications. This move no doubt focused on the fastest growing areas of electronics, but the new division has not been profitable. In recent years, EIS has been drastically trimmed to increase profitability (employment has been cut from 22,900 at the peak to 12,400 in 1987). In January 1988 Ericsson sold most of EIS to the Finnish conglomerate Nokia.

Consumer electronics[18]

As in many other countries, Swedish consumer electronic firms flourished in the 1950s. But in the 1960s, the industry faced increasing competition from abroad, and import penetration rose dramatically. The products were primarily colour TV sets, produced by Luxor (2,500 employees at the peak in 1979) and a Philips subsidiary (1,200 employees in 1979), which later on was closed down. In the late 1970s Luxor tried to diversify into personal computers and satellite receivers, but had to be rescued by the government (1979) and was finally taken over by the Finnish company Nokia (1984).

Instruments

The Swedish electronic instruments industry is specialized in electromedical equipment (see Table 6.2), a pattern based on experiences accumulated through deliveries to the highly developed Swedish health sector. But according to our data, Sweden does not appear to be highly specialized in other types of electronic instruments, which is surprising taking into account the strong engineering sector and the highly developed public sector. However, this may in part be a statistical illusion, caused by the fact that the borderline between engineering and electronic instruments to some extent is

122   B. Dalum, J. Fagerberg and U. Jørgensen

arbitrary. For instance, the Swedish multinational ASEA is one of the world leaders in industrial robots, but in our statistics robots are classified as engineering products, not as electronics.

To sum up, the Swedish electronics industry is today an extremely concentrated branch, totally dominated by one single multinational corporation, whose current position is among the world leaders in its traditional core fields (telephone exchanges and radio communications). But in its new area, computers/office automation, it has been in trouble so far. The future of the Swedish electronics industry seems, thus, extremely dependent on the performance of the Ericsson Company in a few, quite specific subsectors.

3.   The case of Denmark[19]

The industrialization of Denmark was to a high degree based on linkages to the agricultural sector (food-processing, farm machinery and food-processing machinery) and shipping. In contrast to Sweden, small- and medium-sized firms dominate manufacturing industry, and this is characteristic for the electronics industry too. Most firms have less than 500 employees, only three firms more than 2,000 (1986). Total employment is around 30,000, or 6 per cent of total industrial employment. Production and exports have a more even distribution between the different subsectors than in Sweden, with electromedical equipment and other electronic instruments as the leading sectors (30–40 per cent of Danish production and exports of electronics; Table 6.3).

Instruments

Some Danish instrument firms have for long been among the world leaders in specialized areas. Examples are Radiometer (900 employees in 1985), initially a spin-off from the radio industry, and Brüel & Kjær (2,100 employees in 1985), initially triggered off by advances in basic research in electro-acoustics at the Technical University of Denmark. Later, these and other companies used experiences accumulated in the production of measuring equipment and other instruments to enter into electromedical equipment, which in recent years has been among the fastest growing parts of the Danish electronics industry.[20] Today, most Danish electronic instrument firms export 80–90 per cent of their production, some even more than 95 per cent. A common feature of many of the successes has been the close domestic user–producer linkages in the early stages of development, and that the firms were among the early innovators internationally in their specialized fields.

Table 6.3 Denmark: production and exports of electronics

Production	1961	1965	1969	1973	1979	1983		
Computers	1.9	2.2	6.1	3.2	5.7	13.1		
Components	0.0	0.5	0.6	0.4	0.7	0.5		
Telecommunications	27.2	40.3	43.5	41.4	43.2	34.9		
Consumer electronics	54.9	34.8	28.0	28.7	20.0	15.9		
Electromedical	1.6	3.1	3.4	3.7	4.8	8.6		
Other instruments	14.3	19.1	18.4	22.6	25.7	29.9		
Electronics	100	100	100	100	100	100		
Exports	1961	1965	1969	1973	1979	1983	1984	1985
Computers	8.7	7.1	5.7	5.2	8.9	14.6	13.6	17.7
Components	1.1	0.8	1.4	0.9	0.8	1.1	1.6	1.3
Telecommunications	33.3	39.1	43.0	39.1	34.9	29.4	28.5	29.6
Consumer electronics	19.6	22.7	18.2	22.5	17.3	14.6	14.6	12.3
Electromedical	6.6	4.3	4.3	5.0	8.4	11.2	12.0	12.3
Other instruments	30.7	26.0	27.5	27.4	29.8	29.1	29.8	26.8
Electronics	100	100	100	100	100	100	100	100
Export specialization	1961	1965	1969	1973	1979	1983	1984	1985
Computers	0.20	0.26	0.19	0.20	0.22	0.22	0.19	0.24
Components	0.05	0.04	0.07	0.04	0.05	0.04	0.05	0.05
Telecommunications	0.51	0.78	1.04	1.10	1.03	0.78	0.80	0.87
Consumer electronics	0.32	0.59	0.39	0.58	0.56	0.39	0.38	0.35
Electromedical	1.06	0.94	0.91	1.10	1.37	1.59	1.90	1.92
Other instruments	1.09	1.15	1.42	1.75	1.56	1.25	1.37	1.29
Electronics	0.44	0.62	0.61	0.71	0.68	0.50	0.48	0.51

For definitions and sources, see Appendix to this chapter

Consumer electronics

In consumer electronics, Denmark followed the predicted pattern with a large number of rapidly growing firms in the 1950s, which, following increasing competition from abroad, in most cases went out of business during the next two decades. The share of consumer electronics in total Danish production and exports of electronics peaked in 1973 (28.7 per cent of production and 22.5 per cent of exports). Since the mid-1970s one single firm, Bang & Olufsen (B & O—employment 2,900 in 1985), has been dominant. In the last decades a common design of the products has been the most important competitive factor combined with a high reputation for quality. In recent years the company has tried to diversify into telecommunications.

124   B. Dalum, J. Fagerberg and U. Jørgensen

Computers

Triggered off by university research, one Danish company, Regnecentralen (founded in 1955) entered the computer industry in its early phase. A first-generation computer, based on valves, was launched in 1957, a transistorized computer (GIER) was developed in the early 1960s for the Danish Geodetic Institute and in the late 1960s the company launched third-generation computers based on integrated circuits. However, in general it lacked support from governmental bodies which—as in Sweden—favoured IBM solutions. In fact, the governmental computing centre, Datacentralen, tried to stop the GIER project too, but in vain. Thus Regnecentralen never became sufficiently large[21] to compete with IBM and others in the mainframe market (as was its strategy), and after a period of repeated financial problems and reconstruction efforts, it was taken over by ITT in 1979 (from 1986 Alcatel/ITT). During the last decade, it has been specialized in computer networks and customized systems, and presently employs approximately 600 persons (1985).

The 1970s and early 1980s witnessed the rapid growth of another computer company, Christian Rovsing (founded 1963), initially specializing in deliveries to the public health sector. Another important event was a contract from the European Space Agency. Based on an in-house-developed minicomputer, Rovsing in the mid-1970s launched advanced communication networks which were bought by, among others, American Airlines. In the early 1980s Rovsing also launched microcomputers for office automation and products in several other fields. But the rapid expansion came to a halt in 1984 when the company went bankrupt, primarily caused by uncontrolled growth. The activities of Rovsing (employment peaked at 1,200 in 1984) were split and taken over by ITT (later Alcatel/ITT), Great Northern, Olivetti and others. Thus multinationals today control most of what is left of the Danish computer industry.

Telecommunications

As in Sweden, a fairly large company emerged in the previous century in telecommunications, Store Nordiske Telegrafselskab (founded 1869) and a subsidiary, Great Northern Telegraph Works (founded 1875). Great Northern established and ran telegraph networks (cables) in Russia and Asia (China and Japan) before the end of the last century, some of which even today earn rents. But the company was not able, or did not attempt, to keep pace with the technological forefront in telecommunications. Instead, the company followed a 'defensive strategy' (Freeman, 1982). It continued to run telegraph networks, went into production of telephone handsets (GN-Telematic), mobile communications (Storno), as well as a number of other areas. Thus no Danish developments in switching technology ever emerged, and the area was left for subsidiaries of foreign multinationals (Ericsson and

ITT). Thanks to regulations from the PTT, three firms still produce telephones—GN-Telematic, Standard Electric Kirk (taken over by ITT in 1970 and Alcatel/ITT in 1986) and B & O. Probably, this can only continue as long as the domestic market is protected.

A more successful area for Danish firms is radio communications. Accumulated experiences in marine communications and in the research community have given Danish firms a strong competitive position in mobile communications in the last decades. In the 1960s and 1970s, Storno became one of the world leaders in closed mobile communication systems (for taxis, police, ambulances, etc.). In the 1970s only Motorola and General Electric sold more world-wide. However, the mother-company (Great Northern) was unwilling to meet the capital requirements for its expansion, and in 1976 the company was sold to General Electric, and later from General Electric to Motorola (1986). In Denmark, mobile communications equipment is also produced by A.P. Radiotelefon, a Philips subsidiary since 1978, and two small indigenous firms that have entered the business recently, triggered off by the launch of the NMT system in 1981.

To sum up, the Danish electronics industry has its comparative strength in electromedical equipment and other types of instruments, dominated by small- and medium-sized firms with indigenous ownership. These firms are now facing growing international competition. In computers and tele-communications, Danish firms are in general weak and controlled by foreign multinationals. Until about five or ten years ago, marine and mobile communications were important exceptions, but in the latter field the most important firms have now come under the control of foreign multinationals.

4. The case of Norway

Compared to Sweden, Norway is an industrial latecomer. Historically, forestry, fishery and shipping have been very important. As in Sweden a large part of the industrial sector produces raw-materials and semi-finished products, and as in Sweden, shipbuilding has been an important industry. But compared to Sweden and most other industrialized countries, the Norwegian engineering sector is relatively weak. Today the Norwegian electronics industry employs approximately 16,000, or 4 per cent of total industrial employment (1985). Up to the mid-1970s[22] telecommunications and consumer electronics were the most important in terms of production and exports, but the latter industry collapsed in the second half of the 1970s (Table 6.4). In recent years[23] production and exports of computers have increased very fast, caused by the explosive growth of one firm, Norsk Data (3,600 employees in 1986). In 1985 computers accounted for nearly 50 per cent of Norwegian exports of electronics.

126   B. Dalum, J. Fagerberg and U. Jørgensen

Table 6.4   Norway: production and exports of electronics

Production	1961	1965	1969	1973	1979	1983		
Computers	9.0	5.9	2.5	3.0	18.5	28.4		
Components	0.2	0.2	0.3	0.4	1.5	0.2		
Telecommunications	41.1	38.7	50.1	50.5	57.1	52.0		
Consumer electronics	46.2	44.7	35.9	31.1	5.0	3.9		
Electromedical	0.1	0.6	0.8	1.9	0.6	0.6		
Other instruments	3.3	9.9	10.4	13.1	17.4	14.8		
Electronics	100	100	100	100	100	100		

Exports	1961	1965	1969	1973	1979	1983	1984	1985
Computers	32.3	18.1	11.5	5.4	29.0	37.5	43.1	47.8
Components	0.6	0.6	0.4	0.2	0.7	1.0	1.5	1.1
Telecommunications	29.7	24.4	29.1	37.2	43.2	33.6	32.0	28.3
Consumer electronics	27.2	41.6	44.2	44.3	9.0	6.7	4.2	2.9
Electromedical	0.4	2.1	2.0	1.3	1.7	2.1	2.7	3.1
Other instruments	9.9	13.3	12.8	11.6	16.5	19.1	16.5	16.8
Electronics	100	100	100	100	100	100	100	100

Export specialization	1961	1965	1969	1973	1979	1983	1984	1985
Computers	0.67	0.38	0.20	0.13	0.29	0.24	0.21	0.26
Components	0.02	0.02	0.01	0.01	0.01	0.01	0.02	0.02
Telecommunications	0.41	0.28	0.37	0.65	0.51	0.38	0.33	0.32
Consumer electronics	0.40	0.61	0.50	0.71	0.12	0.08	0.04	0.03
Electromedical	0.05	0.26	0.22	0.18	0.11	0.13	0.16	0.18
Other instruments	0.32	0.34	0.35	0.46	0.34	0.35	0.28	0.31
Electronics	0.40	0.35	0.32	0.44	0.27	0.21	0.17	0.20

For definitions and sources, see Appendix to this chapter

Computers

In the early 1950s, demand from the university and the research community led to the construction of a small valve computer (NUSSE, 1953) at a research institute in Oslo, Sentralinstituttet for Industriell Forskning (SI). The computer was based on British design, and a commercial launching was not under consideration.[24] Later, a military research institute, (Forsvarets Forskningsinstitutt, FFI) became the most dynamic centre for digital computer research in Norway. In 1966, FFI got a contract from the European space research organization, ESRO, on computer equipment for a satellite receiving station. The computer, ready in 1967, was the first 'mini' to be produced in Europe.

In 1967 three researchers from FFI founded Norsk Data. Their first machine, Nord 1, was delivered to a Norwegian company specializing in process control on ships, Norcontrol. In the initial phase, Norsk Data competed with Kongsberg Våpenfabrikk (KV), which also started to commercialize FFI's computer concepts. KV, a state-owned manufacturer of defence equipment, was supported by both the government and the military, while Norsk Data, though benefiting from public research, did not receive direct governmental support. However, Norsk Data got indirect support through deliveries to Norwegian research institutes and governmental institutions of tailor-made computer equipment for specific applications, which made it possible for the company to develop its products further. For instance, in 1972 Norsk Data delivered the first 32-bit mini in the world for the Norwegian Meteorological Office (asserted by Heradstveit, 1985).[25]

The major international breakthrough came in 1972–3, when Norsk Data, in competition with DEC and others, won a contract with CERN. Later CERN contracts and a contract for the F-16 fighter plane were some of the major events in the 1970s. While the strength of the company was initially in hardware, its strength in recent years has mainly been in systems (hardware and software) for specific market segments. In spite of rapid growth, the company still is fairly small compared to its competitors,[26] and in spite of rapid internationalization it continues to have strong ties to the domestic market.

KV continued to produce terminals and computers,[27] but mainly as parts of systems for defence purposes, industrial control/automation and other specialized applications. Many of these activities have been split out of KV in the form of small, specialized firms. In recent years, KV has been in serious financial trouble and is no longer an important producer of computers. In addition, Tandberg Data (650 employees in 1986), a spin-off from the consumer electronics firm Tandberg Radio Fabrikk, produces terminal equipment and streamers. However, the company has witnessed financial troubles recently, following a failed attempt to penetrate the US market for streamers.

Telecommunications

Even if the computer sector has grown rapidly in recent years, telecommunications continue to be the largest in terms of production (see Table 6.4).[28] Most of this comes from two companies, Standard Telefon og Kabel (STK, approximately 1,700 employees in electronics in 1986) and Elektrisk Bureau (EB, 3,600 employees in 1986), which used to share the major part of the deliveries to the PTT. Both companies have for a long time been technologically dependent on foreign multinationals, ITT and Ericsson, respectively. In fact, STK (founded in 1915) has been a ITT subsidiary (now Alcatel/ITT) since 1930, while Ericsson has been the major shareholder in EB (founded 1901). More recently the Swedish multinational ASEA has taken control over EB (1987).

128   B. Dalum, J. Fagerberg and U. Jørgensen

In contrast to the telephone sector, Norwegian radio communication firms have to a large extent based their activities on indigenously developed technologies, especially for marine and military applications. Radio-link systems were developed at FFI in the late 1940s and early 1950s, and successfully commercialized by a new firm, Nera, since 1978 a part of EB, which also has gone into satellite communications. Another important firm in this sector is Simrad (marine communications equipment). In addition, several small firms produce internal communications systems.

Instruments

Production of electronic instruments is a relatively small sector in Norway and, as in Denmark, most firms are small. Traditionally, the most important areas have been instruments for ships, equipment for industrial control in shipyards and oceanographic instruments. In the last decades the Norwegian offshore boom created a strong demand for electronic equipment, and several of the largest Norwegian electronic companies have been engaged in delivering electronics for the oil sector. According to Arnestad et al. (1985), these firms include KV, STK, EB, Norsk Marconi, Norsk Data and Simrad.

Consumer electronics

The consumer sector has behaved like the standard 'Vernon case'. During the 1950s, the domestic radio industry flourished, but as in Sweden most companies went out of business during the 1960s, and in the mid-1970s only one company of real importance was left (Tandberg). Tandberg, which at its maximum employed 3,000 (1976), was for a period quite successful, and until the mid-1970s, consumer electronics accounted for between one-third and one half of Norwegian production and exports of electronics (see Table 6.4). Tandberg produced high-quality tape-recorders and TV sets, and made serious efforts to diversify into computer peripherals. But it faced severe management problems, and following increasing financial problems and a failed rescue operation by the government, most of its activities were closed down (1977–8). With Tandberg, the Norwegian consumer electronics industry virtually disappeared. However, some of its activities were taken over by other firms, most important, Tandberg Data.

To sum up, in telephone equipment and consumer electronics, Norway has followed the 'standard' small-developed-country pattern. Thanks to regulations from the PTT, there is a relatively large sector producing telephone equipment, but it is controlled by foreign multinationals. Consumer electronics virtually disappeared in the late 1970s. There are some successful small firms in radio communications and instruments, but compared to the other Nordic countries, this is not an area of strength. In recent years one fast-growing computer firm, Norsk Data has dominated the picture, but this company is still relatively small compared to its main competitors, and appears vulnerable to developments in international markets. In fact, the growth of Norsk Data slowed down considerably in 1987.

5. The case of Finland[29]

The industrialization process started much later in Finland than in the other Nordic countries. Until recently, exports were dominated by industries related to natural resources, especially the forest industry, and simple, manufactured products, especially textiles. But during the last decades, an important transformation of the Finnish economy has taken place. The growth rates of the manufacturing sector in general and electronics in particular have been outstanding, and today (1986) the Finnish electronics industry employs approximately 25,000, or 4 per cent of total industrial employment. Traditionally, the most important products were consumer electronics, but since then the industry has expanded in a number of fields and is probably the most diversified among the Nordic electronic industries. However, one single company, Nokia, dominates the industry (11,600 employees in Finland in 1986, but recent foreign acquisitions in Sweden and Germany have more than doubled the total Nokia employment in electronics). Approximately one-half of Finnish exports of electronics goes to its neigh-bouring countries, the Nordic countries and the Soviet Union, the latter partly due to favourable trade agreements.

Consumer electronics

In the early 1960s, approximately two-thirds of Finnish production of electronics were consumer electronics, delivered by Finnish firms and a Philips subsidiary (which later was closed down). During the late 1960s and early 1970s, exports of consumer electronics grew rapidly, partly due to low wage costs. In 1973 the share of consumer electronics in total Finnish exports of electronics peaked at 61.5 per cent (Table 6.5). In the mid and late 1970s, when competition from low-cost producers from Japan and the NIC coun-tries increased, the Finnish consumer electronics industry faced troubles too, but managed to upgrade the technological character of their products (colour TV sets) and stay in business. According to Lemola and Lovio (Ch. 7 below), this was partly due to the willingness of the Finnish banks to finance the Finnish consumer electronics industry through some difficult years in the 1970s.

The most important company is Salora, from 1984 a part of Nokia, which in that year also acquired the troubled Swedish consumer electronics com-pany Luxor. Salora-Luxor (approximately, 3,500 employees in 1985) has made large losses in recent years, mainly due to problems related to Luxor's original activities (PCs and satellite receivers). In colour TV sets the company

130   B. Dalum, J. Fagerberg and U. Jørgensen

Table 6.5   Finland: production and exports of electronics

Production	1961	1965	1969	1973	1979	1983		
Computers	n.a.	0.0	0.1	1.6	9.5	14.1		
Components	n.a.	0.0	8.5	4.6	0.3	1.0		
Telecommunications	n.a.	22.9	33.4	35.9	36.1	40.7		
Consumer electronics	n.a.	69.5	44.9	38.9	36.4	22.9		
Electromedical	n.a.	0.4	3.2	2.8	8.8	3.0		
Other instruments	n.a.	7.2	9.9	16.2	12.9	18.1		
Electronics	n.a.	100	100	100	100	100		

Exports	1961	1965	1969	1973	1979	1983	1984	1985
Computers	n.a.	6.5	1.5	1.5	8.8	14.8	14.6	24.4
Components	n.a.	1.6	0.9	0.9	2.1	1.2	1.5	1.3
Telecommunications	n.a.	43.3	23.2	24.2	16.8	32.6	28.7	30.4
Consumer electronics	n.a.	28.4	47.4	61.5	45.7	27.9	26.5	20.8
Electromedical	n.a.	4.1	4.8	4.1	4.8	4.8	6.7	5.4
Other instruments	n.a.	16.0	22.2	7.7	21.7	18.7	22.1	17.8
Electronics	n.a.	100	100	100	100	100	100	100

Export specialization	1961	1965	1969	1973	1979	1983	1984	1985
Computers	n.a.	0.04	0.01	0.04	0.13	0.16	0.14	0.27
Components	n.a.	0.02	0.01	0.03	0.07	0.03	0.03	0.04
Telecommunications	n.a.	0.15	0.17	0.45	0.29	0.64	0.57	0.72
Consumer electronics	n.a.	0.13	0.30	1.05	0.85	0.55	0.49	0.47
Electromedical	n.a.	0.15	0.30	0.60	0.46	0.50	0.76	0.67
Other instruments	n.a.	0.12	0.33	0.33	0.66	0.59	0.72	0.69
Electronics	n.a.	0.11	0.18	0.47	0.39	0.37	0.34	0.41

For definitions and sources, see Appendix to this chapter

is more successful, and it is now reported to be the third largest manufacturer in Western Europe. In addition, another Finnish colour TV producer, Lohja (1,100 employees in 1986), has launched electro-luminescence displays among the first world-wide. Although not commercially successful yet, the potential market for flat displays is very large.

Telecommunications

As in Norway, the telecommunications industry was initially dominated by subsidiaries of foreign multinationals, which still are active in the market (Ericsson, approximately 1,000 employees in 1986; Siemens, approximately 500 employees in 1986). In recent years this has changed dramatically. Today approximately one-third of Finnish production and exports of electronics is telecommunications equipment.

A division of Nokia, Telenokia,[30] has launched a switching system (DX 200) for local networks. The development started by the foundation of a governmental development unit, later transformed to a state-owned company, Televa. In 1977 Televa and Nokia joined forces to develop digitalized switching systems, with economic support from the government. Since 1981 the company has been part of Nokia. Telenokia is reported to have around 50 per cent of the Finnish market for switches and is currently trying to penetrate export markets in socialist countries and some developing countries. But in spite of heavy subsidies, these activities are still not profitable. However, Nokia is quite successful in some specific areas, such as data modems and multiplexers.

Another important area is mobile communications, where Mobira, a division of Nokia, was among the first world-wide to launch portable telephones for cars, built on standards of the NMT system. Mobira now claims to be among the world leaders in that field. However, this position may well be vulnerable to the changes in standards underway (the pan-European network) and increasing competition from producers in NIC countries. To meet this challenge, Mobira-Nokia has recently joined forces with Alcatel and AEG in one of the three competing international consortiums in this area (see section 2).

Computers

Nokia launched the first Finnish computers in the mid-1970s in close cooperation with the banks. In 1981 Nokia went into microcomputers as well (the same year as IBM). With the acquisition of Luxor, and later EIS, Nokia has got access to a major part of the Swedish market. Nokia's main aim is not so much to penetrate the (already relatively mature) market for microcomputers, but to establish itself as a major producer of high-quality intelligent terminals which may be connected to different systems. However, in spite of some success in penetrating this market, Nokia appears vulnerable to rapidly growing international competition in this area.

Instruments

By means of indigeneous development efforts a diversity of electronic equipment for the Finnish process industries has been launched, and gradually a fairly strong and internationally competitive industry has emerged. Often these efforts have been made in-house in the large process companies and organized as electronics divisions there.

Industrial control equipment for the forest industry is an outstanding example. The largest manufacturer of paper machinery in the world is the state-owned Valmet, which also has emerged among the world leaders in

132   B. Dalum, J. Fagerberg and U. Jørgensen

electronic control devices in that field (2,300 employees in electronics in 1986). Other examples are Outokumpu, a mining company which has developed electronics for automation in mining and metallurgical processes, Strömberg (1,200 employees in electronics in 1986),[31] an electrical engineering company, which has developed electronic control devices for that field, and Kone (620 employees in electronics in 1986), one of the world leaders in elevators, which has also become one of the leaders in electronics in that area.

Finally, even the electromedical sector has been growing very fast in recent years with three medium-sized firms present in that sector.

To sum up, Finnish electronics have grown from almost nothing to a diversified, internationally oriented industry over a period of less than two decades. The industry is dominated by Nokia, an old forest company (founded in 1856), which has been transformed to a diversified multinational, producing, among others, telecommunications equipment, computers and consumer electronics. In 1986, approximately one-half of Nokia's production is electronics. Strong companies have emerged in electronic instruments, based on linkages to traditional resource based industry, as well as in electromedical equipment.

6.   Conclusion, or is there a lesson to learn?

It is a striking fact that no Nordic country at present is specialized in exports of electronics. In 1985 the export specialization index for electronics as a whole varied from 0.2 (Norway) to 0.9 (Sweden), with an average of 0.5. For all four countries, the 1985 level was well below the 1973 level. These figures may be interpreted in support of the hypothesis of significant small-country disadvantages in electronics.

As noted in section 1, the most marked small-country disadvantages in electronics should be expected in global industries with significant static or dynamic economies of scale, such as active components (semiconductors), computers, especially mainframes, and consumer electronics in the mature phase. On the other hand, the possibilities for small countries should be expected to have been much better in multidomestic industries, such as telecommunications (until recently at least), and industries where economies of scale are less important, such as electromedical equipment and other electronic instruments. On a general level, the experiences of the Nordic countries confirm these expectations. A common feature for all four countries is that export specialization is highest in telecommunications and instruments and/or electromedical equipment, and lowest in semiconductors. In fact, with the partial exception of Ericsson's in-house production, no Nordic country has produced active components on a large scale. As should be expected, the level of export specialization in consumer electronics has declined for all countries from the mid-1970s onwards. No Nordic country produces mainframes and so on.

However, there is also evidence that shows that small-country disadvantages, though existing, may be overcome through interplay between firms and their environments. In these cases governmental policy often turns out to have a crucial effect on the final outcome. We will discuss two examples, from the computer and telecommunications industry, respectively.

Some Nordic research communities started to construct computers already in the 1950s, but in contrast to the US experience these attempts were not adequately supported, neither by governments nor by large private institutions, and failed to give successful commercial spin-offs. In the 1960s, following changes in component technology, several new attempts of entry were made, but again governmental support was at best half-hearted. For instance, in Sweden, and to a large extent in Denmark as well, public institutions were advised by governmental procurement bodies to buy IBM solutions. Thus, it is probably more than a coincidence that the attempts to produce mainframes or minis in Sweden and Denmark all turned to be as unsuccessful. However, the case of Norsk Data shows that it is possible, even in small countries, to establish successful computer firms if they are among the first world-wide to exploit possibilities offered by radical changes in component technology, and manage to combine this with software developments for targeted market segments. Norsk Data, though not directly supported, survived the initial phase mainly because it managed to get contracts, some of them technologically very demanding, from the Norwegian public sector. We hold it as unlikely that Norsk Data would have survived its first years if something similar to the Swedish practice had existed in Norway at that time. Thus in this industry, policy does matter, and in general policies have been unfavourable for the attempts of Nordic firms to enter the market.[32]

All four countries have developed relatively large telecommunications industries, to some degree a reflection of the traditional multidomestic character of these industries and regulations from the PTTs. But even in a period where the industry is turning increasingly global, two Nordic telecommunications firms attempt to compete in the core technology of that industry, digital public switches, albeit one of them is among the industry leaders while the other plays a minor role. Both are relatively large, established companies with long-term strategies and financial bases that allow high development costs and losses in new areas. In both cases, their present technologies in this area were developed in joint ventures with the government (or PTT), which have involved heavy government subsidies (especially Telenokia/Nokia) and the development of a sophisticated public procurement framework (Ellemtel/Ericsson). Thus, even in small countries, governments and firms can interact to create new, long-term technological capability and competitive advantage in a predominantly global sector of an industry.

To conclude, even though small-country disadvantages in electronics exist, these are of a relatively 'soft' character and can in many cases be overcome through exploitation of user–producer linkages, cooperation between the

134   B. Dalum, J. Fagerberg and U. Jørgensen

public sector and firms in creating new technological capabilities and exploiting technological breakthroughs, and—as the experience from the NMT
system shows—cooperation between small countries on systems and standards.

Appendix

The export data used in this paper are based on an elaborated version of
OECD's Trade by Commodities, Series C. This version, the NIKE data
bank, has been established at the Institute of Production, Aalborg University
by the authors, supported by the university computing centre (AUD). The
data bank consists of exports and imports for all OECD countries since 1961
(selected years) in current US dollars, classified according to the revised
version of the Standard International Trade Classification (four-digit SITC
Rev. 1). From 1978, OECD has reported the data according to SITC Rev. 2,
but in the NIKE data bank those data have been converted to Rev. 1. The six
sectors of electronics presented are defined as follows (SITC Rev. 1):

Computers: 714.2 and 714.3;
Components: 729.3;
Telecommunications: 724.9;
Consumer electronics: 724.1, 724.2 and 891.1;
Electromedical equipment: 726.1 and 726.2;
Other instruments: 729.5.

The export specialization figures in Tables 6.2 to 6.5 are calculated as
'Revealed Comparative Advantage' indices (Balassa, 1965):

$$R(ij) = (X(ij)/X(i))/(X(j)/X),$$

where $R(ij)$ is the export specialization index of country i in commodity j,
$X(ij)$ are exports from country i of commodity j, $X(i)$ are total exports from
country i, $X(j)$ are total OECD exports of commodity j, and X are total
OECD exports.

The production data (in current prices too) have been collected from
national industrial statistics. For that purpose, a conversion table between
SITC Rev. 1 and the national versions of BTN/CCCN/NIMEXE has been
constructed by the authors. Firm specific data have been collected from a
variety of sources, as industry associations, newspapers, governmental
reports and so on. Total industrial employment is defined as ISIC 2–4
(*Source: Nordic Yearbook of Statistics 1986*). For a more detailed discussion on
data and sources, the reader is referred to Dalum, Fagerberg and Jørgensen
(1988).

Notes

1. For a more general discussion of the relation between technology, competitiveness and country size, the reader is referred to Chapter 2 above, by Walsh.
2. For a critical overview of different assumptions on technological change and 'path dependency', see Sejersted (1986).
3. On the distinction between static and dynamic economies of scale, see Posner (1961).
4. On the development of the semiconductor industry, see Braun and MacDonald (1982), Freeman, Clarke and Soete (1982), Dosi (1984) and Malerba (1985).
5. However, the initial steps were taken by independent university teams. The first electronic computer was finished in 1946 at the Moore School in Pennsylvania. The team that constructed this machine was swallowed by Rand Remington which launched the Univac computer, the market leader until the mid-1950s. On the early history of the computer industry, see Freeman (1982) and Andersen (1985).
6. For brief surveys of the history of telecommunications, see Guy (1985), *Statens Industriverk* (1982:1) and Granstrand and Sigurdson (1985).
7. For a brief overview of the changing structure of the industry, see *Financial Times*, (1987b).
8. For a survey of 'instrumentation', with some bias towards the UK industry, see Rendeiro (1985). On the importance of users, see also von Hippel (1976).
9. However, in the trade statistics, on which our empirical analyses are based, equipment for industrial control is often difficult to identify. For instance, robots are in most cases classified under the 'machine tool' heading together with a whole range of non-electronic products. For this reason, the data on 'other instruments' presented in this paper should be interpreted with care. For further details, see the appendix to this paper and Dalum, Fagerberg and Jørgensen (1988).
10. In the case of television, see Sciberras (1980).
11. See Eliasson (1980, Appendix) for a brief survey of the history of Ericsson. For a more recent account, see Soete and Tunzelmann (1987).
12. For an analysis of public procurement in telecommunications in Sweden, see Granstrand and Sigurdson (1985). See also van Tulder (Ch. 9 below).
13. The first group consists of Ericsson and the UK Orbitel (Racal/Plessey/GEC); Siemens and Matra are also expected to join. The second of Alcatel, AEG and Nokia, the third of Telenorma (a Bosch subsidiary), Philips and ANT. See *Financial Times*, 24 October and 5 November 1987.
14. For a study of the Swedish computer industry in the 1950s and 1960s, see Annerstedt et al. (1970).
15. In this period, a reorganization of governmental procurements resulted in the creation of a governmental body which in the late 1960s was the largest purchaser of computers in Europe, according to Annerstedt et al. (1970), with a bias toward IBM solutions.
16. See *Statens Offentliga Utredningar* (1981:72) for a detailed account.
17. Datasaab's mainframe activities were already taken over by Sperry Univac.
18. For a more detailed account, see *Statens Industriverk* (1982:11).
19. For a comprehensive study of the development of the Danish electronics industry, see Jørgensen (1986).
20. It should be noted that three Danish firms for several decades have been among

136   B. Dalum, J. Fagerberg and U. Jørgensen

the world leaders in hearing aids. But this group, 899.61 in SITC Rev. 1, has for statistical reasons not been included in our investigation. (It is defined at the five-digit level, while our trade data bank is only disaggregated to the four-digit level—see Appendix to this chapter for further details).

21. In the late 1960s the founder of Regnecentralen in vain tried to persuade the Nordic counterparts in computers to merge their resources in one company. For details, see Sveistrup (1976).
22. For an analysis of the development of the Norwegian electronics industry from the early 1950s to the mid to late 1970s, see Skonhoft (1986).
23. The Norwegian exports of 'computers' were already one-third of total electronics exports in 1961. Most of this came from one company, Jørgen S. Lien, which held a strong position in electromechanical cash registers. The firm reached its peak just before electronics made the electromechanical solutions obsolete, stuck to the old technology too long, and went bankrupt in 1971 (Basberg, 1985).
24. However, this resulted in early know-how which was used in the development of NC-technology for application in shipbuilding (the ESSI-system) and systems for industrial control and construction (at Kongsberg Våpenfabrikk (KV)). It also led to the development of the Autocon-system (at AKER, a large shipyard), a predecessor of CAD/CAM systems. According to Andersen (1986), the Autocon system was one of the few major innovations in Norwegian electronics in the 1960s.
25. The Norwegian Meteorological Office took the risk and asked ND to develop this new machine, just as the Geodetic Institute in Denmark asked Regnecentralen to develop the GIER machine in 1961.
26. In 1984 DEC employment was 67,000, while the size of Data General, Wang, and the German Nixdorf was between 15,000 and 20,000 (*Financial Times*, several issues from 1984).
27. Of a total employment around 4,000, approximately 1,500 were engaged in electronics in the early 1980s.
28. It should be noted that our data show a somewhat larger share of tele-communications in total Norwegian production of electronics than data published by the Norwegian Federation of Electronics Companies (Elektronikkindustriens Bransjeforening, EBF), due to differences in definitions caused by available statistics. Our definition of telecommunications includes microphones, loud-speakers and radio navigation equipment, which they classify as 'professional electronics', and their definition of total electronics is somewhat broader than ours. For instance, they include passive components and equipment for traffic control, which are excluded by us. However, the general picture remains the same (see Arnestad et al., 1985).
29. In this section we have drawn extensively upon Chapter 7 of this book, by Lemola and Lovio. It should be noted, however, that the classification of electronics used in this study is not identical to theirs.
30. On Nokia's telecommunications activities, see the discussion in Soete and Tunzelmann (1987). The Telenokia case has been analysed by Ekberg in Granstrand and Sigurdson (1985).
31. This company has in 1986 been taken over by the Swedish multinational ASEA.
32. In contrast to Norsk Data, the two other major Nordic computer firms, Ericsson and Nokia, both entered the general computer market relatively late and in a rapidly maturing segment (microcomputers). However, they had the financial strength to resist losses, if this was deemed necessary to achieve long-term objectives.

References

Andersen, H.W. (1985), 'Et riss av informationsteknologiens historie', *Working Paper No. 11, The Norwegian Technology History Project, NAVF-NTNF*, Norway.
— (1986), 'Technological Trajectories, Cultural Values and the Labour Process: The Development of NC-Machinery in the Norwegian Shipbuilding Industry', *Working Paper No. 24, The Norwegian Technology History Project, NAVF-NTNF*, Norway.
Annerstedt, J., Forsberg, L. Henriksson, S. and Nilsson, K. (1970), *Datorer och politik*, Zenit/Bo Cavefors, Kristianstad, Sweden.
Arnestad, M. et al. (1985), *Norsk elektronikkindustri. Status og perspektiver*, Elektronikkindustriens Bransjeforening, Oslo.
Balassa, B. (1965), 'Trade Liberalization and "Revealed" Comparative Advantage', *The Manchester School*, 1965, no. 2.
Basberg, B.L. (1985), 'Nølende innovasjon—Utviklingen av elektroniske kassaapparater ved Jørgen S. Lien frem mot konkursen i 1971', *Working Paper No. 12, The Norwegian Technology History Project, NAVF-NTNF*, Norway.
Braun, E. and MacDonald, S. (1982), *Revolution in Miniature*, 2nd ed, Cambridge University Press, Cambridge.
Dalum, B. Fagerberg, J. and Jørgensen, J. (1988), 'The Nordic Electronic Industries Facing the World Markets', *Report for the Norwegian Technology History Project*, forthcoming.
Dosi, G. (1984), *Technical Change and Industrial Transformation*, Macmillan, London.
Duijn, J.J. van (1983), *The Long Wave in Economic Life*, Allen & Unwin, London.
Eliasson, G. (1980), 'Företag, marknader och ekonomisk utveckling—en teori och några exemplifieringar', in E. Dahmén and G. Eliasson (eds.), *Industriell utveckling i Sverige*, Almquist & Wiksell, Stockholm.
Ericsson Connexion, 'Telecommunications in the Nordic Countries: Challenge, Commitment—and Competition', No. 10, August, Ericsson Group, Stockholm.
Financial Times (1982), 'Survey on Computers', 18 January.
— (1984), 'Survey on Finland', 22 May.
— (1986), 'Survey on World Telecommunications', 1 December.
— (1987a), 'Survey on Mobile Communications', 28 April.
— (1987b), 'Survey on International Telecommunications', 19 October.
Freeman, C. (1982), *The Economics of Industrial Innovation*, 2nd ed, Frances Pinter, London.
Freeman, C., Clark, S. and Soete, L. (1982), *Unemployment and Technical Innovation*, Frances Pinter, London.
Granstrand, O. and Sigurdson, J. (eds.) (1985), *Technological Innovation and Industrial Development in Telecommunications: The Role of Public Buying in the Telecommunication Sector in the Nordic Countries*, Nordforsk and Research Policy Institute, Sweden.
Guy, K. (1985), 'Communications', in L. Soete, (ed.), *Electronics and Communications*, Gower, Aldershot.
Heradstveit, P.Ø. (1985), *Eventyret Norsk Data—En bit av framtiden*, J.M. Stenersens Forlag, Oslo.
Hippel, E. von (1976), 'The Dominant Role of Users in the Scientific Instruments Innovation Process', *Research Policy* 5.
Jørgensen, U. (1986), 'Elektronikbranchens etablering og strukturelle udvikling', *Forskningsrapport nr. 11, Institut for Samfunsfag*, Danmarks Tekniske Højskole, Copenhagen.

182   Technology, Growth and Competitiveness

138   B. Dalum, J. Fagerberg and U. Jørgensen

(1988), 'Elektronikproduktionen i Danmark, Norge og Sverige—en reference for udformningen af teknologipolitik', in H. Glimell (ed.), *Industrifornyelse i Norden—til vilket pris?* Forlaget Samfundsfag og Planlægning, Roskilde (forthcoming)

Lundvall, B.-Å. (1985), *Product Innovation and User–Producer Interaction*, Aalborg University Press, Aalborg.

Malerba, F. (1985), *The Semiconductor Business*, Frances Pinter, London.

Nerheim, G. and Nordwik, H.W. (1986), *Ikke bare maskiner. Historien om IBM i Norge 1935–85*, Universitetsforlaget, Oslo.

Patel, P. and Pavitt, K. (1987), 'Is Western Europe Losing the Technological Race?' *Research Policy* 16.

Porter, M. (1980), *Competitive Strategy*, Free Press, New York.

(1985), *Competitive Advantage: Creating and Sustaining Superior Performance*, Free Press, New York.

(1986), 'Changing Patterns of International Competition', *California Management Review* 28(2).

Posner, M.V. (1961), 'International Trade and Technical Change', *Oxford Economic Papers* 13(3).

Rendeiro, J. (1985), 'Instrumentation', in L. Soete (ed.), *Electronics and Communications*, Gower, Aldershot.

Sciberras, E. (1980), 'Technical Innovation and International Competitiveness in the Television Industry', Science Policy Research Unit, Sussex University, Brighton, mimeo.

Sejersted, F. (1986), 'Routine or Choice: The Norwegian Technology History Project', NAVF-NTNF, Norway, mimeo.

Skonhoft, A. (1986), 'Framveksten av ny industriell aktivitet i en liten åpen økonomi', Elektronikk-industrien i Norge, *Working Paper No. 17, The Norwegian Technology History Project*, NAVF-NTNF, Norway.

Soete, L. and Tunzelmann, N. von (1987), *Convergence of Technologies and the European Market for Telecommunications Equipment*, Brookings Institution, mimeo.

Statens Industriverk (1982:1), 'Elektronikindustrin i Sverige—Del 5. Kommunikationselektronik', Liber Forlag, Stockholm.

(1982:11), 'Elektronikindustrin i Sverige-Del 6. Konsumentelektronik', Liber Förlag, Stockholm.

Statens Offentliga Utredningar (1981:72), 'Att avveckla en kortsiktig stödpolitik', Industridepartementet, Stockholm.

Sveistrup, P. (ed.) (1976), *Niels Ivar Bech—en epoke i edb-udviklingen i Danmark*, Data, København.

Vernon, R. (1966) 'International Investment and International Trade in the Product Cycle', *Quarterly Journal of Economics* 80(2).

Walker, W.B. (1979), *Industrial Innovation and International Trading Performance*, JAI Press, Greenwich, Conn.

[11]

Europe at the Crossroads: The Challenge from Innovation-based Growth

JAN FAGERBERG

2.1. Introduction

Europe's performance relative to the US and countries in Asia is a topic that greatly preoccupies policy makers who are concerned that the EU is losing ground compared to other, more dynamic, parts of the world.[1] Although the recent crises in Asia gave a timely reminder that the grass often looks greener on the other side of the fence, this chapter points to trends in EU performance that European policy makers will find disconcerting. Productivity growth has slowed down relative to competitors. Export competitiveness has deteriorated in all areas except agriculture and raw materials. The losses have been manifest in the technologically most sophisticated industries, particularly ICT. Europe has also failed to create employment on a scale at all comparable with the US or Japan, with obvious repercussions for unemployment. While until recently there was a tendency towards convergence in productivity and income between European regions, there are now signs of a reversal of this trend. Redressing this relatively disappointing performance will be neither easy nor quick, but if enduring answers to Europe's problems are to be found, it is essential that the scale and nature of these problems are carefully diagnosed and solutions found.

2.2. A Long View

In terms of productivity (as measured by GDP per capita), Europe seems to be surpassed not only by the United States, but also by Japan and—if the trends from the past decades prevail in the next century—by a number of other Asian economies as well. How did this happen? One or two centuries

[1] This chapter summarizes some of the findings from the TSER project 'Technology, Economic Integration and Social Cohesion' co-ordinated by Bart Verspagen, MERIT, University of Maastricht. It has benefited from comments and suggestions from the editors of this volume, for which I am grateful. An earlier and shorter overview of results from the project has been published as Fagerberg (1999). For a more detailed account the reader is referred to Fagerberg, Guerrieri, and Verspagen (1999a). I wish to thank my co-authors, particularly Iain Begg, Paolo Guerrieri, and Bart Verspagen, for their permission to use our joint work for this purpose.

ago, the situation was entirely different. During most of the nineteenth century the UK was the leading capitalist country in the world, with a GDP per capita about 50 per cent above the average of other leading capitalist countries (Table 2.1). However, during the second half of the century, the United States started to catch up with the UK and eventually—around 1910—surpassed it. In retrospect it becomes clear that US growth was based on a new technological system, based on large-scale production and distribution systems well suited for the large, fast-growing, and relatively homogenous US market (Chandler 1990; Nelson and Wright 1992).

That Europe initially failed to take advantage of these innovations is perhaps not so difficult to explain. The European markets were smaller and less homogenous. Hence, it is not obvious that US methods, if applied to European conditions in this period, would have yielded superior results. This is what Abramovitz (1994) has dubbed a lack of 'technological congruence'. Two world wars and an intermediate period of protectionism and slow growth added to these problems (Abramovitz 1994). Hence, the US lead increased even further and peaked around 1950, when GDP per capita in the United States was about twice the European level.

While the period between 1820 and 1950 was one of divergence in economic performance between leading capitalist countries, the following period has generally been one of convergence. The productivity gap between the United States and Europe has been significantly reduced. This reduction, most of which occurred during the 1950s and 1960s, was related to the potential for rapid productivity advance in Europe through imitation (of superior US technology). European production and exports in industries such as cars, domestic electrical equipment, electronics, and others grew rapidly from the 1950s onwards. The gradual reduction of barriers to trade within Europe from the 1950s onwards has generally been regarded as an important contributing factor to this process, as has the general rise in living standards (Abramovitz 1994; Maddison 1991).

European countries were not alone, however, in exploiting the window of opportunity given by superior US technology. From the 1950s onwards Japan, later joined by other Asian economies, aggressively targeted the very same industries as those that had grown rapidly in Europe (Johnson 1982; Wade 1990). Initially this did not give much reason for concern among European policy makers or industrialists. But during the 1970s and 1980s it became evident that Japanese suppliers outperformed their European and US competitors in many cases, and that this could not be explained solely by low wages. It became clear that the Japanese, as the Americans before them, had made important innovations in the organization of production, innovations that have led to both increased quality and higher productivity (Von Tunzelmann 1995), and which US and European competitors—despite serious efforts—have not yet managed to imitate to the extent that they would have wished.

TABLE 2.1. *GDP per capita in the industrialized world, 1820–1994 (thousand 1990 US$ per head)*

	1820	1870	1910	1950	1970	1980	1990	1994	Growth 1820–1950	Growth 1950–94(90)
USA	1.3	2.5	5.0	9.6	14.9	18.3	21.9	22.6	1.5	2.0
Japan	0.7	0.7	1.3	1.9	9.4	13.1	18.5	19.5	0.8	5.3
Germany	1.1	1.9	3.5	4.3	11.9	15.4	18.7	19.1	1.0	3.4
France	1.2	1.9	2.9	5.2	11.6	15.0	17.8	18.0	1.1	2.8
Italy	1.1	1.5	2.3	3.4	9.5	13.1	16.0	16.4	0.9	3.6
United Kingdom	1.8	3.3	4.7	6.8	10.7	12.8	16.3	16.4	1.0	2.0
Canada	0.9	1.6	3.9	7.0	11.8	16.3	19.6	18.4	1.6	2.2
Belgium	1.3	2.6	4.0	5.3	10.4	14.0	16.8	17.2	1.1	2.7
Netherlands	1.6	2.6	3.7	5.9	11.7	14.3	16.6	17.2	1.0	2.5
Korea[a]				0.9	2.2	4.1	9.0			5.8
Taiwan[a]			1.0	0.9	2.7	5.6	10.3			6.0
Hong Kong[a]				2.0	5.3	10.0	17.1			5.4
Europe(6)[b]										
Mean	1.3	2.3	3.5	5.2	11.0	14.1	17.0	17.4	1.0	2.8
Coeff. of Var.	0.18	0.26	0.22	0.21	0.08	0.07	0.05	0.05		
All countries except Asia NICs										
Mean	1.2	2.1	3.5	5.5	11.3	14.7	18.0	18.3	1.2	2.7
Coeff. of Var.	0.25	0.35	0.32	0.38	0.14	0.11	0.10	0.10		
All countries										
Mean				4.4	9.3	12.7	16.5			3.3
Coeff. of Var.				0.59	0.4	0.32	0.21			

Notes: [a] For Korea, Taiwan, and Hong Kong, the final period is 1950–90, not 1950–94.
[b] Europe (6) is the six European countries in the table.

Sources: Fagerberg, Guerrieri, and Verspagen 1999*b* based on data from Maddison 1995 and unpublished data kindly supplied by Angus Maddison.

48   *Jan Fagerberg*

While Europe, Japan, and other countries started to catch up in many typical 'American way of life' products, US industry leaped forward in another area: science-based industry, in part due to massive public investments in R&D during the Second World War and the 'cold war' that followed. Gradually, however, European countries and Japan started to devote more resources to science and R&D (Table 2.2). By the mid-1970s many of these countries used a larger share of their available resources on civil R&D than did the United States. Hence, the US lead started to be challenged in this area as well. Following the Japanese example, some of the Asian NICs started to invest massively in R&D from the 1970s onwards.

TABLE 2.2. *Estimates of non-defence R&D as a percentage of GDP* (selected years)

	1963	1973	1981	1993
USA	1.5	1.7	1.9	2.1
Japan	1.4	1.9	2.4	2.8
Germany	1.3	2.0	2.4	2.3
France	1.2	1.5	1.7	2.1
Italy	0.7	0.9	1.0	1.3
United Kingdom	1.5	1.6	1.9	1.8
Canada	1.0	1.1	1.2	1.6
Belgium	1.0	1.4	1.4	1.6
Netherlands	2.0	2.0	1.9	2.0
Sweden	0.9	1.4	2.0	3.0
Switzerland	2.5	2.3	2.3	2.6
Korea	0.3	0.3	0.8	2.3
Taiwan	0.4	n.a.	0.7	1.8
Europe (6)				
Mean	1.3	1.6	1.7	1.9
Coeff. of var.	0.3	0.2	0.2	0.2
All countries except Asian NICs				
Mean	1.4	1.6	1.8	2.1
Coeff. of var.	0.4	0.2	0.2	0.2
All countries				
Mean	1.2	1.4	1.7	2.1
Coeff. of var.	0.5	0.4	0.3	0.2

Note: Estimates of civil R&D are available for most OECD countries for selected years. These estimates show that for all but a few countries (notably the USA, the UK, France, and Sweden) differences between civil and total R&D are small. Hence, for some countries and years, total R&D is used instead. Since data are not always available annually, the data reported here will in some cases be based on information from a preceding and/or following year. For definition of Europe (6), see Table 2.1.

Sources: Fagerberg, Guerrieri, and Verspagen 1999*b*, based on data from OECD Science and Technology Indicators Database and UNESCO/national sources (Korea, Taiwan).

During the 1980s European catch-up *vis-à-vis* the United States came to a halt, while Japan continued to increase productivity (GDP per capita) at a faster rate than both the United States and Europe. As a consequence Japan now enjoys a higher level of GDP per capita than Europe. The Asian NICs (Hong Kong, Korea, and Taiwan) have—at least until recently—continued to experience very rapid productivity growth, i.e. to catch-up relative to the United States and other countries.

2.3. Europe in the Global Market

Technological catch-up (or lack of such) and structural changes are intimately related with trade performance. In fact, one of the striking findings from studies of successful catch-up is that it is associated with both a general improvement in trade performance and a radical change in the composition of trade. For instance, the catch-up of Europe and Japan in scale- and capital-intensive technologies from the 1950s onwards was associated with rapidly increasing export market shares for products embodying these technologies. However, since then the locus of growth within manufacturing has changed to science-based industries.

How has Europe adapted to these changes in the global market? To map these developments this chapter makes use of a taxonomy in which industries are allocated to sectors depending on the nature and sources of technological knowledge. In principle this taxonomy, based on earlier work by Pavitt (1984, 1988) and Guerrieri (1992), could have been applied to both goods and services, but because of data limitations the analysis was confined to the former. The taxonomy identifies five type of industries: *agricultural products and raw materials, traditional manufactures, scale-intensive, specialized suppliers* (of various types of machinery, instruments, etc.) and, finally, *science-based* industries (such as professional electronics, pharmaceuticals, and aerospace). The two former depend largely on technology developed in other sectors, while the two latter are typical 'technology producing' sectors serving the entire economy. Scale intensive industry is in an intermediate position in this regard, it receives a lot of its technology from others, but it also has significant in-house technological accumulation (learning). Among these industries, the science-based sector has displayed the highest growth recently. Between 1970 and 1995 the share of science-based products in total world trade more than doubled, largely at the expense of agricultures and raw materials (Fagerberg, Guerrieri, and Verspagen 1999*a*).

Table 2.3 reports market shares (ratio of national exports to world exports) for four major players in the global economy, Europe (15), the United States, Japan, and the Asian NICs between 1970 and 1995. The market shares for Europe reported in the table include intra-European trade, and this explains why Europe's market shares are so high compared to the United States and

TABLE 2.3. Market shares, 1970–1995 (ratio of national exports to world exports[a], per cent)

	Agricultural and raw material Products	Traditional industries	Scale-intensive	Specialized Suppliers	Science-Based	Total
Europe (15)						
1970	24.1	57.0	55.7	61.2	48.6	44.6
1988	30.3	47.6	51.2	56.0	41.3	44.0
1995	31.6	40.1	47.3	47.6	33.8	39.6
Change 1970–95	7.5	−16.9	−8.4	−13.6	−14.8	−5.0
USA						
1970	13.1	7.4	14.5	22.3	29.5	14.8
1988	13.4	5.2	9.4	12.2	19.8	11.6
1995	11.0	6.7	10.3	13.7	17.9	11.8
Change 1970–95	−2.1	−0.7	−4.2	−8.6	−11.6	−3.0
Japan						
1970	1.2	9.3	13.8	6.4	7.7	6.7
1988	1.1	4.1	17.1	15.6	16.7	10.1
1995	1.4	3.2	12.8	15.7	14.3	9.0
Change 1970–95	0.2	−6.1	−1.0	9.3	6.6	2.3
Asian NICs						
1970	2.0	6.1	1.0	0.8	1.0	2.1
1988	2.6	14.5	5.6	4.0	9.1	6.7
1995	3.4	16.2	8.7	8.8	17.8	10.8
Change 1970–95	1.4	10.1	7.7	8.0	16.8	8.7

Notes: Europe (15): Austria, Belgium, Denmark, Finland, France, Germany, Greece, Ireland, Italy, Luxembourg, Netherlands, Portugal, Spain, Sweden, United Kingdom.
Asian NICs: Hong Kong, Korea, Singapore, Taiwan.
[a] Goods exports (trade in services not included). For the definition of sectors see Fagerberg, Guerrieri, and Verspagen 1999b.
Source: Fagerberg, Guerrieri, and Verspagen 1999b, based on UN and OECD data from the SIE World Trade data base.

Japan. However, similar calculations were made excluding intra-European trade, and the trends (changes through time)—which is what commands interest here—were basically the same. Between 1970 and 1995 Japan and the Asian NICs gained market shares at the expense of the United States and Europe. In particular, the Asian NICs showed a spectacular performance; between 1970 and 1995 its overall market share increased more than five times, from 2.1 to 10.8 per cent of the global market. It is also noteworthy that the rapid growth of Japan and the Asian NICs was accompanied by very rapid structural changes that totally changed the specialization pattern of these countries. In the case of Japan, in spite of overall market share growth, the market shares for traditional and scale-intensive industries actually contracted, while those of specialized suppliers and science-based industry increased rapidly, so that by the end of the period Japan had its major strength in the latter (followed by scale-intensive industry). For the Asian NICs a similar development took place, with a much stronger growth in science-based industry and specialized suppliers than in the traditional area of strength (traditional industries).

In contrast to the Asian experience, both Europe and the United States lost overall market shares. Moreover, these losses were generally more manifest in high-technology sectors, particularly science-based industries, than elsewhere. As a consequence, in the 1990s Europe was no longer specialized (i.e. having an above-average market share) in science-based industry. The only area in which Europe gained market shares was agricultural products and raw materials. Hence, European competitiveness, whether measured through its growth or trade performance, is deteriorating. Moreover, slow growth and declining market shares, particularly in the most advanced and fast-growing industries, go hand in hand with increasing unemployment problems (Table 2.4).

2.4. European Economic Integration

It is pertinent to ask what European integration has to do with all this. Forty to fifty years ago, when the first steps towards the present-day European Union

TABLE 2.4. *Unemployment as a percentage of the total labour force*

	1960–73	1974–9	1980–9	1990–5
Europe (15)	2.3	4.6	9.2	9.8
USA	4.8	6.7	7.2	6.4
Japan	1.3	1.9	2.5	2.5
Korea	n.a.	3.8	3.8	2.4

Source and definitions: Fagerberg, Guerrieri, and Verspagen 1999*b*, based on data from OECD Historical Statistics 1960–95.

were taken, priority was given to the creation of a common market for natural resource-based industries such as the coal and steel industries and agriculture. Because of the political sensitivity of these industries, the steps towards a common market were often combined with subsidies for high-cost, uncompetitive producers, and in many cases these subsidies became of a permanent (or semi-permanent) nature. In agriculture, a strong and costly incentive scheme was created, the Common Agricultural Policy (CAP), that encouraged agricultural production. As a result, Europe has become self-sufficient for most agricultural products and a problem of surpluses has occurred that is being resolved through, among other things, subsidized exports. Hence, it comes as no surprise that Europe has increased its market shares internationally for agriculture and raw materials.

The other main element in the European economic integration process has been a continuous drive towards economies of scale through enlargement and homogenization of markets. After the Second World War various schemes were developed in order to facilitate trade across national borders in Europe. From the late 1950s onwards a process of trade liberalization took place within two European trading blocks, EEC and EFTA. By the early 1970s internal trade in manufactures was virtually free of tariffs and other restrictions within these two blocks. These developments clearly strengthened the catch-up of Europe in many scale-intensive industries previously dominated by US industry, such as cars, domestic electrical equipment, and consumer electronics.

The drive towards economies of scale through enlargement of markets continued in the 1970s with the integration of the member countries of the two former trading blocks, EEC and EFTA. By the mid-1980s Western Europe had become a free-trading area for manufactures. However, this failed to produce positive growth effects of the type that had been associated with previous integration efforts. Partly as a result of this the EU launched its plan for a revitalization of the internal European market ('Europe 1992'). This plan was based on the idea that there were large unexploited economies of scale in European industry, the exploitation of which had been prevented by the existence of so-called 'non-tariff barriers' to trade, commonly assumed to be related to discriminatory actions by governments in one way or another. Hence, the heart of the plan has been to abolish these barriers. The fact that Europe's trade performance has been slightly better in scale-intensive industry than in manufacturing as a whole indicates that although it is difficult to detect an effect on overall growth, the strong emphasis on scale in European integration efforts may have had an impact on its pattern of specialization.

To sum up, European integration has favoured natural resource-based and scale-intensive industries, and this is consistent with the observed change in its pattern of specialization. However, given that modern growth is increasingly knowledge-based (Fagerberg 1994), it seems relevant to ask to what extent this move away from the technologically most advanced and fast-growing parts of manufacturing poses a problem for Europe's future growth and welfare.

2.5. Challenges from Innovation-based Growth

Traditional economic theory tells us that specialization is beneficial in itself because it leads to more efficient use of available resources. However, unless this has a positive effect on technological progress (so-called 'dynamic economies of scale'), it will not lead to higher growth in the long run. The evidence (Begg *et al.* 1999) shows that what matters for growth and competitiveness is not so much increasing the degree of specialization in general, as the ability to exploit areas of high technological opportunity, which in recent years have been dominated by information and communication technologies (ICTs).

However, as pointed out above, during the last decades Europe has lost ground in the technologically most progressive industries, and ICT is no exception to this trend. In fact, the research shows that, with the exception of telecommunication equipment, Europe has fallen behind the United States and Japan as suppliers to non-EU markets, and is increasingly vulnerable in software and services as well (Dalum, Freeman, *et al.* 1999). The diffusion of ICT products and services in Europe is also slow (Table 2.5), particularly when compared to the United States, and very uneven across Europe. While some smaller countries, especially the Nordic ones, have diffusion rates similar (or superior) to the US level, most countries in Europe (particularly in the south) are laggards when it comes to use of ICTs.

This raises the issue of what policy makers can and should do to reverse this uncomfortable trend. Arguably, transforming the education and training systems in order to equip individuals with the skills needed for an environment in which the major new technology is pervasive should be high on the policy agenda. The continuing skill shortages in software testify to the failure of Europe to meet this challenge, and it is evident that this deficiency has slowed the diffusion of ICTs beyond the immediate sectors that developed and applied them. However, acquiring skills is only a necessary first step. Skills also have to be put to uses that improve diffusion and learning. Therefore a combination of enhancement of skills and diffusion-oriented policies centred on social needs is required. Mobile communications in the Nordic area is a good example of how public regulation and support managed to bring together new technology, skills, and existing social needs in a way that both led to rapid diffusion of the new technology and—through learning—the development of globally competitive firms and industries (Dalum, Fagerberg, and Jørgensen 1988). The possibility that similar policies also may work for other types of ICT applications should encourage

TABLE 2.5. Some indicators on the use of ICT, 1996

	Cellular phone[a]	Internet hosts[b]	Internet users[b]	Personal computers[a]	ISDN subscribers[b]	Overall rank[c]
Norway	28.7	34.2	113.8	28.5	10.0	1
Finland	29.2	61.3	167.8	19.5	7.0	2
Denmark	25.0	20.3	57.0	30.4	5.7	3
US	16.5	37.9	78.8	36.2	3.3	4
Switzerland	9.3	18.7	52.1	40.9	17.7	5
Sweden	28.2	26.9	90.5	21.5	2.2	6
UK	12.2	12.4	43.0	19.3	4.5	7
Canada	11.4	20.1	66.7	24.4	0.1	7
Germany	7.1	8.4	30.5	23.3	23.7	9
Netherlands	5.2	17.4	58.0	23.2	6.4	10
Japan	21.4	5.8	55.7	12.8	4.2	11
Austria	7.4	11.0	37.2	14.9	5.2	12
Belgium	4.7	6.4	29.5	16.7	5.4	13
Ireland	8.2	7.6	22.7	17.0	0.0	14
France	4.2	4.1	8.6	15.1	7.3	15
Italy	11.2	2.6	10.2	9.2	1.8	16
Portugal	6.7	2.4	23.2	6.7	2.0	17
Spain	3.3	2.9	13.4	9.4	0.9	18
Greece	5.3	1.6	14.3	3.5	0.0	19
Europe[d]	8.8	8.7	29.7	16.9	8.4	—

Notes: [a] subscribers per 100 inhabitants, [b] per 1000 inhabitants, [c] mean rank of previous 5 columns, [d] weighted mean of countries above.

Source: Dalum et al. 1999, based on data from ITU World Telecommunications Development Report, 1998.

policy makers to experiment further with diffusion-oriented policies centred on users and social needs.

In a way the challenge for policy makers is no less than devising solutions which restore the dynamism and creativity that characterized the European economy in earlier periods. Part of the answer has to do with getting a proper understanding of the 'system of innovation', the mix of characteristics, infrastructure, and policies that determines how well an economy is able to exploit opportunities afforded by new technologies. In fact, differences in invention and innovation would not matter much if knowledge spread readily from region to region. However, the research reveals that the greater the geographical distance between regions, the lower the degree of knowledge flows between them (Maurseth and Verspagen 1999). Moreover, knowledge flows are greater within countries than between them, suggesting that the national element in innovation systems remains strong. The research also shows that knowledge flows are most intense between regions with similar or complementary specialization patterns, as well as between technologically linked sectors. These results suggest powerful influences leading to the formation of geographically concentrated clusters of technologically related activities at work in Europe's economy.

Economic and social cohesion—usually defined in terms of equity considerations such as regional disparities or social inclusion—is a fundamental aim of the EU articulated in Article 2 of the Treaty. However, research shows that regional disparities in economic performance remain substantial, and have increased in many member countries in the last decade (Fagerberg and Verspagen 1996; Cappelen, Fagerberg, and Verspagen 1999), see Table 2.6. This gap is especially marked as regards innovative activity. Hence, what seems to be a fairly robust finding is that there exists a subgroup of high

TABLE 2.6. *Dispersion of GDP per capita in EU regions and countries, 1960–1995*

	1960	1970	1980	1995
Regional standard deviation EU9	0.34	0.27	0.20	0.21
National standard deviation EU9	0.26	0.23	0.18	0.17
Share of total regional dispersion in EU9 due to:				
Between country dispersion in per cent	64	79	52	41
Within country dispersion in per cent	36	21	48	59

Note: Regional standard deviation measures the dispersion across European regions independent of which country the regions belong to. National standard deviation measures the dispersion across European countries (disregarding the dispersion between regions within countries). EU 9 includes Denmark, Be-Ne-Lux, France, Germany, Ireland, Italy, and UK. All figures based on PPS (purchasing power standard). The regional disaggregation is more detailed from 1980 onwards, and this biases the figures before 1980 for EU9 downwards.

Source: Cappelen, Fagerberg, and Verspagen 1999, based on data from EUROSTAT (REGIO Data Base).

R&D, high-income regions in Europe with its own internal dynamics. What distinguishes these high R&D regions from the rest is mainly that R&D matters a lot in the former, while it is of little importance (or contributes negatively) in the latter. Thus, there is a risk that a faster rate of innovation, which is vital for European growth and competitiveness in general, might further aggravate regional disparities.

Although data are scarce on many factors of potential relevance for regional growth, the evidence clearly indicates that most low-income regions have failed to exploit the potential for technology diffusion. This points to a need for policies aimed at enhancing the capacity of such regions to absorb new technologies, especially ICTs. Similar issues arise in relation to the eastern enlargement anticipated in the next few years (Grabbe, Hughes, and Landesmann 1999). The research also drew attention to the potential for the local science base, in the form of university research, to contribute to local learning processes and, hence, regional development (Dalum, Holmen, *et al.* 1999). Furthermore, the low rate of diffusion is often associated with a structure of activity dominated by agriculture or 'older' industries, and a corresponding lack of high-tech activities, often combined with relatively high unemployment. One strategy for change would be to reorient policies in this area towards accelerating structural change. But it is important to design policies in a way that does not lead to a further increase in long-term unemployment, as this is itself a factor hampering diffusion and growth (Fagerberg, Verspagen, and Caniëls 1997).

Perhaps the most important problem facing EU policy makers is how to combat the persistent high rate of unemployment in Europe (Table 2.4), which threatens social cohesion. It is important to stress that innovation is, in itself, no 'quick fix' for unemployment. Product innovation may increase employment through increased demand for products embodying the new technologies. But process innovation aimed primarily at rationalization of existing production processes may also reduce employment in a specific industry and/or location, if not compensated by indirect income and demand effects. In contrast to the situation in the other parts of the 'triad', the latter (employment-reducing) type of outcome is in fact the most common in Europe (Pianta and Vivarelli 1999). This is especially evident in industry (Table 2.7). What this implies is that Europe's industrial structure is orientated towards sectors most open to labour saving, mostly mature industries characterized by a high degree of process innovations.

Thus the challenge for policy makers is not only to increase innovation diffusion but also to do so in a way that is more 'employment friendly'. This requires a shift from the traditional emphasis on process innovations and reduction of labour costs to a stronger focus on product innovations and increases in quality. It should be evident that Europe can never hope to compete with newly industrialized countries in Asia and elsewhere on the basis of labour costs alone, and that the long-run outlook for Europe is also influenced by

The Challenge from Innovation-based Growth   57

TABLE 2.7. *The relationship between growth of employment and growth of GDP/value added (elasticity), 1975–1996*

Country	Whole economy	Industry	Services
United States	0.6	0.4	0.6
Japan	0.3	0.2	0.4
Europe (15)	0.1	−1.2	0.4

Source: Pianta and Vivarelli 1999, based on data from the OECD, UN, and Datastream.

the quality of what it produces. The research shows that there is great scope for raising quality as the core competitive advantage of the EU through a strategy based on product innovation, upgrading of skills, and increased R&D efforts (Jansen and Landesmann 1999).

2.6. Conclusions

To some extent Europe's current problems are the price to be paid for past successes. European integration, most recently through the single market programme, has made product and factor markets more open and paved the way for the realization of economies of scale and a more efficient allocation of resources. From a long-run perspective, these policies have been extremely successful. Without them, it is doubtful whether Europe would have managed to catch up with the United States to the extent that it did. However, the rewards to catch-up in capital- and scale-intensive sectors producing for the mass markets have been cashed in long ago, and now the rules of the game have changed. In the last decades, science-based industries, especially those drawing heavily on ICTs, have become the main driver of technological change and economic growth. Although the ICT revolution has been under way for a long time, its major effects are just beginning to be felt and it is clear that Europe's performance in ICT, however measured, is far from satisfactory. Arguably, if appropriate steps are not taken now, the current trends towards slow growth, increasing inequality and unemployment are likely to persist, threatening social cohesion, the social model, and the democratic values that Europeans hold dear.

The story is easily told. Slow growth is mainly the result of failure to exploit the technological opportunities inherent in new and fast-growing technologies. This is not mainly a question of failing to be competitive in, say, the production of computers or other products embodying ICT, but embedding the new technology in society at large. Regional disparities have been exacerbated by the very uneven diffusion of new technology, which has, hitherto, disproportionately favoured high-income, high-R&D regions specialized in high-tech manufacturing and—above all—services. By contrast, traditional agricultural regions or regions in the rustbelt have benefited very little if at all. Rather, what has happened is that the relative prices of their products and factor services have declined. High unemployment is the flip side of this coin. Europe's continuing specialization in increasingly mature industries characterized by labour-saving innovation has meant that relatively few new jobs have been created. Low labour mobility has made matters worse by inhibiting effective redeployment of resources and has, arguably, been an impediment to technological advance (Fagerberg, Verspagen, and Caniëls 1997).

Although the diagnosis is clear, agreeing on remedies is much less easy. What makes the problem so challenging is the need for actors and trends at very different levels to pull together. On the one hand, as the research shows, the creation of technological advantage is in most cases a very local affair. At the other extreme, radical technological changes, particularly the ICT revolution, affect nearly all aspects of life, so that a holistic approach to change aimed at exploiting the opportunities afforded by these new technologies is needed. Because of path dependency in local technological, institutional, and economic systems, and the complex conditions for getting the most out of ICT, this is very difficult to realize in practice. Thus, there is a large co-ordination problem here, and this emphasizes the need for a strategic view on European growth. Arguably, what is needed is a much more prominent role for the EU, not only in policy co-ordination, but in discussing policy change, experimenting with policy alternatives, evaluating the results, and providing benchmarking for government at various levels. Moreover, a much greater emphasis needs to be placed on stimulating more rapid, pervasive, and effective innovation in technologies, organizations, and institutions.

The core message from the research presented in this chapter is that the problems that Europe faces in key areas such as growth, equality, and employment are all related to its failure to take sufficient advantage of technological advances, particularly the ICT revolution. Consequently, a coherent European strategy for upgrading technological capability and quality competitiveness is long overdue. This cannot be limited to providing support to selected industries (or companies) in order to make them more competitive in global markets. Rather, what Europe has to do is to take steps to embed new technologies in society. This should bring together macroeconomic policy, regulation, science and technology policy, and employment initiatives. The complementarities between policy areas, in particular, should be stressed. Equally, it is vital at the outset to recognize that change will not happen overnight and that boosting the long-run ability of the economy to create and use new technologies will require concerted action.

REFERENCES

ABRAMOVITZ, M. (1994). 'The origins of the postwar catch-up and convergence boom', in J. Fagerberg, B. Verspagen, and N. von Tunzelman (eds.), *The Dynamics of Technology, Trade and Growth*. Aldershot: Edward Elgar.

BEGG, I., DALUM, B., GUERRIERI, P., and PIANTA, M. (1999). 'The Impact of specialization in Europe', in J. Fagerberg, P. Guerrieri, and B. Verspagen (eds.), *The Economic Challenge for Europe: Adapting to Innovations-based Growth*. Aldershot: Edward Elgar.

CAPPELEN, A., FAGERBERG, J., and VERSPAGEN, B. (1999). 'Lack of regional convergence', in J. Fagerberg, P. Guerrieri, and B. Verspagen (eds.), *The Economic Challenge for Europe: Adapting to Innovations-based Growth*. Aldershot: Edward Elgar.

CHANDLER, A. D., Jr (1990). *Scale and Scope. The Dynamics of Industrial Capitalism*. Cambridge, Mass.: The Belknap Press.

DALUM, B., FAGERBERG, J., and JØRGENSEN, U. (1988). 'Small countries in the world market for electronics: The case of the Nordic countries', in B.-Å. Lundvall and C. Freeman (eds.), *Small Countries Facing the Technological Revolution*. London: Pinter Publishers.

DALUM, B., FREEMAN, C., SIMONETTI, R., VON TUNZELMANN, N., and VERSPAGEN, B. (1999). 'Europe and the information and communication technologies revolution', in J. Fagerberg, P. Guerrieri, and B. Verspagen (eds.), *The Economic Challenge for Europe: Adapting to Innovation-based Growth*. Aldershot: Edward Elgar.

DALUM, B., HOLMEN, M., JACOBSSON, S., PRÆST, M., RICKNE, A., and VILLUMSEN, G. (1999). 'Changing the regional system of innovation', in J. Fagerberg, P. Guerrieri, and B. Verspagen (eds.), *The Economic Challenge for Europe: Adapting to Innovation-based Growth*. Aldershot: Edward Elgar.

FAGERBERG, J. (1994). 'Technology and international differences in growth rates'. *Journal of Economic Literature*, 32: 147–75.

——(1999). 'The need for innovation-based growth in Europe'. *Challenge*, 42: 63–79.

——VERSPAGEN, B., and VON TUNZELMAN, N. (1994) (eds.). *The Dynamics of Technology, Trade and Growth*. Aldershot: Edward Elgar.

—— ——(1996). 'Heading for divergence? Regional growth in Europe reconsidered'. *Journal of Common Market Studies*, 34: 431–48.

—— ——and CANIËLS, M. (1997). 'Technology, growth and unemployment across European regions'. *Regional Studies*, 31: 457–66.

——GUERRIERI, P., and VERSPAGEN, B. (1999a) (eds.). *The Economic Challenge for Europe: Adapting to Innovation-based Growth*. Aldershot: Edward Elgar.

—— ——and——(1999b). 'Europe-a long view', in J. Fagerberg, P. Guerrieri, and B. Verspagen (eds.), *The Economic Challenge for Europe: Adapting to Innovation-based Growth*. Aldershot: Edward Elgar.

GRABBE, H., HUGHES, K., and LANDESMANN, M. (1999). 'The implications of EU enlargement for EU integration, convergence and competitiveness', in J. Fagerberg, P. Guerrieri, and B. Verspagen (eds.), *The Economic Challenge for Europe: Adapting to Innovation-based Growth*. Aldershot: Edward Elgar.

GUERRIERI, P. (1992). 'Technological and trade competition: The changing position of US, Japan and Germany', in M. C. Harris and G. E. Moore (eds.), *Linking Trade and Technology Policies*. Washington, DC: National Academy Press.

JANSEN, M., and LANDESMANN, M. (1999). 'European competitiveness: Quality rather than price', in J. Fagerberg, P. Guerrieri, and B. Verspagen (eds.), *The Economic Challenge for Europe: Adapting to Innovation-based Growth*. Aldershot: Edward Elgar.

JOHNSON, C. (1982). *MITI and the Japanese Miracle: The Growth of Industrial Policy, 1925–1975*. Stanford: Stanford University Press.

MADDISON, A. (1991). *Dynamic Forces in Capitalist Development*. New York: Oxford University Press.

——(1995). *Monitoring the World Economy, 1820–1992*. Washington, DC: OECD.

MAURSETH, P., and VERSPAGEN, B. (1999). 'Europe: one or several systems of innovation?', in J. Fagerberg, P. Guerrieri, and B. Verspagen (eds.), *The Economic Challenge for Europe: Adapting to Innovations—based Growth*. Aldershot: Edward Elgar.

NELSON, R. R., and WRIGHT, G. (1992). 'The rise and fall of American technological leadership: The postwar era in historical perspective'. *Journal of Economic Literature*, 30: 1931–64.

PAVITT, K. (1984). 'Sectoral patterns of technical change: Towards a taxonomy and a theory'. *Research Policy*, 13: 343–74.

——(1988). 'International patterns of technological accumulation', in N. Hood and J. E. Vahlne (eds.), *Strategies in Global Competition*. London: Croom Helm.

PIANTA, M., and VIVARELLI, M. (1999). 'Employment dynamics and structural change in Europe', in J. Fagerberg, P. Guerrieri, and B. Verspagen (eds.), *The Economic Challenge for Europe: Adapting to Innovations-based Growth*. Aldershot: Edward Elgar.

VON TUNZELMANN, G. N. (1995). *Technology and Industrial Progress. The Foundations of Economic Growth*. Aldershot: Edward Elgar.

WADE, R. (1990). *Governing the Market. Economic Theory and the Role of Government in East Asian Industrialization*. Princeton: Princeton University Press.

PART III

TECHNOLOGY AND COMPETITIVENESS

[12]

The Economic Journal, **98** (*June* 1988), 355–374
Printed in Great Britain

INTERNATIONAL COMPETITIVENESS*

Jan Fagerberg

Measures of the international competitiveness of a country relative to other countries are frequently used, especially in mass media, governmental reports and discussions of economic policy. But, in spite of this, it is rather rare to see the concept of international competitiveness of a country defined. However, few would probably disagree with the view that it refers to the ability of a country to realise central economic policy goals, especially growth in income and employment, without running into balance-of-payments difficulties. Following this, what a theory of international competitiveness must do is to establish the links between the growth and balance-of-payments position of an open economy and factors influencing this process.

Even if there exist many measures of the international competitiveness of a country,[1] by far the most popular and influential is 'growth in relative unit labour costs' $(RULC)$.[2] In the small open economies of Western Europe this measure seems to be as important for policy-making as certain monetary aggregates have been in the United States and the United Kingdom in recent years. If unit labour costs grow more than in other countries, it is argued, this will reduce market shares at home and abroad, hamper economic growth and increase unemployment. However, available empirical evidence shows that the fastest growing countries in terms of exports and GDP in the post-war period have at the same time experienced much faster growth in relative unit labour costs than other countries, and vice versa.[3] This fact, sometimes referred to as the 'Kaldor paradox' after Kaldor (1978), indicates that the popular view of growth in unit labour costs determining international competitiveness is at best too simplified. But why?

Section I discusses the main theoretical arguments in favour of a detrimental effect of 'growth in relative unit labour costs' on market shares and growth. It

* The ideas set forth in this paper owe much to discussions with Ådne Cappelen, Bengt Åke Lundvall and Nick von Tunzelman. I am also indebted to Jens C. Andvig, Lennart Erixon, Wynne Godley, Kalle Moene and Anders Skonhoft for comments on various drafts, and to the editors and referees of this JOURNAL for helpful comments and suggestions during the final stage of the work. Financial support from the Norwegian Research Council for the Social Sciences and the Humanities (NAVF) is gratefully acknowledged. An earlier version of the paper was presented at the Second Annual Congress of the European Economic Association in Copenhagen August 22–4, 1987.

[1] These measures range from indicators of economic performance (market shares (Chesnais (1981), profitability (Eliasson, 1972)), single-factor indicators based on price or cost development, to complex composite indexes reflecting economic, structural and institutional factors (EMF, 1984).

[2] Unit labour costs (ULC) in manufacturing are wages and social costs for workers at current prices divided by gross product at constant prices. Relative unit labour costs $(RULC)$ are ULC converted to an international currency and divided by the average ULC for the country's trading partners. $RULC$ may grow (1) because wages and social costs for workers in national currency are rising faster than in other countries, (2) because the exchange rate is improving relative to other countries, or (3) because productivity growth is lower than in other countries.

[3] Several studies, including Fetherston *et al.* (1977), Kaldor (1978) and Kellman (1983) have shown that the effects of growing relative costs or prices on exports or market shares seem to be rather weak and sometimes 'perverse'.

[355]

also considers an alternative, although closely related, approach advocated by Thirlwall (1979), which focuses on differences between countries in 'income elasticities of demand' as a possible source of international growth rate differentials. The common shortcoming of these approaches, we shall argue, is that they fail to take factors other than price competition and demand explicitly into account. Sections II and III of this paper, then, develop a model of international competitiveness which relates growth in market shares to three sets of factors: the ability to compete in technology, the ability to compete in price, and the ability to compete in delivery (capacity). The remaining part of the paper presents a test of the model on pooled cross-sectional and time-series data from 15 OECD countries between 1961–83. The results indicate that factors related to technology and capacity are indeed very important for medium and long run differences across countries in growth of market shares and GDP, while cost-competitiveness plays a more limited role than commonly assumed. These results are shown to provide a reasonable explanation for the seemingly paradoxical findings by Kaldor and others.

I. TRADITIONAL WISDOM QUESTIONED

The most popular approach to international competitiveness is that which focuses on the detrimental effects of growth in relative unit labour costs ($RULC$) on market shares and growth. What are the theoretical arguments in favour of this view? First, it may be noted that this approach is incompatible with neoclassical equilibrium theory. In perfect competition, prices and quantities will always adjust, resources (including labour) be fully utilised and balance-of-payments equilibrium ensured. Thus, economists defending the hypothesis of the detrimental effects of growing relative unit labour costs, have always had to assume some degree of imperfect competition or disequilibrium.

For instance, let us assume that each country produces one good which is an imperfect substitute for the goods produced by the other countries. As a consequence, each country faces a downward sloping demand curve both at home and abroad. To bring unit labour costs into the picture, assume that prices are determined by unit labour costs with a mark-up (other cost factors than labour costs ignored), and that unit labour costs are determined outside the model. The model is closed by assuming balanced trade.

The following symbols will be used: Y = GDP (volume), X = Exports (volume), M = Imports (volume), W = World demand (volume), P = Price per nationally produced product (dollar), P_w = World Market price (dollar), U = Unit labour costs at home (dollar) and U_w = Unit labour costs abroad (dollar).

The coefficients a and b are the price elasticities of demand on the world market and the national market respectively, while c and h are the corresponding income elasticities.

$$X = A(P_w/P)^a \, W^c, \text{ where } A, a \text{ and } c \text{ are constants,} \tag{1}$$

$$M = B(P/P_w)^b \, Y^h, \text{ where } B, b \text{ and } h \text{ are constants,} \tag{2}$$

$$XP = MP_w \text{ (the balance-of-trade restriction)}, \tag{3}$$

$$P_i = U_i(1+t), \text{ where } t \text{ is a constant, } i = \text{home, world.} \tag{4}$$

This way of modelling export and import growth has a long tradition in applied international economics, and examples may be found in many national and international macroeconomic models, including, for instance, the OECD INTERLINK model (Samuelson, 1973). In its present version (1–3), it was first presented by Thirlwall (1979). The main lesson to be learned from the model is set out in equations (5)–(6) below.

$$\frac{dY}{Y} = \frac{1-(a+b)}{h}\left(\frac{dP}{P} - \frac{dP_w}{P_w}\right) + \frac{c}{h}\frac{dW}{W}. \tag{5}$$

By substituting (4) into (5) we get:

$$\frac{dY}{Y} = \frac{1-(a+b)}{h}\left(\frac{dU}{U} - \frac{dU_w}{U_w}\right) + \frac{c}{h}\frac{dW}{W}. \tag{6}$$

Thus, on these assumptions, economic growth may be written as a function of growth in relative unit labour costs and world demand. However, this model has given rise to rival interpretations. The most common is no doubt that higher growth in relative unit labour costs than in other countries decreases exports, increases imports and slows down economic growth. As is evident from equation (6) above, a necessary condition for this is that the Marshall-Lerner condition is strictly satisfied $(a+b > 1)$. This is often taken for granted, but, as noted in the introduction, several studies indicate that the effects of growing relative unit labour costs on exports or imports are rather weak. For instance, a report from the British Treasury points out:

> 'Recent experience suggests that cost-competitiveness may have a significantly less important or more delayed influence on export volumes than was thought a few years ago' (Treasury (1983), p. 4)

According to this report, the long-term elasticities of growth in relative unit labour costs in the Treasury model were as a result adjusted downwards to 0.5 for exports and 0.3 for imports. Consider, also, the following regression of growth in relative unit labour costs ($RULC$) and growth in OECD imports (W) on GDP growth (GDP) on a pooled cross-country time-series data set[4] for the period 1961–83 (95 % confidence intervals in brackets):

$$GDP = \underset{(-0.08/1.36)}{0.64} + \underset{(-0.07/0.20)}{0.06\,RULC} + \underset{(0.38/0.60)}{0.49W}, \qquad \begin{aligned} &R^2 = 0.60\ (0.58) \\ &\text{SER} = 1.36 \\ &\text{DW}(g) = 1.23 \\ &N = 60. \end{aligned}$$

Where R^2 in brackets is R^2 adjusted for the degree of freedom, SER is standard

[4] The data cover the 15 industrial countries for which data on unit labour costs exist. Average values of the variables covering whole business cycles were calculated, using the 'peak' years 1968, 1973, 1979 and 1983 (final year) to separate one cycle from the next. For further information on data and methods, see Section IV and Appendix.

error of regression, DW(g) is the Durbin-Watson statistics adjusted for gaps[5]
and N is the number of observations included in the test.

For the Marshall-Lerner condition to be strictly satisfied, the estimate of
RULC should be negative and significantly different from zero at the chosen
level of significance. The test suggests that this hypothesis should be rejected.
Since serial correlation in the residuals of the cross-sectional units cannot be
ruled out, an additional test was carried out including one dummy variable for
each country. To test for the sensitivity of lags, a three year distributive lag of
the RULC variable was introduced. However, neither of these additional tests
changed the result.

The second interpretation (Thirlwall, 1979) starts off with the assumption
that relative prices in the long run will be roughly constant,[6] so the first term
can be neglected. On this assumption, equation (6) reduces to:

$$\frac{dY}{Y} = \frac{c}{h}\frac{dW}{W}. \tag{7}$$

or, alternatively

$$\frac{dY}{Y} = \frac{1}{h}\frac{dX}{X}. \tag{8}$$

In this case differences in economic growth between countries will be
determined exclusively by differences in income elasticities of exports and
imports (7), or, in the case of exogenously given export growth, by differences
in income elasticities of imports alone (8). Using estimates of income elasticities
from Houthakker and Magee (1969), Thirlwall (1979) showed that equation
(8) gave fairly good predictions of the differences in growth rates between
countries.

However, Thirlwall's conclusions have been subject to some controversy.[7]
First, it is pointed out that the test carried out by Thirlwall, a nonparametric
one, is rather weak, and that more appropriate tests question his results.
Secondly, it is argued that since Thirlwall tests a reduced form of the model,
his test cannot be legitimately quoted in support of the underlying assumptions.
Thirdly, it is not clear what meaning should be attached to the 'income
elasticities of demand' in equations (1)–(2). Why, for instance, is the estimated
income elasticity for imports to the United Kingdom so much higher, and the
estimated income elasticity for exports from the United Kingdom so much
lower, than for other countries on approximately the same level of income per
capita? One possible answer to this question is, as indicated by Thirlwall
(Thirlwall, 1979, pp. 52–3), that UK producers did not manage to compete

---

[5] This test, which is designed for first order serial correlation in the residuals within the cross sectional
units, was suggested to me by Professor Ron Smith of Birkbeck College, London. For a more thoroughgoing
discussion of serial correlation in regressions with pooled data sets, see Section IV. The difference between
this test and the one commonly used in time-series analysis, is that the differences between the residuals of
different cross sectional units, and the corresponding residuals, are left out from both the numerator and the
denominator of the Durbin-Watson statistics. This reduces the number of observations in the test by one per
country.

[6] This is a strong assumption which may be difficult to justify (and deserves to be tested). For a discussion
of this point, see McGregor and Swales (1985, 1986) and Thirlwall (1986).

[7] See McCombie (1981), Thirlwall (1981, 1986) and McGregor and Swales (1985, 1986).

successfully on non-price factors during the period for which the estimation was carried out, and that the estimates of c and h capture the effects of this. This interpretation is also shared by Kaldor, who points out that the income elasticities of this model reflect 'the innovative ability and adaptive capacity' of the producers in different countries (Kaldor, 1981, p. 603). However, if true, it would be preferable to include these factors in the equations for exports and imports instead of relying on estimated proxies (which may be subject to different interpretations).

II. TECHNOLOGY, COSTS AND CAPACITY

In recent years, there has been an increasing awareness among economists, especially in the field of international economics, of the importance of technological competition. One of the early forerunners, Joseph Schumpeter, described the importance of this vividly as follows:

> 'Economists are at long last emerging from the stage in which price competition was all they saw. (...) But in capitalist reality, as distinguished from its textbook picture, it is not that kind of competition which counts, but the competition from the new commodity, the new technology, the new source of supply, the new type of organization (...) – competition which commands a decisive cost or quality advantage and which strikes not at the margins of the profits and the outputs of the existing firms but at their foundations and their very lives.' (Schumpeter, 1943, p. 84)

A logical conclusion from this would be to include both technological competitiveness and price competitiveness in the exports and imports functions. However, even if a country is very competitive in terms of technology and prices, it is not always able to meet the demand for its products because of a capacity constraint. Similarly, lack of competitiveness in terms of technology or prices may sometimes be compensated by a high ability to meet demand, if some other country faces a capacity constraint. Thus, the growth in market shares for a country at home and abroad does not only depend on technology and prices, but also on its ability to deliver. We will assume that the rest of the world's ability to deliver is unlimited, i.e. that there is always some country which is able to deliver if the national producers face a capacity constraint.

Let the technological competitiveness of a country be T/T_w, price competitiveness P/P_w and capacity C. How these variables may be measured will be discussed in section IV. Let the market share for exports be $S(X) = X/W$. In the usual multiplicative form, $S(X)$ may be written:

$$S(X) = AC^v(T/T_w)^e(P/P_w)^{-a}, \qquad (9)$$

where A, v, e and a are positive constants. By differentiating with respect to time this may be written:

$$\frac{dS(X)}{S(X)} = v\frac{dC}{C} + e\left(\frac{dT}{T} - \frac{dT_w}{T_w}\right) - a\left(\frac{dP}{P} - \frac{dP_w}{P_w}\right). \qquad (10)$$

We will assume that growth in the ability to deliver depends on three factors: (a) the growth in technological capability and know-how that is made possible by diffusion of technology from the countries on the world innovation frontier to the rest of the world (dQ/Q), (b) the growth in physical production equipment, buildings, transport equipment and infrastructure (dK/K) and (c) the rate of growth of demand (dW/W). Demand enters the function because capacity at any given point of time is given, while demand may vary.[8] If demand outstrips the given level of capacity, exports will remain constant, but the market share for exports will decrease, because other countries will increase their exports. If we assume a multiplicative form as above, the growth in the ability to meet demand may be written:

$$\frac{dC}{C} = z\frac{dQ}{Q} + r\frac{dK}{K} - l\frac{dW}{W}, \tag{11}$$

where z, r, l are positive constants.

As is customary in the literature on diffusion, we will assume that growth in free knowledge follows a logistic curve:

$$\frac{dQ}{Q} = f - f\frac{Q}{Q*}, \tag{12}$$

where f is a positive constant, and $Q/Q*$ is the ratio between the country's own level of technological development and that of the countries on the world innovation frontier. This contribution will be zero for the frontier countries. By substituting (11)–(12) into (10) we finally arrive at the following:

$$\frac{dS(X)}{S(X)} = vzf - vzf\frac{Q}{Q*} + vr\frac{dK}{K} - vl\frac{dW}{W} + e\left(\frac{dT}{T} - \frac{dT_w}{T_w}\right) - a\left(\frac{dP}{P} - \frac{dP_w}{P_w}\right). \tag{13}$$

For the sake of exposition, this exercise was carried out for the market share for exports only. But exactly the same logic applies to the import share, or the 'rest of the world's' market share in a specific country's home market, with the exception that the demand variable in this case is GDP(Y). However, all effects now enter the equation with the opposite signs of those in (13). For instance, growth in relative prices decreases the export share, but increases the import share etc. Carrying out the same exercise for the import share $S(M)$, using bars to distinguish the coefficients in the two equations, leaves us with the following equation:

$$\frac{dS(M)}{S(M)} = -\bar{v}\bar{z}\bar{f} + \bar{v}\bar{z}\bar{f}\frac{Q}{Q*} - \bar{v}\bar{r}\frac{dK}{K} + \bar{v}\bar{l}\frac{dY}{Y} - \bar{e}\left(\frac{dT}{T} - \frac{dT_w}{T_w}\right) + \bar{a}\left(\frac{dP}{P} - \frac{dP_w}{P_w}\right). \tag{14}$$

Thus, equations (13–14) state that growth in the market shares for exports and imports depends on technological factors (scope for imitation, growth in technological competitiveness), growth in physical production capacity, growth in relative prices and growth of demand.

---

[8] Since these constraints (or critical levels of demand) vary across the different export sectors, the relation between $S(X)$ and W is likely to be continuous, as in equation (11) below.

III. COMPETITIVENESS AND GROWTH

This section focuses on the relation between market shares for exports and imports and economic growth. First, how do changes in market shares affect economic growth? Secondly, how does economic growth feed back on market shares?

The first question relates to the assumption of balanced trade made in section I:

$$XP = MP_w. \tag{3}$$

Following the previous section, define the export share as $S(X) = X/W$ and the import share as $S(M) = M/Y$. By substituting these expressions into (3), differentiating with respect to time and rearranging, (3) may be written:

$$dY/Y = dS(X)/S(X) - dS(M)/S(M) + (dP/P - dP_w/P_w) + dW/W. \tag{15}$$

Basically, what is assumed is that countries do not wish, or are not able, continually to increase debts or claims to the rest of the world, so that the balance-of-payments, with the exception of short run fluctuations, will have to balance through its current account.[9] This implies that, in the medium and long run, actual growth has to adjust to the balance-of-trade equilibrium growth rate, or the growth rate 'warranted' by the current account, to use a Harrodian term. We will assume that the government plays an important role in this process by adjusting fiscal and monetary policies towards this end.

The second question refers to the possible feedbacks of economic growth on factors influencing the growth of market shares for exports and imports. For instance, higher economic growth is likely to lead to higher growth in both wages and productivity. However, with respect to unit labour costs, these effects tend to counteract each other. The net effect will crucially depend on the institutions and the working of the national system of income distribution, which we in the present context have chosen to regard as exogenously determined.

Furthermore, economic growth may influence technological competitiveness through demand-induced innovation (Schmookler, 1966). The importance of demand-induced relative to supply-induced innovation has been subject to much debate in recent years. The available evidence shows that there is no easy link between changes in demand conditions and innovative activity. Clusters of innovations have appeared in booms as well as in slumps, and on the whole innovative activity seems to depend more on technological opportunity and the quality and quantity of the resources devoted to innovation than on demand conditions (Freeman *et al.*, 1982).

Finally, economic growth may affect the ability to compete in delivery. An increase in domestic demand may lead to a situation where demand outstrips capacity in certain sectors, and as a consequence domestic suppliers may lose market shares to foreign suppliers, and vice versa. This has already been taken into account in the import share function (14). But the effect of increased

[9] It should be noted, though, that the United States is in a special position because of the demand for dollars for international monetary transactions.

demand on capacity utilisation may also have a secondary effect on the ability to deliver, by stimulating investments in new productive capacity. This effect is supported by economic theory and should be taken into account in the model. For instance, the effect of growth in demand on investment may be represented by a simple accelerator mechanism:

$$dK/K = dY/Y. \tag{16}$$

However, viewed as an explanation of differences between countries in investment behaviour, this model will not do, because investment behaviour is also influenced by other factors. Some of these will be highly country specific, others of a more general nature. Among the latter, many emphasise the 'crowding out' mechanism: the higher the share of output devoted to governmental activities, it is argued, the less the scope for investments in new production capacity. However, this argument rests on the assumption of a supply constraint, an assumption which, while certainly relevant in some cases, cannot be said to be generally valid.

According to the approach of this paper, investment in physical production capacity should be analysed as one of several factors necessary for generating technological capability. This implies that growth of physical production capacity should be seen as complementary to the growth of other resources such as the number of scientists and engineers, R & D facilities, advanced electronic equipment etc. Some of these are scarce, and to the extent that the government succeeds in attracting these at the expense of the market sectors of the economy, this may hamper investment in physical production capacity too. As pointed out by Kaldor *et al.* (1986), the probability for this to happen is much larger for the military than for other types of governmental activities. Thus, following Smith (1977) and Cappelen *et al.* (1984), we have chosen to include the shares of output devoted to military and non-military governmental expenditures ('welfare state expenditures') in the accelerator-based investment function. What we should expect, then, is that military expenditures have a significantly more negative effect on investment behaviour than welfare-state expenditures.

Let us take a brief look at the model as developed so far. It consists of five equations:

$$dY/Y = dS(X)/S(X) - dS(M)/S(M) + (dP/P - dP_w/P_w) + dW/W, \tag{15}$$

$$\frac{dS(X)}{S(X)} = vzf - vzf\frac{Q}{Q*} + vr\frac{dK}{K} - vl\frac{dW}{W} + e\left(\frac{dT}{T} - \frac{dT_w}{T_w}\right) - a\left(\frac{dP}{P} - \frac{dP_w}{P_w}\right), \tag{13}$$

$$\frac{dS(M)}{S(M)} = -\overline{vzf} + \overline{vzf}\frac{Q}{Q*} - \overline{vr}\frac{dK}{K} + \overline{vl}\frac{dY}{Y} - \overline{e}\left(\frac{dT}{T} - \frac{dT_w}{T_w}\right) + \overline{a}\left(\frac{dP}{P} - \frac{dP_w}{P_w}\right), \tag{14}$$

$$dK/K = -g\,MIL - h\,WELF + dY/Y, \tag{17}$$

where *MIL* and *WELF* are the shares of military and non-military governmental expenditures in total output, respectively.

From (4) we have:

$$dP_i/P_i = dU_i/U_i \quad (i = \text{home, world}) \tag{18}$$

The working of the model is as follows: growth in relative prices is determined by growth in relative unit labour costs (18). Together with technological factors, growth in physical production and demand, growth in relative prices determine the growth in market shares for exports and imports (13)–(14). Growth in market shares, growth in relative prices and growth of world demand jointly determine the balance-of-trade equilibrium growth rate, to which the actual growth rate is assumed to adjust (15). The actual growth rate then feeds back on the import share (14) and the growth of physical production equipment etc (17).

The actual outcome of the adjustment process depends on the relative strength of the two feedback effects, since they counteract each other. For example, let us assume that the balance-of-trade equilibrium growth rate, y_b, is below the actual growth rate, y_a, and that the government seeks to adjust the actual growth rate to the balance-of-trade equilibrium growth rate by successive incremental cuts in demand of given size until a new equilibrium ($y_a = y_b = y^*$) is reached.[10] The new equilibrium y^* will be between the initial values of y_a and y_b provided that the positive effect on the balance-of-trade of reduced imports outweighs the negative effect of reduced capacity, or formally:

$$0 > [(vr + \overline{vr}) - \overline{vl}]. \tag{19}$$

If on the contrary the negative effect of reduced capacity outweighs the positive effect of reduced imports, we will have a 'vicious' circle, with the new equilibrium below the initial value of y_b, or formally:

$$1 > [(vr + \overline{vr}) - \overline{vl}] > 0. \tag{20}$$

IV. TESTING THE MODEL

(a) *Data*

The model was tested on pooled cross-country and time-series data for the period 1960–83 covering the 15 industrial countries for which data on unit labour costs exist. Average values of the variables covering whole business cycles were calculated, using the 'peak' years 1968, 1973, 1979 and 1983 (final year) to separate one cycle from the next. In principle, it would have been preferable to begin by estimating the model for each country and test whether pooling is appropriate or not, but because of lack of annual data for the technology variables, this was not possible.

The following variables were used:

GDP_i = Growth of gross domestic product in country i at constant prices,
ME_i = Growth in export market share (volume) for country i on the world market,
MI_i = Growth in import share (volume) in country i,
$TERMS_i$ = Growth in terms of trade for country i,
$RULC_i$ = Growth in relative unit labour costs in common currency for country i,

[10] The condition for a stable solution is: $1 > [(vr + \overline{vr}) - \overline{vl}]$.

W = Growth of world trade at constant prices,

TL_i = Technological level of country i relative to the most advanced country of the sample ($= 1$),

TG_i = Growth in country i's technological competitiveness,

$WELF_i$ = Non-military governmental consumption as percentage of GDP in country i,

INV_i = Gross fixed investment as percentage of GDP in country i,

MIL_i = Military expenditures as a percentage of GDP in country i.

Most of these variables, with an exception for the technology variables, are self-explanatory (the reader is referred to the appendix for details on sources and methods).

The major problem in testing the model was to find proxies for the technology variables. Many other studies have used GDP per capita, measured in various ways, as a proxy for the level of technological development. While defensible for countries on very different levels of development as, for instance, developed and less developed countries, this practice becomes more questionable for a sample of developed countries. Contrary to less developed countries, developed countries also regularly publish data on technological activities which could be used to construct a proxy for the level of technological development.

Data on technological activities may roughly be divided in two groups, 'technology input' and 'technology output' data (Soete, 1981). Among the former, expenditures on research and development (R & D) may be mentioned, among the latter, patenting activity. The advantages and problems of different types of data on technological activities are discussed in more detail elsewhere (Fagerberg, 1987) and will not be repeated here. However, both R & D and patent statistics are imperfect measures in the sense that they neglect important aspects of technological activity. Some sectors of the economy do a lot of R & D, but do not patent, while others patent a lot without being especially R & D-intensive. At the national level, however, cross-country studies show a close correlation between levels of R & D and levels of patenting activity (Soete, 1981; Fagerberg, 1987). If both variables were to be included in the same model, a high degree of multicollinearity should be expected. These considerations seem to suggest that the best measure of technological activity would be a weighted average of R & D-based and patent-based measures. In principle we would have given the two variables an equal weight, but since the variances of the two variables differ substantially, we used weights that adjusted for these differences.

Thus, the proxy for technological development, TL, is a weighted average of (*a*) civil R & D as percentage of GDP, and (*b*) external patent applications per capita adjusted for differences in the openness of the economy.[11] Following the

---

[11] Civil R & D is total R & D less military R & D. Military R & D was excluded because, if included, it would bias the measure in favour of countries with a large military sector, and because several studies show that the economic spin offs of military R & D are small (Kaldor *et al.*, 1986). The number of external patent applications of country i is the total number of patent applications filed by residents in country i in all other

discussion in section II, both variables were divided by the highest value found in the sample in each period. The index, then, varies between 1 (the country on the world innovation frontier) and 0 (a hypothetical country with no technological activity). In a similar way, a proxy for growth in technological competitiveness, TG, can be constructed as a weighted average of (a) annual percentage growth in Civil R & D[12] for country i, less the average growth for the countries in the sample, and (b) annual percentage growth in external patent applications for country i, less the average growth for the countries in the sample. This index, then, has a zero average in each period.

Regarding the growth of 'physical production equipment, transport equipment and infrastructure', we would have preferred a proxy based on some measure of physical capital, but unfortunately no such measure was available for all the countries concerned and for sufficiently long time spans. As a number of other studies, therefore, we chose to use gross investment as a percentage of GDP as a proxy.

(b) The empirical model

The model tested is the one set out in the previous section subject to a few modifications.

First, in order to test the assumption of a one-to-one correlation between actual growth and the balance-of-trade equilibrium growth rate (BAL), we have introduced a separate equation for this (in addition to the balance-of-trade equilibrium growth rate identity). Second, in actual practice growth in relative prices (terms of trade) is influenced by a number of factors, many of them country specific, that do not relate to the price- or cost-competitiveness of firms. Since we believe growth in relative unit labour costs to be a better measure of price- and cost-competitiveness of firms than growth in terms of trade, we have substituted growth of relative unit labour costs into the two equations for growth in market shares, and introduced a separate equation where growth in terms of trade is set out to be a function of growth in relative unit labour costs, country dummies (see later) and a POST-73 dummy. The POST-73 dummy is supposed to catch the effect of the loss in terms trade that most of these countries experienced because of the oil price shocks.

---

countries than country i. To arrive at a patent based index of technological development, we adjusted for the size and openness of the economy (the number of patent applications filed abroad reflect both the size of the country and the importance of foreign markets relative to the domestic market (Fagerberg, 1987)). In general, changes in international patent regulations have made it difficult to compare data from years prior to 1978–9 with data from later years. However, in the present context, this does not represent a serious problem, because we have used 1979 to separate the third cycle from the fourth and, in the case of growth of external patent applications, adjusted for the common within-period trend.

[12] Annual data for R & D were available for a few countries only, so we had to use a proxy for growth in civil R & D. In general, R & D efforts (as a percentage of GDP) and income per capita tend to be closely correlated (Soete, 1981; Fagerberg, 1987). If the R & D efforts of a country are much above what should be expected from the level of income in the country, this may be interpreted as an effort by the country to upgrade its technological level, and vice versa. Following this, the proxy chosen is the difference between actual R & D (as a percentage of GDP) and what should be expected assuming a linear relation between R & D and income per capita. It was calculated as the ratio between civil R & D per capita and GDP per capita, subtracted by the average value of the ratio (for all countries) in each period.

The empirical model, then, is the following:

$$GDP = a_{10} + a_{11} BAL, \text{ where we expect } a_{10} = 0, a_{11} = 1, \tag{21}$$

$$BAL \equiv ME - MI + TERMS + W \tag{22}$$

$$TERMS = a_{31} RULC - a_{32} POST_{73} + DUMMIES, \tag{23}$$

$$ME = a_{40} - a_{41} TL + a_{42} INV - a_{43} W + a_{44} TG - a_{45} RULC, \tag{24}$$

$$MI = a_{50} + a_{51} TL - a_{52} INV + a_{53} GDP - a_{54} TG + a_{55} RULC, \tag{25}$$

$$INV = a_{60} - a_{61} MIL - a_{62} WELF + a_{63} GDP. \tag{26}$$

Since all coefficients are defined as positive, the expected signs are the ones above. Note, however, that since we use a proxy for growth in physical production capacity, we cannot any longer make inferences from the theoretical model about the expected signs of the constant terms in (24)–(26).

(c) Estimation

To avoid simultaneous equation bias, the two stage least squares method (2SLS) was adopted. To test for first-order serial correlation within the cross-sectional units, we used the Durbin-Watson statistics adjusted for gaps, to test for heteroscedasticity, we applied a Glejser test. Furthermore, to test for the possibility of structural change, a Chow test was used.

There is a special problem involved in estimation on pooled cross-country time-series data. For instance, assume that there is one time-invariant omitted variable for each country, representing country-specific factors such as differences in culture, institutions, composition of output etc. In this case we would expect least-squares methods to produce results where the residuals of each country are serially correlated. If this type of serial correlation is a serious one, more efficient estimates may be obtained by methods that adjust for the part of the total variance which can be attributed to country-specific factors.

Several methods are available. The most widely used is to introduce country dummies (the LSDV method). This method automatically leaves out the part of the total variance which refers to differences in country-variable means, and is therefore not applicable in cases where these differences are considered to be relevant. Another class of methods treats the country specific effects as random variables[13] (random effects method). The problem in this case is that the 'true' variances are not known and have to be estimated.

The choice of estimation method depends crucially on the nature of the

---

[13] In the case of a linear relation between a dependent and a set of independent variables, let the dependent variable be denoted by y_{jt} (country j, period t), the independent variables by x_{ijt} (variable i, country j, period t), the 'adjustment-factor' by c ($1 > c > 0$) and let 'bar' denote within-country mean of a variable. It is suggested, then, that estimates obtained by estimating the equation

$$(y_{jt} - c\bar{y_j}) = a_i(x_{ijt} - c\bar{x_{ij}})$$

will give more efficient estimates than estimates obtained by ordinary least squares. Let the disturbance term be $u(j,t) = b(j) + w(j,t)$, where $b(j)$ is the country-specific 'random effect', and let the expected variance of the country-specific effects and the rest of the disturbance term be $V(b)$ and $V(w)$, respectively. The adjustment factor may then be written:

$$c = 1 - \{V(w)/[V(w) + T V(b)]\}^{0.5},$$

hypothesis under test. Consider, for instance, the relation between growth in terms of trade and growth in relative unit labour costs (23). Ordinary least squares implies a test of the hypothesis that growth in terms of trade is determined by growth in relative unit labour costs (and the *POST*-73 dummy) only. To apply the LSDV method implies a test of the hypothesis that growth in terms of trade is determined by country-specific trends, reflecting differences in specialisation patterns and other time-invariant factors, but that deviations from these trends are determined by growth in relative unit labour costs (and the *POST*-73 dummy). Since we, as pointed out in the previous subsection, hold the latter to be the most likely, the LSDV method is the most appropriate method in this case.

Similar arguments may be put forward for the relation between actual growth and the balance-of-trade equilibrium growth rate (21). To use 2SLS without dummy variables implies a test of the hypothesis that the balance-of-trade equilibrium growth rate and the actual growth rate are identical. This is a strong hypothesis, that may be contested. For instance, the United States is in a special position, because of the demand for dollars for international monetary transactions. Furthermore, large, unexpected changes in the balance-of-trade position may lead to very long adjustment processes, as the experiences of the major oil-producing countries suggest. The use of two-stage LSDV, then, allows for the existence of stable, country-specific deviations from the balance-of-trade equilibrium growth rate. This implies a test of the weaker hypothesis that a change in the balance-of-trade equilibrium growth rate will be accompanied by an equal change in the actual growth rate. Since both hypotheses are interesting, we report both estimates.

In the case of the equations for growth in market shares for exports and imports (24–25), the hypotheses under test suggest a different procedure. For instance, would we consider a large scope for imitation, or a high investment share, compared to other countries throughout the period to be irrelevant to the growth in market shares? Certainly not. To apply the LSDV method in this case would mean wrongly attributing a large part of the effects of these variables to unknown country-specific factors. A similar argument may be put forward in the case of the investment equation (26). In these cases, if serial correlation in the residuals within the cross-sectional units is considered to be important, it is better to re-estimate the equation by the random effects model discussed above.

(d) Results

Table 1 reports results from the test. For the sake of space, we do not report the estimates of the country dummies.

---

where T is the number of time periods (Maddala, 1971; 1977; Johnston, 1984). The problem is that the true variances are not known and have to be estimated. Several methods are suggested in the literature, but Monte Carlo studies show that the differences between the estimates obtained by the various methods are small (Nerlove, 1971; Maddala and Mount, 1973). The estimates of $V(b)$ and $V(w)$ used in this paper are based on the 2SLS residuals, with $V(b) = [\text{Sum}(i)\,u(i)^2]/(n-1)$ and $V(w) = \{\text{Sum}(i, t)\,[u(it)-u(i)]^2\}/[n(T-1)]$, where n is the number of countries and $u(i)$ within-country means of the observed residuals $u(it)$.

The limiting cases $c = 1$ and $c = 0$ may be shown to correspond to LSDV and ordinary least squares, respectively (Johnston, 1984).

Table 1
The Model Tested ($N = 60$)

---

(21) 2SLS

$$GDP = 0.96 + 0.67BAL$$
$$(2.13) \ (6.43)$$

$R^2 = 0.31 \ (0.30)$
SER $= 1.76$
DW$(g) = 1.62$
DF $= 58$

(21) 2SLS–LSDV

$$GDP = 1.16BAL + DUMMIES$$
$$(4.01)$$

$R^2 = 0.41 \ (0.19)$
SER $= 2.66$
DW$(g) = 2.47$
DF $= 44$

(22) 2SLS–LSDV

$$TERMS = 0.23RULC - 0.92POST73 + DUMMIES$$
$$(3.02) \qquad (-2.45)$$

$R^2 = 0.50 \ (0.30)$
SER $= 1.45$
DW$(g) = 2.03$
DF $= 43$

(24) 2SLS

$$ME = -2.03 - 2.70TL + 0.24INV - 0.35W + 0.27TG - 0.29RULC$$
$$(-1.16) \ (-2.31) \quad (3.56) \quad (-4.56) \quad (4.49) \quad (-3.14)$$

$R^2 = 0.55 \ (0.51)$
SER $= 1.81$
DW$(g) = 2.09$
DF $= 54$

(24) 2SLS–WLS

$$ME = -3.25 - 2.64TL + 0.30INV - 0.36W + 0.25TG - 0.34RULC$$
$$(-2.25) \ (-2.98) \quad (-5.01) \quad (-5.42) \quad (4.68) \quad (-4.59)$$

$R^2 = 0.67 \ (0.63)$
SER $= 1.10$
DW$(g) = 1.97$
DF $= 54$

(25) 2SLS

$$MI = 2.65 + 3.47TL - 0.27INV + 1.22GDP - 0.17TG + 0.23RULC$$
$$(1.47) \ (2.75) \ (-3.39) \quad (7.20) \quad (-2.55) \quad (2.45)$$

$R^2 = 0.47 \ (0.42)$
SER $= 1.85$
DW$(g) = 1.85$
DF $= 54$

(25) 2SLS-Random effects method

$$MI = 0.88 + 3.46TL - 0.23INV + 1.25GDP - 0.21TG + 0.21RULC$$
$$(0.62) \ (1.84) \quad (-2.00) \quad (7.72) \quad (-2.34) \quad (2.38)$$

$R^2 = 0.54 \ (0.49)$
SER $= 1.59$
DW$(g) = 2.33$
DF $= 54$

(26) 2SLS

$$INV = 28.52 - 1.48MIL - 0.23WELF + 0.75GDP$$
$$(13.01) \ (-6.95) \quad (-2.34) \qquad (3.60)$$

$R^2 = 0.65 \ (0.64)$
SER $= 2.48$
DW$(g) = 0.75$
DF $= 56$

(26) 2SLS-Random Effects model

$$INV = 9.21 - 1.32MIL - 0.29WELF + 0.50GDP$$
$$(12.47) \ (-4.33) \quad (-2.78) \qquad (3.09)$$

$R^2 = 0.55 \ (0.52)$
SER $= 1.45$
DW$(g) = 1.89$
DF $= 56$

R^2 in brackets $= R^2$ adjusted for degrees of freedom.
SER $=$ Standard error of regression.
DW$(g) =$ Durbin–Watson statistics adjusted for gaps.
$N =$ Number of observations included in the test.
DF $=$ Degrees of freedom.
The numbers in brackets below the estimates are t-statistics.

The test suggests that even though the balance-of-trade equilibrium growth rate and the actual growth rate are strongly correlated, the assumption of strict equality between the two does not hold. However, the introduction of two dummies, one for the United States and one for Norway, the 'Kuwait' of the North, is enough to challenge this (95 % confidence intervals in brackets):

$$GDP = \quad 0.21 \qquad + 0.87\,BAL + 2.00US - 1.96\,NORWAY, \text{ (2SLS)}$$
$$(-0.97/1.39) \quad (0.59/1.15)$$

Futhermore, the test suggests that we can accept the weaker hypothesis of a one-to-one correlation between changes, or deviations, in the balance-of-trade equilibrium growth rate and changes, or deviations, in the actual growth rate.

In the case of the equations for growth in the market shares for exports and imports, all coefficients turned up with the expected signs, most of them significantly different from zero at the 1 % level.[14] Furthermore, the estimates of the coefficients in the two equations did not differ significantly, except for the demand variables. The latter result is in accordance with the fact that world trade in the post war period has grown more than twice as fast as GDP. In the case of the equation for growth in the export market share, the Glejser test indicated violation of the assumption of homoscedasticity. To check the implications for the estimates, we re-estimated the equation with weighted least squares, but this did not change the result significantly. For the equation for growth in the import share, the test for serial correlation was inconclusive, so we re-estimated the equation with the random effects method to check whether this would affect the estimates (it did not.)[15]

For investment, 2SLS produced serial correlation between the residuals within each cross-sectional unit. The random effects method gave a lower estimate of the feedback of economic growth on investment. In both cases military expenditures had a significantly larger negative effect on investments than welfare state expenditures.

Finally, to test for the possibility of structural change, we tested the assumption that the 15 post-1979 observations are not generated by the same model as the entire data set, using a Chow test. Table 2 reports the results of

Table 2

Chow Test of Structural Change (F-statistics)

GDP	GDP (lsdv)	TERMS (lsdv)	ME	MI	INV
1.73	2.48	2.01	0.74	1.80	0.47
(*)	(*)	(*)	(*)	(*)	(*)

* denotes rejection of the assumption of structural change at the 1 % level of significance.

[14] Except for the constant terms, for which no assumptions could be made, due to the introduction of proxies.
[15] Note that since these additional tests imply a transformation of the whole data set, the estimate of the constant term cannot be compared to 2SLS.

the test for the regressions in Table 1 above (except the additional WLS and random-effects tests). The test suggests that in all cases, the assumption of structural change can be rejected at the 1% level of significance.

V. 'THE KALDOR PARADOX' ONCE MORE

We will now return to the seemingly paradoxical findings by Kaldor and others. What Kaldor (1978) did was to compare growth in relative unit labour costs and growth in market shares for exports, when measured in value, for 12 countries over the period 1963–1975. He found that for some of these countries, the relation between growth in relative unit labour costs and growth in market shares seemed to be positive, or the opposite of what is commonly assumed ('perverse'). Table 3 reproduces Kaldor's findings for three countries[16] for which he found a strong 'perverse' relationship, Japan, the United Kingdom and the United States, and compares these findings with the same relationship as predicted by the model.[17]

Table 3

The Kaldor Paradox

	Kaldor 1963–75		Our 1961–73	
Country	RULC	Growth in market share (value)	RULC	Growth in market share (value (predicted))
Japan	27·1	72·0	31·0	103·3
UK	−21·4	−37·9	−25·7	−16·2
USA	−43·7	−17·8	−33·9	−29·8

Thus, in these cases, the model actually predicts a strong 'perverse' relationship between growth in relative unit labour costs and market shares for exports (value). To see how this may be explained, consider Table 4 below. The decomposition suggests that Japan's large gains in market share during this period should be explained by a combination of (*a*) a rapid increase in technological competitiveness, (*b*) a large scope for imitation, and (*c*) a high level of investment. Note, also, that since the estimated (negative) effect of growth in relative unit labour costs on the market share for exports measured in volume, is not significantly different from the estimated (positive) effect of

[16] Kaldor found four examples of a strong 'perverse' relationship, Japan, Italy, the United Kingdom and the United States. Our model does predict this for all but one (Italy). A closer look at the export performance of Italy shows a very erratic development (an export boom in the early mid-sixties followed by a weak performance in the late sixties and early seventies) which our model fails to replicate.

[17] The predicted growth in the market share for exports measured in value was obtained as the sum of the predicted growth in the market share measured in volume and the predicted growth in the terms of trade (country dummies not included). The coefficients were taken from the 2SLS-estimates given in Table 1. Note that the predictions are for total exports, while Kaldor reported data for manufacturing only. For these and other reasons, predicted and actual export performance (as reported by Kaldor) should only be expected to show a similar pattern, not coincidence.

Table 4
An Explanation of the Kaldor Paradox

Country	(1) + (2) + (3) Growth in market share (value (predicted))	(1) Technology (*TG*)	(2) Costs (*RULC*)	Of which		(3) Delivery (total)	Of which due to	
				trough volume (*ME*)	effects on terms of trade (*TERMS*)		diffusion (*TL*)	investment and demand (*INV, W*)
Japan	103·3	66·9	−0·9	−7·8	6·9	37·4	20·9	16·5
UK	−16·2	6·9	0·8	7·9	−7·1	−23·9	15·9	−39·8
USA	−29·8	−0·6	1·6	12·4	−10·8	−30·8	7·3	−38·2

growth in relative unit labour costs on relative prices (terms of trade), the net effect of growth in relative unit labour costs on the growth of market shares for exports measured in value turns out to be negligible.

In the case of the United States, it may be argued that a certain loss in market share would have been difficult to avoid, given the cost of being close to the world innovation frontier in a number of areas. This is also partly confirmed. However, for both the United States and the United Kingdom, the main factor behind the losses in market shares during this period seems to have been slow growth in productive capacity caused by the unusually low shares of national resources devoted to investments. The model (equation (26)) suggests that the main factor behind the low investment shares in these two countries is the high share of national resources used for military purposes.

VI. CONCLUDING REMARKS

The most commonly held approach to international competitiveness focuses on differences in the growth of relative unit labour costs (RULC) as the major factor affecting differences in competitiveness and growth across countries. However, as several studies have pointed out, this view is at best too simplified. The results of this paper suggest that the main factors influencing differences in international competitiveness and growth across countries are technological competitiveness and the ability to compete on delivery. Regarding the latter, this paper especially points out the crucial role played by investments, and factors influencing investments; in creating new production capacity and exploiting the potential given by diffusion processes and growth in national technological competitiveness. Cost-competitiveness does also affect competitiveness and growth to some extent, but less so than many seem to believe.

Norwegian Institute of International Affairs, Oslo

Date of receipt of final typescript: October 1987

REFERENCES

Cappelen, Å., Gleditsch, N. P. and Bjerkholt, O. (1984) 'Military spending and economic growth in the OECD countries.' *Journal of Peace Research*, vol. 21, no. 4, pp. 361–73.
Chesnais, F. (1981). *The Notion of International Competitiveness*. Discussion Paper DSTI/SPR/81.32 Paris:OECD.
Eliasson, G. (1972). *International Competitiveness – an Empirical Analysis of Swedish Manufacturing*. Federation of Swedish Industries, Mimeographed Series B3, September. Stockholm.
EMF (1984). *Report on International Industrial Competitiveness*. Geneva: European Management Forum.
Fagerberg, J. (1987). 'A technology gap approach to why growth rates differ.' *Research Policy*, vol. 16, nos. 2–4, pp. 87–99.
Fetherston, M., Moore, B. and Rhodes, J. (1977). 'Manufacturing export shares and cost competitiveness of advanced industrial countries.' *Cambridge Economic Policy Review*, no. 3, pp. 87–99.
Freeman, C., Clark, J. and Soete, L. (1982). *Unemployment and Technical Innovation*. London: Frances Pinter.
Houthakker, H. S. and Magee, S. P. (1969) 'Income and price elasticities in world trade.' *Review of Economics and Statistics*, vol. 51, no. 2, pp. 111–25.
Johnston, J. (1984). *Econometric Methods*. New York: McGraw-Hill.
Kaldor, M., Sharp, M., and Walker, W. (1986). 'Industrial competitiveness and Britain's defence.' *Lloyds Bank Review*, no. 162.
Kaldor, N. (1978). 'The effect of devaluations on trade in manufactures', In *Further Essays on Applied Economics*. London: Duckworth, pp. 99–118.
—— (1981). 'The role of increasing returns, technical progress and cumulative causation in the theory of international trade and economic growth.' *Economie Appliquie (ISMEA)*, vol. 34, no. 4, pp. 593–617.
Kellman, M. (1983). 'Relative prices and international competitiveness: an empirical investigation'. *Empirical Economics*, vol. 8, nos. 3–4, pp. 125–38.
Maddala, G. S. (1971). 'The use of variance components models in pooling cross-section and time-series data.' *Econometrica*, vol. 39, no. 2, pp. 341–58.
—— (1977). *Econometrics*. New York: McGraw-Hill.
—— and Mount, T. D. (1973). 'A comparative study of alternative estimators for variance components models.' *Journal of the American Statistical Association*, vol. 68, no. 342, pp. 324–8.
McCombie, J. S. L. (1981). 'Are international growth rates constrained by the balance of payments? A comment on Professor Thirlwall.' *Banca Nazionale del Lavoro Quarterly Review*, vol. 34, no. 139, pp. 455–8.
McGregor, P. G. and Swales, J. K. (1985). 'Professor Thirlwall and balance of payments constrained growth'. *Applied Economics*, vol. 17, no. 1, pp. 17–32.
—— —— (1986). 'Balance of payments constrained growth: a rejoinder to Professor Thirlwall.' *Applied Economics*, vol. 18, no. 12, pp. 1265–74.
Nerlove, M. (1971). 'Further evidence on the estimation of dynamic economic relations from a time series of cross sections.' *Econometrica*, vol. 39, no. 2, pp. 359–82.
Samuelson, L. (1973). *A New Model of World Trade*. OECD Occasional Studies, December. Paris: OECD.
Schmookler, J. (1966). *Invention and Economic Growth*. Cambridge, MA.: Harvard University Press.
Schumpeter, J. (1943). *Capitalism, Socialism and Democracy*. London: Unwin.
Smith, R. (1977). 'Military expenditure and capitalism'. *Cambridge Journal of Economics*, vol. 1, no. 1, pp. 61–76.
Soete, L. (1981) 'A general test of technological gap trade theory'. *Weltwirtschaftliches Archiv*, vol. 117, no. 4, pp. 639–59.
Thirlwall, A. P. (1979). 'The balance of payments constraint as an explanation of international growth rate differences.' *Banca Nazionale del Lavoro Quarterly Review*, vol. 32, no. 128, pp. 45–53.
—— (1981). 'A reply to Mr McCombie'. *Banca Nazionale del Lavoro Quarterly Review*, vol. 34, no. 139, pp. 458–9.
—— (1986). 'Balance of payments constrained growth: a reply to McGregor and Swales.' *Applied Economics*, vol. 18, no. 12, pp. 1259–63.
Treasury (1983). 'International Competitiveness', *Economic Progress Report* no. 158, July.

APPENDIX

1. *Definitions and Methods*

Growth rates are calculated as geometric averages for the periods 1960–68, 1968–73, 1973–79 and 1979–83, while levels and shares are calculated as arithmetic averages for the periods 1960–67, 1968–73, 1974–79 and 1980–83, or the nearest period for which data exist.

The growth of the export market share of a country is defined as the growth of exports less the growth of world trade (OECD imports), both in constant prices.

The growth of the import share of a country is defined as the growth of imports less the growth of GDP, both in constant prices.

The data on exports and imports used in this paper comprise both goods and services.

The technological level of a country i (TL_i) is defined as the weighted average of a patent-based index (P_i) and a R & D-based index (R_i), using the standard deviations as weights:

$$TL_i = \{\text{std } (R)/[\text{std } (P) + \text{std } (R)]\}P_i + \{\text{std } (P)/[\text{std } (P) + \text{std } (R)]\}R_i.$$

The patent-based index (P) is defined as the number of external patent applications (PAT), divided by the number of inhabitants in the country (POP) and the degree of the openness of the economy, measured through exports as a percentage of GDP(XSH), $P_i = PAT_i/(POP_i*XSH_i)$. The R & D-based index (R) is defined as civil research and development expenditures as a percentage of GDP. Each index is normalised to the range 0, 1 by dividing all observations from period t with that observation from period t which has the highest value.

The growth in country i's technological competitiveness relative to other countries (TG_i) is defined as the weighted average of a patent-based index (PG_i) and a R & D based index (RG_i), using the standard deviations as weights:

$$TG_i = \{\text{std } (RG)/[\text{std } (PG) + \text{std } (RG)]\}PG_i$$
$$+ \{\text{std } (PG)/[\text{std } (PG) + \text{std } (RG)]\}RG_i.$$

The patent-based index (PG) is defined as growth in external patent applications for country i, less the average growth rate for all countries. The R & D based index (RG) is defined as the ratio between civil R & D expenditures as a percentage of GDP (RD) and GDP per capita (T) for country i, less the average ratio for all countries in each period. Let 'bar' denote within-period mean. Then

$$RG_i = RD_i/T_i - (\overline{RD_i/T_i}).$$

The TG index, then, has a zero average in each period.

2. Sources

Growth in relative unit labour costs in common currency: IMF International Financial Statistics and OECD (Finland).

External patent applications: OECD/STIIU DATA BANK and World International Property Organization (WIPO): Industrial Property Statistics.

The R & D data are estimates based on the following sources: OECD Science and Technology Indicators, Basic Statistical Series (vol. B (1982) and Recent Results (1984)).

Military R & D expenditures were, following the OECD, assumed to be negligible in all countries except the United States, France, Germany, Sweden and the United Kingdom. The R & D data for these countries were adjusted downward according to OECD estimates. The estimates were taken from OECD, Directorate for Science, Technology and Industry: The problems of estimating defence and civil GERD in selected OECD member countries (unpublished). For other countries, civil and total R & D as a percentage of GDP were assumed to be identical.

Military expenditure as percentage of GDP: SIPRI Yearbook.

Non-military governmental consumption as percentage of GDP: SIPRI Yearbook and OECD Historical Statistics.

Other variables: OECD Historical Statistics and OECD National Accounts.

3. *Supplementary tables*

A set of supplementary tables is available on request from the author at the following address: NUPI, Box 8159 DEP, 0033 Oslo 1, Norway.

[13]

Cambridge Journal of Economics 1995 **19**, 243–256

User–producer interaction, learning and comparative advantage

Jan Fagerberg*

Michael Porter's book *The Competitive Advantage of Nations* (1990) has led to increasing attention to the favourable impact that 'advanced domestic users' may have on competitiveness. This paper presents a critical appraisal of the theoretical and empirical evidence on this relationship. An econometric test of the hypothesis—of a positive impact of advanced domestic users on competitiveness—on data for 16 OECD countries between 1965 and 1987 is presented. In general, the results give strong support to the hypothesis under test. The relationship appears to be stronger in cases where the home market is exposed to international competition.

1. Introduction

Michael Porter's book *The Competitive Advantage of Nations* (1990) has led to increasing attention to the favourable impact that the domestic market, through 'advanced domestic users', may have on the international competitiveness of a country. The idea that the domestic market may affect competitiveness positively, is by no means a new one: it dates back at least to List (1841). However, neoclassical trade theorists have normally regarded it as 'theoretically unsound' and as a cover for protectionism. This paper presents a critical appraisal of the theoretical and empirical evidence on this hypothesis. Based on an empirical method initially developed by Andersen *et al.* (1981), the hypothesis—of a positive impact of the domestic market on the competitiveness of a country—is tested on data for 16 OECD countries between 1965 and 1987.

2. Why should 'advanced domestic users' matter?

Traditionally, most attempts to explain the specialisation patterns of countries in international trade have focused on supply conditions. According to standard neo-classical theory of international trade, countries ought to specialise in areas of production that make intensive use of factors of production with which the country is relatively well

Manuscript received 15 March 1993, final version received 12 June 1993.

*Norwegian Institute for International Affairs, Oslo. This paper builds on and extends earlier work by the author on the same subject (Fagerberg 1992, 1994). An earlier version was presented at the conference 'Technology Collaboration: Networks, Institutions and States', Manchester, April 21–23, 1993. The ideas owe much to discussions with members of the IKE group at the University of Aalborg, especially Esben Sloth Andersen, Bent Dalum and Bengt-Ake Lundvall. Furthermore, I wish to thank Bent Dalum and Vibeke Jakobsen, both at the University of Aalborg, for assistance in data work. The final version has also benefited from comments from Daniele Archibugi and two anonymous referees. Financial support from the Nordic Economic Research Council is gratefully acknowledged.

0309–166X/95/010243+14 $08.00/0

equipped. In spite of the dominant role played by traditional neoclassical theory in this area, there has always been a strand of thought that has emphasised *learning* as a potential source of comparative advantage. This tradition points to the potential effects of relations between firms or sectors, within the domestic economy, on innovation and learning, and the impact of this on the international competitiveness of the country and its specialisation pattern in international trade.[1]

The first systematic attempt to discuss the implications of these ideas for trade theory was made by Linder (1961). His argument runs as follows. First, a need that cannot be sufficiently satisfied by existing products arises on the demand side. Since entrepreneurs for various reasons (culture, language, proximity) tend to be better informed about developments in the home market than in markets elsewhere, they will usually be the first to react to the demand for new or improved products arising in the domestic market. The outcome of this activity, i.e., the innovation, then enters a period of testing and revision in which the home market is assumed to play a critical role. If the new product is a success at home, it will probably be introduced on the export market too. Thus, in the case of developed countries, he suggested that it is demand-induced innovation *within each country*, not supply factors, that determines comparative advantage.

Recently, Porter (1990) has presented an evolutionary scheme of economic development based on similar ideas. Echoing Linder, he argues that traditional supply factors, although important in the earlier stages of development, are not among the prime determinants of 'competitive advantage' in more advanced countries, where growth is assumed to be innovation-driven. The most competitive industries in an advanced country, he argues, tend to be highly integrated ('clustered'), both vertically and horizontally, with favourable consequences for learning, innovation and 'competitive advantage'. In Porter's scheme, this typically starts with integration between customers in traditional industries and suppliers of machinery and other types of advanced equipment, then widens through spill-overs and feed-backs to and from related and supporting industries (Porter, 1990, p. 554–5).

In this paper, we shall focus on the first of these two mechanisms, emphasised by both Linder and Porter, i.e. that a high degree of integration between customers and suppliers (or users and producers) may affect international competitiveness/comparative advantage positively. This hypothesis is intuitively appealing, and there is a large amount of descriptive evidence that can be used in its defence (see Porter, 1990). However, in spite of the growing popularity of this approach, many still probably feel that it is a phenomenon in search of a theory. We shall sketch briefly a possible framework for the analysis.

Let us assume that the development of new technology in many cases requires close communication and interaction between *users* and *producers of technology* (Lundvall, 1985, 1988). To achieve this end, a channel—and a common code—of communication must exist. The establishment of channels and codes of communication involves fixed costs, and this implies that in a stable user–producer relationship, the cost per transaction is decreasing. This is clearly an argument for keeping relationships stable. Furthermore, lower transaction costs are likely to lead to a higher volume of transactions. Hence, a higher rate of innovation should be expected in a market characterised by enduring user–producer relationships, compared to a more 'atomistic' market structure. To the

---

[1] Writers who have emphasised the importance of relations between firms or sectors, within the domestic economy, for industrialisation, growth and competitiveness include Perroux (1955), Hirschman (1958), Linder (1961) and Dahmén (1970). For an overview, see Dosi and Soete (1988).

extent that the parties of a stable user–producer relationship can prevent the (immediate) diffusion to others of the innovations they make, as seems likely, they may (for some time at least) keep the benefits for themselves.[1] Indeed, the fact that the relationship is of an enduring character, and is recognised as such by both parties, may significantly increase the probability of appropriating the benefits. Thus, a stable user–producer relationship may be interpreted as an institution that reduces the costs—and increases the pace—of innovation and learning, while at the same time making it easier to appropriate the economic benefits.[2] As a result, the competitive positions of the participating firms are likely to improve. To some extent, this holds for both users and producers, but in this paper we shall focus mainly on the latter.

However, the importance of stable relationships may vary across industries. It should be expected to be of special importance in industries characterised by complex and user-specific technology. In these cases, the need for close communications and interaction between users and producers of technology is likely to be large, and the costs of establishing new relationships of this kind high. In other cases, products and technologies may be highly standardised: both transaction costs and the need for enduring user–producer relationships will be low.

To the extent that this type of interaction takes place mainly *within country borders*, this should be expected to affect patterns of export specialisation (or comparative advantage) of countries as well. Since, as pointed out by both Linder and Porter, the costs associated with communication and interaction increase with distance and differences in culture, language, institutional settings etc., this may be a reasonable assumption to make. Porter even holds that the importance of the domestic market for competitive advantage is growing.

While globalization of competition might appear to make the nation less important, instead it seems to make it more so. With fewer impediments to trade to shelter uncompetitive domestic firms and industries, the home nation takes on growing significance because it is the source of the skills and technology that underpin competitive advantage. (Porter, 1990, p. 19)

However, it may also be argued that the increasing role of multinationals in world production has reduced the costs of communication and interaction significantly, and that the Linder–Porter hypothesis therefore was more relevant in the past than it is now. The empirical evidence presented in this paper may shed some light on this controversy.

Another issue raised by Porter is to what extent a competitive market structure is a necessary condition for a positive impact of user–producer interaction on competitiveness. He argues that 'favourable demand conditions ... will not lead to competitive advantage unless the state of rivalry is sufficient to cause firms to respond to them' (1990, p. 72). Porter seems to be most concerned with competition among producers (suppliers) of technology.[3] However, a similar argument holds for the user side: users that are under continuous pressure to improve their performance, are more likely than

---

[1] Several factors may contribute to this. New knowledge may be very specific and difficult to transfer ('tacit knowledge'). Secrecy and legal procedures (patents and trade marks) are other means.

[2] This way of looking at things shows some similarity with parts of the 'new growth' literature (see Verspagen, 1992 for an overview). However, this literature (Romer, 1986, and others), as well as the older literature in this area (Arrow, 1962; Kaldor and Mirrlees, 1962), discusses externalities of *activities internal to firms* (investment and/or production). This paper focuses on the effects of *interaction between different firms*.

[3] Porter emphasises especially the importance of domestic rivalry, but acknowledges that, for small open economies, foreign competitors may serve a similar function (1990, p. 121).

246   J. Fagerberg

others to demand improvements from their suppliers. Here, Porter emphasises especially the importance of international competition:

One competitive industry helps to create another in a mutually reinforcing process. Such an industry is often the most sophisticated buyer of the products and services it depends on. Its presence in a nation becomes important to developing competitive advantage in supplier industries. (1990, p. 149).

3. Data and methods

The hypothesis that we want to test is the following:

There is a positive relationship between the existence of advanced, domestic users and the competitiveness of domestic producers that supply these users with advanced equipment.

Most empirical work in this area is descriptive (case studies). These studies are often interesting and perceptive, but it is of course difficult to know how representative they are. To allow more general statements on the empirical relationships, we have, following Andersen *et al.* (1981), chosen a different method. The essence of this is the use of trade statistics to measure both the *competitiveness of the producers of technology* and *how advanced the domestic users are*. It is argued that one may approximate 'advanced domestic users' with 'internationally competitive (domestic) users'. This does not seem unreasonable. Firms that compete favourably on the world market, and want to continue to do so, have a clear incentive to acquire superior technology. This is also consistent with Porter's view (see the previous section).

One problem with this interpretation is that it limits the investigation to export products and home market sectors where the trade statistics allow a link to be made. Equipment that is used in many sectors, and sectors that mainly make use of such equipment, cannot be included. For instance, some well known 'high-tech' industries, most notably the computer industry, had to be left out of the investigation for this reason. This, of course, does not mean that user–producer interaction is unimportant in these cases, just that these links can not be explored by the methodology adopted here. Another consequence is that users in the service sectors of the economy (not covered by the trade statistics) are excluded. To remedy this somewhat, an attempt was made to construct special 'home market indexes' for three important service sectors. These sectors are health care, telecommunications and shipping (two of which are dominated by public-sector services).

Table 1 lists the 23 pairs of export products and home market sectors. The sample includes 'advanced' export products for which the commodity classification (SITC, Revision 1, four-digit level) allowed a link to a home market sector to be made.[1] The 23 pairs were divided into 5 groups, depending on *the character of the home market*. The first group includes export products with users in the food-producing sector, mostly agriculture. These user sectors are strongly regulated in all countries. As a consequence, there is in most cases little competition. The second and third groups include export products with users in the manufacturing sector, in 'traditional manufacturing' and 'transport equipment' respectively, for which the degree of competition is generally high. The services group is divided in two: shipping and public sector services. Shipping is a

---

[1] 'Advanced' is used here in a broad sense. Only products based on natural resources and relatively unsophisticated ('mature') manufactures were excluded.

Table 1. *Export products and home market sectors*

SITC (REV 1)	Export product	SITC (REV 1)	Home market sector
(A) Home market: agriculture			
6951	Hand tools for agriculture and forestry	04-08(-0814), 24	Agricultural products, wood products
7121, 7122	Agricultural machinery for preparing soil and harvesting	04-08(-0814)	Agricultural products
7123	Milking machines	02	Dairy products
7125	Tractors	04-08(-0814)	Agricultural products
7129	Agricultural machinery N.E.S.	04-08(-0814)	Agricultural products
7183	Food processing machinery	0(-00)	Food
7191	Heating and cooling equipment	01-03	Meat, dairy products, fish and eggs
(B) Home market: producers of traditional manufactures			
7151, 7152	Machine tools for working metals	69	Metal manufactures
7171	Textile machinery	65	Textiles
7172	Leather machinery	61	Leather
7173	Sewing machinery	84	Clothing
7181	Paper working machinery	25,64	Pulp and paper, paper products
7182	Printing machinery	829	Printed matter
7184, 7185	Construction and mining machinery, machinery for mineral crushing, etc.	27, 28	Crude minerals and metals
(C) Home market: producers of transport equipment			
6291	Rubber tyres and tubes	732-734	Road motor vehicles
7114	Aircraft engines	734	Aircraft
7115	Internal comb. engines	732	Road motor vehicles
7294	Automotive electrical equipment	732	Road motor vehicles
(D) Home market: shipping			
735	Ships and boats		Shipping[a]
(E) Home market: (public sector) services			
54	Pharmaceuticals		Health[a]
7249	Telecommunications		Tele[a]
726	Electromedicals		Health[a]
8617	Medical instruments N.E.S.		Health[a]

[a] For the definition of this indicator, see the text and appendix 1.
Explanatory note (example): 04-08 means 04, 05, 06, 07, 08; 08(– 0814) means 08 less 0814.

typical global industry (Porter, 1990), with very competitive markets. Public sector services, in contrast, have until recently been strongly regulated in all countries, with little competition domestically as well as internationally.[1]

To measure competitiveness, we use the familiar index for revealed comparative advantage (the RCA index, see Balassa, 1965). For a particular country and product, this index is the *ratio between the market share of the country on the world market for this particular product and the market share of the country on the world market for all products.* Letting X denote exports, i the exporting country and j the export product, the index for revealed comparative advantage (S) for country i in product j can be presented as follows:

$$S_{ij} = \frac{X_{ij} / \sum_n X_{nj}}{\sum_m X_{im} / \sum_n \sum_m X_{nm}} \tag{1}$$

where $n=, 1, \ldots i, \ldots, N$, and $m = 1, \ldots, j, \ldots, M$. This index has the property that the weighted mean is identical to unity for each country across all commodity groups, and for each commodity group across all countries. Thus, a country is said to have a revealed comparative advantage (be specialised) in a product if the RCA index exceeds unity.

It was argued above that one may approximate 'advanced domestic users' with 'internationally competitive (domestic) users'. Thus, RCA indices were calculated also for the home-market sectors ('home-market indexes', S_{ik}). The indices for the service sectors were constructed to make them comparable to the RCA index. For instance, if the index for a specific country for shipping exceeds unity, this implies that the market share of the country for shipping services (merchant fleet registered in the country) exceeds the market share of the country for goods and services in general. For telecommunications and health services, which, until recently at least, were not traded on the world market to the same extent, the population of the country was used as a deflator. Thus, in these cases, a value larger than one implies that the per capita 'quality' of these services in the country is higher than the OECD average. For telecommunications we used data for the number of telephone lines in the country, for health services we equated 'quality' with the economic resources devoted to this purpose. A problem with the latter may be that possible differences in health sector efficiency across countries are not accounted for. (For details and sources, the reader is referred to the Appendix.)

The trade data used in this paper were collected from OECD Trade Series C, using the IKE Data Base at the University of Aalborg. Three years were included; 1965, 1973 and 1987. Since the theory is only expected to hold for developed countries, we excluded the industrially less developed of the OECD countries.[2] The countries included in the sample were: Canada, the USA, Japan, Austria, Belgium, Denmark, Finland, France, Germany, Italy, the Netherlands, Norway, Spain, Sweden, Switzerland and the UK.

---

[1] As follows from Table 1, we have assumed that the health sector is the 'user' of pharmaceutical products, although strictly speaking the final users are the individual patients/consumers. However, it is the health sector that decides on standards etc., which is what matters in the present context.

[2] Australia and New Zealand were excluded owing to lack of data for some of the years covered by the investigation.

4. Testing the hypothesis

In a general form, the model to be tested is the following:

$$S_{ij}^\tau = f(S_{ik}^\tau, C_i^\tau), \quad dS_{ij}^\tau / dS_{ik}^\tau > 0. \tag{2}$$

This model includes two independent variables, the home-market index S_{ik} and a country-specific variable C_i. The inclusion of the latter reflects the possibility that there may exist additional, country-specific factors that affect comparative advantage, and which should be taken into account to avoid biased results.[1] For instance, a country with a comparative advantage in natural-resource based products (SITC 0–4), will by definition not have a comparative advantage for manufactured products (SITC 5–9). Since the dependent variable in all 23 cases belongs to the manufactured group, this implies that the dependent variable may be biased against countries specialising in natural-resource based products. The inclusion of a country specific constant term may correct for this type of bias.

In principle, the choice of functional form should be based on theory. But, as is common in testing of hypotheses, we have in this case no particular theoretical reasons for preferring one specific functional form. However, to get a better approximation to the assumption of normally distributed variables, a logarithmic form is preferred.[2] A Box–Cox test of functional form came up with the same suggestion. Since there were zeros in the data matrix, we had to add a small positive number to all observations to allow the transformation to be made.

Thus, the tested model is as follows:

$$\log(S_{ij}^\tau + 0 \cdot 1) = c_i + a \log(S_{ik}^\tau + 0 \cdot 1). \tag{3}$$

When in the following we refer to the variables S_{ij} and S_{ik}, it should be understood that these are in log-form, as in eqn (3).

The questions we want to ask are:

(1) Is there a positive relationship between the two specialisation indexes, as argued by Linder and Porter, i.e. is the coefficient a positive?

(2) Does the impact of the home-market variable (S_{ik}) decline over time, i.e., is the coefficient a less significant in 1987 than in earlier years?

(3) To what extent does the introduction of a time-lag for the home-market variable (S_{ik}) improve the explanatory power of the model?

(4) Are there significant differences across countries, or home markets, in the impact of the home-market variable (S_{ik})?

To answer the first two questions, eqn (3) was tested on data for 1965, 1973 and 1987, with and without the country-specific variable C_i. The results are reported in Table 2. In all cases, the coefficient a turned up significantly larger than zero at the 1% level, as the Linder–Porter hypothesis would predict. The numerical estimate of a was remarkably stable across both time and differences in specification (the estimate varied between 0·43 and 0·49). Furthermore, there was no tendency towards a decrease in the numerical

---

[1] This is the so-called 'least-squares dummy variables method' (LSDV), which is developed for use in pooled data sets. For details, see Johnston (1984).

[2] The index of revealed comparative advantage (S) has a skew distribution, with a long tail to the right. This creates problems in regression analysis, because it violates the assumption of normality. A logarithmic transformation of the data reduced this problem significantly.

250   **J. Fagerberg**

Table 2. *The hypothesis tested*

1965
$$S_{ij} = -\ 0\cdot37 + 0\cdot43\ \ S_{ik}$$
$$(7\cdot54)\ \ (8\cdot14)$$
$$\ \ \ \ *\ \ \ \ \ \ \ *$$
$R^2 = 0\cdot15\ (0\cdot15)$ (2.1)
$SER = 0\cdot90$

$$S_{ij} = C_i + 0\cdot43\ S_{ik}$$
$$(9\cdot00)$$
$$\ \ \ \ *$$
$R^2 = 0\cdot39\ (0\cdot36)$ (2·2)
$SER = 0\cdot78$

1973
$$S_{ij} = -\ 0\cdot26 + 0\cdot47\ \ S_{ik}$$
$$(5\cdot69)\ \ (8\cdot62)$$
$$\ \ \ \ *\ \ \ \ \ \ \ *$$
$R^2 = 0\cdot17\ (0\cdot17)$ (2.3)
$SER = 0\cdot85$

$$S_{ij} = C_i + 0\cdot49\ S_{ik}$$
$$(9\cdot58)$$
$$\ \ \ \ *$$
$R^2 = 0\cdot36\ (0\cdot33)$ (2.4)
$SER = 0\cdot76$

1987
$$S_{ij} = -\ 0\cdot21 + 0\cdot45\ \ S_{ik}$$
$$(4\cdot76)\ \ (8\cdot15)$$
$$\ \ \ \ *\ \ \ \ \ \ \ *$$
$R^2 = 0\cdot15\ (0\cdot15)$ (2.5)
$SER = 0\cdot81$

$$S_{ij} = C_i + 0\cdot49\ S_{ik}$$
$$(9\cdot19)$$
$$\ \ \ \ *$$
$R^2 = 0\cdot33\ (0\cdot30)$ (2·6)
$SER = 0\cdot74$

$N = 368$

Method of estimation: Ordinary least squares, absolute t-values in brackets. R^2 in brackets is adjusted for degrees of freedom.
*Significance at 1% level.

value of the estimate for a or its significance. The only notable difference between the tests reported in Table 2 relates to the impact of the country-specific variable C_i. In all cases the inclusion of this variable significantly increased the explanatory power of the model, but less so in 1987 than for earlier years, indicating that the importance of the country-specific factors may be reduced somewhat during this period.

Patterns of comparative advantage may be viewed as the result of a long-term historical process. Thus, there may be rather long lags present in the impact of user–producer interaction on comparative advantages. To shed some light on this issue we have included in Table 3 some tests where the independent variable is lagged one or two periods. Given that patterns of comparative advantage change only slowly, the home market variables should be expected to be strongly correlated across years, which was indeed the case. To avoid multicollinearity in cases where two annual observations of S_{ik} were to be included, we had to put one of them in first differences [eqns (3.2) and (3.4)].

The results of the tests with lagged variables in Table 3 should be compared to the result without lags in Table 2 [eqn (2.6)]. It then becomes clear that the explanatory power of the instantaneous relationship [eqn (2.6)] is not inferior to any of the lagged relationships, when adjustments for differences in degrees of freedoms are made. Thus, surprisingly perhaps, there is not strong support in the data for long lags. This is also confirmed by the low weights given to the lagged independent variables in eqns (3.2) and (3.4).[1] These findings may indicate a two-way relationship between 'users' and 'producers', e.g. that the competitiveness of both parties is affected. As noted in Section

[1] In eqn (3.2), the implicit weight is $0\cdot16$ for S_{ik65} and $0\cdot34$ for S_{ik87}, while in eqn (3.4), the implicit weight is $0\cdot10$ for S_{ik73} and $0\cdot39$ for S_{ik87}.

Table 3. *Testing for lags (1987)*

$$S_{ij87} = C_i + 0.39 \ S_{ik65} \qquad\qquad R^2 = 0.31 \ (0.28) \qquad (3.1)$$
$$(8.46) \qquad\qquad\qquad\qquad SER = 0.75$$
$$*$$

$$S_{ij87} = C_i + 0.50 \ S_{ik65} + 0.34 \ (S_{ik87} - S_{ik65}) \qquad R^2 = 0.34 \ (0.30) \qquad (3.2)$$
$$(9.37) \qquad\quad (3.85) \qquad\qquad\qquad SER = 0.74$$
$$* \qquad\qquad *$$

$$S_{ij87} = C_i + 0.43 \ S_{ik73} \qquad\qquad R^2 = 0.31 \ (0.28) \qquad (3.3)$$
$$(8.64) \qquad\qquad\qquad\qquad SER = 0.75$$
$$*$$

$$S_{ij87} = C_i + 0.49 \ S_{ik73} + 0.39 \ (S_{ik87} - S_{ik73}) \qquad R^2 = 0.33 \ (0.30) \qquad (3.4)$$
$$(9.20) \qquad\quad (2.97) \qquad\qquad\qquad SER = 0.74$$
$$* \qquad\qquad *$$

$$N = 368$$

Method of estimation: Ordinary least squares, absolute t-values in brackets. R^2 in brackets is adjusted for degrees of freedom.
*Significance at 1% level.

Table 4. *Testing for pooling*

	1965	1973	1987
16 country sample[a]	2·03 **	1·98 **	1·58
13 country sample[b]	1·53	1·44	1·59

[a]All countries, F-statistics with degrees of freedom 15,336.
[b]All countries less Austria, France and UK, F-statistics with degrees of freedom 12,273.
*Significance at 1% level.
**Significance at 5% level.

2, this would not be inconsistent with the theory, but we shall not discuss this issue further here. No attempt was made to test for the direction of causality.

In the tests reported so far we have implicitly assumed that all countries are identical except for the constant term, which was assumed to reflect sector-invariant, country-specific factors. Although we have no prior information that leads us to believe that the impact of the home market variable on comparative advantage differs substantially across countries, this possibility cannot be excluded *a priori*. To account for this possibility we have included a test of the restriction that $a_1 = a_2 = \ldots = a_i = \ldots = a_N = a$. The results (Table 4) are ambiguous. In no case can the hypothesis of a common coefficient a for all countries be rejected at the 1% level. However, for 1965 and 1973—but not for 1987—the tests indicate that the hypothesis of a common coefficient can be rejected if the weaker criterion of a 5% significance level is adopted.

Table 5 lists the unrestricted estimates for the coefficient a. The results suggest that the countries of our sample may be divided roughly in four groups, depending on the strength of the relationship. For five countries (Japan, Denmark, Finland, Norway and Switzerland) the estimates of the coefficient a are positive, significant at the 1% level, for

Table 5. *Unrestricted estimates for* $S_{ik}{}^a$

	1965	1973	1987
Canada	0·28 (1·52) ***	0·20 (1·01)	0·42 (2·15) **
USA	0·43 (1·38) ***	0·37 (1·78) **	0·38 (1·49) ***
Japan	0·78 (4·08) *	0·78 (4·18) *	0·51 (3·38) *
Austria	0·26 (1·45) ***	0·11 (0·59)	0·16 (0·79)
Belgium	0·13 (0·35)	0·14 (0·45)	0·43 (1·76) **
Denmark	0·58 (3·95) *	0·56 (3·72) *	0·77 (4·78) *
Finland	0·50 (3·69) *	0·47 (2·93) *	0·51 (2·78) *
France	− 0·20 (0·43)	− 0·09 (0·45)	− 0·09 (0·02)
Germany	0·31 (1·34) ***	0·42 (1·50) ***	0·31 (0·80)
Italy	0·19 (0·69)	0·41 (1·46) ***	0·54 (2·15) **
Netherlands	0·10 (0·43)	0·32 (1·37) ***	0·36 (1·74) **
Norway	0·42 (3·03) *	0·57 (3·85) *	0·60 (3·73) *
Spain	0·33 (2·61) *	0·39 (2·21) **	0·23 (1·09)
Sweden	1·00 (5·13) *	0·47 (2·08) **	0·10 (0·50)
Switzerland	0·78 (4·16) *	0·92 (5·45) *	1·12 (5·77) *
UK	− 0·16 (0·66)	− 0·17 (0·60)	0·40 (0·78)

^{a}Estimated with country dummies (C_i).

Method of estimation: ordinary least squares, absolute-t values in brackets.

*Significant at 1% level, one-tailed test.

**Significant at 5% level, one-tailed test.

***Significant at 10% level, one-tailed test.

all three years. Clearly, for these countries there is strong support for the hypothesis of a positive relationship between the two indices. Then follows a group of seven countries where there is some support, although weaker (positive, significant at the 10% level, for at least two years): Canada, the USA, Germany, Italy, The Netherlands, Spain and Sweden. For Belgium and Austria too, a positive relationship was reported, though significant for one year only (at the 5% and 10% level, respectively). However, for France and the UK, the results give no support at all for the hypothesis of a positive relationship between the two indices. Taking this information into account, we repeated the test of the restriction (a common value of a for all countries) on a sample that excluded Austria, France and the UK. For this sample it was not possible to reject the restriction for any year (Table 4).

The fact that the hypothesis is not supported empirically for some countries deserves an explanation. First, it cannot be excluded that this—to some extent at least—is the result of imperfect data or methods. It can be shown that there is a positive relationship between the statistical significance of the estimate a and the variance of the dependent variable, i.e. that countries with a 'flat' structure of export specialisation (low variance) generally have poor results. Low variance is a common problem in small samples, and it is possible that the results would have improved if the number 'pairs' included in the test had been larger. This was not possible with the available data. The problem of a 'flat' structure of export specialisation was especially pronounced for Belgium and France, and it is possible that the poor results for these countries may be explained by data limitations. This explanation is less probable for the UK and Austria, where the reported variances do not differ much from that of the sample as a whole. Unfortunately, we do not have a good alternative explanation to offer. In general, the reported results show no clear relation to variables commonly used in cross-country analyses of specialisation patterns, such as—for instance—country size or income level (past or present). Arguably, a much more detailed analysis of economic, institutional and cultural factors seems to be required.[1]

The possibility of differences across home markets—in their impact on the competitiveness of suppliers—is perhaps more interesting. At least, here we have a well-argued case (Porter, 1990) for assuming that home markets exposed to international competition are more conducive than others to fostering internationally competitive suppliers. This can be tested in a similar way as for the differences across countries. The results (Table 6) indicate that there may be significant differences between different types of home markets. Generally speaking, the relationship between the two indices appears to be much stronger for home-market sectors exposed to international competition (traditional manufacturing, production of transport equipment and shipping) than for the more 'sheltered' sectors (agriculture and public sector services). For public sector services the results may be affected by the problem of finding reliable indicators. Still, the results lend clear support to Porter's view on the importance of competition.

The results reported in this paper may to some extent be compared with those reported by Andersen et al. (1981), although differences in both sample and methods exist.[2] In particular, it must be kept in mind that their sample was much smaller. Results for 1954, 1960, 1966 and 1972 were reported. In general, a significant relationship was found for

---

[1] See Tylecote (1993) for an interesting attempt to explain cross-country differences in the degree of inter-firm collaboration with the help of some of these factors.

[2] See Fagerberg (1992) for a more detailed presentation and discussion of the contribution by Andersen et al. (1981).

254   **J. Fagerberg**

Table 6. *Testing for differences between home market sectors, 1987*

$$S_{ij} = C_i + \underset{(2 \cdot 74)}{0 \cdot 23} \ S_{ik}^{\text{agriculture}} + \underset{(5 \cdot 74)}{0 \cdot 52} \ S_{ik}^{\text{traditional}}$$

$$+ \underset{(6 \cdot 59)}{0 \cdot 68} \ S_{ik}^{\text{transport}} + \underset{(5 \cdot 12)}{0 \cdot 89} \ S_{ik}^{\text{shipping}}$$

$$+ \underset{(1 \cdot 67)}{0 \cdot 55} \ S_{ik}^{\text{public}}$$

$$R^2 = 0 \cdot 36 \ (0 \cdot 32)$$
$$\text{SER} = 0 \cdot 72$$
$$N = 368$$
$$F_{(5,347)} = 3 \cdot 89$$
$$(\star)$$

[a]Method of estimation: ordinary least squares, absolute t-values in brackets. R^2 in brackets is adjusted for degrees of freedom. $F_{(5,347)}$ is an F-test of whether there are significant differences across home market sectors.
★Significance at 1% level.

approximately half of the countries included in their sample. The countries for which they found no support for the hypothesis were Belgium, France and the United Kingdom (Austria was not included). This is in line with the results presented here. Furthermore, as in the present study, there was no sign of a weakening of the relationship: in fact, the best results were reported for the most recent years.

5. Concluding remarks

The view that the home market may have a positive impact on the competitiveness of domestic producers is by no means a new one. Indeed, it has been widely held for at least a century, although neoclassical trade theorists have condemned it as 'theoretically unsound'. Often it has been regarded as a pure cover for protectionism. More recently, however, Michael Porter (1990) has made a major effort to increase the credibility of this view, and with considerable success, especially among policy makers and industrialists.

This paper has attempted to give an appraisal of the theoretical and empirical evidence on the hypothesis of a positive impact of the domestic market, through 'advanced domestic users', on the international competitiveness of a country (the 'Linder–Porter hypothesis'). It was suggested that a positive impact of this kind may be explained by a theory that focuses on *interaction between users and producers of technology* as a major impetus to technological change. Interaction, however, involves costs. It was argued that these are a decreasing function of both the stability of the user–producer relationship and the degree of 'proximity', defined to include factors such as language, the legal system, the education system etc. Hence, most stable user–producer relationships are of a *national* character. The above, together with the assumption that a country's comparative advantage in the long run will be in areas where its rates of learning and innovation are high (compared to other countries), suggests that countries in the long run tend to develop comparative advantages in areas where, by a comparative standard, there are many advanced domestic users.

Most previous empirical work in this area has been of a descriptive character. This paper, in contrast, has presented an econometric test of the hypothesis of a positive impact of advanced domestic users on competitiveness. The data set included 16 countries, 23 pairs of products and three selected years (1965, 1973 and 1987). The main empirical findings were:

(1) There is strong support in the data for the hypothesis of a positive impact of advanced domestic users on competitiveness.

(2) There is no evidence of a weakening of this relationship during the period 1965–1987.

(3) The time lag between the initial stimulus (from the domestic market) and the impact on competitiveness appears to be relatively short.

(4) For most countries there is some support for the hypothesis. The most notable exceptions are France and the UK.

(5) The relationship appears to be stronger in cases where the home market is exposed to international competition.

In general, these findings are consistent with the predictions made by Linder (1961) and Porter (1990).

The theoretical and empirical evidence presented in this paper indicate that stable relationships between domestic users and producers of technology may have a positive impact on both technological progress and international competitiveness. This is especially so if these relationships develop in a competitive environment, i.e. that the positions of both users and producers may be contested. Thus, contrary to the belief of many economists, this approach does not favour protectionism. However, the emphasis in this approach on a competitive environment does not necessarily imply that every individual contract has to be open to public tender. Arguably, a competition policy of this kind would in practice make stable user–producer relationships very difficult to maintain. Thus, the old Schumpeterian theme of the uneasy balance between static and dynamic efficiency may apply also in this case.

Bibliography

Arrow, K. 1962. The economic implications of learning by doing, *Review of Economic Studies*, vol. 29, 155–173

Andersen, E. S., Dalum, B. and Villumsen, G. *International Specialization and the Home Market*, Aalborg, Aalborg University Press

Balassa, B. 1965. Trade liberalization and revealed comparative advantage, *The Manchester School*, vol. 33, 99–123

Dahmén, E. 1970. *Entrepreneurial Activity and the Development of Swedish Industry 1919–1939*, Homewood, American Economic Association Translation Series

Dosi, G. and Soete, L. 1988. Technical change and international trade, in Dosi, G. *et al.* (eds), *Technical Change and Economic Theory*, London, Pinter

Fagerberg, J. 1992. The 'home-market hypothesis' reexamined, in Lundvall, B. Å. (ed.), *National Systems of Innovation—Towards a Theory of Innovation and Interactive Learning*, London, Pinter

Fagerberg, J. 1994. Domestic demand, learning and comparative advantage, in Johansson, B. *et al.* (eds), *Patterns of a Network Economy*, Berlin–Heidelberg, Springer

Hirschman, A. O. 1958. *The Strategy of Economic Development*, New Haven, CT, Yale University Press

Johnston, J. 1984. *Econometric Methods*, New York, McGraw-Hill

Kaldor, N. and Mirrlees, J. A. 1962. A new model of economic growth, *Review of Economic Studies*, vol. 29, 174–192

Linder, S. B. 1961. *An Essay on Trade and Transformation*, Uppsala, Almquist & Wicksell

List, F. 1841. *Das Nationale System der Politischen Ökonomie*, Stuttgart/Tubingen, J. G. Cotta

Lundvall, B. Å. 1985. *Product Innovation and User–Producer Interaction*, Aalborg, Aalborg University Press

Lundvall, B. Å. 1988. Innovation as an interactive process—from user–producer interaction to the National System of Innovation, in Dosi, G. *et al.* (eds), *Technical Change and Economic Theory*, London, Pinter

Perroux, F. 1956. Note sur la notion de pôle de croissance, *Economie Appliquée*, vol. 7, 307–320

Porter, M. E. 1990. *The Competitive Advantage of Nations*, London, Macmillan

Romer, P. M. 1986. Increasing returns and long-run growth, *Journal of Political Economy*, vol. 94, 1002–1037

Tylecote, A. 1993. Managerial Objectives and Technological Collaboration in National Systems of Innovation: The Role of National Variations in Cultures and Structures', *CRITEC Discussion Paper* No. 2, Sheffield, Sheffield University Management School

Verspagen, B. 1992. Endogenous innovation in neo-classical growth models: a survey, *Journal of Macroeconomics*, vol. 14, 631–662

Appendix

The trade data used in this paper were calculated from OECD Trade Series C (value data) using the IKE data base on trade statistics at the Aalborg University Centre. Data for health care were taken from OECD: Health Care Systems in Transition, OECD, Paris, 1990, data for merchant fleets and telephone lines were taken from UN *Statistical Yearbook*, various editions. Other data from OECD *National Accounts*.

Construction of home market indicators

Tele and health. T_j = telephone lines in country $j(i = 1, \ldots, j, \ldots, n)$; N_j = number of inhabitants in j. The index may then be written:

$$I_j = \frac{T_j}{N_j} / \frac{\sum_i T_i}{\sum_i N_i} \cdot$$

Similarly for health services, where T_j = total (public and private) expenses for health services in current prices in common currency.

Shipping. S_j = merchant fleet registered in country j, in 1000 tons; X_j = total exports of goods and services from country j in current prices in common currency.

$$I_j = \frac{S_j}{\sum_i S_i} / \frac{X_j}{\sum_i X_i} \cdot$$

[14]

Is there a large-country advantage in high-tech?

*Jan Fagerberg**

1 Introduction

High-tech is a commonly used catch-word for industries that use a relatively large share of their resources on R&D and develop many new products and processes. Sometimes it is argued that one should also include industries that make intensive use of products with a high R&D content, even if they do not spend much on R&D or develop much new technology themselves. Although this broader definition may be interesting for some purposes, in this paper we will stick to the more commonly used, narrow definition. This restricts the concept, high-tech, to industries that innovate.

To explain why high-tech is important, we need to focus on the links between innovation, growth and trade. The classic reference is Schumpeter (1934, 1939, 1943). In his theory of industrial development, innovation is assumed to be the single most important competitive factor. Innovative firms have a temporary monopoly which allows them to charge higher prices and, hence, be more profitable than other firms. They will also grow faster, partly because they have the market temporarily to themselves, and partly because their higher innovative ability implies that they are more competitive in the marketplace. There is also a stimulus from the demand side, since the growth of demand for goods based on new technology generally outstrips the growth of demand for goods based on older technologies. For technological as well as economic reasons, Schumpeter expected innovations to cluster in some (R&D-intensive) industries. Hence, production in these industries should be expected to experience above average growth. The same goes for trade. In fact, from the 1960s to the 1980s the share of high-tech in world trade (as defined in this study) roughly doubled.

Thus, high-tech means high growth, and this probably explains the general concern in many countries for the fate of high-tech industries. Indeed, it seems to be a widespread view among policy-makers that success in high-tech industry (and exports) is a good recipe for high growth in national income. Recently, this view has obtained greater academic credibility through the advent of 'new growth theories' emphasizing the importance of innovation and organized R&D for economic growth (Romer 1990; Grossman and Helpman 1991; for an overview see Verspagen 1992). But what determines the extent to which a country succeeds in specializing in high-tech? When this question was first raised in the 1960s, it became apparent that traditional trade theory (Hecksher–Ohlin) had relatively little to say about the subject. This led to the formulation of so-called 'neotechnological' trade theories, to a large extent inspired by Schumpeterian perspectives (for an overview, see Dosi and Soete 1988). These theories and subsequent empirical work based on this perspective suggested a link between a strong competitive position in high-tech trade and domestic R&D efforts: 'All roads lead to a link between export performance and R&D' (Gruber, Metha and Vernon 1967, p. 22).[1] The importance of R&D and innovation for trade performance was also demonstrated empirically by Lacroix and Scheuer (1976). More recently, Soete (1981, 1987) and Dosi and Soete (1983) have provided additional evidence for the view that national technological activity, measured through R&D or patent statistics, matters for export performance in high-tech (and some not-so-high-tech) industries.

The policy implication of much of this seems to be that a country can increase its chance of success in high-tech industries by devoting resources to R&D. However, some recent theoretical work indicates that it may not be so simple. For instance, some 'new growth theories' suggest that while R&D efforts matter for high exports, so does country size (see Grossman and Helpman 1991). These theories emphasize that R&D efforts generate technological spillovers that facilitate (reduce the cost of) subsequent R&D projects (or innovations). Since a large country does much more R&D than a small one, there will be more spillovers and lower costs of innovative activity in the large country. Hence, in the long run a large country may gain the upper hand in high-tech even if it at the outset devotes a smaller share of its resources to organized R&D than a smaller one.[2] This argument, which rests on the assumption of geographical limitations on technology spillovers, may have important implications for policy.

To the best of our knowledge there is not much empirical work that investigates the joint impact of national technological activity, country size and other factors on export performance. This paper is a modest attempt to throw some more light on this issue.

2 The design of the test

The analysis that follows is based on the commonly used assumption that (a) *a country's specialization pattern in international trade* results from the interaction between (b) *industry-specific conditions of competition* and (c) *country-specific capabilities*. Knowledge about any two of these may then be used to make inferences about the third element, in this case the conditions of competition at the industry level. Basically, this is the methodology proposed by Leamer (1974). However, while Leamer starts from the traditional factor abundance theory, our point of departure will be the Schumpeterian-inspired models discussed in the preceding paragraph.

The model to be tested is set out in equation 1 below. For reasons that will become apparent, a log-linear form was preferred:

$$\log S_{ij} = a_o + \sum_{l=1}^{m} a_i \log C_{lj} \tag{1}$$

where S_{ij} is the specialization index (RCA) for country j in commodity group i; and C_{lj} is the set of capabilities (l) for country j.

To measure specialization, we use the familiar index for revealed comparative advantage (Balassa 1965). For a particular country and product, this index is the *ratio between the market share of the country on the world market for this particular product and the market share of the country on the world market for all products*. This index has the property that the weighted mean is identical to unity for each country across all commodity groups, and for each commodity group across all countries. Thus, a country is said to have a revealed comparative advantage (be specialized) in a product if the RCA index exceeds unity. However, the index has a skew distribution, with a long tail to the right. This may create problems in regression analysis, because it violates the assumption of normality. Since a logarithmic transformation of the data reduces this problem significantly, a log-linear functional form was preferred (equation 1 above).

The calculation of the RCA index draws from a database[3] on OECD trade (value data).[4] The data were aggregated into 41 product groups (see Table 1). Great care was taken to ensure that R&D-intensive products as well as products based on important, commercially successful innovations in the not-too-distant past were specified as separate products, while more mature products and raw materials were treated in a more aggregative way. The identification of the R&D-intensive products was based on other studies (Kelly 1977; Aho and Rosen 1980; OECD 1985). While the two earlier studies were based solely on US data, the last one uses data for a group of OECD countries. However, with a few exceptions, these studies end up with rather similar rankings of products according to R&D intensity (expenditures on research and development as a share of output or sales).[5]

From the 41 products included in the classification, raw materials, where comparative advantage to a large extent depends on the domestic supply of natural resources, and residual categories were excluded from the investigation. The remaining 28 products accounted for 61.2% of total OECD exports in 1983. The single largest group was cars, which alone accounted for 11.0% of total OECD exports in that year. The share of the others varied from 0.2% to 5.7%.

Table 1   List of products

Product Groups	SITC Revision 1
101 Products based on natural resources	
1 Animals, meat and meat preparations	00, 01, 091.3, 411.3
2 Dairy products and eggs	02
3 Fish and fish preparations	03, 411:1
4 Cereals and cereal preparations	04
5 Feeding-stuff for animals	08
6 Skins and leather manufactures	21, 61
7 Wood and wood manufactures	24, 63
8 Pulp and paper	25, 64
9 Textiles	26, 65
10 Iron ore	281
11 Iron, steel and ferro alloys	67
12 Aluminium	684
13 Other products based on natural resources	Rest 0–4 and 6, less 33, 34, 69

Table 1 cont.

Product Groups	SITC Revision 1
102 Oil and gas	
14 Oil and gas	33, 34
103 Chemicals	
15 Organic chemicals	512
16* Inorganic chemicals	513, 514
17 Dyestuffs, colouring materials	53
18* Pharmaceuticals	54
19 Fertilizers	56
20* Plastics	581.1 and 2
21 Other chemicals	Rest 5
104 Machinery and transport equipment	
22* Power-generating machinery	711
23 Machinery for special industries or processes	712, 715, 717, 718, 719.3, 5 and 8
24 Heating and cooling equipment	719.1
25 Pumps and centrifuges	719.2
26* Typewriters and office machines	714.1 and 9
27* Computers and peripherals	714.2 and 3
28* Semiconductors	729.3
29* Telecommunications	724.9
30* Machinery for production and distribution of electricity	722, 723, 729.9
31* Consumer electronics	724.1 and 2, 891.1
32 Domestic electrical equipment	725
33* Scientific instruments, photographic supplies, watches/clocks	726, 729.5 and 7, 861, 862, 864
34* Cars (road motor vehicles)	732
35* Aircraft	734
36 Ships and boats (incl. oil rigs)	735
37 Other engineering products	Rest 7, less 719.4
105 Traditional industrial products	
38 Manufactures of metal	69, 719.4, 812.1 and 3
39 Furniture	82
40 Clothing	84
41 Industrial products n.e.c.	Rest 8–9

* = high-tech.

One of the problems in this study, as in most econometric studies of export specialization, is the selection of explanatory variables and proxies. Indeed, the potential number of factors that could have been taken into account is very large. Here we have to rely on theoretical considerations and the specific purpose of the study. The basic model will be one in which comparative advantage is created through technological capability, measured through R&D or patent statistics, and continually challenged by imitators exploiting cost advantages (low wages). To this framework we add variables reflecting various factors that are often alleged to have an important impact on export specialization. One of these, which follows from the purpose of this study, is the country size or scale variable, here proxied by the size of the population. Since it is often argued that military demand has been an important factor for the creation of competitive advantage in many high-technology industries, we also included military expenditures as a percentage of GDP as a possible explanatory factor. Finally, to be able to account for the possibility of differing requirements for capital across industries, we included gross investment as a share of GDP. Since raw materials were excluded from the investigation, we did not include any variable reflecting relative 'abundance' of natural resources. Admittedly, many of these variables are of a rather crude nature and, as in most other econometric studies of export specialization, the results should be taken as just indicative. Below follows a list the explanatory variables included in the test. For sources, see the appendix.

- Research and development (RD): total R&D expenditure as a percentage of GDP.
- Patents (PAT): external patent applications adjusted for country size and the openness of the economy.[6]
- Wages (WAGE): wage per hour in common currency.
- Scale (POP): population of the country.
- Military demand (MIL): military expenditure as a percentage of GDP.
- Investments (INV): gross investments as a percentage of GDP.

As will often be the case, some of these variables may be open for rival interpretations. For instance, the investment and wage variable could be interpreted as reflecting 'endowments' of capital and labour respectively (the traditional factor proportion – or Hecksher–Ohlin – theory). By stretching the argument somewhat, R&D expenditure could be interpreted as reflecting the 'endowment of skilled labour' on which R&D activity obviously depends (the so-called neo-factor proportion theory). Patents, scale and military expenditure, however, are variables that hardly fit into a neo-factor proportion framework. In any case, considerable doubts may be raised about the usefulness of the neo-factor approach. Arguably, to label something 'endowment' – when it clearly reflects conscious human behaviour – does not constitute much of an explanation.

The data refer to different time periods between 1960 and 1983, and 19 OECD member countries were included.[7] For the dependent variable indices were calculated for 1969, 1973, 1979 and 1983. The data for the independent variables were calculated as average values for the preceding periods (1960–67, 1968–73, 1974–79 and 1980–83), allowing for an average lag of roughly three years. Since the dependent variable, the revealed comparative advantage index, is a normalized variable, we decided to normalize all the independent variables in the same way. This implies that, for each country (and year), the value of each independent variable was divided by the across-country mean of that variable.[8]

3 Results

Three different tests were carried out: a pooled test (all time periods combined), a mean test (regression between the within-country means across years of each variable) and a difference test (a regression between the difference between the final observation and the first observation of each variable).

The advantage of a pooled test is that it combines information on the static and dynamic aspects of the model, and allows for a much larger sample than could otherwise have been used. The problem is that specification problems, in particular the omission of country-specific variables, may result in residual correlation within the cross-sectional units. To test for this we applied the Durbin–Watson test adjusted for gaps. The test indicated that residual correlation within the cross-sectional units was a problem. Methods to remedy this consist of excluding, totally or in part, that share of the total variance that can be associated with the within-country means of the variables (Maddala 1977; Johnston 1984). These methods are problematic in cases where the within-country means are considered to be important as explanatory factors, especially if some of them do not change much through time, as is the case for many of the variables considered here. We decided, therefore, following one of the suggestions made in the econometric literature,[9] to supplement the pooled test with separate tests for the statics and dynamics of the model.

The interpretation of the two additional tests is as follows. The mean test is a test of the long-run implications of the model, or to what extent *the structure of comparative advantage* (or export specialization) within each product group for the period as a whole can be explained by *the independent variables* included in the test. The difference test, on the other hand, tests the extent to which *the changes in the structure of comparative advantages* during the period of investigation can be explained by *changes in the independent variables* included in the test. This allows for the possibility that the determinants of the existing pattern of specialization across countries differ from those explaining the dynamics of this pattern.

In each case a backward search for the model with the least variance was used. The reason why we included both an R&D-based measure and a patent-based measure in the regressions, even though these are known to be heavily correlated across countries (Fagerberg 1987, 1988), is that other studies have shown that the significance of these two variables differs across sectors. So, even if only one of them will usually be retained, we found it advisable to start the search with both variables included.

The results are reported in Tables 2–4. Restricted R^2 and variables that were significant at a 10% level or more are included (for the others we accepted the proposition that their impact was not significantly different from zero).

Table 2   Regression results (pooled test)

		R^2	RD	PAT	INV	WAGE	POP	MIL
8	Paper	0.18	−0.58 (1.89) ***			1.09 (2.85) *	−0.26 (2.05) **	
9	Textiles	0.22	0.34 (1.92) ***			−1.05 (4.67) *		
11	Steel	0.12			1.36 (2.30) **	−0.41 (1.75) ***	0.18 (2.17) **	
12	Aluminium	0.24			2.17 (2.70) *	0.67 (2.02) **	−0.24 (2.29) **	0.80 (2.63) *
15	Organic chemicals	0.34	0.66 (2.77) *	0.22 (1.69) ***		−1.06 (4.30) *		0.34 (1.79) ***
16	Inorganic chemicals	0.34		−0.35 (3.74) *	2.25 (3.82) *		0.25 (3.48) *	1.02 (5.04) *
17	Colouring materials	0.47		0.72 (5.49) *		−1.17 (4.62) *	−0.31 (3.98) *	
18	Pharmaceuticals	0.47	0.43 (1.82) ***	0.58 (4.38) *	−2.65 (5.15) *	−1.15 (4.82) *	−0.37 (4.74) *	
19	Fertilizers	0.27	0.75 (2.09) **	−1.00 (5.24) *			0.28 (2.46) **	
20	Plastics	0.39	0.72 (4.39) *			−0.96 (4.78) *		0.56 (2.67) *
22	Power-generating machinery	0.55		0.39 (5.71) *			0.25 (4.44) *	
23	Special machinery	0.62	−0.24 (1.78) ***	0.71 (9.25) *		−0.55 (4.13) *		
24	Heating and cooling equipment	0.25	−0.54 (2.25) **	0.55 (4.34) *				
25	Pumps	0.50	−0.31 (1.72) ***	0.67 (7.04) *		−0.60 (3.29) *		0.29 (2.17) **

Table 2 cont.

	R^2	RD	PAT	INV	WAGE	POP	MIL
26 Office machinery	0.52		0.42 (3.28) *	−1.46 (2.91) *	−0.65 (2.80) *	0.26 (3.35) *	
27 Computers	0.33	0.48 (2.36) **				0.33 (3.76) *	
28 Semiconductors	0.48	1.08 (4.81) *			−0.92 (3.37) *	0.38 (4.34) *	
29 Telecommunication equipment	0.34	0.78 (4.92) *		−0.76 (2.66) *		0.14 (2.19) **	
30 Machinery for production & distribution of electricity	0.69		0.63 (12.5) *		−0.96 (8.31) *		
31 Consumer electronics	0.53	0.98 (5.55) *				0.29 (3.80) *	−1.51 (8.45) *
32 Domestic electrical equipment	0.15	−0.50 (2.00) **	0.33 (2.38) **		−0.74 (3.01) *		
33 Instruments	0.64	0.85 (4.64) *	0.47 (4.95) *	0.86 (1.76) ***	−0.50 (2.82) *		−0.49 (2.68) *
34 Cars	0.45	0.58 (2.15) **	−0.32 (2.24) **			0.58 (6.75) *	
35 Aircraft	0.72	0.34 (1.78) ***		−1.49 (2.84) *		0.41 (6.87) *	0.67 (3.62) *
36 Ships	0.19	−0.90 (2.58) *		4.95 (4.07) *			0.96 (2.22) **
38 Metal products	0.48		0.34 (5.57) *		−0.79 (7.47) *		
39 Furniture	0.15	−0.54 (1.75) ***			−0.60 (1.91) ***	−0.27 (2.75) *	
40 Clothing	0.49		0.20 (2.00) **	−2.07 (3.56) *	−1.56 (6.52) *		

*   Significant at 1% level, two-tailed test.
**   Significant at 5% level, two-tailed test.
*** Significant at 10% level, two-tailed test.

Table 3   Regression results (mean test)

		R^2	RD	PAT	INV	WAGE	POP	MIL
8	Paper	0.09						
9	Textiles	0.12				−0.93 (1.89) ***		
11	Steel	0.08						
12	Aluminium	0.19					−0.38 (1.90) ***	1.22 (2.09) ***
15	Organic chemicals	0.32	1.18 (3.19) *			−0.99 (2.02) **		
16	Inorganic chemicals	0.33		−0.43 (2.06) ***	3.63 (2.31) **		0.31 (1.94) ***	1.43 (2.86) **
17	Colouring materials	0.44		0.91 (4.12) *		−1.21 (2.39) **	−0.27 (1.76) ***	
18	Pharmaceuticals	0.38		0.78 (3.34) *	−2.86 (2.39) **	−1.21 (2.38) **	−0.36 (2.13) ***	
19	Fertilizers	0.20		−0.76 (2.61) **				1.36 (1.97) **
20	Plastics	0.37	0.90 (2.82) **			−1.17 (2.61) **		
22	Power-generating machinery	0.54		0.39 (2.68) **			0.31 (2.65) **	
23	Special machinery	0.58		0.67 (5.13) *		−0.73 (2.29) **		
24	Heating and cooling equipment	0.23		0.51 (2.71) **				
25	Pumps	0.45		0.64 (4.08) *				
26	Office machinery	0.59			−1.91 (1.90) ***	−0.87 (1.90) ***	0.27 (1.90) ***	

Table 3 cont.

	R^2	RD	PAT	INV	WAGE	POP	MIL
27 Computers	0.40					0.39 (2.60) **	
28 Semiconductors	0.50	1.03 (2.48) **			−1.17 (2.24) **	0.41 (2.51) **	
29 Telecommunication equipment	0.33	0.73 (2.48) **					
30 Machinery for production & distribution of electricity	0.69		0.69 (6.34) *		−1.17 (4.36) *		
31 Consumer electronics	0.52	1.04 (2.83) **				0.33 (2.15) **	−1.55 (4.32) *
32 Domestic electrical equipment	0.10				−0.81 (1.75) ***		
33 Instruments	0.57	1.12 (2.36) **	0.44 (1.92) ***				
34 Cars	0.46					0.69 (4.06) *	
35 Aircraft	0.76					0.43 (4.07) *	0.73 (2.37) **
36 Ships	0.22	−1.43 (1.89) ***		8.43 (2.74) **			1.99 (1.97) ***
38 Metal products	0.54		0.32 (3.69) *		−0.99 (4.58) *		
39 Furniture	0.05						
40 Clothing	0.42				−1.94 (3.82) *		

*   Significant at 1% level, two-tailed test.
**   Significant at 5% level, two-tailed test.
***   Significant at 10% level, two-tailed test.

Table 4   Regression results (time difference test)[a]

		R^2	ΔRD	ΔPAT	ΔINV	ΔWAGE	ΔPOP	ΔMIL
8	Paper	0.12		−0.49 (1.95) ***		0.83 (2.13) ***		−1.18 (1.77) ***
9	Textiles	0.21	0.39 (1.95) ***					
11	Steel	0.04						
12	Aluminium	0.16				1.05 (2.29) **		−1.49 (1.91) ***
15	Organic chemicals	0.57			4.22 (5.17) *			
16	Inorganic chemicals	0.18			1.48 (2.23) **			
17	Colouring materials	0.14						0.70 (1.95) ***
18	Pharmaceuticals	0.53	0.89 (4.14) *		−1.02 (2.03) **	−0.40 (1.90) ***		
19	Fertilizers	0.29	1.65 (2.84) *					
20	Plastics	0.28			1.19 (1.83) ***			
22	Power-generating machinery	0.48	0.78 (2.81) **		2.35 (3.37) *	0.79 (2.36) **		
23	Special machinery	0.35		0.34 (2.67) **				0.68 (2.08) ***
24	Heating and cooling equipment	0.71			2.56 (3.55) *			
25	Pumps	0.62			2.06 (4.58) *	0.35 (1.78) ***		
26	Office machinery	0.23	−1.03 (2.06) ***	0.70 (2.00) ***				

Table 4 cont.

		R^2	ΔRD	ΔPAT	ΔINV	ΔWAGE	ΔPOP	ΔMIL
27	Computers	0.72			3.53 (3.10) *			3.32 (3.38) *
28	Semiconductors	0.33	0.94 (2.21) **		1.86 (1.94) ***			
29	Telecommunication equipment	0.68		0.63 (4.40) *		−0.66 (2.80) **	0.37 (2.60) **	1.77 (4.67) *
30	Machinery for production & distribution of electricity	0.66		0.20 (2.15) **	0.94 (2.71) **			0.65 (2.23) **
31	Consumer electronics	0.52	0.82 (2.17) **		1.86 (2.08) ***			−1.36 (1.98) ***
32	Domestic electrical equipment	0.12						
33	Instruments	0.53		0.31 (3.25) *		−0.47 (2.97) *		0.92 (3.67) *
34	Cars	0.50	0.75 (2.77) **			0.80 (2.95) *		
35	Aircraft	0.07						
36	Ships	0.06						
38	Metal products	0.02						
39	Furniture	0.03						
40	Clothing	0.42	0.72 (2.37) **	−0.45 (2.21) **				−1.02 (2.15) **

a   Final period observation less first period observation.
*   Significant at 1% level, two-tailed test.
**   Significant at 5% level, two-tailed test.
***   Significant at 10% level, two-tailed test.

The main results may be summarized as follows:

1. If we restrict ourselves to products where one or more factors were significant at a 1% level in the pooled test, and at a 5% level in at least one of the two supplementary tests, there were twenty products that met these criteria and eight that did not. The latter were: paper, textiles, steel, aluminium, fertilizers, office machinery, domestic electrical equipment and furniture. Together these eight products accounted for 13.4% of total OECD exports in 1983 (or roughly one-fifth of our sample). Of these eight products, six come from industries processing raw materials. For these a possible explanation may be that success depends on 'relative abundance' of important resources (including, perhaps, cheap energy) not taken into account in the test.

2. Clearly the most important factor according to the above criteria was technology, which was significant in fourteen of the twenty cases mentioned above. But also the wage level was found to be important (ten cases). The scale variable turned out to be significant in six cases, and the two remaining factors, military demand and investments, in two cases each. The explanatory power of the different factors (in terms of number of significant estimates) is reflected in the different sizes of the circles in Figure 1. If the products had been weighted according to their shares in total OECD trade, the differences in explanatory power between the technology, wage and scale variables would have been smaller, but technology would still have been the most important factor. In 1983 the share in total OECD exports of the products for which technology was found to be an important factor was 29.9%. The shares for products where wages and scale were relevant were 24.3% and 20.7% respectively.[10] The shares of products in which the two remaining factors, military demand and investments, were important were 3.0% and 2.2% respectively, that is, not very large.

3. As Figure 1 shows, there are many cases of overlap between the various factors, especially between technology on the one hand, and wages and scale on the other. But there was only one case of overlap between wages and scale, namely semiconductors, for which also technology was found to be an important factor. Thus, with the exception of semiconductors, the products for which technology was found to be an important factor divide neatly in three: one group where technology and scale (but not wages) are important (two products), another where technology and wages (but not scale) are important (eight products) and finally one where only technology matters (four products). The most important of these, numerically and economically, is the one where technology and wages matter. In 1983 this group alone accounted for 21.5% of total OECD trade.

4. If we adopt the stricter criteria of products where one or more factors were found to be significant at a 1% level in the pooled test and at a 5% in *both* the supplementary tests, the dominant role played by technology is strengthened. In this case technology was found to be a significant factor in eight products, compared with one product each for scale and investments and no products for wages and military demand. Thus, technology is the only factor that has sufficient explanatory power to explain both the statics and the dynamics of the model.

5. When the dynamics is tested separately (Table 4), the important role played by technology is again confirmed. If the 5% level of significance is adopted, technology turns out to be a significant factor (with the correct sign) in eleven products, compared with two for wages and one for scale.[11] It is interesting to note, however, that the investments variable performs much better in this test (significant at a 5% level in seven products) than in the other two, that is, that growth in comparative advantage and growth in investment activity are positively correlated in many cases.[12] The same applies, although not to the same extent, to growth in comparative advantage and growth in military expenditure (four products).

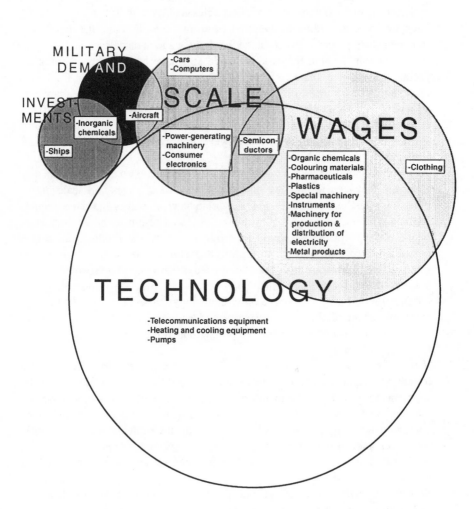

Figure 1   Factors affecting export specialization

If we compare the results obtained here with the R&D intensity of products as reported by other sources (see Table 1), some important similarities, as well as differences, emerge. First, out of the thirteen goods that are classified as R&D-intensive in Table 1, eight are included in the group where technology was found to have a significant impact. All but one belong to the group of products for which technology was found to affect both the statics and dynamics of the model (see point 4 above). The remaining five R&D-intensive products are distributed, with three in the group where scale was found to be the most important factor (cars, computers and aircraft – the latter in overlap of military demand), one in the group where investment matters most (again in overlap with military demand) and one in the group for which no significant explanatory factor was found. The latter, office machinery, was one of a few products that were classified as R&D-intensive prior to 1973 but not later, indicating increasing maturity (and, hence, change of explanatory factors) during the period of investigation.

The findings of this study suggest that *a distinction must be made between technology (including R&D) as an input in the process of production and as the most decisive factor in the process of global competition.* Industries such as aircraft, computers and – to a lesser extent – cars are clearly among the most R&D-intensive, but comparative advantage in these industries is determined by access to a large domestic market rather than by differences between countries in R&D efforts.[13] This finding lends some support to the argument by some new growth theorists that large countries are more likely to develop a comparative advantage in high-tech.

However, the results of this study also point to another difference between R&D as an input and technology as an important competitive factor. *The list of products for which technology was found to be an important factor is broader than the list of R&D-intensive products or industries.* In particular it includes a larger part of the machinery and chemical sectors. This relates, for instance, to various types of general and specialized equipment for use in the industrial sector. As is clear from Tables 2–4 it is the inclusion of the patent variable that produces this result. Thus, in these industries, competition through technological innovation is important, but it is not necessarily related to the intensity of R&D. This result is in accordance with the findings of a number of innovation studies showing that innovations in these sectors are more related to engineering activities, often in interaction with customers and suppliers, than to organized R&D (Pavitt 1984). Since scale factors do not seem to be important in these industries, the opportunities for small countries are probably better here. But, in contrast to the cases where scale factors were found to be important, most of these industries are also exposed to cost competition (wages).

How are these findings to be explained? One possibility suggested in the literature (Pavitt 1984; Nelson and Wright 1992) is that the process of technological progress differs in character between industries. In some industries, it is argued, innovations are science-based (result from organized R&D), written down (codified) and replicable. In other industries technological improvements continue to result from learning (by doing, interacting and so on) and are, in contrast to the science-based ones, often 'tacit' (uncodified) and 'organizational' in character. Although these latter industries also use legal instruments (patents) to protect their innovations, the 'tacit' and 'organizational' character of the innovation process implies a high degree of protection in itself, that is, that innovations from these industries are often not easily replicable. From this one might conjecture, using the language of the new growth theorists, that technological externalities are much more frequent in the science-based industries than in the 'learning'-based ones. Since the hypothesis of a large-country advantage in high-tech is based on the assumption that technological externalities are frequent, it is perhaps not surprising that this hypothesis does not fit all industries where innovation and technological competition have been found to be important. This implies, however, that the new growth theorists have not succeeded in modelling technological progress in an all-encompassing way, and thus puts some limitations on the validity of the predictions that can be obtained from this framework. Another critical point is that geographical limitations on technological externalities, which play an important role for some of these predictions, cannot merely be assumed, but have to be explained (Fagerberg 1994).

There is also the possibility of alternative explanations of the impact of the scale, or country size, variable. The six industries for which scale was found to be important were aircrafts, computers, semiconductors, consumer electronics, power-generating machinery and cars. These are all industries where non-tariff barriers to trade are known to be important. Governmental favouritism and subsidies have also been frequent. Thus, a more conventional explanation based on scale economics and trading costs[14] – caused by various forms of protectionism – might perhaps do the trick. The present study cannot discriminate between these different versions of the scale argument.

4   Comparison with other studies

There are few other studies that can be compared directly with this one. Studies based on correlation between some measure of export performance on the one hand and R&D performance on the other, such as Walker (1979), tend to turn up with a more narrow definition of high-technology products than the one suggested here.[15] The methodology applied in many of these studies also differs from the one adopted here, by using industry-specific data, often based on the US experience, for the independent variables. One study, closer to the framework adopted here, is that of Lacroix and Scheuer (1976). They regress exports from fifteen different industries on a set of country-specific variables, including scale factors, industry-specific R&D outlays, human capital and capital intensity. The level of aggregation does not allow for a detailed comparison with the results presented here. However, the general result was that R&D turned out to be important in a broad range of industries, including most chemical and mechanical industries. The impact of scale factors, however, is more difficult to assess because of the inclusion of two variables related to scale, GDP and population (the results indicate that a multicollinearity problem may be present).

A methodology similar to that of Lacroix and Scheuer has been applied by Soete (1987) and Dosi and Soete (1983).[16] In Soete (1987) the market share for exports was regressed on a set of country-specific variables reflecting sectoral innovative activity (external patents in the United States), population, capital intensity and 'distance', for 40 sectors in 1977 (1963–1977 average for the patent variable). As in the present study technology was found to be an important factor in many sectors. This includes some of the (R&D-intensive) sectors mentioned earlier, where our study points to scale, not technology, as the most important competitive factor. The scale variable turned out to be significant in a few sectors only, and with the exception of cars, in other sectors than the ones found here. However, as in the case of Lacroix and Scheuer, the way the variables are handled makes this result difficult to assess. Indeed, with the exception of the 'distance' variable, all variables included in the test by Soete depend on the size of the country.

It should be noted that there is an important difference between the tests conducted here and those of Lacroix and Scheuer and Soete in the way the technology variables are defined. In our study these variables are calculated for the country as a whole and are assumed to reflect national technological capabilities. Lacroix and Scheuer and Soete, however, use sector-specific data for the technology variable and aggregated data for the others. The implication is that the hypothesis under test is not exactly the same as in our study. While we test for the impact of national technological capabilities, they test for the impact of sector-specific technological efforts. These do not have to be related (although they often are). For instance, a country may for some reason be specialized in a particular product or industry where technological competition is important, and – consequently – have a high level of R&D and patents in that particular field, even if the general level of technological activity in the country is rather low.

Another difference between the tests by Lacroix and Scheuer and Soete and the tests presented here is that neither of them included a cost variable. However, this has been done by Dosi and Soete (1983) on roughly the same data. But in that study the scale variable was omitted and the cost variable defined in a way which made it a mixture of costs and income distribution. Thus, it is not possible to make direct comparisons between the results of our study and those obtained in earlier studies in this respect.

Still, here, as in earlier studies, technology is found to be the single most important explanatory factor of export performance/export specialization. Table 5 compares the results obtained in our study with those presented by Soete (1987) with respect to the estimated technology elasticities. As is clear from the table the results are almost identical for non-electronic machinery. For electronics the results are more difficult to compare. In general, in our study these products appeared to be more related to R&D than to patents. The definitions of the product groups also differ somewhat. However, when note is taken of the fact that the mean of the estimated elasticities is higher for R&D than for patents, the results may be interpreted as being broadly similar. For chemicals, however, our study generally reports higher and more significant elasticities than those reported by Soete. Partly, this is due to the inclusion of R&D as an explanatory variable, but it does also hold for the cases for which patents were found to be the most significant factor.

5   Concluding remarks

This paper has raised the question of whether or not there exists a large-country advantage in high-tech industries. *The results indicate that there exists a group of R&D-intensive products where access to a large domestic market appears to be an important competitive factor, sometimes (but not always) in combination with a high share of military expenditure in GDP.* This includes aircraft, cars, power-generating

Table 5   Ranking according to technology elasticity

	Our (mean test)	Soete (1987)[a]
Patents matter:		
1. Colouring materials (17)	0.91	0.33/NS
2. Pharmaceuticals (18)	0.78	0.34
3. Machinery for production and distribution of electricity (30)	0.69	0.67/0.62
4. Special machinery (23)	0.67	0.68/0.66/0.57
5. Pumps (25)	0.64	(0.49)
6. Heating and cooling equipment (24)	0.51	0.51
7. Power-generating machinery (22)	0.39	0.47
8. Metal products (38)	0.32	0.35
R&D matters:		
1. Organic chemicals (15)	1.18	NS
2. Consumer electronics (31)	1.04	NS
3. Semiconductors (28)	1.03	(0.46)
4. Plastics (20)	0.90	0.31
5. Telecommunications (29)	0.73	(0.46)
Both patents and R&D matter:		
Instruments (33)		
Patents	0.44	0.74
R&D	1.12	

[a]   This column contains estimates as reported by Soete for comparable (not identical) product groups. All estimates refer to patents.
Brackets: his classification is more aggregated than ours.
Several numbers: his classification is more disaggregated than ours.
NS = not significant.

machinery and a large part of electronics. The results also indicate that most of these products are not very sensitive to cost competition (wages).[17] The significant impact of country size on comparative advantage in these industries is consistent with the predictions of some new growth theorists (based on the assumption that technology spillovers are national rather than international in scope). Another possible interpretation of these results is that there is a story of large-country protectionism to be told here, as much circumstantial evidence indeed suggests. To the extent that protectionism is present, this reinforces the well-known argument from the trade literature that small countries have most to gain from reduced trade barriers (see, for instance, Krugman 1988).

However, this study also shows that technology is an important competitive factor in a large number of products or industries where scale factors are of little importance.

These include a large number of engineering and chemicals industries. But with some exceptions, these products are also exposed to cost competition (wages). Thus, the challenges from industrializing, low-cost countries may be of greater importance for small than for large countries (although the public attention on this is at least as great in the latter). Nonetheless, the results also indicate that wage costs, although important, play a more passive role in global competition than technology.[18] The option for small developed countries appears to be to compensate for higher costs by a higher level of innovation and a more rapid process of diffusion. Hence, technology policy may be important in small countries as well. However, small countries should avoid imitating the technology policies of the large countries, which often concentrate resources on areas where large-country advantages seem to be present. Instead, small countries ought to focus on the large number of industries where technology – and innovation through learning – is important, but scale matters less.

Appendix: data sources (independent variables)

- External patent applications: OECD/STIIU DATA BANK and World International Property Organization (WIPO): Industrial Property Statistics.
- R&D: OECD Science and Technology Indicators.
- Military expenditure as percentage of GDP: SIPRI Yearbook.
- Other variables: OECD Historical Statistics and OECD National Accounts.

Notes

*   An earlier version of this paper was presented at the International Joseph A. Schumpeter Society, Fifth Conference, Münster, Germany, 17–20 August 1994. I wish to thank the participants at the session and colleagues at the Norwegian Institute of International Affairs for comments and suggestions, retaining full responsibility for what remains.

1.   Another suggestion was that innovation was facilitated by advanced domestic demand (Linder 1961; Vernon 1966). For an empirical test of this view see Fagerberg (1995).

2.   This may be seen as a special version of the more general prediction of so-called 'new trade theory' (Helpman 1984); that countries with small domestic markets may face a potential disadvantage in industries where economies of scale prevail if products are differentiated or there are barriers to trade (protectionism and so on).

3.   The database was constructed jointly by Bent Dalum (at the University of Aalborg) and the author from OECD Trade Series C. See Fagerberg (1986) for details.

4.   It is often suggested that it would be preferable to use volume data instead of value data, but this was not possible at a sufficiently disaggregated level. Furthermore, volume data are problematic in cases where substantial technological changes occur and become, for the very same reason, less reliable when the time span under consideration grows.

5.   It should be noted, though, that a few products classified as R&D-intensive in the two earlier studies did not appear as such in the last study (non-electronic office machinery such as typewriters and so on, consumer electronics and cars). Probably this reflects that these products, by the early 1970s, had entered the mature phase of the product cycle. We have chosen to regard these as R&D-intensive prior to 1973, but not later. Thus, we end up with two lists of high-tech products, a broad one, applicable for the 1960s and early 1970s, and a more narrow one, assumed to be appropriate for the most recent period.

6.   The reason for adjusting the index for differences in the degree of openness of the economy is that the propensity to patent in foreign markets is assumed to depend on the importance of export markets relative to the domestic market (see Fagerberg 1987).

7.   These are: the United States, Japan, Germany (West), France, the United Kingdom, Italy, Canada, Austria, Belgium, Denmark, the Netherlands, Norway, Sweden, Switzerland, Finland, Ireland, Spain, New Zealand and Australia.

8.   Some countries had values for the RCA index close to zero in some sectors. In order to avoid extreme values in the regressions (a logarithmic specification was used), we restricted the lower end of the

observations to 0.1 by adding 0.1 to all observations of the dependent and the independent variables. Thus, the average for each variable in each year is 1.1, not 1.0.

9. See Maddala (1977 p. 326) and Johnston (1984 pp. 405–6).
10. It should be noted, however, that the size of the share for the scale factor depends very much on one product group, cars, which alone accounted for 11.0% of total OECD exports in 1983.
11. In the case of the scale variable, it should be mentioned that since this variable is relatively stable through time, it should be expected to lose much of its impact in a test of this type irrespective of whether the hypothesis under test is true or false. The same applies – although perhaps not to the same extent – to some of the other variables.
12. It might be suggested that this result supports the factor abundance theory. However, this theory would also predict a positive relation between the level of comparative advantage and the level of the investment ratio (as a proxy for capital intensity). As follows from Table 3, this was the case for two products only (inorganic chemicals and ships).
13. Van Hulst et al. (1991) also found that technology variables had little explanatory power in some 'very high-tech' industries.
14. See the survey by Helpman (1984) on trade models with imperfect competition and economies of scale.
15. The recent study by Magnier and Toujas-Bernate (1994) is an exception to this rule. Their analysis, based on pooled time-series data for five countries and twenty industries (in the 1980s), suggests that the positive impact of R&D on market shares extends to some 'low-tech' industries (such as wood, paper, textiles and food). Due to the handling of the data (normalization procedure), the results from their study are not comparable with the others discussed in this section. However, it may be seen as a more refined version of our difference test on a smaller sample (and using industry-specific data for the independent variables). The results for typical 'low-tech' industries differ, however.
16. See also Dosi, Pavitt and Soete (1990), where many of the empirical studies by Soete and others, including the two discussed here, are summarized and discussed.
17. Indeed, for one group (cars), the results indicate that increasing comparative advantage and increasing wage costs vis à vis competitors are positively related (see Table 4). This result is significant at the 1% level. If the level of significance is set to the 5% level, similar results were found for two other groups, aluminium and power-generating machinery.
18. This is shown by the fact that wage costs, with two exceptions (telecommunications and instruments (5% level)), failed to contribute to explanation of the changes in comparative advantages during the period of investigation (see Table 4). By comparison, there were eleven products where one of the technology variables was shown to have an impact on these changes (5% level).

References

Aho, M.C. and H.F. Rosen (1980) *Trends in Technology Intensive Trade: With Special Reference to US Competitiveness*, US Department of Labor

Balassa, B. (1965) Trade Liberalization and 'Revealed' Comparative Advantage, *The Manchester School*, Vol. 33, pp. 99–123

Dosi, G. and L. Soete (1983) Technology Gaps and Cost-based Adjustment: Some Explorations of the Determinants of International Competitiveness, *Metroeconomica*, Vol. 35, pp. 357–82

Dosi, G. and L. Soete (1988) Technical Change and International Trade, in G. Dosi et al. (eds), *Technical Change and Economic Theory*, Pinter, London

Dosi, G., K. Pavitt, H. and L. Soete (1990) *The Economics of Technical Change and International Trade*, Harvester Wheatsheaf, London

Fagerberg, J. (1986) Norden og strukturendringene på verdensmarkedet, En analyse av de nordiske lands handel med hverandre og de øvrige OECD-landene 1961–1983, *Rapport fra Statistisk Sentralbyrå*, 86/18, Statistisk Sentralbyrå, Oslo

Fagerberg, J. (1987) A Technology Gap Approach to Why Growth Rates Differ, *Research Policy*, Vol. 16, pp. 87–99

Fagerberg, J. (1988) Why Growth Rates Differ, in G. Dosi et al. (eds), *Technical Change and Economic Theory*, Pinter, London

Fagerberg, J. (1994) Technology and International Differences in Growth Rates, *Journal of Economic Literature*, Vol. 32, pp. 1147–75

Fagerberg, J. (1995) User–Producer Interaction, Learning and Comparative Advantage, *Cambridge Journal of Economics*, Vol. 19, pp. 243–56

Grossman, G.M. and E. Helpman (1991) *Innovation and Growth in the Global Economy*, MIT Press, Cambridge

Gruber, W., D. Metha and R. Vernon (1967) The R&D Factor in International Trade and International Investment of US Industries, *Journal of Political Economy*, Vol. 75, pp. 20–37

Helpman, E. (1984) Increasing Returns, Imperfect Markets and Trade Theory, in R.W. Jones and P.B. Kenen (eds), *Handbook of International Economics*, Volume 1, North-Holland, Amsterdam

Johnston, J. (1984) *Econometric Methods*, McGraw-Hill, New York

Kelly, R. (1977) *The Impact of Technological Innovation on International Trade Patterns*, US Department of Commerce

Krugman, P. (1988) EFTA and 1992, *Occasional Paper*, No. 23, EFTA, Geneva

Lacroix, R. and P. Scheuer (1976) L'Effort de R&D, l'Innovation et le Commerce International, *Revue Economique*, No. 6, pp. 1008–29

Leamer, E. (1974) The Commodity Composition of International Trade in Manufactures: An Empirical Analysis, *Oxford Economic Papers*, Vol. 26, pp. 350–74

Linder, S.B. (1961) *An Essay on Trade and Transformation*, Almqvist & Wiksell, Uppsala

Maddala, G.S. (1977) *Econometrics*, McGraw-Hill, New York

Magnier, A. and J. Toujas-Bernate (1994) Technology and Trade: Empirical Evidence from Five Industrialized Countries, *Weltwirtschaftliches Archiv*, Vol. 130, pp. 494–520

Nelson, R. and G. Wright (1992) The Rise and Fall of American Technological Leadership: The Postwar Era in Historical Perspective, *Journal of Economic Literature*, Vol. 30, pp. 1931–64

OECD (1985) *Trade in High Technology Products: An Initial Contribution to the Statistical Analysis of Trade Patterns in High Technology Products*, DSTI/SPR/84/66 (1st Revision)

Pavitt, K. (1984) Sectoral Patterns of Technical Change: Towards a Taxonomy and a Theory, *Research Policy*, Vol. 13, pp. 343–73

Romer, P.M. (1990) Endogenous Technological Change, *Journal of Political Economy*, Vol. 98, pp. 1002–37

Schumpeter, J. (1934) *The Theory of Economic Development*, Harvard University Press, Cambridge, MA

Schumpeter, J. (1939) *Business Cycles I–II*, McGraw-Hill, New York

Schumpeter, J. (1943) *Capitalism, Socialism and Democracy*, Harper, New York

Soete, L. (1981) A General Test of Technological Gap Trade Theory, *Weltwirtschaftliches Archiv*, Vol. 117, pp. 638–60

Soete, L. (1987) The Impact of Technological Innovation on International Trade Patterns: The Evidence Reconsidered, *Research Policy*, Vol. 16, pp. 101–30

Van Hulst, N., R. Mulder and L. Soete (1991) Exports and Technology in Manufacturing Industry, *Weltwirtschaftliches Archiv*, Vol. 127, pp. 246–64

Vernon, R. (1966) International Investment and International Trade in the Product Cycle, *Quarterly Journal of Economics*, Vol. 80, pp. 190-207

Verspagen, B. (1992) Endogenous Innovation in Neo-classical Models: A Survey, *Journal of Macroeconomics*, Vol. 14, pp. 631–62

Walker, W.B. (1979) *Industrial Innovation and International Trading Performance*, JAI Press, Greenwich

3. Competitiveness, scale and R&D

Jan Fagerberg

---

1 INTRODUCTION

Recent theorizing on growth and trade points to the importance of R&D and spillovers from this to other firms, industries and countries. According to this literature, the geographical boundaries of such spillovers are of prime importance for trade patterns. Country size may also play an important role. However, until recently, applied work in this area has had relatively little to say about these issues. This chapter begins with a short review of the theoretical and applied literature in this area. Based on the lessons learned, an eclectic model is formulated and applied to data for ten OECD countries and 20 industries in 1985. The data set includes, among other things, data for direct R&D and R&D acquired indirectly through purchase of capital goods and intermediary products. The results give some support to theories that focus on the importance of R&D investments and spillovers for exports.

2 THE AGENDA

The interest in the relationship between technology and competitiveness dates back to the so-called neo-technological trade theories of the 1960s (technology gap, product cycle and so on; for an overview see Dosi and Soete, 1988). These may be seen as attempts to overcome the rigidity of the standard neoclassical approach to international trade, which had become apparent for many observers. Most of these attempts were, explicitly or implicitly, based on Schumpeter's analysis of innovation and diffusion as the driving forces behind the competitiveness of firms (and economic growth in general).[1] Writers in this tradition pointed to the importance of R&D and innovation for trade flows and possible differences across industries and countries in this respect.

Since this issue was first introduced by Posner (1961), Vernon (1966) and others, economic theory has changed considerably. Trade theorists started to apply the insights from models of imperfectly competitive markets to the analysis of international trade and worldwide competitiveness (the so-called 'new trade theory'; see Helpman, 1984 for an overview). In this literature the existence of

38

fixed costs, such as, for instance, investment in R&D, plays an important role (since they give rise to economies of scale). Thus, following this approach, R&D investment may be an important competitive factor. The size of the domestic market also plays an important role in such models. One possible outcome[2] in a world characterized by imperfect competition, economies of scale and trading costs (that are neither too small, nor prohibitive) is, other things being equal, that countries specialize in products for which there is a relatively large domestic market – the so-called 'home-market effect' (Krugman, 1990). Furthermore, if some industries are characterized by economies of scale while others are not, one might expect the large countries to specialize in the former and the small countries in the latter.

More recently, growth theorists started to introduce the Schumpeterian insight of the importance of innovation-diffusion into formal growth models based on the assumption of imperfectly competitive markets (the so-called 'new growth theory'; for an overview see Grossman and Helpman, 1995). These models also point to the importance of R&D for growth of GDP and exports. While much of the earlier literature in this area emphasized the direct impact of the R&D effort of a firm, industry or country, the new growth literature focuses more sharply on the impact of diffusion or 'technological spillovers'. Following this approach, it matters a lot what the actual boundaries of these spillovers are. If technological spillovers are (mainly) national in scope, a large country will benefit more from investments in new technology (R&D) than a small one. Hence, on this assumption, a large country should be considered more likely to gain a competitive advantage in R&D-intensive activities than a small country.

Differences across countries in the efficiency of R&D and other technological activities have also been emphasized by the recent literature on 'national systems of innovation' (Lundvall (ed.), 1992; Nelson (ed.), 1993). This literature stresses the systemic aspects of innovation, the importance of interaction across firms, industries and sectors and the advantage of a coherent national system in this area. A related perspective is that of Porter (1990), who also emphasizes the potential benefits of close links and interaction between producers and their (domestic) customers and suppliers, often referred to as 'clustering' or 'agglomeration'.[3] This phenomenon is also consistent with a perspective that focuses on scale economics, for instance among domestic suppliers of goods and services, see Venables (1994). What is of interest here is that all these approaches suggest that a high reliance of domestic sources of technology may imply a competitive advantage.

3 THE EVIDENCE

Empirically, analysts have tried to highlight the relationship between competitiveness and technology by regressing a measure of export performance on a technology variable, usually based on R&D or patent statistics, and – in some cases – other variables that were deemed relevant for the analysis. Generally, the relationship is the following:

$$X = f(T, O), \tag{3.1}$$

where X is a measure of export performance, T is a technology proxy and O is a set of other variables.

A distinction may be made between cross-sectional work, using data for a number of industries and countries at one point in time (the static case), and applications on time-series data (the dynamic case). Among the former, Lacroix and Scheuer (1976), Walker (1979), Soete (1981, 1987), Dosi and Soete (1983), Dosi, Pavitt and Soete (1990) and Fagerberg (1995a) may be mentioned. Generally, the results of these studies support the hypothesis of a positive relationship between competitiveness and technological activity for a large number of industries, not only those that are commonly regarded as 'high tech'. However, tests that use R&D instead of a patent-based technology indicator tend to come up with a narrower list of industries for which technology matters. Some of these studies also included a variable assumed to reflect scale factors (population). Fagerberg (1995a), in a cross-sectional study of 19 OECD countries and 40 industries, found scale factors to be important in only a few industries, covering about one-fifth of total OECD trade.

A dynamic version of equation 3.1 was suggested by Fagerberg (1988) and applied to pooled cross-sectional time-series macro data for a number of industrialized countries. Time-series estimates for the macro level have also been presented by Amendola et al. (1993). Magnier and Toujas-Bernate (1994) and Amable and Verspagen (1995) both analysed pooled time-series and cross-sectional data for five large OECD countries in the 1970s and 1980s. Generally, the results from these studies confirm much of the previous evidence from cross-sectional samples, but the role of scale factors was largely ignored.

4   DATA AND METHOD

The applied literature surveyed above has generated a lot of insights and knowledge on the impact of R&D and innovation (and other factors) on trade performance across countries and industries. However, many questions remain open, in particular those related to the possible impact of technology flows across firms, industries and countries. The purpose of this chapter is to add to the existing literature in this area by exploring the relationship between competitiveness, scale and R&D with the help of the OECD STAN and ANBERD Data Bases and the recent work by the OECD on embodied technology flows. The ensuing data set is unique in the sense that it provides data for a number of variables – including direct R&D and R&D acquired through purchase of capital goods and intermediates – at the level of the industry (mostly in current prices).

Ten countries, 22 industries[4] and (roughly) two decades are included. We excluded two industries on the grounds that they were ill defined (two residual categories). For some of the technology variables data were available for selected years only (in some cases only one year). This made a regular time series difficult. What will be presented here is a cross-sectional analysis for 1985, the only year for which the technology variables are available for all ten countries (even then about 5 per cent of the observations are missing because of a lack of data for certain variables, industries and countries).

International competitiveness at the industry level may be defined as the ability to sell products in international markets in competition with suppliers from other countries. Exports seem to be a natural indicator for that, and most of the applied literature on competitiveness also uses an export-based indicator.[5] The model we wish to apply is an eclectic one in which the international competitiveness of a country at the industry level is explained by technological factors (direct R&D efforts and its ability to profit from R&D acquired indirectly through purchase of inputs, whether of domestic or foreign origin), cost competitiveness (wage level), the rate of investment and the size of the domestic market. More formally, we have:

$$X = f(RD, DIF, FOR, INV, WAGE, HOME), \qquad (3.2)$$

where:

X is exports,
RD (direct R&D) is business enterprise R&D,
DIF (indirect R&D) is R&D acquired indirectly through purchases of capital
    goods and intermediate goods from domestic and foreign suppliers,
FOR (foreign share) is indirect R&D acquired through purchases of capital
    goods and intermediate goods from foreign suppliers as a percentage of
    total indirect R&D (both foreign and domestic),
WAGE is labour costs per worker,
INV is gross fixed capital formation,
HOME is domestic demand (measured as production + imports – exports).

All variables are measured in current prices in a common currency (US dollars) and are country and industry specific. The data for R&D acquired through purchases of capital goods and intermediates were calculated by the OECD and supplied as shares of production (these data were then scaled up by using data for production in 1985). In their calculation of indirect R&D acquired through domestic sources the OECD applied an input–output methodology, based on the so-called Leontief inverse (Papaconstantinou et al., 1996). This means that the indirect R&D from domestic sources for a particular industry in a particular country reflects not only the direct R&D carried out by its domestic suppliers but also the R&D acquired by these suppliers through their use of domestically produced capital goods and intermediates. For various reasons, indirect R&D acquired from foreign sources was calculated using a less sophisticated methodology, weighting direct R&D in the supplying (foreign) industries with actual import shares for the industry and country in question. As noted by the OECD, this implies an underestimation of the total amount of foreign R&D. Probably this does not constitute a serious problem in the present context, since the impact on the variables used here is likely to be small.[6]

Consistent with most theoretical perspectives in this area we expect a positive impact of both R&D and investment in physical capital (*INV*) on exports. Which of them is the most efficient way to enhance competitiveness is a matter of controversy. Some theories predict that the impact of investment in R&D (Romer, 1990; Grossman and Helpman, 1991) or physical capital (Romer, 1986) is more prominent in large countries; we will be able to test for that as well. If there are important positive externalities stemming from the use of product-embodied R&D, we might expect a large positive impact of indirect R&D (*DIF*). An unresolved issue is, as mentioned, to what extent national boundaries matter for the impact of technology flows; the *FOR* variable was designed to throw some light on that. If the estimated impact is deemed to be not different from zero, this implies that the source (domestic or foreign) does not really matter. If, on the other hand, the estimated impact is negative, this means that indirect R&D from domestic sources is valued more highly, consistent with the suggestion from some theories in this area. Cost competition figures prominently in the public debate on competitiveness and in some theories as well (the product-cycle theory, for example). To take this possibility into account, we included the *WAGE* variable. We also included the *HOME* variable to allow for an impact of market size on competitiveness, consistent with some of the suggestions of 'new trade theory' (the 'home-market effect'). Finally we test for the widely held view, often associated with the product-cycle theory (Vernon, 1966), that the impact of R&D and other factors vary systematically across broad classes of industry ('high tech' versus 'medium' or 'low tech'). Following this theory R&D and market size should be of prime importance for competitiveness in innovative, high-tech industries; while in mature, low-tech industries investments in physical capital and low wages should be assumed to matter most.

5 A PREVIEW OF THE DATA

Table 3.1 gives summary statistics (total manufacturing) for the ten OECD countries included in the investigation for the year 1985.[7] There is a large spread in direct R&D efforts (as a percentage of production), with the USA far ahead of the others (3.5 per cent). The remaining nine countries divide neatly into two groups, five in the area 2–2.5 per cent, and four between 0.7 and 1 per cent. In the former we find the Netherlands, Japan, France, the UK and Germany, in the latter Italy, Australia, Canada and Denmark. As could be expected there is also a marked difference between large and small countries with respect to the importance of domestic versus foreign indirect R&D, with the large ones benefiting almost exclusively from the former and the small countries mostly geared towards the latter. This is clearly reflected in the share of foreign indirect R&D in total indirect R&D: column four in Table 3.1 (the 'foreign share').

Table 3.1   Summary statistics - 10 OECD countries, 1985

	Direct R&D	Domestic indirect R&D	Foreign indirect R&D	Foreign share	Relative wage level	Market size	Investment share
USA	3.5	0.8	0.1	11.1	146.5	39.8	3.9
Netherlands	2.0	0.2	0.7	77.8	107.1	1.7	5.8
Japan	2.0	0.7	0.1	12.5	73.3	20.2	6.3
Italy	0.7	0.2	0.2	50.0	87.7	7.4	5.5
UK	2.2	0.3	0.4	57.1	94.2	7.4	4.1
France	2.0	0.4	0.3	42.9	106.9	7.1	5.0
Denmark	1.0	0.1	0.4	80.0	74.5	0.6	5.6
Germany	2.5	0.6	0.2	25.0	102.7	11.0	4.1
Canada	1.0	0.2	0.6	75.0	117.3	3.3	4.5
Australia	0.9	0.3	0.3	50.0	89.8	1.6	5.2

Table 3.2 ranks the 22 industries in our sample after their direct R&D intensity (calculated as direct business R&D divided by production). More information about the definition of each of these industries is given in the Appendix. If one adopts the criterion that an industry with R&D efforts of 1.5 times the average or higher is 'high tech', and one with efforts between 0.5 and 1.5 times the average 'medium tech', we end up with five high-tech industries (aerospace, computers, drugs, telecommunication/semiconductors and instruments) and five medium-tech industries (electrical machinery, other transport, cars, industrial chemicals and non-electrical machinery). The remaining 12 industries, many of which are related to the use of natural resources in one way or another, are all 'low tech' by this definition.

Table 3.2 R&D intensity, production, 1985 (per cent)

High		Medium		Low	
Aerospace	20.08	Electrical machinery	3.26	Stone, glass	1.10
Computers	10.41	Other transport	3.03	Plastics	1.01
Drugs	9.01	Cars	2.83	Non-ferrous metals	0.89
Telecommunications	7.88	Industrial chemicals	2.76	Petroleum refining	0.78
Instruments	6.10	Non-electrical machinery	1.68	Fabricated metal products	0.64
				Other manufacturing	0.64
				Ferrous metals	0.61
				Ships	0.36
				Food, drinks	0.29
				Paper	0.23
				Textiles	0.19
				Wood, furniture	0.16

Notes
High: R&D intensity 1.5 times the mean R&D intensity or higher.
Low: R&D intensity 0.5 times the mean R&D intensity or lower.
Medium: R&D intensity between 0.5 and 1.5 times the mean R&D intensity.

6.   RESULTS

The small sample (8–10 observations per industry, 17–20 observations per country) does not allow for very extensive testing of differences across industries and countries on the impact of the variables included in our investigation. What we do is to pool all the data and then test for the sensitivity of allowing the coefficients to vary across high-, medium- and low-tech sectors and, where appropriate, also across countries of different sizes. All equations are estimated in logs by OLS. As part of the estimation procedure, tests for heteroscedasticity were conducted and heteroscedastic consistent standard errors (HCSEs) calculated (White, 1980). The results indicate that heteroscedasticity is not an important problem in this case, that is, the HCSEs did not differ much from standard errors as calculated by OLS. Hence, we report the latter.

It is common in analyses of this type to adjust for differences in size across countries and sectors. We do this by including a full set of country and industry dummies. What these do is to adjust for factors that affect competitiveness in the same way for each country (independent of industry) and industry (independent of country). These include size but also a host of other factors that impact on the propensity to export, such as distance and transport costs. Thus, even if we had divided all variables by a measure of size such as, say, the labour force or GDP of the country, we would still have had to include dummies and, except for the dummies, the estimates thus obtained would have been identical to the ones reported here.[8]

Table 3.3 contains the main results from the estimations. Four different models are presented. The first (3.3.1) is our basic model (see equation 3.2). The three others extend the basic model by allowing for differences in the impact of variables across technology classes and country groups. In Table 3.4 we test the different models against each other. Finally, we test for the sensitivity of changes in the specification and the way data are handled. Some of the more interesting results from these tests are included in Table 3.5.

Generally, the results (3.3.1) confirm many of our priors. Both direct R&D, indirect R&D and investment are positively correlated with competitiveness at the 1 per cent level of significance. It is noteworthy that the estimated impact of indirect R&D is about twice as high as that of direct R&D. The foreign share had a significant negative impact, as suggested by several theories in this area. Contrary to popular belief, wage levels were found to be uncorrelated with competitiveness.[9] This confirms the finding from Wolff in this volume (Chapter 1) that low wages do not seem to be an important competitive factor among OECD countries. The size of the domestic market (*HOME*) has a significant negative impact, in contrast to the predictions of some theories emphasizing economies of scale.

Table 3.3   Factors affecting exports, 1985

Equation	3.3.1	3.3.2			3.3.3	3.3.4		
		High tech.	Medium tech.	Low tech.		High tech.	Medium tech.	Low tech.
Direct R&D	0.18 (2.76) *	0.52 (3.22) *	0.15 (1.00)	0.18 (2.45) **	0.12 (1.63) ***	0.47 (2.52) **	0.14 (0.87)	0.17 (1.87) ***
Indirect R&D	0.37 (3.24) *	0.32 (1.81) ***	0.59 (2.05) **	0.52 (2.99) *	0.44 (3.79) *	0.33 (1.87) ***	0.69 (2.32) **	0.53 (2.93) *
Foreign share	−0.25 (2.14) **	−0.56 (2.25) **	−0.24 (1.11)	−0.26 (1.96) ***	−0.34 (2.86) *	−0.45 (1.70) ***	−0.10 (0.44)	−0.32 (2.34) **
Investment	0.69 (6.63) *	0.34 (1.43) ****	0.51 (2.04) **	0.68 (5.28) *	0.67 (5.54) *	0.36 (1.41) ****	0.48 (1.83) ***	0.73 (4.76) *
Wage	0.06 (0.18)	−0.09 (0.42)	0.47 (0.89)	−0.05 (0.16)	−0.00 (0.01)	−0.20 (0.46)	0.24 (0.45)	0.32 (0.08)
Home market	−0.51 (2.87) *	−0.51 (1.79) ***	−0.41 (1.35) ****	−0.85 (3.77) *	−0.64 (3.66) *	−0.56 (1.91) ***	−0.46 (1.46) ****	−0.93 (3.97) *
R&D – large	—	—			0.44 (3.90) *	0.24 (1.37) ****		
R&D – medium	—	—			0.09 (1.42) ****	−0.01 (0.15)		
Investment – large	—	—			−0.21 (1.28)	−0.06 (0.30)		
Investment – medium	—	—			−0.15 (1.26)	−0.09 (0.69)		
Country dummies	yes	yes			yes	yes		
Product dummies	yes	yes			yes	yes		
$R^2(\overline{R}^2)$	0.86 (0.83)	0.89 (0.85)			0.88 (0.85)	0.89 (0.85)		

Notes
Estimated in log-form. For definition of variables, see text. $N = 192$. Absolute *t*-statistics in brackets. * = Significant, 1% level. ** = Significant, 5% level. *** = Significant, 10% level. **** = Significant, 20 % level.

Table 3.4   Testing for inclusion of additional variables

Country and product dummies	3.3.1 (against $3.3.0^1$)$F_{(28,157)}$	$= 10.03^*$
High, medium and low R&D sectors	3.3.2 (against 3.3.1) $F_{(12,145)}$	$= 2 59^*$
	3.3.3 (against 3.3.1) $F_{(4,153)}$	$= 4.86^*$
Large-country advantages (R&D and investment)	3.3.4 (against 3.3.2) $F_{(4,141)}$	$= 1.28$
	3.3.4 (against 3.3.3) $F_{(12,141)}$	$= 1.37$

Notes
1. 3.3.1 without country and product dummies (a common constant term), $R^2 = 0.61$, not reported.
*   Significance of test, 1% level.

When the impact of the variables was allowed to vary across high-, medium- and low-tech sectors (3.3.2), the explanatory power of the model increased somewhat. The test (Table 3.4) suggests that this is a real improvement, indicating that there are important differences across sectors in the way variables work. The impact of direct R&D, for example, is about twice as large in high-tech as in low-tech industries. Indirect R&D and investment in physical capital, on the other hand, appear to matter more in low-tech industries. To some extent these results resemble the kind of 'stylized' facts that led Vernon (1966) to formulate the product-cycle theory. However, low wages do not seem to matter, not even in low tech, where cost-competition – following Vernon – should be expected to have a sizeable impact. Following Vernon one might also have expected market size to be positively correlated with competitiveness in high-tech industries. The results suggest that competitiveness is negatively correlated with market size in all three sectors, but less so in high-tech than in the other sectors.

A division of countries into large, medium-sized and small can be made along the same lines as for the technology classes. If this methodology is adopted, two countries appear as large: the USA and Japan. The medium-sized countries are Italy, the UK, France and Germany. According to new growth theory, the rewards from investments in R&D and/or physical capital should be larger in large countries. We test for this by allowing the estimated impact of R&D and investment in large and medium-sized countries to deviate from the rest of the sample, that is, the small countries (3.3.3). For physical capital there is little evidence of large-country advantages. If anything it is the other way around. However, there is strong support for the hypothesis that direct R&D has a higher impact on exports in large countries. Furthermore, the test in Table 3.4 also suggests that the version allowing for large-country advantages (3.3.3) should be preferred when tested against the basic model (3.3.1).

Table 3.5   Testing for changes in specification

Equation	3.5.1	3.5.2	3.5.3[1]	3.5.4[1]	3.5.5	3.5.6
Dependent variable	Export–import ratio	Export–import ratio	Exports per worker	Exports per worker	Exports	Exports
Direct R&D	0.22 (2.62) *	0.14 (1.55) ****	0.20 (2.92) *	0.12 (1.60) ****	0.17 (2.54) *	0.19 (1.48) ****
Indirect R&D	0.37 (2.59) *	0.48 (3.35) *	0.29 (2.44) **	0.32 (2.66) *	0.25 (2.33) **	0.37 (2.45) **
Foreign share	−0.62 (4.16) *	−0.70 (4.85) *	−0.18 (1.52) ****	−0.25 (2.03) **	−0.23 (1.93) ***	−0.32 (2.31) **
Investment	0.85 (6.49) *	0.79 (5.33) *	0.50 (4.01) *	0.65 (4.16) *	0.59 (5.88) *	0.74 (5.25) *
Wage	0.33 (0.80)	0.27 (0.69)	0.29 (0.82)	0.26 (0.74)	0.02 (0.06)	0.02 (0.06)
Home market	−0.84 (3.77) *	−1.07 (4.96) *	−0.43 (3.01) *	−0.31 (2.02) **	—	−0.70 (3.11) *
RSE (human capital)	—	—	—	—	—	−0.00 (0.03)
R&D – large	—	0.56 (4.09) *	—	0.38 (3.35) *	—	—
R&D – medium	—	0.11 (1.39) ****	—	0.09 (1.31) ****	—	—
Investment – large	—	−0.07 (0.34)	—	−0.66 (2.87) *	—	—
Investment – medium	—	−0.17 (1.15)	—	−0.37 (2.06) **	—	—
Country dummies	yes	yes	yes	yes	yes	yes
Product dummies	yes	yes	yes	yes	yes	yes
$R^2(\bar{R}^2)$	0.62 (0.53)	0.68 (0.60)	0.80 (0.76)	0.82 (0.77)	0.86 (0.82)	0.86 (0.82)
N	192	192	192	192	192	152

Notes
1. In this equation, all variables except 'foreign share' are divided by the number of workers in the industry and country in question.
Estimated in log-form. For definition of variables, see text. Absolute t-statistics in brackets.
* = Significant, 1% level. ** = Significant, 5% level. *** = Significant, 10% level. **** = Significant, 20 % level.

What is the interpretation of this? That large countries specialize in high-tech industries is no secret. Apparently they also get more out of their investments in R&D. However, do they specialize in high tech because they gain higher rewards to R&D, or do they enjoy higher rewards because they specialize in high tech? Unfortunately we are unable to tell. As is evident from Tables 3.3–4, if we start out with one of these assumptions (sector or size differences), then adding the other does not increase the explanatory power of the model in a significant way. This might perhaps have been different for a larger sample of countries including, for instance, some small high-tech countries such as Sweden and Switzerland. For the present sample, however, sector and size differences go hand in hand.

Some of the implications of these results might be clearer by way of an example. Assume that we want to know the impact on exports of reallocating a part, say 1 per cent, of a country's investments in physical capital to direct R&D. Since on average the OECD countries invest twice as much in physical capital as in R&D, this means that an average country would have to increase direct R&D by 2 per cent. Our basic model (3.3.1), which we use here, estimates that a 1 per cent reduction in investment in physical capital reduces exports by 0.69 per cent, while a 2 per cent increase in direct R&D increases it by 0.36 per cent, indicating a net loss in exports of 0.33 per cent from this operation. For the economy as a whole, however, this may be different, because a general increase in direct R&D also implies a rise in the R&D content of the goods and services that firms acquire from their domestic suppliers. For simplicity we abstract from any change that might occur in the demand or price level of domestic inputs as a result of the reallocation from investment in physical capital to R&D. Furthermore, let us assume – as seems reasonable – that the ratio between direct and indirect R&D is constant, so that a 2 per cent increase in direct R&D implies a 2 per cent increase in the domestic part of the total indirect R&D. On these assumptions (and based on the estimates in 3.3.1) the impact on exports of increased domestic indirect R&D, caused by a 2 per cent increase in direct R&D, can be calculated to be 0.87 per cent.[10] This indirect gain more than outweighs the direct loss, indicating a net gain of 0.54 per cent for the country as a whole. Thus, for the average country, R&D appears to be a more potent competitive factor than investments in physical capital. For the individual firm, however, this may not be so clear, because the lion's share of this effect accrues to other domestic firms. This resembles the familiar case from the literature, where a large gap between social and private returns to R&D justifies an R&D subsidy.

This example may also be applied to countries of different sizes. It then becomes clear that the basic model generates some unwarranted results. Since small countries do much less R&D compared to what they invest than large countries, an increase in R&D equivalent to 1 per cent of investment translates itself into a much larger percentage increase in direct R&D in a small country than in a large one. If, as in the basic model, the impact of direct R&D on exports is assumed to be the same across industries and countries, this implies that this effect is much larger in small countries than in large ones. If this was the case, then firms in small countries should face a stronger (private) incentive to invest in R&D than firms in large countries. This is, of course, contrary to what we observe. Allowing for a differential impact of investment in R&D and physical capital across technology classes or countries of different size adjusts for this. For instance, when large-country advantages are allowed (3.3.3), an increase in direct R&D equivalent to 1 per cent of investment yields a 0.59 per cent increase in exports in a small country compared to 0.92 per cent for a large one, consistent with the observation that firms in small countries devote much less resources to R&D than firms in large countries. The total (combined direct and indirect) effect is also stronger in large countries than in small ones if large-country advantages are allowed. However, the conclusion of the previous paragraph, that is, that the total impact on exports of an investment of given size is larger for R&D than for physical capital, still holds for all countries (independent of size).

We are not aware of any study that may be directly compared to this one. There are, however, some attempts to quantify the impacts of direct and indirect R&D on productivity, see in particular the recent study by Coe and Helpman (1995). Arguably, for a sample of high-income countries, competitive advantages and superior productivity should be expected to go hand in hand,[11] so perhaps something may be learned by comparing their results to ours. What they find, based on evidence for OECD countries in the last decades, is that the returns to R&D investments are high, especially in the larger and medium-sized countries. This is consistent with the findings reported here. Furthermore, they report that for the larger countries, domestic R&D matters most, while for the small countries R&D acquired indirectly through imports is the most important source of technological advance. To see how this latter finding compares to the results of this study, assume a 1 per cent increase in R&D world-wide that leads to a similar increase in indirect R&D (this leaves the ratio between foreign and domestic indirect R&D unaffected). Using the estimates in 3.3.3 (allowing for large-country advantages) the combined direct and indirect impact on exports from domestic sources can be shown to be 0.21 per cent for the small, 0.39 per cent for the medium-sized and 0.85 per cent for the large countries. Similar estimates for the foreign contribution are 0.29 per cent for the small, 0.14 per cent for the medium-sized and 0.04 per cent for the large countries. Hence, for the largest countries, inflows of technology through trade are of negligible importance compared to technology from domestic sources, while for the small countries the foreign contribution is what matters most. Thus, our results, although based on different data and methods, are consistent with those reported by Coe and Helpman.

How sensitive are the results reported here for changes in specification? We tested this extensively, and the results appear reasonably robust. The first two columns in Table 3.5 (3.5.1–2) report the result from substituting the dependent variable (log exports) with the log of the export–import ratio, a measure of export specialization. The results were only marginally different from those reported in Table 3.3 apart from, perhaps, that the detrimental impact of relying heavily on technology import (the foreign share) was even more pronounced. In the two next columns (3.5.3–4) we report the result of deflating all level variables (all variables except 'foreign share') with the number of workers in the industry and country in question. This implies a slight change in the meaning of the test, since this way of doing things excludes that part of the total variance which refers to cross-country differences in the employment structure, that is, patterns of specialization. Still, the results were not qualitatively different, although the numerical values of the estimates were lower in most cases. We also checked for the impact of excluding the HOME variable, since the estimated impact of this variable, although highly significant, was contrary to expectations. Again, the numerical estimates were lower, but not qualitatively different. Finally we made an attempt to include a variable reflecting 'human capital' (*RSE*), defined as (the log of) the share of researchers, scientists and engineers in the labour force of the industry and country in question (*source*: OECD), even if this implied a marked reduction in the size of the sample (3.5.5). However, the *RSE* variable turned out to be uncorrelated with competitiveness.[12]

7 CONCLUDING REMARKS

The purpose of this study has been to explore the relationship between competitiveness, scale and R&D with the help of OECD data bases and the ongoing work in the OECD on embodied technology flows. The results suggest that both direct and indirect R&D have a significant, positive impact on competitiveness. Indirect R&D from domestic sources appear to be more conducive to competitiveness than indirect R&D from abroad. On average the total (direct and indirect) impact of a given investment in R&D on exports is about twice as large as the impact of an investment of similar size in physical capital. The impact of R&D investment appears to be especially high in large countries and R&D-intensive industries.

However, the preliminary and exploratory character of the study should be stressed. What is presented here is a pure cross-sectional analysis. As is well known, this does not allow for testing of causality. The most we can do is to use our theoretical knowledge as a guide for presenting and analysing the structure (and relationships) of the data and compare the findings thus obtained with the theoretical predictions. Furthermore, the number of countries included is small, and this may bias the results, in particular since many of the omitted countries are small. Finally, although these data go much further than most other data sets in quantifying knowledge flows, disembodied knowledge flows are clearly not accounted for. Further research and more extensive data are necessary to validate these results and dig deeper into the question of how scale, R&D and other factors interact in the competitive process.

NOTES

*   This chapter is based on data supplied by the OECD Directorate for Science, Technology and Industry (DSTI) as part of a project there. I am grateful to the DSTI for allowing me to use them for this chapter. An earlier version was presented at the conference on 'Technology and International Trade' in Oslo, 6–8 October 1995. I wish to thank the participants, in particular the commentator and my fellow editors, for comments and suggestions, retaining sole responsibility for the final version.

1.   See Dosi, Pavitt and Soete (1990) for an elaboration and empirical application of this perspective.

2.   As shown by Melchior (Chapter 5 in this volume), in general the predictions for trade patterns in such models depend very much on the specific assumptions made in each case.

3.   See Fagerberg (1995b) for an empirical test of the relationship between export performance and the strength of advanced domestic users.

4.   See the Appendix for a complete listing of products/industries.

5.   There may be different ways to handle the data (such as deflation); see the section on results for how this is done.

6.   To see this, recall that on average the share of domestic indirect R&D in total domestic R&D (direct and indirect) varies between one-tenth and one-quarter across OECD countries (Table 3.1). For the OECD as a whole this share is 20 per cent. Similarly, for the OECD as a whole, the share of foreign indirect R&D in total indirect R&D (DIF) is 23 per cent. This means that on average the underestimation of DIF is ($100*0.23*0.20$) per cent = 4.6 per cent, not a very large number. Note also that in the case of the FOR-variable, foreign indirect R&D enters both in the numerator and the denominator, reducing the problem even further.

7.   For the sake of exposition the variables in this table have been deflated. Market size (domestic demand) is deflated by total OECD demand, wages by average OECD wages, the others are presented as share of production in the country in question. All variables in per cent

8.   An additional reason for including dummies in this case would be that the relationship between the propensity to trade and country size is clearly non-linear. For instance, large countries export much less compared to their size than small countries do.

9.   The wage level is sometimes used as a proxy for skills; thus one might perhaps have expected a high correlation with direct R&D efforts. However, the result that $WAGE$ is uncorrelated with exports holds even when direct R&D is excluded (not reported).

10. The formula used for calculating the total indirect effect (including the decrease in the foreign share) is $b(1 - f)(0.37) + (-b(1 - f)(-0.25))$ where b is the increase in direct R&D (0.02) and f the foreign share (0.23).

11. See the discussion and empirical evidence in Wolff (Chapter 1) and Gustavsson et al. (Chapter 2) in this volume.

12. This might be due to multicollinearity with the direct R&D and/or wage variables. However, even when these variables were excluded (not reported), the RSE variable failed to make a significant impact.

REFERENCES

Amable, B. and B. Verspagen (1995), 'The role of technology in market shares dynamics', *Applied Economics*, **27**, 197–204.

Amendola G., G. Dosi and E. Papagni (1993), 'The Dynamics of International Competitiveness', *Weltwirtschaftliches Archiv*, **129**, 451–71.

Coe, D.T. and E. Helpman (1995), 'International R&D Spillovers', *European Economic Review*, **39**, 859–87.

Dosi, G., K. Pavitt and L. Soete (1990), *The Economics of Technical Change and International Trade*, London: Harvester Wheatsheaf.

Dosi, G. and L. Soete (1983), 'Technology Gaps and Cost-based Adjustment: Some Explorations of the Determinants of International Competitiveness', *Metroeconomica*, **35**, 357–82.

Dosi, G. and L. Soete (1988), 'Technical change and international trade', in G. Dosi, C. Freeman, R. Nelson, G. Silverberg and L. Soete (eds), *Technical Change and Economic Theory*, London: Pinter, pp. 401–43,

Fagerberg, J. (1988), 'International Competitiveness', *Economic Journal*, **98**, 355–74.

Fagerberg, J. (1995a), *Is there a large-country advantage in high-tech?*, Working Paper, No. 526, January, Oslo: Norwegian Institute of International Affairs.

Fagerberg, J. (1995b), 'User–Producer Interaction, Learning and Comparative Advantage', *Cambridge Journal of Economics*, **19**, 243–56.

Grossman, G.M. and E. Helpman (1991), *Innovation and Growth in the Global Economy*, Cambridge, Ma: MIT Press.

Grossman, G.M. and E. Helpman (1995), *Technology and Trade*, Discussion Paper Series, No. 1134, February, London: CEPR.

Helpman, E. (1984), 'Increasing Returns, Imperfect Markets and Trade Theory', in R.W. Jones and P.B. Kenen, *Handbook of International Economics*, Volume 1, Amsterdam: North Holland, pp. 325–65.

Krugman, P. (1990), *Rethinking International Trade*, Cambridge, MA: MIT Press.

Lacroix, R. and P. Scheuer (1976), 'L'Effort de R&D, l'Innovation et le Commerce International', *Revue Economique*, No. 6, 1008–29.

Lundvall, B.Å. (1985), *Product Innovation and User-Producer Interaction*, Aalborg: Aalborg University Press.

Lundvall, B.Å. (1988), 'Innovation as an Interactive Process – from User-Producer Interaction to the National System of Innovation', in G. Dosi, C. Freeman, R. Nelson, G. Silverberg and L. Soete (eds), *Technical Change and Economic Theory*, London: Pinter, pp. 349–69.

Lundvall, B.Å. (ed.) (1992), *National Systems of Innovation – Towards a Theory of Innovation and Interactive Learning*, London: Pinter.

Magnier, A. and J. Toujas-Bernate (1994), 'Technology and Trade: Empirical Evidence from Five Industrialized Countries', *Weltwirtschaftliches Archiv*, **130**, 494–520.

Nelson, R. (ed.) (1993), *National Innovation Systems, A Comparative Study*, Oxford: Oxford University Press.

Papaconstantinou, G., N. Sakurai and A. Wyckoff (1996), 'Embodied Technology Diffusion: An Empirical Analysis for 10 OECD Countries', *OECD Working Paper*, **4** (8).

Porter, M.E. (1990), *The Competitive Advantage of Nations*, London: Macmillan.

Posner, M.V. (1961), 'International Trade and Technical Change', *Oxford Economic Papers*, **13**, 323–41.

Romer, P.M. (1986), 'Increasing Returns and Long-Run Growth', *Journal of Political Economy*, **94**, 1002–37.

Romer, P.M. (1990), 'Endogenous Technological Change', *Journal of Political Economy*, **98**, S71–102.

Soete, L. (1981), 'A General Test of Technological Gap Trade Theory', *Weltwirtschaftliches Archiv*, **117**, 638–60.

Soete, L.(1987), 'The Impact of Technological Innovation on International Trade Patterns: The Evidence Reconsidered', *Research Policy*, **16**, 101–30.

Venables, A. (1994), 'Economic Integration and Industrial Agglomeration', *Economic and Social Review*, **26**, 1–17.

Vernon, R. (1966), 'International Investment and International Trade in the Product Cycle', *Quarterly Journal of Economics*, **80**, 190–207.

Walker, W.B. (1979), *Industrial Innovation and International Trading Performance*, Greenwich, CT: JAI Press.

White, H. (1980), 'A heteroskedastic-consistent covariance matrix estimator and a direct test for heteroskedasticity', *Econometrica*, **48**, 817–38.

APPENDIX　STAN CLASSIFICATION

ISIC codes	STAN names	Our names
3100	Food, drink and tobacco	Food, drinks
3200	Textiles, footwear and leather	Textiles
3300	Wood, cork and furniture	Wood, furniture
3400	Paper and printing	Paper
351+352		
−3522	Industrial chemicals	Industrial chemicals
3522	Pharmaceuticals	Drugs
353+354	Petroleum refining	Petroleum refining
355+356	Rubber and plastics products	Plastics
3600	Stone, clay and glass	Stone, glass
3710	Ferrous metals	Ferrous metals
3720	Non-ferrous metals	Non-ferrous metals
3810	Fabricated metal products	Fabricated metal products
382–3825	Non-electrical machinery	Non-electrical machinery
3825	Office machinery and computers	Computers
383–3832	Electrical machinery	Electrical machinery
3832	Electronic equipment and components	Telecommunications, semiconductors
3841	Shipbuilding	Ships
3842+3844 +3849	Other transport equipment	Other transport
3843	Motor vehicles	Cars
3845	Aerospace	Aerospace
3850	Instruments	Instruments
3900	Other manufacturing	Other manufacturing
30000	Total manufacturing	

TECHNOLOGY AND COMPETITIVENESS

JAN FAGERBERG

ESST, University of Oslo, and Norwegian Institute of International Affairs[1]

I. INTRODUCTION

'Technology' and 'competitiveness' are two of the most popular buzz-words of our time. Increasingly policy-makers on both sides of the Atlantic link the two. But what do we really mean when we talk about the international competitiveness of a country? And what does technology have to do with it? Is there a theory behind this link? What about the empirical evidence? This paper addresses these questions from a long-run perspective.[2]

II. THE COMPETITIVENESS ISSUE

Many concepts used by economists in professional discourse are virtually unknown to the broader public. Who, for instance, has heard about 'Ricardian equivalence' (and knows what it means)? Probably not many outside the inner circle. Not so with 'international competitiveness'. Almost everybody seems to know something about—and even have an opinion on—the international competitiveness of their country.

How can that be? The reason is simple. It is not a concept invented by theoreticians, but by practical people close to the policy-making process. Although it is widely used, some theoreticians detest it. Paul Krugman, for instance, has gone so far as to talk about the concern for the international competitiveness of a country as a 'dangerous obsession' (Krugman, 1994). This led to a spirited debate in the American journal, *Foreign Affairs*, in 1994.

Why does the issue attract so much attention, not to say emotion? Let us start by stating a few simple facts regarding the concept and its use. First, it is

[1] I want to thank Andrea Boltho and three referees for helpful comments and suggestions, while retaining sole responsibility for remaining errors and omissions.

[2] Hence, the paper does not deal with the short-run variations in costs or prices that people often associate with changes in competitiveness.

39

applied at several levels (e.g. whole economies, sectors, and firms). What has been the prime focus of the debate, and what we will focus on here, is its application to a country. Second, it is a relative term. What is of interest is not a country's absolute performance, however that may be defined, but how well it does relative to other countries. Some dislike this comparative perspective. But, after all, it is a perspective found in nearly all aspects of social life, work, sports, business, etc., among individuals as well as collectives. So why not at the level of countries? I see no compelling reason against its use.[3] Third, when applied to a country, it has a double meaning, since it relates both to the economic well-being of the citizens as well as to the nation's trade performance.[4] The underlying assumption, then, is that these things are intimately related. This is perhaps not so controversial in itself, but the nature and cause of this relationship may be. In the next section we discuss this issue in more detail.

However, the recent controversy seems to have had little to do with these points. Rather, what Krugman is aiming his criticism at is the common American attitude of blaming shortcomings in its economic performance on foreigners (and acting accordingly). If American producers do not meet the standards of international competition, then this failure is more or less automatically explained by unfair practices by foreign competitors and/or governments, and Congress is lobbied for protection. Although the tendency to blame others for one's own failures may be universal, it has never been a real option in smaller economies. The reason is simple; if one depends on export markets for a large share of what one produces, the last thing one would do would be to give other governments an incentive to impose import restrictions. By and large, this has also been the situation for most medium-sized developed countries such as, for instance, the UK. However, in a large country such as the USA, in which about 90 per cent of output is sold on the domestic market, foreign retaliation may not be seen as a real threat. Arguably, this may also hold for the EU when considered as a whole. I agree that the tendency to blame one's own failures on others is unhealthy. Rather, one should focus on one's own performance, on which domestic well-being ultimately depends, as Krugman correctly points out. But if there is an obsession here, it is not with competitiveness *per se*, but with trade policy/protectionist politics.

Another pitfall in this area has been to equate international competitiveness solely with indicators of relative unit costs or prices. This was sometimes justified by the absence of data on so-called 'non-price' factors. Kaldor (1978) was among the first to point out the seriousness of omitting such factors. He showed for a number of countries that, over the long term, market shares for exports and relative unit costs or prices tended to move together, i.e. that growing market shares and increasing relative costs or prices went hand in hand (the so-called 'Kaldor paradox'). This was, of course, the opposite of what one would have expected from the simplistic, though at the time widely diffused, approach which focused exclusively on the (assumedly negative) impact of increasing relative costs or prices on market shares.

Table 1 updates and extends Kaldor's investigation to the more recent 1978–94 period. The countries included are the world's 12 largest exporters (in the 1990s). The table shows that Kaldor's paradox also holds good for this more recent period. Thus, growing market shares and growing relative unit labour costs tend to be positively associated (rather than the other way round, as commonly assumed). The table also includes data for two other variables often invoked in discussions of competitiveness: productivity growth (proxied by the growth of GDP per capita) and increases in research and development (R&D) expenditures (as a share of GDP). The latter may be interpreted as a rough indicator of change in technological capability.[5] It turns out

---

[3] Dunn (1994) and Moran (1996) both defend this comparative perspective by pointing to the relationship between economic performance and power.

[4] There are many definitions around, most of which reflect this 'double meaning' in one way or another. A typical example is the following: competitiveness is 'the degree to which, under free and fair market conditions, a country can produce goods and services which meet the test of foreign competition while simultaneously maintaining and expanding the real income of its people' (OECD, 1992, p. 237). Porter (1990, ch. 1) and Reinert (1995) provide an extended discussion.

[5] Changes in R&D expenditure as a share of GDP may reflect both general changes (common to all industries) and changes in industrial composition. Differences in R&D, as a percentage of GDP or of production, are known to be much greater across industries than across countries (within an industry). Large changes in R&D expenditure, such as those reported for Korea and Taiwan, are therefore likely to reflect changes in those countries' industrial composition from low to high R&D industries.

J. Fagerberg

Table 1
The Kaldor Paradox Re-examined, Twelve Industrialized Countries, 1978–94

	Growth in market share for exports[a]	Growth in relative unit labour cost[a]	Growth in GDP per capita at constant prices[a]	Change in R&D as a share of GDP[b]
USA	0.08	−1.17	1.36	0.24
Japan	0.95	0.82	2.94	1.10
Germany	−1.03	1.62	1.65	0.23
France	−0.98	−0.18	1.36	0.54
Italy	−0.16	−1.13	2.00	0.59
UK	−0.89	0.81	1.57	−0.01
Canada	−0.10	−0.38	0.97	0.36
Belgium–Luxembourg	−0.89[c]	−2.85[c]	1.70	0.31
Netherlands	−1.53	−1.60	1.23	0.13
Korea	4.85	1.89	6.33[c]	1.16
Taiwan	4.68	3.77	5.94[d]	1.13
Hong Kong	8.36	2.58	5.35[c]	n.a.
Regression on growth in market share[e]	slope	1.17 (0.36)	1.43 (0.21)	4.48 (0.94)
	R^2	0.52	0.82	0.71

Notes: [a] Annual rate of growth. [b] Difference between 1992 and 1979 levels of R&D as a share of GDP. [c] 1978–92. [d] 1978–91. [e] Estimated by ordinary least squares with constant term (not reported), standard deviation in brackets, 12 observations except for R&D (11 observations).
Sources: OECD (GDP per capita and relative unit labour cost); IMF (merchandise exports); and EMF/IMD–World Economic Forum and national sources (R&D).

that the growth of market share is strongly positively correlated with both. Hence, as a rule, countries that gain market share also display faster productivity growth and increase their technological capability more than other countries.

The facts are reasonably clear. But how are they to be explained?

III. TECHNOLOGY, TRADE, AND THE WEALTH OF NATIONS

Until recently, the competitiveness issue was mostly neglected by neoclassical theoreticians. The single most important reason for this was, perhaps, that neoclassical theory did not attach much importance to trade as a growth-promoting factor.[6] Following the standard neoclassical approach to growth, it did not really matter whether goods were sold at home or abroad. It is true that the so-called factor-proportion theory postulated that there were some gains from trade through increased specialization in sectors using intensively the factors with which countries were relatively well endowed. However, these gains were essentially of a once-and-for-all nature. Moreover, empirical work on trade based on this perspective indicated that they were rather small (Robson, 1987).

This traditional neoclassical view on growth and trade rested on very restrictive assumptions. In particular, it neglected demand as a source of growth, it did not allow for economies of scale, and it assumed away technological differences across countries. Alternative views on the subject relax one or more of these assumptions.

Keynesian theories, attempting to come to grips with the growth of open economies, came to focus

---

[6] For an overview of the literature on trade and growth, see Dowrick (1996).

41

OXFORD REVIEW OF ECONOMIC POLICY, VOL. 12, NO. 3

on the demand for exports as a source of growth in its own right. While domestic demand was assumed to be more or less endogenous, export demand was seen as an autonomous force that could propel growth (through various multipliers). Anything that raised export demand would also raise growth (Beckerman, 1962; Kaldor, 1970).

A problem with this perspective was that no allowance was made for the need to balance trade, if not in the short at least in the longer term. It was thus possible that projections based on this approach might give growth paths that were unsustainable because they implied ever-increasing accumulations of reserves or of foreign debt. This could be remedied by introducing a balance of trade constraint and assuming, for instance, that governments would modify fiscal and monetary policies towards this end. Such a model was suggested by Thirlwall (1979). In this model the growth of an open economy was shown to depend on the growth of international trade, on changes in relative prices (price competitiveness), and on the ratio of the income elasticity of demand for exports to that for imports.[7] Thus, assuming everything else constant, the higher the income elasticity for exports relative to that for imports, the higher the rate of growth of the economy, and vice versa. Using estimates from Houthakker and Magee (1969), Thirlwall claimed that this simple model gave a remarkably good approximation to the growth experience of many countries in the first half of the post-war period, even when the impact of changing relative prices was ignored. This was taken as a demonstration of the importance of so-called non-price factors, which the estimated income elasticities were assumed to reflect (and also of the relatively modest impact of price factors). Such results were, of course, consistent with the seemingly paradoxical findings of Kaldor (1978).

Thirlwall's model and its explanatory power have been the subject of considerable controversy, a full account of which would require a paper of its own, if not a whole book (as was suggested by McCombie, 1992).[8] Table 2 updates Thirlwall's calculations[9] to the more recent 1979–93 period. An estimate for the preceding period (1960–79) is also provided. A cursory look at the data reveals that the model reproduces correctly some of the qualitative features of the post-war growth experience (such as the relatively rapid growth of Japan and the slow growth of the UK). However, it systematically over-predicts these differences, and this tendency becomes more manifest through time (as shown by the coefficient of variation). None of this is necessarily surprising. First, the model is based on the assumption of balanced trade, which might not hold for all countries.[10] Second, price effects are ignored altogether, which is, it has to be said, quite a drastic simplification. Third, and perhaps most important, the non-price factors, which the estimated income elasticities are assumed to reflect, are themselves likely to change through time. Thus, in the long run, these elasticities should be considered as variables rather than as exogenously given constants.[11]

This raises the question of how these non-price factors can be identified and measured. There are, of course, many factors that could be considered potentially relevant, and it is beyond the purpose of this paper to discuss all of these in great detail.[12] One prime candidate, though, is differences in technological capabilities, as originally suggested by Kaldor (1981, p. 603):

Basically in a growing world economy the growth of exports is mainly to be explained by the income elasticity of foreign countries for a country's products; but it is a matter of the innovative ability and adaptive capacity of its manufacturers whether this income elasticity will tend to be relatively large or small.

---

[7] The income elasticity of demand for exports is the growth in exports resulting from a 1 per cent increase in world demand, holding relative prices constant (and ignoring cyclical factors), and similarly for imports.

[8] This book has since been published (McCombie and Thirlwall, 1994).

[9] The estimates reported here are based on equation (8) in Thirlwall (1979), disregarding the price term, since, following McCombie and Thirlwall (1994, p. 341), this is the most appropriate specification.

[10] This is not so restrictive as it seems, since the formal model can actually accommodate a constant surplus or deficit (as a percentage of exports or imports).

[11] Several studies for the UK conclude that these elasticities (and/or the underlying trends which they reflect) are not stable through time (Landesmann and Snell, 1989; Anderton, 1992; Blake and Pain, 1994)

[12] A more general discussion of the impact of non-price factors on trade may be found in McCombie and Thirlwall (1994, ch. 4).

J. Fagerberg

Table 2
'Thirlwall's Law' Re-examined, Nine Industrialized Countries, 1979–93

	Ratio of income elasticity for exports to that for imports[a]	Actual growth 1960–79	Predicted growth[b] 1960–79	Actual growth 1979–93	Predicted growth[b] 1979–93
USA	0.66	3.46	2.92	2.27	1.41
Japan	2.89	7.71	12.84	3.57	6.20
Germany	1.16	3.70	5.14	2.11	2.48
France	0.92	4.58	4.10	1.80	1.98
Italy	1.35	4.79	5.99	1.97	2.89
UK	0.52	2.59	2.30	1.71	1.11
Canada	1.18	5.02	5.23	2.27	2.52
Belgium	0.94	4.05	4.20	1.83	2.03
Netherlands	0.99	4.14	4.43	1.79	2.14
Coefficient of variation	0.55	0.30	0.55	0.25	0.55
Regression on actual growth[c] slope			0.44 (0.05)		0.35 (0.06)
R^2			0.90		0.81

Notes: [a] Estimate of income elasticities, based on data for the period 1951–66, from Houthakker and Magee (1969). [b] Predicted growth is calculated as the ratio of the income elasticity for exports to that for imports multiplied by the average growth of the countries in the sample. [c] Estimated by OLS with constant term (not reported), standard deviation in brackets.
Source: GDP figures from OECD.

A natural conclusion from this would be to include indicators of technological competitiveness (or innovative ability and adaptive capacity) directly in the equations for exports and imports. This was the route taken by Fagerberg (1988).[13] He related changes in the market shares of a country at home and abroad to the change in its technological capacity (whether resulting from innovation or from exploiting the potential for imitation). The growth in productive capacity, proxied by gross investment in physical capital, changing relative unit labour costs, and growth of demand were also taken into account. The empirical results, based on data for 15 OECD countries from the early 1960s to the early 1980s, generally confirmed the importance of growth in technological and productive capacity for competitiveness,[14] while the impact of cost factors was

found to be relatively marginal. These results provided a reasonable explanation of the Kaldor paradox.

The idea that in capitalist economies it is technological, rather than price, competition that matters most, is not a new one. This thesis had been forcefully argued by Schumpeter (1934, 1939, 1943) and by Marx before him. But in the theoretical universe of the neoclassical theorist of the 1950s and 1960s (that of so-called perfect competition) this was not an idea that could be easily accommodated. Hence, it tended to be ignored. However, the idea popped up now and then, in particular when researchers encountered empirical phenomena that the established theory could not explain. Such an incident occurred in the 1950s when Leontief (1954) provided evi-

[13] Fagerberg also departed from the Thirlwall framework by introducing a direct test of the assumed equality of the actual growth rate and the one that would be consistent with balanced trade. He found that this was a reasonable approximation for most (though not all) countries. The exceptions were the USA, the printer of world money, and Norway, which during this period started to produce oil on its continental shelf.

[14] McCombie and Thirlwall (1994) argue that these results depend to some extent on the inclusion of Japan in the data set.

OXFORD REVIEW OF ECONOMIC POLICY, VOL. 12, NO. 3

dence that the specialization pattern of the USA in international trade seemed to deviate from what neoclassical theory predicted. In particular, it did not seem to rest in capital-intensive industry, as would have been expected. Several authors responded to this by suggesting that the real competitive strength of US industry lay not in its capital abundance, but in its superior technological capability. This led to the formulation of the so-called neo-technological trade theories of the 1960s, which emphasized the importance of cross-country differences in technological capability and their impact on trade (Posner, 1961; Vernon, 1966; and others; for an overview, see Dosi and Soete, 1988).

A particularly clear and influential account of the neo-technological perspective was the one given by Posner (1961). The essence of his reasoning can be captured by a two-country model, in which one country is more innovative than the other (and consequently has a technological lead), while the other (the technological laggard) relies more on imitation. New technologies emerge in the leading country, which for a period enjoys a temporary monopoly. However, in the course of time, the technological laggard will learn to cope with these technologies, and competition between producers from the two countries will arise. Generally, the level of income will be higher in the leading country, with the size of the income gap depending on the size of the technological gap (or on the time needed for the lagging country to imitate the innovations of the leader).

Formal models based on this logic began to emerge in the 1970s. These models—often called north–south models[15]—envisaged an innovating north, paying high wages, and an imitating south, exploiting cost advantages (low wages), with the wage gap between north and south depending on the balance between innovation (north) and imitation (south). Assuming everything else constant, technological catch-up (increased speed of imitation) by the south would reduce the wage gap and, under certain assumptions, also northern welfare. To prevent this from happening, northern industrialists were left with no other choice than to increase the speed of

innovation. Krugman (1979, p. 262), one of the theoretical contributors in this area, formulated this vividly as follows: 'Like Alice and the Red Queen, the developed region has to keep running to stay in the same place.'

There has recently been a surge of new formal contributions in this area. While the first generation of north–south models considered innovation in the north as exogenous, the most recent modelling efforts have sought to endogenize innovation, hence the terms 'endogenous' or 'new growth' theory.[16] There are basically two strands in this literature, one that analyses technological progress as learning by doing (Romer, 1986; Lucas, 1988), and another that emphasizes investments in R&D (Romer, 1990; Grossman and Helpman, 1991). In both cases long-run growth is explained by (*a*) private incentives to investment in activities that lead to innovation (learning) and (*b*) the spill-overs from this process on future investment of this kind.

In the first strand it is pertinent to mention the contribution by Lucas (1988). He assumes large differences across sectors in the scope for technological progress (learning). Hence, countries which specialize in the technologically progressive (high-tech) industries may experience faster growth than those which do not. Because of the cumulative character of technological progress, existing patterns of specialization will tend to be reinforced through time. Thus, market forces may actually strengthen a specialization pattern that implies slow growth (a low-growth trap). In this situation, Lucas argues, it may actually pay off for a country to change its specialization by a combination of subsidies and protection.

The most interesting contributions from the perspective of this paper belong, perhaps, to the class of models that emphasizes the importance of R&D and spill-overs for growth and trade (see Grossman and Helpman, 1991). Countries that devote a large share of their resources to R&D, and countries with large domestic markets, will—according to this perspective—be more likely than others to specialize in high-tech industries and may display faster

---

[15] For an overview, see Goglio (1991).

[16] The following does not attempt to survey 'new growth' theory, but just to point to some contributions that are important in the present context. A good, condensed overview is provided by Verspagen (1992).

J. Fagerberg

growth. However, the outcome also depends on the geographical reach of spill-overs.[17] If, for instance, spill-overs are national rather than global in scope, a 'lock in' situation may occur, where small initial inter-country differences lead to a divergence in specialization patterns and in growth. As in the Lucas model above, this is a situation where policy intervention may have a large impact. To the extent that presence in foreign markets is required to benefit from technology flows, trade may enhance growth (Coe and Helpman, 1995).

There is now, therefore, quite a large (and diverse) literature suggesting that the link between technology, competitiveness, and growth is an important one. In the older Keynesian approach, exports were considered exogenous and growth endogenous. Hence, according to that approach, causation runs from trade to growth. At a deeper level the exogenous factors are those having an impact on trade performance, in particular non-price factors, among which technology has been recognized as a prime candidate. Models that allow for technology playing a role in global competition point to the balance between innovation and imitation as the main force explaining both trade and growth. However, in reality, innovation and imitation are not exogenous, but depend on factors such as incentives, skills, and the environment in which they are carried out. Recent modelling efforts in this area attempt to push the analysis further by incorporating some of these aspects.

IV. TECHNOLOGY AND EXPORTS

Empirically, analysts have tried to highlight the relation between competitiveness and technology by regressing a measure of export performance on a technology variable and other variables that were deemed relevant for the analysis. Generally, the functional relation is the following:

$$X = f(T, O) \qquad (1)$$

where X is a measure of export performance, T is a technology proxy, and O is a set of other variables. The following paragraphs discuss the main results from this work (a more comprehensive overview may be found in Wakelin, 1995). Similar analyses have also been carried out with imports or performance on the domestic market as the dependent variable, and have yielded roughly similar results.[18] Trade in services, on the other hand, has been completely neglected.

The technology variables used in these analyses can be divided into technology-input and technology-output measures (Soete, 1981). Among the former, the most popular choice is R&D spending, but scientific personnel has also been used. Technology-output measures include patent-based measures (Soete, 1981), innovation counts (Greenhalgh, 1990; Greenhalgh *et al.*, 1994), and various measures of productivity (Milberg, 1991; Wolff, 1995, 1996). Composite measures combining two or more of these alternatives have also been suggested (Aquino, 1981; Fagerberg, 1988).

None of these measures is perfect. For instance, innovations made by engineers as a result of learning by doing, using, etc. do not have a clear-cut relationship with R&D as normally recorded (Patel and Pavitt, 1994). The propensity to patent is known to vary widely across industries. Some industries do much R&D, without patenting a lot, and others do the reverse (Pavitt, 1982). Productivity measures have at best an indirect relationship with innovation. However, at the national level, R&D, patents, and productivity-based measures are closely correlated (Fagerberg, 1987).[19]

The first analyses of this kind were undertaken in the late 1960s following the advent of the neo-technological trade theories, and focused on US export performance, using data for a cross-section of industries. Initial results seemed to support the emphasis in these theories on the importance of R&D for export performance (Gruber *et al.*, 1967).

---

[17] Little is known for sure on the geographical reach of spill-overs. Some studies suggest that these are often rather local in nature (Jaffe, 1989; Jaffe *et al.*, 1993), i.e. that proximity is an important factor. There is also some evidence indicating that technology flows less freely across than within countries (Sjöholm, 1996). However, Nelson and Wright (1992) and Nadiri (1993) both argue that the international flow of technology has accelerated in recent years, and that the main vehicle for this is the trans-national corporation (TNC), i.e. that spill-overs are increasingly becoming global. Others stress the continuing ties between TNCs and their home countries (Patel and Pavitt, 1991). See also Globerman (1996).

[18] See Hughes (1986) and Buxton *et al.* (1994) for the UK, and Fagerberg (1988) for a group of OECD countries.

[19] For a discussion of indicators and measurement, see Archibugi (1992) and Patel and Pavitt (1995).

Later Sveikauskas (1983), in a very thorough study, convincingly showed that the competitiveness of US exporters rested on R&D and on innovation (rather than on the supply of skilled labour or of other factors). More recently, much of the applied literature in this area has focused on British evidence. Hughes (1986) demonstrated the importance of both R&D (absolute and relative to foreign competitors) and skilled labour for British exports.[20] A strong relationship between R&D and the international competitiveness of British industry has also been reported by Buxton *et al.* (1994). Similarly, Greenhalgh (1990) and Greenhalgh *et al.* (1994), using different data and methods, showed the importance of 'home-grown' innovation for British trade performance. There is also some scant evidence from other countries indicating that indigenous R&D and innovation may have an influence on trade performance (even though the country may not be specialized in high-tech industries).[21]

However, analyses for single countries across industries, interesting as they may be, fail to test for possible differences across sectors in the impact of technology and other variables. The latter may be investigated by applying equation (1) to a cross-section of countries for single industries. Such analyses typically use data for all or most OECD countries (Lacroix and Scheuer, 1976; Soete, 1981; Dosi and Soete, 1983; Fagerberg, 1995). There are also some studies that pool cross-sectional and time-series data, but for a smaller number of countries (Magnier and Toujas-Bernate, 1994; Amable and Verspagen, 1995). As these studies use different sectoral classifications and include different variables, the results are not directly comparable. However, to facilitate comparison, results from a number of studies are presented in one common table (Table 3). Preparation of this table has involved a considerable element of judgement, and the table should only be read as an indication of the state of the art in this area. Readers interested in particular studies or industries are urged to consult the original sources.

Generally, the results of these studies support the hypothesis of a positive relation between technological activity and export performance for a large number of industries. The most consistent results supporting such a relationship are found for the chemical (drugs, industrial chemicals, and plastics) and machinery industries. Among the latter the evidence is particularly strong for non-electrical machinery, a very broad category covering a wide range of specialized and general machinery, as well as instruments and computers. There is also quite strong evidence linking technology and exports in the car industry. However, the evidence of such a link is not confined to industries commonly regarded as high-tech (or R&D-intensive), although the evidence is generally stronger for these industries. Among the less high-tech industries for which technological competition appears important, metal products and food and drinks may be mentioned. It is noteworthy that there is only one industry (petroleum refining) for which there is no evidence whatsoever of a positive impact of technology on export performance.

On the importance of price competition, the evidence is more mixed. Price competition appears to be significant in chemicals, for which technology was also found to be an important factor. For machinery and transport equipment the evidence of price competition is rather weak, with the exception of electrical machinery (which includes many consumer products) and electronics (semiconductors). As might be expected, price competition appears to be of importance in many low-tech industries, such as textiles and clothing. The investment variable—usually measured per worker—fails to have a significant impact in all but a few cases.

Some studies also include a variable assumed to reflect the size of the country or of its domestic market. But—with the exception of Fagerberg (1995)—the reported results are difficult to assess, since several variables included in these tests to some extent already reflect scale factors. Fagerberg (1995) found such scale factors to be important in a few industries only, covering around one-fifth of total OECD trade. The findings suggested that a distinction should be made between technology (including R&D) as an input in the process of production and as the most decisive factor in the

---

[20] She also found support for a simultaneous relationship between exports and R&D, consistent with the Kaldorian ideas of 'cumulative causation' and 'virtuous and vicious circles' (Kaldor, 1981).

[21] Lundberg (1992) applied Hughes's model to Swedish evidence and reached similar results. For an analysis of the impact of R&D efforts on Australian foreign trade, see Engelbrecht (1992).

J. Fagerberg

Table 3
Impact of Technology and Other Factors on Trade Performance

	R&D intensity (expenditure in % of production, 1985)	Technology						Price/cost			Investment					Scale	
		R&D			Patents												
		L	F	M	S	F	A	F	M	A	L	S	F	M	A	S	F
Aerospace	20	–	–	x	x	–	–	–	x	–	–	–	–	(–)	x	–	x
Computers	10	x[e]	–	x	x	–	x	–	x	–	–[e]	–	–	x	x	–	x
Electronics	8	x[e]	x	–	x		–	x[d]	x	–	–[e]	–	–	x	–	–	x[d]
Instruments	6	x[e]	x	–	x	x	x	–	x	x	–[e]	–	–	x	–	–	–
Electrical machinery	3	x[e]		–	x	x	–	x	–	–	–[e]	–	–	–	–	–	–
Non-electrical machinery	2	x		x	x	x	x	x[b]	–	–	–	–	–	–	–	x/–	x[c]
Cars	3	x[f]	–	x	x	–	x	–	–	–	–[f]	–	–	–	(–)	x	x
Other transport	3	x[f]		–			–	–	x	–	–[f]			–	–		
Ships	0	x[f]	(–)		–	–	–	–	–	–	–[f]	–	x	–	–	–	–
Drugs	9	x		–	x	x	x	x	x	–	–	–	(–)	x	–	–	(–)
Industrial chemicals	3	x	x[a]	x	x		x	x[a]	x	x	–	–	–	–[a]	–	x	–[a]
Plastics	1	x	x	–	x		x	x	–	x	–	x	–	x	–	x	–
Petroleum refining	1	–		–	–				x		–	x		–		–	
Ferrous metals	1	x[g]	–	–	x	–	x	–	x	x	–[g]	–	–	–	–	x	–
Non-ferrous metals	1	x[g]	–	–	x	–	–	–	x	–	–[g]	x	–	–	–	–	(–)
Metal products	1	x[g]		x	x	x	–	x	x	x	–[g]	–	–	–	–	x	–
Stone, glass, and clay	1	–		–	x		x	–	x		–	–		–	(–)	x	
Wood and wood products	0	–		x			x	x	x		–			–			
Paper	0	x	–	x		–		–	x		–		–	–			–
Textiles, clothing	0	–	–	x	–	–	x	x	x	x	–	–	–	–	–	x	–
Food and drinks	0	x		x	–		x		x	x	–	–	–	–	–	–	

Symbols: x = significant, correct sign; x/– = conflicting evidence; – = not significant; (–) = significant, incorrect sign; blank = not included.

Notes: [a] Organic chemicals. [b] Special machinery. [c] Power-generating machinery. [d] Semiconductors. [e] Electrical machinery (broadly defined) and instruments. [f] Transport equipment (excluding aerospace). [g] Metals and metal products.

Sources: R&D intensity = Fagerberg (1996).
L = Lacroix and Scheuer (1976); 15 sectors/12–17 countries, 1968.
F = Fagerberg (1995); 28 sectors/19 countries, 1960–83 (average values).
M = Magnier and Toujas-Bernate (1994); 20 sectors/5 countries, 1980–87.
S = Soete (1981); 40 sectors/22 countries, 1977.
A = Amable and Verspagen (1995), 18 sectors/5 countries, 1970–91.

process of global competition. Industries such as aircraft, computers, and—to a lesser extent—cars are clearly among the most R&D-intensive, but according to this study, comparative advantage in these industries is determined by access to a large domestic market rather than by differences between countries in R&D efforts.[22]

Until recently, most studies have focused on the impact of direct R&D and innovation by firms on exports. The impact of technology flows from other firms, industries, and countries, though potentially important according to recent theorizing in this area, has received far less attention. The reason is, of course, that little is known about these flows. However, Fagerberg (1996), in a study based on data for ten OECD countries and 20 industries in the mid-1980s, included both direct R&D and R&D acquired indirectly through purchase of capital goods and intermediary products from domestic and foreign sources as possible determinants of exports. The results from that study indicate that although both direct and indirect R&D have a significant, positive impact on export performance, the impact (i.e. the estimated elasticity) of the latter is about twice that of the former.[23] Indirect R&D from domestic sources appeared more conducive to improved competitiveness than indirect R&D from abroad. This naturally favours firms in large countries, since these source a greater share of their inputs domestically. Also, the impact of direct R&D on exports was found to be larger in large countries, consistent with the predictions of 'new growth' theory, and with the fact that firms in such countries actually devote a much greater share of their resources to R&D than firms in small countries. Yet, R&D appears as a very potent factor for competitiveness in small countries as well, since the total impact on exports of an investment in R&D was found to exceed the impact of an investment of similar size in physical capital in both large and small economies.

Market size is only one among several factors that may contribute to different developments across countries. Exploiting the time-series dimension of the data, several authors have looked at the extent to which the impact of specific variables differs across countries (parameter constancy, speed of adjustment, etc.). For instance, Magnier and Toujas-Bernate (1994) find that R&D has a much larger impact in Japan than elsewhere. On the other hand, Amable and Verspagen (1995), using patents instead of R&D, point to the USA, and not to Japan, as the country in which technology has the largest impact on exports. However, they do find a much higher speed of adjustment in Japan than elsewhere. This leads them to conclude that 'the general institutional arrangements in Japan may substantially differ from those in Germany, the USA, the UK or Italy' (Amable and Verspagen, 1995, p. 201). Pain and Wakelin (1996), analysing the aggregate export performance of 14 countries in the 1970s and 1980s, report that both prices and technology (measured by patents) matter in most cases. But, according to this study, the evidence of a positive impact of technological activity on export performance is weaker for the USA than for most other economies. Moreover, the estimated impact of technology on Japanese exports is not particularly large. In fact, according to the authors, France is the country for which technology matters most for trade. Thus, although several studies indicate that there may be some heterogeneity among countries in the way technology and other variables affect competitiveness, the present evidence does not allow us to draw strong conclusions about its precise nature.

V. LESSONS

The notion of 'the international competitiveness of a country' has attracted much attention, not to say emotion, lately. However, the basic idea behind it is sound and simple: people care about how well they do compared to others, individually as well as collectively. A consensus definition of international competitiveness might perhaps be that it reflects the ability of a country to secure a high standard of living for its citizens, relative to the citizens of other countries, now and in the future. At the same time, it is usually assumed that the concept is related to trade. This is perhaps not so controversial in itself; what is at stake is rather the direction of causality.

---

[22] Van Hulst *et al.* (1991) also found that technology variables had little explanatory power in some 'very high-tech' industries.
[23] To the best of my knowledge, there are no other studies on this subject. But studies of indirect R&D on productivity have arrived at estimates of roughly the same order of magnitude (see Nadiri, 1993).

A number of arguments have been considered, focusing on the demand as well as on the supply side. While growth obviously affects trade, there are also good reasons to assume a feedback from trade on growth, i.e. that causation goes both ways. Thus, it makes considerable sense to look at indicators reflecting both income (or productivity) and trade when assessing international competitiveness.

While there may be many factors having an impact on trade in the short term, this paper has focused on the long term, and on the role of technology in particular, since theoretical work in this area increasingly suggests that technology has an impact on trade performance. There is also a large and growing applied literature on the subject. Three central findings may be noted. First, R&D and innovation play an important role in many industries, and not only in those that are commonly regarded as high-tech (although the impact is perhaps more pronounced in the latter). Second, in some 'very high-tech' industries, competitiveness seems to be strongly affected by the size of the domestic market. (This is true for aerospace, but may also apply to other industries.) Thus, while R&D and innovation may be important for competitiveness in both large

and small countries, the latter should be careful not to use the specialization pattern of the former as a kind of yardstick of success. Third, R&D does not only matter for the firm or sector of origin, but spills over to other firms and sectors, and these spill-overs are at least as important as the direct effects. This is, of course, an argument for public support of R&D in private firms, since under such circumstances there tends to be underinvestment in R&D. To the extent that national borders act as a barrier to technology flows (as some research suggests), firms in small countries may find themselves at a disadvantage. For Europe this points to the need to speed up cross-country technology flows by means of appropriate policies.

A concern for international competitiveness is sometimes seen as a support for a zero-sum game. But this is in no way a necessary consequence. If it is recognized that the most efficient way to enhance competitiveness in the longer term is to support innovation and diffusion of technology, this may actually lead to higher growth worldwide, and higher welfare all round. This is especially so since countries traditionally specialize in different areas and devote their resources to R&D and innovation accordingly.[24]

REFERENCES.

Amable, B., and Verspagen, B. (1995), 'The Role of Technology in Market Shares Dynamics', *Applied Economics*, 27(2), 197–204.

Amendola, G., Guerrieri, P., and Padoan, P. C. (1992), 'International Patterns of Technological Accumulation and Trade', *Journal of International and Comparative Economics*, 1, 173–97.

Anderton, R. (1992), 'UK Exports of Manufactures: Testing for the Effects of Non-price Competitiveness Using Stochastic Trends and Profitability Measures', *The Manchester School*, 60(1), 23–40.

Archibugi, D. (1992), 'Patenting as an Indicator of Technological Innovation: A Review', *Science and Public Policy*, 19, 357–68.

—   Pianta, M. (1994), 'Aggregate Convergence and Sectoral Specialization in Innovation', *Journal of Evolutionary Economics*, 4, 17–33.

Aquino, A. (1981), 'Changes over Time in the Pattern of Comparative Advantage in Manufactured Goods', *European Economic Review*, 15(1), 41–62.

Beckerman, W. (1962), 'Projecting Europe's Growth', *The Economic Journal*, 72(4), 912–25.

Blake, A. P., and Pain, N. (1994), 'Investigating Structural Changes in UK Export Performance: The Role of Innovation and Direct Investment', Discussion Paper No. 71, London, National Institute of Economic and Social Research.

Buxton T., Mayes, D., and Murfin, A. (1994), 'Research and Development and Trading Performance', in T. Buxton, P. Chapman, and P. Temple (eds), *Britain's Economic Performance*, London, Routledge.

Coe, D. T., and Helpman, E. (1995), 'International R&D Spillovers', *European Economic Review*, 39(7), 859–87.

[24]   The resulting specialization patterns are surprisingly sticky. For evidence, see Amendola *et al.* (1992), Papagni (1992), and Archibugi and Pianta (1994).

Dosi, G., and Soete, L. (1983), 'Technology Gaps and Cost-based Adjustment: Some Explorations on the Determinants of International Competitiveness', *Metroeconomica*, **35**(3), 197–322.

— —(1988), 'Technical Change and International Trade', in G. Dosi *et al.* (eds), *Technical Change and Economic Theory*, London, Pinter.

Dowrick, S. (1996), 'Trade and Growth: A Survey', in J. Fagerberg *et al.*, forthcoming.

Dunn, M. H. (1994), 'Do Nations Compete Economically?', *Intereconomics*, **29**(6), 303–8.

Engelbrecht, H.-J. (1992), 'Australia's Industrial R&D Expenditure and Foreign Trade', *Applied Economics*, **24**(5), 545–56.

Fagerberg, J. (1987), 'A Technology Gap Approach to Why Growth Rates Differ', *Research Policy*, **16**(2–4), 87–99.

— (1988), 'International Competitiveness', *The Economic Journal*, **98**(2), 355–74.

— (1995), 'Is There a Large-country Advantage in High-tech?', Working Paper No. 526, January, Oslo, Norwegian Institute of International Affairs.

— (1996), 'Competitiveness, Scale and R&D', in J. Fagerberg *et al.*, forthcoming.

— Hansson, P., Lundberg, L., and Melchior, A. (forthcoming), *Technology and International Trade*, Aldershot, Edward Elgar.

Globerman, S. (1996), 'Decentralization of Research and Development by Multinational Companies: Determinants and Future Prospects', in J. Fagerberg *et al.*, forthcoming.

Goglio, A. (1991), *'Technology Gap' Theory of International Trade: A Survey*, Geneva, UNCTAD.

Greenhalgh, C. (1990), 'Innovation and Trade Performance in the United Kingdom', *The Economic Journal*, **100**(Conference 1990), 105–18.

— Taylor, P., and Wilson, R. (1994), 'Innovation and Export Volumes and Prices—A Disaggregated Study', *Oxford Economic Papers*, **46**(1), 102–34.

Grossman, G. M., and Helpman, E. (1991), *Innovation and Growth in the Global Economy*, Cambridge, MA, MIT Press.

Gruber, W., Metha, D., and Vernon, R. (1967), 'The R&D Factor in International Trade and International Investment of United States Industries', *Journal of Political Economy*, **75**(1), 20–37.

Houthakker, H. S., and Magee, S. P. (1969), 'Income and Price Elasticities in World Trade', *Review of Economics and Statistics*, **51**(2), 111–25.

Hughes, K. (1986), *Exports and Technology*, Cambridge, Cambridge University Press.

Jaffe, A. B. (1989), 'Real Effects of Academic Research', *American Economic Review*, **79**(5), 957–70.

— Trajtenberg, M., and Henderson, R. (1993), 'Geographical Localization of Knowledge Spillovers as Evidenced by Patent Citations', *Quarterly Journal of Economics*, **108**(3), 577–98.

Kaldor, N. (1970), 'The Case for Regional Policies', *Scottish Journal of Political Economy*, **17**(3), 337–48.

— (1978), 'The Effect of Devaluations on Trade in Manufactures', in N. Kaldor, *Further Essays on Applied Economics*, London, Duckworth.

— (1981), 'The Role of Increasing Returns, Technical Progress and Cumulative Causation in the Theory of International Trade and Economic Growth', *Economie appliquée*, **34**(4), 593–617.

Krugman, P. (1979), 'A Model of Innovation, Technology Transfer and the World Distribution of Income', *Journal of Political Economy*, **87**(2), 253–66.

— (1994), 'Competitiveness: A Dangerous Obsession', *Foreign Affairs*, **73**(2), 28–44.

Lacroix, R., and Scheuer, P. (1976), 'L'effort de R&D, l'innovation et le commerce international', *Revue économique*, **27**(6), 1008–29.

Landesmann, M., and Snell, A. (1989), 'The Consequences of Mrs Thatcher for UK Manufacturing Exports', *The Economic Journal*, **99**(1), 1–27.

Leontief, W. (1954), 'Domestic Production and Foreign Trade: The American Capital Position Re-examined', *Economia Internazionale*, **7**(1), 3–32.

Lucas, R. E. (1988), 'On the Mechanisms of Economic Development', *Journal of Monetary Economics*, **22**(1), 3–42.

Lundberg, L. (1992), 'The Structure of Swedish International Trade and Specialization: "Old" and "New" Explanations', *Weltwirtschaftliches Archiv*, **128**(2), 266–87.

Magnier, A., and Toujas-Bernate, J. (1994), 'Technology and Trade: Empirical Evidence for the Major Five Industrialized Countries', *Weltwirtschaftliches Archiv*, **130**(3), 494–520.

McCombie, J. S. L. (1992), ' "Thirlwall's Law" and Balance of Payments Constrained Growth: More on the Debate', *Applied Economics*, **24**(5), 493–512.

— Thirlwall, A. P. (1994), *Economic Growth and the Balance-of-Payments Constraint*, London, Macmillan.

Milberg, W. S. (1991), 'Structural Change and International Competitiveness in Canada: An Alternative Approach', *International Review of Applied Economics*, **5**(1), 77–99.

J. Fagerberg

Moran, T. H. (1996), 'Power and Plenty in Grand Strategy', *International Organization*, 50, 175–205.

Nadiri, M. I. (1993), 'Innovations and Technological Spillovers', NBER Working Paper No. 4423, Cambridge, MA, National Bureau of Economic Research.

Nelson, R. R., and Wright, G. (1992), 'The Rise and Fall of American Technological Leadership: The Postwar Era in Historical Perspective', *Journal of Economic Literature*, 30(4), 1931–64.

OECD (1992), *Technology and the Economy: The Key Relationships*, Paris, Organisation for Economic Co-operation and Development.

Papagni, E. (1992), 'High-technology Exports of EEC Countries: Persistence and Diversity of Specialization Patterns', *Applied Economics*, 24(8), 925–33.

Pain, N., and Wakelin, K. (1996), 'Foreign Direct Investment and Export Performance', paper for presentation at the 23rd European Association for Research in Industrial Economics (EARIE), Vienna, September 7–10.

Patel, P., and Pavitt, K. (1991), 'Large Firms in the Production of the World's Technology: An Important Case of Non-globalisation', *Journal of International Business Studies*, 22(1), 1–21.

— — (1994), 'The Continuing, Widespread (and Neglected) Importance of Improvements in Mechanical Technologies', *Research Policy*, 23, 533–45.

— — (1995), 'Patterns of Technological Activity: Their Measurement and Interpretation', in P. Stoneman (ed.), *Handbook of the Economics of Innovation and Technological Change*, Oxford, Blackwell.

Pavitt, K. (1982), 'R&D, Patenting and Innovative Activities: A Statistical Exploration', *Research Policy*, 11, 33–51.

Porter, M. E. (1990), 'The Competitive Advantage of Nations', *Harvard Business Review*, 68(2), 73–93.

Posner, M. V. (1961), 'International Trade and Technical Change', *Oxford Economic Papers*, 13(3), 323–41.

Reinert, E. (1995), 'Competitiveness and its Predecessors—A 500-year Cross-national Perspective', *Structural Change and Economic Dynamics*, 6, 23–42.

Robson, P. (1987), *The Economics of International Integration*, 3rd edn, London, Allen & Unwin.

Romer, P. M. (1986), 'Increasing Returns and Long-run Growth', *Journal of Political Economy*, 94(5), 1002–37.

— (1990), 'Endogenous Technological Change', *Journal of Political Economy*, 98(5:2), S71–102.

Schumpeter, J. (1934), *The Theory of Economic Development*, Cambridge, MA, Harvard University Press.

— (1939), *Business Cycles I–II*, New York, NY, McGraw-Hill.

— (1943), *Capitalism, Socialism and Democracy*, New York, NY, Harper.

Sjöholm, F. (1996), 'Knowledge Inflow to Sweden: Does Geography and International Trade Matter?', in J. Fagerberg *et al.*, forthcoming.

Soete, L. G. (1981), 'A General Test of Technological Gap Trade Theory', *Weltwirtschaftliches Archiv*, 117(4), 638–60.

Sveikauskas, L. (1983), 'Science and Technology in United States Foreign Trade', *The Economic Journal*, 93(3), 542–54.

Thirlwall, A. P. (1979), 'The Balance of Payments Constraint as an Explanation of International Growth Rate Differences', *Banca Nazionale del Lavoro Quarterly Review*, 32(1), 45–53.

Van Hulst, N., Mulder, R., and Soete, L. G. (1991), 'Exports and Technology in Manufacturing Industry', *Weltwirtschaftliches Archiv*, 127(2), 246–64.

Vernon, R. (1966), 'International Investment and International Trade in the Product Cycle', *Quarterly Journal of Economics*, 80(2), 190–207.

Verspagen, B. (1992), 'Endogenous Innovation in Neo-classical Models: A Survey', *Journal of Macroeconomics*, 14(4), 631–62.

Wakelin, K. (1995), 'Empirical Studies on the Relationship between Trade and Innovation', doctoral thesis presented at the European University Institute, Florence, September.

Wolff, E. N. (1995), 'Technological Change, Capital Accumulation and Changing Trade Patterns over the Long Term', *Structural Change and Economic Dynamics*, 6, 43–70.

— (1996), 'Productivity Growth and Shifting Comparative Advantage on the Industry Level', in J. Fagerberg *et al.*, forthcoming.

Appendix: A formal presentation of the "technology gap model"

This note shows how the technology-gap model of economic growth applied in Chapter 2 (and later chapters as well) can be derived formally. The note is based on Fagerberg, J. (1988) "Why growth rates differ", in Dosi, G. et al. (eds), *Technical Change and Economic Theory*, Pinter, London, pp. 432–57.

Assume that the level of production in a country (Q) is a multiplicative function of the level of knowledge diffused to the country from abroad (D), the level of knowledge created in the country (N), the country's capacity for exploiting the benefits of knowledge whether internationally or nationally created (C), and a constant (Z).

$$Q = ZD^{\alpha} N^{\beta} C^{\tau}, \tag{1}$$

where Z is a constant.

By differentiating and dividing through with Q, letting small-case letters denote growth rates:

$$q = \alpha d + \beta n + \tau c \tag{2}$$

Assume further, as customary in the diffusion literature, that the diffusion of internationally available knowledge follows a logistic curve. This implies that the contribution of diffusion of internationally available knowledge to economic growth is an increasing function of the distance between the level of knowledge appropriated in the country and that of the country on the technological frontier (for the frontier country, this contribution will be zero). Let the total amount of knowledge, adjusted for differences in size of countries, in the frontier country and the country under consideration be T_f and T, respectively:

$$d = \mu - \mu (T/T_f) \tag{3}$$

By substituting (3) into (2) we finally arrive at:

$$q = \alpha\mu - \alpha\mu (T/T_f) + \beta n + \tau c \tag{4}$$

Thus, following this approach, economic growth depends on three factors:

- the diffusion of technology from abroad (imitation): the contribution of this factor increases with the distance from the (world) technology frontier;
- the creation of new technology within the country (innovation);
- the development of the country's capacity for exploiting the benefits offered by available technology, whether created in the country or elsewhere ('efforts').

Name index

Abramovitz, M. 3, 4, 26, 54, 83, 87, 116, 184
Ahmad, J. 43
Aho, M.C. 108, 143, 237
Alesina, A. 44
Amable, B. 258, 281–3
Amendola, G. 258
Amsden, A.H. 31
Andersen, E.S. 221, 224, 231
Andersen, H.W. 180
Anderton, R. 277
Annerstedt, J. 179
Aquino, A. 280
Arnestad, M. 172, 180
Arrow, K. 92, 98

Balassa, B. 236
Baldwin, R.E. 128–30
Barro, R. 27, 53, 55–6, 73, 76, 102
Basberg, B.L. 180
Baumol, W.J. 61, 89
Beckerman, W. 277
Belsley, D.A. 27
Bernanke, B. 45
Blake, A.P. 277
Blanchard, O.J. 71, 74
Brakman, S. 133
Buxton, T. 281

Caniëls, M.C.J. 61, 194, 196
Cappelen, A. 193, 208
Caves, R.E. 142
Chandler, A.D. 184
Chesnais, F. 201
Choi, K. 117
Clark, S. 157
Coe, D.T. 104, 268, 280
Cohen, W.M. 58
Cornwall, J. 3, 4, 8, 16–22, 25–8, 102, 116
Cornwall, W. 28
Cripps, F. 18

Dahmén, E. 222
Dalum, B. 142, 178, 192, 194
De Long, B. 89
Denison, E.F. 3, 83
Domar, E. 80, 98
Dosi, G. 53, 235–6, 250, 258, 279, 281

Dunford, M. 76
Dunn, M.H. 275
Durlauf, S.N. 61

Eliasson, G. 201

Fagerberg, J. 53–4, 70, 73, 75, 117, 147, 178, 185–9, 193–4, 196, 210, 250, 258, 278, 280–83
Freeman, C. 5, 31, 99, 142, 157–8, 168, 207

Gerschenkron, A. 30, 87, 116
Gertler, M. 45
Giersch, H. 108
Gomulka, S. 3, 4
Gouyette, C. 53, 55–6, 70, 74
Grabbe, H. 194
Greenhalgh, C. 280–81
Griliches, Z. 5
Grossman, C.M. 31, 54, 73, 235–6, 257, 260, 279
Gruber, W. 236, 280
Guerrieri, P. 185–9

Harnhirum, S. 43
Harrod, R. 80, 98
Helpman, E. 31, 54, 73, 104, 235–6, 253, 256–7, 260, 268, 279–80
Heradstveit, P.Ø. 171
Hirsch, S. 4, 108, 141
Hirschmann, A.O. 222
Holmen, M. 194
Houthakker, H.S. 204, 277–8
Hufbauer, G. 141
Hughes, K. 194, 281

Jaffe, A.B. 280
Jansen, M. 195
Johnson, C. 31, 184
Johnson, P.A. 61
Johnston, J. 213, 240
Jones, C. 95
Jørgensen, U. 178

Kaldor, N. 17, 18, 26, 86, 91–2, 98, 201–2, 205, 208, 210, 216–17, 275, 277
Katz, L.F. 71, 74
Katzenstein, P. 117